Understanding Marx, Understanding Modernism

UNDERSTANDING PHILOSOPHY, UNDERSTANDING MODERNISM

The aim of each volume in **Understanding Philosophy, Understanding Modernism** is to understand a philosophical thinker more fully through literary and cultural modernism and consequently to understand literary modernism better through a key philosophical figure. In this way, the series also rethinks the limits of modernism, calling attention to lacunae in modernist studies and sometimes in the philosophical work under examination.

Series Editors:
Paul Ardoin, S. E. Gontarski, and Laci Mattison

Volumes in the Series:

Understanding Bergson, Understanding Modernism
Edited by Paul Ardoin, S. E. Gontarski, and Laci Mattison

Understanding Deleuze, Understanding Modernism
Edited by S. E. Gontarski, Paul Ardoin and Laci Mattison

Understanding Wittgenstein, Understanding Modernism
Edited by Anat Matar

Understanding Foucault, Understanding Modernism
Edited by David Scott

Understanding James, Understanding Modernism
Edited by David H. Evans

Understanding Rancière, Understanding Modernism
Edited by Patrick M. Bray

Understanding Blanchot, Understanding Modernism
Edited by Christopher Langlois

Understanding Merleau-Ponty, Understanding Modernism
Edited by Ariane Mildenberg

Understanding Nietzsche, Understanding Modernism
Edited by Douglas Burnham and Brian Pines

Understanding Derrida, Understanding Modernism
Edited by Jean-Michel Rabaté

Understanding Adorno, Understanding Modernism
Edited by Robin Truth Goodman

Understanding Marx, Understanding Modernism
Edited by Mark Steven

Understanding Cavell, Understanding Modernism (forthcoming)
Edited by Paola Marrati

Understanding Flusser, Understanding Modernism (forthcoming)
Edited by Aaron Jaffe, Rodrigo Martini, and Michael F. Miller

Understanding Marx, Understanding Modernism

Edited by Mark Steven

BLOOMSBURY ACADEMIC
NEW YORK • LONDON • OXFORD • NEW DELHI • SYDNEY

BLOOMSBURY ACADEMIC
Bloomsbury Publishing Inc
1385 Broadway, New York, NY 10018, USA
50 Bedford Square, London, WC1B 3DP

BLOOMSBURY, BLOOMSBURY ACADEMIC and the Diana logo are trademarks of Bloomsbury Publishing Plc

First published in the United States of America 2021
This paperback edition published 2022

Copyright © Mark Steven and Contributors, 2021

Cover design by Namkwan Cho
Cover image by Fine Art Images / Heritage Images / Getty Images

All rights reserved. No part of this publication may be reproduced or transmitted in any form or by any means, electronic or mechanical, including photocopying, recording, or any information storage or retrieval system, without prior permission in writing from the publishers.

Bloomsbury Publishing Inc does not have any control over, or responsibility for, any third-party websites referred to or in this book. All internet addresses given in this book were correct at the time of going to press. The author and publisher regret any inconvenience caused if addresses have changed or sites have ceased to exist, but can accept no responsibility for any such changes.

Library of Congress Cataloging-in-Publication Data
Names: Steven, Mark, editor.
Title: Understanding Marx, understanding modernism / edited by Mark Steven.
Description: New York : Bloomsbury Academic, 2021. | Series: Understanding philosophy, understanding modernism | Includes bibliographical references and index. | Summary: "Explores and illuminates Karl Marx's profound influence on literary modernism"– Provided by publisher.
Identifiers: LCCN 2020033880 | ISBN 9781501351112 (hb) | ISBN 9781501351129 (ebook) | ISBN 9781501351136 (epdf)
Subjects: LCSH: Marx, Karl, 1818-1883–Influence. | Modernism (Literature) | Literature–Philosophy. | Communism and literature.
Classification: LCC HX39.5 .U63 2021 | DDC 335.4–dc23
LC record available at https://lccn.loc.gov/2020033880

ISBN: HB: 978-1-5013-5111-2
PB: 978-1-5013-7230-8
ePDF: 978-1-5013-5113-6
eBook: 978-1-5013-5112-9

Series: Understanding Philosophy, Understanding Modernism

Typeset by Deanta Global Publishing Services, Chennai, India

To find out more about our authors and books visit www.bloomsbury.com and sign up for our newsletters.

Series Preface

Sometime in the late twentieth century, modernism, like philosophy itself, underwent something of an unmooring from (at least) linear literary history in favor of the multi-perspectival history implicit in "new historicism" or, say, varieties of "presentism." Amid current reassessments of modernism and modernity, critics have posited various "new" or alternative modernisms—postcolonial, cosmopolitan, transatlantic, transnational, geomodernism, or even "bad" modernisms. In doing so, they have not only reassessed modernism as a category but also, more broadly, rethought epistemology and ontology, aesthetics, metaphysics, materialism, history, and being itself, opening possibilities of rethinking not only which texts we read as modernist but also how we read those texts. Much of this new conversation constitutes something of a critique of the periodization of modernism or modernist studies in favor of modernism as mode (or mode of production) or concept. The "Understanding Philosophy, Understanding Modernism" series situates itself amid the plurality of discourses, offering collections focused on key philosophical thinkers influential both to the moment of modernism and to our current understanding of that moment's geneology, archeology, and becomings. Such critiques of modernism(s) and modernity afford opportunities to rethink and reassess the overlaps, folds, interrelationships, interleavings, or cross-pollinations of modernism and philosophy. Our goal in each volume of the series is to understand literary modernism better through philosophy as we also better understand a philosopher through literary modernism. The first two volumes of the series, those on Henri Bergson and Gilles Deleuze, have established a tripartite structure that serves to offer accessibility both to the philosopher's principle texts and to current new research. Each volume opens with a section focused on "conceptualizing" the philosopher through close readings of seminal texts in the thinker's oeuvre. A second section, on aesthetics, maps connections between modernist works and the philosophical figure, often surveying key modernist trends and shedding new light on authors and texts. The final section of each volume serves as an extended glossary of principal terms in the philosopher's work, each treated at length, allowing a fuller engagement with and examination of the many, sometimes contradictory, ways terms are deployed. The series is thus designed both to introduce philosophers and to rethink their relationship to modernist studies, revising our understandings of both modernism and philosophy, and offering resources that will be of use across disciplines, from philosophy, theory, and literature, to religion, the visual and performing arts, and often to the sciences as well.

Contents

Introduction: Modernist Marx, Marxist Modernism *Mark Steven* 1

Part One Conceptualizing Marx

1 Greek Ideology and Modern Politics in Marx's First Works *Giacomo Bianchino* 15

2 Before the *Manifesto*: Märchen and the Impulse to Exorcism *Peter Riley* 30

3 *The Communist Manifesto* and the Exhumation of Literature *Alex Niven* 40

4 On France: Revolutions and Communes *Owen Holland* 50

5 Jupiter against the Lightning-Rod: Literary Form in the *Grundrisse* *Dominick Knowles* 64

6 The Voices of *Capital*: Poetics of Critique beyond Sentiment and Cynicism *Daniel Hartley* 74

7 The Dialectics of Utopia: *Critique of the Gotha Program* *Regenia Gagnier* 86

8 Posthumous Publications: Capitalism's Circuits and Reading for Totality *Treasa De Loughry and Miles Link* 99

Part Two Marx in Modernism

9 Marx in the Modernist Novel *Julian Murphet* 115

10 Marx and Modernist Poetry *Kristin Grogan* 124

11 Marx and Cinema *Angelos Koutsourakis* 134

12 Theatrical Proletarians *Michael Shane Boyle* 146

13 Marx, Music, Modernism *Sarah Collins* 162

14 Constructing Socialism: Marxism, Modernism, and Architecture *Tyrus Miller* 172

15 Marx and Popular Modernism *Esther Leslie* 184

Part Three Glossary of Key Terms

16 The Commodity *Josh Jewell* — 197
17 Labor *Veronica Brownstone* — 200
18 Value *Rory Dufficy* — 202
19 Money *Marina Vishmidt* — 204
20 The General Formula of Capital *Adam David Morton* — 207
21 Class *Elinor Taylor* — 209
22 Technology *Trevor Strunk* — 211
23 Family *Kate Montague* — 214
24 Ideology *Harry Warwick* — 217
25 Alienation *Ana Tomcic* — 219
26 Materialism *Fiona Allen* — 221
27 Colonization *Paul Young* — 223
28 Nature *Margaret Ronda* — 226
29 Revolution *Colleen Lye* — 229
30 Communism *Conall Cash* — 231
31 Utopia *Cat Moir* — 234

Notes on Contributors — 237
Index — 241

Introduction

Modernist Marx, Marxist Modernism

Mark Steven

"Aren't there already more than enough interpretations of Marx?" asked Marshall Berman in a book written over four decades ago. "Do we really need a modernist Marx, a kindred spirit of Eliot and Kafka and Schoenberg and Gertrude Stein and Artaud?"[1] This second and more exacting question, which projects a spectral image of the bearded thinker onto the conceptual stage alongside those figures whose names are as good as synonymous with modernism, also animates and directs the collective labor of the present volume. Like ours, Berman's answer is resolutely affirmative. "Marx," he suggests, "can tell us as much about modernism as it can tell us about him."[2] But the significance of this combination will not just be to the benefit of critics, and neither is the combination itself a belated critical invention, or at least it's not just that. The combination of Marx and modernism is, as this volume will demonstrate, native and immanent to both of those entities, with each internal to the other. In the delimited fields of theory and criticism, the ideas originating with Marx and the texts we now theorize as modernist will continue to prove mutually generative, but there are arguments to be made, and which are made all throughout the following chapters, that Marx and modernism are also causally related—that Marx and modernism are woven through one another's material substance, in ways that condition critical and cultural production in either instance. While Berman achieved more than most in documenting some of the connections, the sense of bilateral illumination between these two distinct phenomena— Marx's thinking and writing and persona, on the one hand, and that mangle of ideas and practices and artworks called modernism, on the other—has only heightened in the time since Berman was writing. The reasons for this heightening are both economic and institutional; they are felt transformatively within the aesthetic regime no less than in the body of ideas we associate with the name Marx; and they respond to a series of historical coincidences that have as much to do with the formation of an archive now canonized as modernism as they do with the critical reception and revaluation of that canon with all the benefits of scholarly hindsight.

Perhaps it goes without saying here that the period of high modernism, arguably running from the final decades of the nineteenth century through the first half of the twentieth, belonged to a cultural matrix alongside what Leszek Kołakowski once described as a "golden age" for the radical, anti-capitalist Left. "Its influence," Kołakowski says of Marx's thinking, "extended beyond the immediate circle of the faithful, to historians, economists, and sociologists who did not profess Marxism as a whole but adopted particular Marxist ideas and categories."[3] This idea will be familiar to anyone with even a passing interest in the history of emancipatory politics. Weighing up the cultural proliferation of Marxism between 1880 and 1914, for instance, Eric Hobsbawm explains the global penetration by this radical ideology and critical science: "The dramatic expansion of labor and socialist movements associated with the name Karl Marx in the 1880s and 1890s inevitably spread the influence of his theories (or what were considered to be his theories) both inside these movements and outside them."[4] The reach of Marx, however, has not been limited to labor and socialist movements—which, in the early-industrializing core nations, tended to be more white and more male than any totalizing theory of emancipation could be said to champion uncritically.

Where collective identities seek liberation from economic and political oppression, Marxism has served as analytic framework and emancipatory catalyst, also being taken up by feminist thinkers, decolonial activists, and critical race scholars—or, to use Frantz Fanon's expression, Marx's ideas often find themselves "slightly stretched" to be redeployed within struggles that remain irreducible to a narrowly defined class politics but which nevertheless pit themselves against the depredations of capital and its hierarchies.[5] Indeed, Walter Rodney approached the imperative to stretch Marx's ideas as a necessary political challenge. "Marxism," he claimed, "comes to the world as an historical fact, and it comes in a cultural nexus . . . loaded with conceptions of the historical development of Europe itself. So that method and factual data were obviously interwoven, and the conclusions were in fact in a specific historical and cultural setting." The challenge, then, is "making sure that Marxism does not simply appear as the summation of other people's history, but appears as a living force within one's history," and this, he insists, "is the task of anybody who considers himself or herself a Marxist."[6] Other thinkers have committed themselves to precisely this task within and across disparate yet intersecting struggles. "Since Marx," begins Silvia Federici's landmark work of feminist counter-history, *Caliban and the Witch* (1998),

> studying the genesis of capitalism has been an obligatory step for activists and scholars convinced that the first task on humanity's agenda is the construction of an alternative to capitalist society. Not surprisingly, every new revolutionary movement has returned to the "transition to capitalism," bringing to it the perspectives of new social subjects and uncovering new grounds of exploitation and resistance.[7]

According to W. E. B. Du Bois, for whom Marxism underwrites the critical account of racialization, black slaves abandoning their plantations and organizing during the Civil War fomented "one of the most extraordinary experiments of Marxism that the world, before the Russian Revolution, had seen."[8]

Marx didn't just offer ways of understanding history; his intellectual and political legacy, what we call Marxism, is history in and of itself. Writing from another conjuncture, Rosa Luxemburg employed this argument in her assessment of Marxism's revolutionary efficacy. "Marx's theory," she reflected, "proves to be true continuously with every new proletarian who supports class struggle. So Marx's theory is at the same time part of the historical process and is also itself a process," to such an extent that actual "revolution" is the only "final chapter" worthy of Marx's name.[9] Taking the question of influence to the outer limits of materialist plausibility, Louis Althusser once wrote an ostensibly speculative account of how Marx and Marxism have impressed themselves onto the wider world, shaping the general intellect as a very specific kind of collective literacy:

> Of course, we have all read, and all do read *Capital*. For almost a century, we have been able to read it every day, transparently, in the dramas and dreams of our history, in its disputes and conflicts, in the defeats and victories of the workers' movement which is our only hope and our destiny. Since we "came into the world," we have read *Capital* constantly in the writings and speeches of those who have read it for us, well or ill, both the dead and the living, Engels, Kautsky, Plekhanov, Lenin, Rosa Luxemburg, Trotsky, Stalin, Gramsci, the leaders of the workers' organizations, their supporters and opponents: philosophers, economists, politicians. We have read bits of it, the "fragments" which the conjuncture had "selected" for us. We have even all, more or less, read *Volume One*, from "commodities" to the "expropriation of the expropriators."[10]

The proposition that "reading" history is to simultaneously "read" Marx might prove far less scandalous than it initially sounds, but only if we pay attention to the two senses that inform its verb. Provided here is a list of familiar names and historical events that mediate between the written critique of political economy and the lived experience of capitalist modernity; and together, these names and the events with which they are associated orchestrate the transfer of energies between those two primary terms. So we are not meant to interpret the proposition either metaphorically or literally at the expense of one meaning or the other; instead, both meanings occupy a kind of parallax view. While Marx can be read in the details of everyday life under capitalism, because that is what he grasped as an integrated system of economic fetishes, those revolutionaries listed here have also re-inscribed his thought, word-for-word or slightly augmented, into historical discourse. This double mediation is what legitimizes and perhaps even actualized the potentially rarefied notion of a modernist Marx. Before we can introduce this idea at greater length, it will be necessary to clarify what we are talking about when we talk about Marx in the first place.

Marx was a radical thinker and writer who lived from 1818 to 1883 and whose cultural impact is to be measured with real historical transformation as much as it is by academic citation and opinion polls. In a frequently quoted sentence written in the spring of 1845, Marx issued what reads as a statement of intent. "The philosophers," he claimed, "have only *interpreted* the world, in various ways; the point is to *change* it."[11] There is no philosopher for whom these words are a more accurate description than Marx, forefather of modern communism and, as this book will want to show, herald for modernism. Thinking, for Marx, would not be enough to achieve the freedom of all humans. For that kind of freedom, we need to change the material conditions and social relations through which we live, and we do so with revolution, by making the tiger's leap of history from one mode of production into another: from feudal aristocracies to industrial empires, and then from the capitalist inferno into the paradise of communism. After socialist revolutions in Russia, China, Cuba, Venezuela, and elsewhere, for much of the twentieth century nearly four out of every ten people on earth lived under governments that claimed to follow Marx's ideas and to aspire toward communism. That legacy persists today, despite the market liberalization and re-colonization by capital of these erstwhile revolutionary states. To mark the second centenary of Marx's birth in 2018, Xi Jinping—general secretary to the Chinese Communist Party—ordered study sessions on Marx for "the broad masses of party members, cadres and especially senior cadres." The purpose of these sessions, Xi told members of the CCP's ruling body, is "enhancing the party's ability to use Marxist principles to solve the problems facing contemporary China."[12] While there is good reason to debate China's statewide commitment to Marxism, which is more symbolic than practical, lionizing moves like this nevertheless signal the ongoing deployment of Marx as a figurehead for anti-capitalist mobilizations in the twenty-first century, in ways that outlive most of what we understand as modernism.

Marx's most famous works are *The Manifesto of the Communist Party* (1848), which he coauthored with Friedrich Engels, and the first volume of *Capital: A Contribution to the Critique of Political Economy* (1867). Between these, Marx developed a theory of society propelled by economic forces and internal contradiction, and by the conflict of interests between property owners and dispossessed workers. Marx showed that, rather than creating wealth from nothing, capitalism and its beneficiaries are ruthless expropriators. "The history of all hitherto existing society is the history of class struggle," we read in the *Manifesto*'s first chapter. "Society as a whole is more and more splitting up into two great hostile camps, into two great classes directly facing each other—Bourgeoisie and Proletariat."[13] This core idea will be uncontroversial to anyone familiar with the fact that, in 2018, the world's richest 1 percent accrued 45 percent of all global wealth. And, while statistics fail to capture the social sedimentations of class hierarchy, the actual experience of dispossession with its hunger and its deprivation, or the massive hierarchical differences within that other 99 percent of all persons, Marx also showed that the so-called free market—from which the wealthiest distil their riches—perpetuates exploitation and coercion. "Freedom" under capitalism is freedom to purchase, to buy what you choose, but this "freedom" is a precondition for a second, negative sense of that term: the freedom to sell one's own labor, which becomes an imperative, insofar as it is required for subsistence, whereby only those who work are permitted to purchase their food and shelter and basic dignity. In this account, the capitalist economy results from manufactured dispossession, compelled in equal measure by legislative rule and coercive force, and the subsequent reabsorption of the dispossessed now as workers, from whom profits might be engineered. In the decline of feudalism, governments affixed prohibitively expensive prices to the land, bequeathing real estate to the aristocracy and the bourgeoisie, thereby compelling a landless working class to earn wages that are in turn extorted back from them as ground rent. This historical and systemic account of capitalism is the one advanced by Marx, but it will also read as obvious and true to anyone who has ever had to work in order to eat and who is subject to the laws of tenancy for their shelter. Finally, as populations grow in negative correlation with capital's capacity or willingness to absorb labor, we encounter that freedom to work now severed from the freedom to purchase, with the vast swathes of persons left to fend for themselves beyond that relative safety of waged employment.

While, on these points, Marx's account of capitalism might be as accurate of the twenty-first century as it was for England and Europe and the emergent world-system between the nineteenth century's industrial revolutions, controversy arrives with the proposed alternative: a classless, stateless society, arranged according to cooperation; material equality between all people as realized through the abolition of private property; or, in Yanis Varoufakis' ultra-humanist precis, what Marx and Engels propose is nothing short of "authentic human happiness and the genuine freedom that must accompany it."[14] The proper name for this society, with its happiness and its freedom, is communism, a way of living together that does not and cannot belong to any one state or nation. "We call communism," they clarify, "the real movement which abolishes the present state of things."[15] That abolitionary movement is what we are beginning to see in resurgence with left-wing action the world over, not in official parliamentary politics but in real practice: in the efflorescence of strikes and occupations, of riots and insurrections, all geared toward some final, climactic abolition. So ends the *Manifesto*:

> The Communists disdain to conceal their views and aims. They openly declare that their ends can be attained only by the forcible overthrow of all existing social conditions. Let the ruling classes tremble at a communist revolution. The proletarians have nothing to lose but their chains. They have a world to win.[16]

Of course this idea is controversial. For those at the top, for whom we work and to whom we pay rent, that fight and our victory will mean the loss of something aside from chains: to say we are their "gravediggers" is not entirely metaphorical. The opposite of this is true for the dispossessed proletariat, whose subjects are comprised by a class which, in its contradiction with capital at a given time, wields the potential to abolish capital, all classes that exist within capitalism, and therefore capitalism itself. The driving force from here to communism begins with a collective subject saying no to capital and embracing the fight for real change—and this subject speaks not in words but with action, in a language made up of strikes and riots, of barricades and looting, of occupations and insurrection. Marx described this process of communization using forms and figures taken from aesthetic modernity. "The social revolution of the nineteenth century cannot take its poetry from the past but only from the future," he prophesied. "The revolution of the nineteenth century must let the dead bury their dead in order to arrive at its own content. There the phrase went beyond the content—here the content goes beyond the phrase."[17]

Within the present context, let us hypothesize that Marx's critique of capitalism, which forms the material undercurrent to communism's poetry of the future, is also a theory of modernism. If we can agree with Fredric Jameson's argument that "artistic or aesthetic 'modernism' essentially corresponds to a situation of incomplete modernization," and if we also take heed of his advice to substitute "capitalism for modernity in all the contexts in which the latter appears," we must have realized that modernism occupies a period defined by fierce competition between an incomplete monopoly capitalism and emergent communist revolutions.[18] From this perspective, the key actors in "those aesthetic and philosophical revolutions were people who still lived in two distinct worlds simultaneously," or in multiple "socioeconomic temporalities, which the first modernists had to negotiate in their own lived experience."[19] Modernism, in other words, is the cultural logic of industrial, monopoly capitalism before capitalism secured a global market with no alternative—if it ever did so at all—and at a time when it was subject to real challenges from the anti-capitalist and frequently Marxist Left. Speaking in the recalcitrant language of political commitment or at least economic resistance, modernism is when art—and literature—attaches itself to forms and forces that do not reconcile into capitalism. In other words, modernism is one last attempt at autonomous world-creation before everything is subsumed into a single (uneven and combined) global market. It is, in Theodor Adorno's august description, "the true consciousness of an age in which the real possibility of utopia—that given the level of productive forces the earth could here and now be paradise—converges with the possibility of total catastrophe."[20] This is why T. J. Clark is correct to define modernism as socialism's "shadow," as part of a "struggle to imagine modernity otherwise" during a period in which, because of the unfinished character of modernization, such an otherwise still existed: if modernism is socialism's shadow, this is true because both desire a way through and beyond capitalism.[21]

While the discursive success or at least global uptake of Marx and Marxism in the first decades of the twentieth century, during the moment of high modernism, indexes a series of economic crises that gave birth to imperialist wars of extermination but also socialist and communist revolutions, this volume joins the field at a time when modernism and modernist studies have experienced a seemingly exponential expansion of intellectual fortunes within and beyond the academy. What remains unstated about this "rebirth" of modernist studies—which announced itself as full-fledged in 2008, with Douglas Mao and Rebecca Walkowitz surveying the newly expanded field for *PMLA*—is its coincidence with a renewed interest in Marx and Marxism across the English-speaking world, one that compares to the late 1960s and early 1970s return to Marx in the wake of insurrectionary upsurge and economic downturn. "The New Modernist Studies," as Mao and Walkowitz identified their field, acquired its title in the first year of the subprime mortgage crisis, which soon turned into a global financial crisis, which was then followed the world over by riot and rebellion. What this meant is that a critical return to modernism, as an object of interest and a conceptual strategy for world-creation, coincided with a hemorrhaging of capitalism in the core states and, with that, a renewed if not newfound enthusiasm for Marx and Marxism. Working across multiple fields and disciplines, established Marxists like David Harvey (geography), Giovanni Arrighi (sociology), Jodi Dean (political science), and Terry Eagleton (literature) have all enjoyed an enlarged readership. Their ongoing work has been flanked by a range of new Marxist writing, the best of which utilizes online distribution, as with the militant communism of *Endnotes* (launched 2008), *Viewpoint* (2011), *Commune* (2018), *Pinko* (2019), and *Spectre* (2020) as well as the widely read socialist magazines *Jacobin* (2011) and *Tribune* (2018). The connections between the New Modernist Studies and Marxism have also been made in more localized instances. For example, urgent Marx-inflected scholarship is starting to emerge on the causal links between financialization, austerity, precarity, and the shape of modernist studies in the disappearance of previous generations' employment opportunities. For Alys Moody and Stephen J. Ross, writing in the summer of 2019, "academic precarity is simply another iteration of changes in labor relations under neoliberalism, and the response here must be the same as elsewhere: a shift towards collective action and solidarity."[22] It is against this historical and disciplinary backdrop that we should reemphasize the degree to which modernism, as a unique aesthetic phenomenon, is also coherent with the Marxist view of history and with capitalism's tendency toward precisely these kinds of crisis and their revolutionary counterforces.

The moment of modernism and of modernist studies through the second decade of the twenty-first century is not only the moment of capitalism in crisis but also a moment of revolt, of uprising, and—potentially—of revolution. While the popular ascendency of a far-right has taken hold from within the institutions of state power and formed, in its explicitly neo-Nazi constructions, something like a fascist cultural front, a leftist opposition gathers in disparate though related movements such as Antifa, Black Lives Matter, BDS, and Occupy, not to mention its filtration through the intensifying frequency of rank-and-file insurgencies, wildcat strikes, and fighting on the streets. These movements, none of which takes place in isolation from one another, suggest a moment when the old divisions between capitalism and its revolutionary antitheses apply less to geopolitical blocs within the interstate system or even to parties within a given state than to antagonisms flaring up all across the world and irrespective of sovereign boundaries. And all of this, erupting the world over, is in dialogue with the thing we call modernism—these movements, like it, are attempting in their fire and their fury to remake the world anew and as something other than capitalist. If Marx and modernism each have lessons to teach us about the other, this is the context in which those lessons must now be received: modernism and modernist studies, in their spiraling declensions, are responsive to the dynamic forms of capitalism today and to the possibility, or even potential, of capitalism's imminent demise.

And yet, for all of this, we do not possess a thoroughgoing or comprehensive guide to these two interlocking forces, to the intersections and overlaps between Marx and modernism. The precedents for this kind of thinking are to be found in the critical outpourings of the Frankfurt School and with the inheritors of their legacy, like Berman and Jameson, for whom modernist artistic production means the aesthetic regime attempting to resist capitalism. The historical arguments have been bolstered and reenergized by Soviet-centered modernist scholarship, from art historians like Clark but also in the expansive cultural histories of Susan Buck-Morss and Boris Groys. The potentially idiosyncratic field of poetics hosts a burnished theoretical apparatus indexed to a critique of the value-form: this is what we find, in its most openly Marxist configuration, in those poets associated with Commune Editions, whose stated mission is to make good on the old situationist maxim, itself an inversion of modernist aestheticism: "it is not a question of putting poetry at the service of revolution, but rather of putting revolution at the service of poetry."[23] Joining these discussions are several dedicated books on the question of Marx and modernism. Exceptional among these is Martin Puchner's *Poetry of the Revolution: Marx, Manifestos, and the Avant-Gardes* (2005), which takes its title and point of departure directly from Marx. This book compares aesthetic and political manifestos based on the theoretical assumption that, within this genre, it is the manifestos' "form, not their particular complaints and demands, that articulates most succinctly the desires and hopes, maneuvers and strategies of modernity: to create points of no return; to make history; to fashion the future."[24] While aesthetically compelling and narratively eloquent, this ultra-formalist argument links two textual archives without paying much attention to historical specificity, or to the mediating forces of economic and social history, and so Puchner's Marx all but ceases to be identifiably Marxist, decoupled from questions of political economy, without which any Marxism is inevitably going to be superficial. This, however, is to say that interventions within the new modernist studies have cleared a path without necessarily pursuing it, opening up the possibilities of a modernist Marx and a Marxist modernism without conjuring those entities into existence. There is an articulate desire for such a conjuring. According to Ruth Jennison's characteristically sharp assessment, the most pressing task for modernist scholarship, which has otherwise been preoccupied with the artwork's complicities with capitalist modernity and its right-wing excrescences, is to "study the relationship between modernism and the less widespread, but equally compelling periodization of the twentieth century as one of transformative left utopianism."[25] That, an aggressively and unapologetically leftist vision, is what this collection aims to provide its readers, with hopes of doing so in such a way that it will be useful as well as polemical: an introduction to Marx and Marxism for the modernists, and an introduction to modernism for the Marxists—and so, together, an object lesson in the enduring relevance of these critical and cultural forces as well as and especially in combination today.

There is a logical progression to the structure of this book—or, in the spirit of Marx, a dialectical movement between its multiple parts. The first two sections, which make up the majority of the book's content, are near inversions of one another, together reading Marx as a thinker whose work absorbed artistic and cultural modernity as much as his writing then helped shape it into what we now call modernism. The format here follows that of other volumes in the series, which allows the title's repeated verbal-noun, "understanding," to describe a plurality of ambitions: to provide that introduction to a figure and a field in ways that will interest advanced undergraduates, graduate students, and other scholars new to the subject but at the same time to generate new insights for established scholars, experts, and long-term comrades and fellow travelers. That plurality, on which this book's chapters make good and then some, also reproduces the plurality of Marx, that he is and has been many things to many people and many movements. This is why, in describing what might be called the "Marxism-Event," Slavoj Žižek explains Marx as a multiplicity that inspires different responsive subjectivities with these examples:

(1) fidelity (communism, Leninism); (2) reactive re-integration (social democracy); (3) outright denial of the evental status (liberalism, Furet); (4) catastrophic total counter-attack in the guise of a pseudo-Event (fascism); (5) total enforcement of the Event, which ends up in an "obscure disaster" (Stalinism, the Khmer Rouge); (6) renewal of Marxism (Lenin, Trotsky, Mao).²⁶

In this volume, our sense is that modernism and modernist artworks can and do convoke within any one or any combination of these subjectivities, not all of them faithful or positive. In these ways, Marx has had a decisive impact on at least half the thinkers already treated in the "Understanding Philosophy, Understanding Modernism" series, looming large in the work of Maurice Blanchot, Gilles Deleuze, Michel Foucault, Maurice Merleau-Ponty, Jacques Rancière, Theodor Adorno, and Jacques Derrida, "It will always be a fault not to read and reread and discuss Marx," Derrida reminded us after the collapse of the Soviet Union, "to go beyond scholarly 'reading' or 'discussion.' It will be more and more a fault, a failing of theoretical, philosophical, political responsibility."²⁷

The unique tripartite structure of the books in this series works especially well for our volume on Marx. This is because Marx's thinking and writing was preoccupied with aesthetic inheritance as much as Marxism would go on to define modernism in and across multiple media. The book's first part, "Conceptualizing Marx," comprises close readings of Marx's central philosophical texts in relation to his artistic and primarily his literary antecedents, from Epicurus and Dante through Shakespeare and Dickens. The point of Part One is to show how Marx evolved as a thinker and a writer, from the earliest stages through the posthumous works, and to show how that evolution was tempered not just by his understanding and experience of political economy and materialist philosophy but also of literature and culture. While Marx's principal collaborator, Engels, would claim to have learned more about French society from the novels of Balzac than from "all of the professed historians, economists, and statisticians of the period together," it is well known that Marx planned a complete, critical study of the novelists' works, just as soon as his critique of political economy was complete.²⁸ This part, which advances chronologically through Marx's biography, begins with the youthful writer's enthusiasm for ancient Greece; proceeds through his affection for the gothic as well as his engagement with the classical literary genres; goes on to speculate on the rhetorical forms taken by his published and unpublished writings, from totalizing epic ambition to choric polyphony; and, while doing so, the chapters all seek to explain how Marx arrived at the ideas and thoughts and concepts we now associate with Marxism, not purely through the apprehension and critique of political economy but also in conversation with aesthetic and especially literary history. By looking at the way such literary influences irradiated Marx's thought at every turn of his career, this part aims to re-contextualize Marx and Marxism within the space of cultural modernity—doing so in a way that delivers incisive new interpretations that will appeal to readers embedded within but also coming to this from beyond the discourse of Marxism.

Part Two, "Marx in Modernism," is concerned with recognizably modernist aesthetics and demonstrates how Marx and Marxism were taken up by key modernists. The chapters included in this section go beyond Marxist readings of modernist texts to show how Marx and Marxism were coiled into the DNA of modernism. If, as Clark proposed, "there could and can be no modernism without the practical possibility of an end to capitalism existing," this part makes a similar argument for the importance of Marx to modernism, because no philosopher has ever expended as much scientific rigor and militant enthusiasm in the pursuit of that possibility, which he single-handedly elevated from utopian ideal to material truth.[29] Making good on such a proposition, this part includes discussion of the afterlife of texts by Marx, or how modernists working across disparate forms and genres and media all drew inspiration from Marx. The chapters in Part Two are organized around form and genre, rather than theme, in order to show how different media and different expressive modalities grapple with the legacy of Marx and Marxism in their own specific ways. Chapters here focus on the novel, the poem, cinema, theater, music, and architecture, before a wide-ranging essay on Marx and "popular modernism" refocuses attention on the visual regime as its own kind of mass-produced industry. The modernist texts encountered in this part as they are brought into contact with Marx or shown to have absorbed some kind of Marxism should be considered object lessons to be taken up elsewhere for either more thoroughgoing or more focused studies of modernism's Marxism.

The book's third and final part is a glossary of shorter chapters on some of Marx and Marxism's thorniest concepts, selected primarily because of their currency in or relevance to modernist thought. Rather than include myriad disconnected entries that would all need to be endlessly cross-referenced in order to push back against the atomizing force of ideational fetishism, this glossary clusters its terms and concepts under broader categories. Each entry in this section is self-contained, having been written in such a way as to engender specifically Marxist literacies built from a precise and generative technical vocabulary. Nevertheless, this part has a narrative of its own, and one that holds loosely to Marx's own explanatory model, matching the totalizing, maximalist drive of dialectical thought. The part thus begins with the constitutive building blocks for a Marxist critique of capitalism (with the commodity and its fetishism before working up through labor and value and money toward a picture of capital as a whole, its general formula), from which proceeds a series of social formations (class, family, technology, colonization, nature) and relational dynamics (ideology, alienation, materialism), and then anti-capitalist counterforces (revolution, communism, utopia). The entries in the glossary are written to be exported into and beyond the field of modernist studies. We hope that together they serve as the conceptual roadmap to a properly Marxist understanding of modernism, and individually as a set of concepts and ideas with which to accurately and lucidly theorize not only modernism but also the world that modernism and its critical interpreters have been forced to inhabit, namely capitalism, which collectively we shall overthrow.

Notes

1. Marshall Berman, *All That Is Solid Melts into Air: The Experience of Modernity* (London: Verso, 2010), 89–90.
2. Berman, *All That Is Solid Melts into Air*, 90.
3. Leszek Kołakowski, *Main Currents of Marxism*, trans. P. S. Falla (New York: Norton, 1976), 356.
4. Eric Hobasbawm, *How to Change the World: Tales of Marx and Marxism* (Great Britain: Little Brown, 2011), 212.
5. Frantz Fanon, *The Wretched of the Earth* (London: Penguin, 1963), 30–1.
6. Walter Rodney, "Marxism and African Liberation" (Speech at Queen's College, New York, 1975). https://www.marxists.org/subject/africa/rodney-walter/works/marxismandafrica.htm, accessed August 20, 2019.
7. Silvia Federici, *Caliban and the Witch: Women, the Body and Primitive Accumulation* (Brooklyn: Automedia, 2004), 11. For a useful account of Marxist-feminism, see Michèle Barrett, *Women's Oppression Today: The Marxist/Feminist Encounter* (London: Verso, 1980).
8. W. E. B. Du Bois, *Black Reconstruction in America* (New York: Harcourt, 1935), 358.
9. Rosa Luxemburg, "Marxist Theory and the Proletariat," 64.14 *Vorwärts* (March 1903). https://www.marxists.org/archive/luxemburg/1903/03/14-abs.htm, accessed August 20, 2019.
10. Louis Althusser and Étienne Balibar, *Reading Capital*, trans. Ben Brewster (London: Verso, 1968), 13.
11. Marx, "Theses on Feuerbach," in *The Marx-Engels Reader*, ed. Robert C. Tucker, 2nd ed. (London: Norton, 1978), 145. This edition will be used for many texts cited throughout the volume. It has been chosen not as the authoritative edition of Marx's writing, which it is not, but for reasons of accessibility: for a relatively comprehensive collection, this is a book that seems to appear just about everywhere in the English-speaking world—in every library, online as a PDF, on many syllabi, and on the throwaway tables of innumerable second-hand bookstores. Moreover, considering Marxism is also if not primarily a practical revolutionary project, let us remind ourselves that revolutionary literature cannot just be an object to display or a theory to be read in the comfort of the study or at the lectern: instead, it should find its home within the backpack alongside munitions, rations, and other supplies, and should be easily disposable in the case of a police raid or arrest. This edition meets that standard. So: next time you're admiring a comrade's books, or browsing the library at an occupation or autonomous zone, keep an eye out for its red spine!
12. Nectar Jan, "A New Class Struggle: Chinese Party Members Get Back to Communist Manifesto Basics," *South China Morning Post* (April 29, 2018). https://www.scmp.com/news/china/policies-politics/article/2143841/new-class-struggle-chinese-party-members-get-back, accessed August 20, 2019.
13. Marx and Engels, "Manifesto of the Communist Party," in *The Marx-Engels Reader*, 474.
14. Yanis Varoufakis, "Marx Predicted Our Present Crisis—And Points the Way Out," *The Guardian* (April 20, 2018). https://www.theguardian.com/news/2018/apr/20/yanis-varoufakis-marx-crisis-communist-manifesto, accessed August 20, 2019.
15. Marx and Engels, "The German Ideology" in *The Marx-Engels Reader*, 162.

16　Marx and Engels, "Manifesto of the Communist Party," 500.
17　Marx, "The Eighteenth Brumaire of Louis Bonaparte," in *The Marx-Engels Reader*, 597.
18　Fredric Jameson, *A Singular Modernity: Essay on the Ontology of the Present* (London: Verso, 2002), 141, 215.
19　See Jameson, "The End of Temporality," *Critical Inquiry* 29.4 (Summer 2003): 695–718.
20　Theodor Adorno, *Aesthetic Theory*, trans. Robert Hullot-Kentor (London and New York: Continuum, 1997), 33.
21　T. J. Clark, *Farewell to an Idea: Episodes from a History of Modernism* (New Haven: Yale University Press, 2001), 9.
22　Alys Moody and Stephen J. Ross, "On Global Modernism and Academic Precarity: A Reply to Claire Barber-Stetson," *The Discipline, Modernism/Modernity Blog* 4.2 (June 20, 2019). https://modernismmodernity.org/forums/posts/academic-precarity-reply, accessed August 20, 2019.
23　Laura Carter, "Interview with Commune Editions: Small Presses on the Move," *Jacket 2* (September 30, 2015). https://jacket2.org/commentary/interview-commune-editions, accessed August 20, 2019.
24　Martin Puchner, *Poetry of the Revolution: Marx, Manifestos, and the Avant-Gardes* (Princeton, NJ: Princeton University Press, 2006), 2.
25　Ruth Jennison, *The Zukofsky Era: Modernity, Margins, and the Avant-Garde* (Baltimore: Johns Hopkins University Press, 2012), 2.
26　Slavoj Žižek, *Less Than Nothing: Hegel and the Shadow of Dialectical Materialism* (London: Verso, 2012), 836.
27　Jacques Derrida, *Specters of Marx: The State of the Debt, the Work of Mourning and the New International*, trans. Peggy Kamuf (London: Routledge, 1994), 14.
28　Marx and Engels, *On Literature and Art* (Moscow: Progress, 1976), 91.
29　Clark, *Farewell to an Idea*, 9.

Part One

Conceptualizing Marx

1

Greek Ideology and Modern Politics in Marx's First Works

Giacomo Bianchino

Philosophy, like the owl of Minerva, takes flight at the end of the day. There is a pathos for anyone who recognizes the significance of this statement. It takes from each individual thinker the right to the "last word." Pronouncing the absolute truth of a statement like this means embracing the irony of one's own finitude. To be Hegelian is to commit absolutely to the reality of a dialectic by which all historical declarations of the absolute eventually become relativized. No less, one would imagine, for the "Master" himself. Ultimately, Hegel would have had to understand that this fate awaited his own "universal" project of thought. His attempts to bring the dialectic to bear on old metaphysical notions revolved around the ways thought can *situate* itself in the present. Those who adopted the owl as their sigil, then, would do so in permanent reference to the problem of their "modernity." Only thought that recognized "the philosophy of Hegel . . . has pronounced sentence upon itself" could overcome metaphysical abstraction and make philosophy the act of a historical subject.[1] The pursuit of modernity, insofar as it was taken up by thinkers in the Hegelian aftermath, was the means by which an atmospheric "negativity" was transformed into an active and determinate "negation."[2]

Perhaps the most ruthless attempt at situating thought in history came from the youthful works of Karl Marx. As early as 1837, Marx told his father of a felt need to "acquire modernity and the standpoint of the contemporary scientific view."[3] His modernity was an attempt to go beyond metaphysics and to locate himself in the determinate problems of the day. This project was to "discover" its protagonist in the model of the proletariat Marx developed in the years between 1842 and 1845.[4] The proletarian view, unencumbered by the class interests that constrained bourgeois thought, was Marx's answer to the problem of modernity. It would take him beyond mere "interpretation" and toward the effort of building a subject capable of "changing" the finite reality in which all subjectivity found itself. It was in the process of elaborating a proletarian view of reality that Marx developed the critical method he would leave to posterity: historical materialism. The realization that *economic struggle* and not philosophical speculation would liberate humanity drove the young thinker, after 1845, to examine the material conditions of the world. This meant negating the Hegelian edifice to develop a totally situated project: the attempt to determine the forces of production "with the precision of a natural science" and to study the material world "without any foreign admixture."[5]

It would produce some interesting monsters, then, if we are to ask the *literary* question of Marx's primitive modernism. Modernity was, in Marx's youthful imagination, an entire register of analysis. In fact, the first struggle in Marx's career was against the "spiritual situation at that time," whose lyrical mood transformed everything real into "a remote beyond."[6] On leaving home, his first "idealistic" attitude produced works of verse and drama. The verse, compiled and sent to Jenny in several volumes, was characterized "by attacks on the present times, by broad and formless feelings thrown together."[7] His appetite for modernity, however, prompted the realization that the "complete opposition of what is and what should be" was rhetorical rather than philosophical. This led him to the unforgiving idea that philosophy must be supreme, and "poetry may only and should only be an accompaniment."[8]

As the "discovery" of Hegel pushed him to "bring genuine pearls into the light of day," Marx began a short-lived attempt to use literature as a vehicle for philosophical explication.[9] In his student years, he wrote a long and "forced" comedy on a range of philosophical themes called *Scorpio and Felix*, and an "unsuccessful . . . fantastic drama" on political romanticism called *Oulanem*. The last work that can be called properly literary in Marx's canon is 1837's *Cleanthes, or the Starting Point and Necessary Continuation of Philosophy*. Moving beyond the "moonshine" of his early poetry, this defense of the dialectical model of philosophy was cashed out in the form of Greek dialogue, with the stoic Cleanthes as its protagonist. Even as early as this "philosophical dialectical account of divinity and how it manifests itself conceptually, as religion, as nature, and as history," however, Marx clearly had no scruples sacrificing literary unity to philosophical ambition.[10] His interest in acquiring the "modern scientific view" drove him further from self-conscious poetics to the use of literary flair as pure "accompaniment."

Marx's tilt into Hegelianism gave a new set of structures to his developing interest in history. His pursuit of philosophical modernity and his attempt to situate thought in history prompted him to develop an acute and often brutal sense of his own place in history. He found himself in the "iron times" that come after a "great philosophy" has animated the world. In this light, he saw himself chiefly as a "carrier" of the Hegelian sequence, whose role was to make the system "worldly."[11] This project was ultimately informed by precedents he discovered in the proponents of what he called "Greek Enlightenment."[12] In the late 1830s, Marx began to weave a modern view from the frayed threads of the Greek Fleece he found in the work of the Alexandrian schools of the fourth and third centuries BC. It was in his dissertation, *On the Difference between the Democritean and Epicurean Philosophies of Nature*, that he developed his own model of philosophical history. By focusing on the Hellenistic inheritors of Aristotle, Marx developed original theories about the German interpretation of Hegel. His understanding of the Greek antiquity was thus recoded by the modern parameters of the struggle developing in Germany between the "Left" and "Right" Hegelians. In this way, the ancient world shed light on the current situation, with Marx seeking to provide the conditions under which both were comparable. Epicurus, the "greatest representative" of Greek Enlightenment, had worth for Marx so long as he illuminated the universal conditions of the worldly reception of philosophy.[13]

Marx's philosophical theory of influence and reception, then, demanded he become a certain kind of reader. As with Epicurus' critical ingestion of Aristotle, Marx set himself the task of reading reality as if it were an established, Hegelian text. His approach to this text was at times quodlibetarian and at times critical. On the one hand, Marx sought to protect the authorial integrity of the "giant thinker" from the moral reproaches of his critics and followers.[14] Living in the wake of this "master" meant searching for traces of absolute Spirit in history. The irony that Marx recognized better than any other, however, was that this intellectual machinery would eventually claim Hegel as collateral. Moving beyond the German Right's enthusiasm for "mediocrity" as the "normal manifestation" of absolute Spirit also meant putting everything, including Hegel, in its place.[15]

This appetite for the dialectical method of relativizing old absolutes infused Marx's style of reading with an attitude that can only be called satirical. He himself was aware of the historical necessity of this parodic impulse. In the dissertation, Marx identified both the young Hegelians and the receivers of Aristotle as revellers in a "carnival of philosophy" (*Fastnachzeit der Philosophie*) that develops after a world-system makes itself "total" and self-sufficient in its own abstraction. In this carnival, philosophy "throws itself on the breast of the world" and seeks to resolve its theoretical issues practically. Having "expanded to be the whole world," thought now "turns against the world of appearances" to find truth.[16] The *Fastnachzeit*, literally the *Mardi Gras* before Lent, allows and requires the total overturning of convention and orthodoxy. It means inverting philosophy's own preconceptions and evaluating against the reality from which it emerged. It is in the *iron* time that philosophy itself becomes *ironized*, transforming its own ambient negativity into an active and subjective process of negation.

The young Marx drew his own critical "modernity" from the "carnival" philosophy of Epicurus. In this conjunction, "objective universality" is transformed into "subjective forms of individual consciousness."[17] These subjective forms evaluate the majesty of the formal system by their own discrete and concrete needs as individuals. His "ruthless" negative position made Marx a powerful critical reader. But he soon realized that the Epicurean subjectivism was only able to tie itself in contradictions. Marx came to recognize "real and true science" as something that had to constitute itself in a struggle against the view of any individual subject.[18] The attempt to elaborate the philosophical sequence "subjectively" ultimately meant asserting his project's own finitude and pronouncing sentence on itself. For Marx, acquiring modernity meant moving beyond "philosophy as philosophy" and seeking a model that could be "determined with the precision of natural science."[19] This pivot toward materialism meant reprising philosophy as just one "ideological form in which men become conscious" of class conflict "and fight it out."[20] The so-called mature Marx is thus born in the assertion of philosophy's contingency as just one site of the class struggle.

Taking the complexity of the young thinker's carnivalesque criticism as the starting point, what remains of this chapter traces the explicit movement of the Greek influence in his *bildung*. The first two sections examine Marx's development through the analysis of Greek thought in the dissertation. The major problem that emerges from this is the role that the individual subject plays in elaborating the "objective universality" of scientifically-deduced truths. The third section examines Marx's application of the Epicurean subjectivism to his own time. The inadequacies that he discovered in his attempt at this historical generalization are taken up in the fourth and final section. Here, a new narrative of ideological development through the early works is traced from a semi-Epicurean position of negative "critique" to a positively "scientific" position. This is elaborated in the concluding statements on the idea of "proletarian genericity." It is the overall contention that his youthful internalization of Epicurean irony eventually made Marx impatient with the very foundations of philosophy. Specifically, his ironic sense of his own historical place in the carnival of Hegel's philosophy prepared the way for his move beyond the purely critical-textual and toward "the modern view" of historical materialism. It was this "generic orientation of thought," unbeholden to *any* ideological subject, that is the main legacy of the thinker as he transformed from reader to writer in the mid-1840s.[21]

The Dissertation: Epicurus' Carnival and Abstract-individual Self-Consciousness

The Greek origins of Marxian modernity are on full display in his earliest works. In the dissertation, which was his first sustained piece of academic writing, Marx's central concern was German thought's Greek heritage. Composed between 1839 and 1841, *The Difference between the Democritean and Epicurean Philosophies of Nature* sought to interpret the world-historic value of the atomist schools of the Hellenistic period. The thesis was to constitute one episode of a "larger work in which I shall present in detail the cycle of Epicurean, Stoic and Sceptic philosophy in their relation to the whole of Greek speculation."[22] Though Marx is clearly working with a Hegelian ambition for world history here, he is already concerned with the shortcomings of the old master's apparatus. The need for a restoration of the Hellenistic atomists was, in Marx's estimation, a result of Hegel's own underestimation of the importance of these schools. "In the admirably great and bold plan of his history of philosophy," he writes, "the great thinker was hindered by his view of what he called speculative thought *par excellence* from recognising in these systems their great importance for the history of Greek philosophy and for the Greek mind in general."[23] This is why, in his dissertation, Marx sets out to dignify the Hellenistics in a story of the development of Spirit, ultimately demonstrating that "these systems are the key to the true history of Greek philosophy" and so discovering the cunning of reason where Hegel saw only contingency.[24]

For Marx, the importance of the Epicurean school does not lie in its concrete scientific contributions. Instead of the "metaphysical characteristics" of the Epicurean physics, Marx seeks the "spiritual" importance of the Alexandrian philosophy for thought as a whole.²⁵ In restoring Epicurus to history, the main challenge is differentiating him from the figure to whom he is often subordinated: Democritus.²⁶ Above all else, what makes Epicurus unique among Greeks is his capacity to read philosophy *against* philosophy. What interests Marx from a world-historical perspective is the Alexandrian's problematization of science's foundations: questioning the role that investigation played in the overall life of the human mind. In mounting a philosophical criticism of Aristotelian science, the Hellenistics enacted the "double-edged demand" of all carriers of a world philosophy, to "turn against the world" as well as "against philosophy itself."²⁷

The double assault against the material world and abstract theory is what makes this conjuncture of thought a "carnival of philosophy." The carnival and its revellers hold up a worldview to the laughter of the world that formulated it. Parody here should not be confused with its modern pejorative deployment. The Hegelian interpretation of the "parodic" attitude in Greek literature was something aptly explained a century after Marx by the Russian literary theorist Mikhail Bakhtin. In *The Dialogic Imagination*, written between Kimry and Moscow in the 1930s and 1940s, Bakhtin pointed out that ancient satire or criticism did not operate as a force of obliteration so much as one of negation and sublation. In the imagination of classical and Hellenistic writers, the parody was not a devaluation but a fulfillment of tragedy, or of discourse more generally. The "fourth drama," the satyr-play, is said to complete the tragic fiction and inoculate it against the outside world by including it in the play's machinery. "It is as if such mimicry rips the word away from its object, disunifies the two and shows that a given straightforward generic word . . . is one-sided, bounded, incapable of exhausting the object."²⁸ The afterlife of tragedy in satire is, within this context, the condition of its worldly fulfillment.

Marx's image of the ancient philosophy is based on a consonant view of the dramatic and ironic in the Greek and Roman imagination. For him, the "carnival of philosophy" seeks to fulfill and complete philosophy by bringing it down to earth. The parodic-satirical lens reads philosophy according to the very concrete needs of an "abstract-individual self-consciousness."²⁹ This union of science with the needs of the historical subject makes the Epicurean edifice a choice candidate for the explication of Hegel's dialectics of Spirit. More than the Aristotelian system, which was agnostic on its own historical status, the Hellenistic thinkers were able to transform the scientific study of nature into a category of historical reflexivity. By the logic of this subjectivist system, "sensuous nature is only the objectified, empirical, individual self-consciousness."³⁰ It is the historical subject's own discrete and individual needs that become the critical standard for all philosophy and knowledge.³¹

Epicurus' subordination of truth to the needs of an abstract "subject" leads to some interesting developments in his philosophy of science. The Alexandrian, in his own writings, asserts that the condition of science is that humanity was "troubled by our suspicions of the phenomena of the sky and about death, and also by our failure to grasp the limits of pains and desires."³² Without these decidedly individual but apparently human problems, we would have "no need of natural science."³³ This evaluation of science by subjective need generated the standard of ataraxy (*ataraxia*): the serenity of a human soul. For Epicurus, science must be evaluated by its ability to generate and maintain this serenity. Philosophy has importance only insofar as it provides us with "real health," which it does by creating practical knowledge and freeing us from troubling myths.[34] In the final instance, the justification of the entire philosophical edifice is derived from "prudence": a thorough and realistic estimation of one's own powers in relation to outside forces. Philosophy thus becomes a tool for maintaining ataraxy through knowledge of what one can and cannot control.[35]

This is an extreme conditioning of science by the needs of the individual. Even in the positivistic and concrete criticisms of Hegel developed by the German theorists of the Right, nobody would think to attribute him such a radical solipsism. But for a Marx more Hegelian than Hegel, Epicurus is paradigmatic because he develops atomistic science (including the famous *clinamen* or atomic swerve) from "the consequence of the principle itself."[36] While Democritean empiricism "considers properties of the atom only in relation to the formation of differences in the world of appearances," Epicurus subordinates empirical observation to the transcendental necessity of ideals.[37] What constitutes necessity in this case is that which preserves the ataraxy of Epicurus' abstract subject. The worldly carnival fulfills and inoculates the system of philosophy critically by grounding it in the human realm that forms its basis. The elevation of the subject, an "abstract-individual self-consciousness," to the condition of science is what distinguishes Epicurus from earlier Greek thought and particularly Democritus. And it is this that makes him, for Marx, "the greatest representative of Greek Enlightenment."[38]

Greek Enlightenment and Greek Ideology: In the Garden of Meteors

Marx learned Epicurean irony too well to remain faithful to it for long. Indeed, as with all historical absolutes, the effusive presentation of Epicurus as the leading figure of Greek science contains an internal negativity. Insofar as Epicurus elevated "abstract-individuality" to an "absolute principle," his thought forms the "prototype of the Roman mind, the shape in which Greece wandered to Rome."[39] But in its own self-awareness, Epicurean philosophy gives up its claim on truth and absoluteness. The "satirical" or "carnivalesque" aspect of Epicureanism is found in its recognition that the truth of its conclusions is contingent on the needs of the historical subject. This philosophy relates itself to the absolute precisely by historicizing and negating its own scientific edifice. Indeed, Epicurus laughs at the dogmatic assuredness of philosophers who think they are committed to anything other than their own "health," and this laughter echoes through his own system, finitizing any totalizing claims he might be inclined to make. Epicurus' elaboration of this dialectical principle means differentiating existence from essence and proceeding to the latter through negation. For this reason, all appearance is subordinated to the presiding figure of "contingency." Marx is aware of the consequences of this move. For him, Epicurus' model of self-consciousness has "the intrinsic urge to affirm itself in the things themselves in which it can only affirm itself by negating them."[40] In this way, the Alexandrian thinker puts himself permanently on the edge of mysticism and total solipsism.

At the end of the dissertation, Marx takes up the problem of atomism's active auto-negation. His final chapter is on the heavily-criticized Epicurean theory of meteors.[41] The Greek thinker treats these heavenly bodies, seemingly unbeholden to terrestrial laws, with a total agnosticism. In their obscurity to reason, they fall under the same category as speculation or myth. In Epicurus' view, the imputation of any cause for heavenly motion is simultaneously justified and unjustified: it is undecidable. Assigning them a single cause with any conviction is a "foolish notion of astrology."[42] He condemns the mythic explanation of their movement as a "superstition" that is not only unfounded but which also threatens ataraxy.[43]

For Marx, Epicurus' agnosticism on the planets is a rejection of the only point in external nature that ostensibly justifies his system. The remoteness of heavenly bodies from questions of human need leaves them available as a means to study the "principle" of atomic physics without the problem of essence and appearance. "In the celestial system matter has received form into itself, has taken the individuality into itself and has thus achieved its independence."[44] The movement of the planets should be a justification of the Epicurean system because everything is held in abstract space and governed by pure laws of movement. But, as Marx observes, precisely this positive instantiation of the principle is made impossible by the Epicurean philosophy of science, which relies on the preservation of a distinction wherein "the senses are the only criteria in concrete nature, just as abstract reason is the only criterion in the world of the atoms."[45] The alienated relation of appearance to essence means that sensuous nature can never be taken as a positive substantiation of the atomic movement. "Where Epicurus' principle becomes reality it will cease to have reality for him."[46] The principle of the noncoincidence of the real, atomic world and its sensuous alienation in experience is the condition of ataraxy and the foundation of science. "Nothing is eternal which destroys the ataraxy of individual self-consciousness."[47]

What, according to Marx, does this mean for philosophy in and after the Epicurean world? Precisely where one should find the justificatory moment at which theory becomes "worldly," the world is renounced. "If abstract individual self-consciousness is posited as an absolute principle, then, indeed, all true and real science is done away with [*aufgehoben*] inasmuch as individuality does not rule within the nature of things themselves."[48] At the moment "universality" becomes "concrete" and matter takes Spirit into itself, the study of this universality becomes impossible.[49] Marx is forced to accept that Epicurus' carnival of philosophy ends with the renunciation of science. "Abstract-individual self-consciousness" opposes itself to the universal and to knowledge as a whole, and science is done away with.[50]

This irreducible contradiction is what David Stanley refers to as the Greek ideology: a species of "alienated thought," whereby a mind estranges itself from the world and finds peace in its own self-sufficiency. "Epicurus' abstract-individual freedom, now freed from constraints," Stanley reflects, "only serves to open the way for *arbitrary pragmatic constructions* for securing ataraxy; this allows Epicurus to turn away from nature and from the world as such: he remains in his garden."[51] For Marx, by prioritizing "abstract-individual self-consciousness" the Epicurean philosophy fails to apprehend its fulfillment in the "concrete individuality, universality" of the world.[52] Its form of "critique" does not measure the false by the true but the world by the individual. If Epicureanism bestows humanity with anything, it is the troubling conclusion that the self-consciousness of the abstract-individual subject is *incompatible* with the scientific study of the material world. For a student of Hegel, this problem would have to be resolved to avoid the total relativization of the system in which he moved.

Living in Iron Times

Marx was keenly aware of the problems his Epicurean discovery posed for any sort of Hegelian project. His reflections on Greek philosophy are posed only in the way they cast light on the present. The dissertation's broader conclusions are more about the reception of thought than its germination: the process of elaboration and critical reading. Following on from the Hegelian story of Spirit, the young thinker developed an episodic logic of historical development to explain how the Idea informs science and subjects. This Idea, the Hegelian "principle," stands above historical development as the shared outcome of all science: something to which all other (lower case) ideas are related as particular "concepts" or "notions." By seeking the Idea as a shared norm of all science, Marx was able to link the world of Epicurus to his own. In the notebooks to the dissertation, he divided the history of philosophy into moments of condensation and diffusion. On the one hand, he envisioned "nodal points which raise philosophy in itself to concretion" and "apprehend abstract principles in a totality."[53] On the other hand, he proposed "moments when philosophy turns its eyes to the external world, and no longer apprehends it, but, as a practical person, weaves, as it were, intrigues with the world."[54] Both the Hellenistics and the followers of Hegel are engaged in the latter demand, to make thought intrigue with the world. It is in this that they share their status as revellers in the philosophical carnival.

There are also similarities in the details of how Epicurus and Marx's contemporaries "intrigued" with the great philosophies that preceded them. Epicurus tries to reconcile the philosophical system with the world through the reason of the private individual. He elevates the latent aspects of the world-system into activities. "What," claims Marx, "formerly appeared as growth is now determination, what was negativity existing in itself has now become negation."[55] The German followers of Hegel were forced to face the same necessity of making the Master's thought practical. Both Left and Right, for Marx, consciously or unconsciously maintained a separation of philosophy from the world it inhabits. While the Right responded to this separation by criticizing philosophy from a position of the "positive" or empirical reality, the "liberal" (Marx's term for the Left) party remained "the party of the concept."[56] Like Epicurus, they set out to resolve concrete issues in the remoteness of the principle. The "historicist" school of Hegelian criticism, led by theorists like Karl Daub and Johann Philipp Gabler, emphasized the rationality of the state apparatus and the practical resolution of theoretical issues. On the Left, theorists like Bruno Bauer and Arnold Ruge (a close friend and collaborator of Marx) turned against the Right's defense of the state by emphasizing the contingency of the present in relation to the absolute.

Marx's ambiguous position on Epicurus casts light on the relationship he bore to the Hegelian "schools" at this time. It has become commonplace to align Marx with the Left's project of critique: the measuring of "the individual existence by the essence, the particular reality by the Idea."[57] As Stanley has noted, however, the Marx of 1841 is not completely clear about his allegiances.[58] In his notes for the dissertation, Marx insisted that both "sides" of the Hegelian dilemma had their share of "slugs."[59] Marx commits himself to rising above either of these positions, parodically finding each group, in the words of Bakhtin, "one-sided, bounded, incapable of exhausting the object."[60] Instead, he seeks the conditions of their mutual composability as outgrowths of the historical opposition between the system and the world. Together they constitute "two sides of the dilemma facing Hegelianism."[61] Individually they are, according to Marx, equally "ideological" in their attempt to transform a scientific problem into a problem of subjectivity. Insofar as they are unable to recognize the real cause of their antagonism, they are condemned to entertain what Althusser would eventually describe as an "*imaginary* relationship . . . to the real conditions of experience."[62]

Taking at least one cue from Epicurus, Marx sought precisely to study the reality behind the dogmatic Left and Right mystifications. His sense that the Hegelian schools were ideologically alienated from the reality of their situation prompted Marx to cultivate his signature textual cynicism. In the view of the dissertation's notebooks, the cynic was one of the *Fastnachzeit* revellers who arrived to the party disguised "as a dog."[63] They take no position, and instead subject all those around them to excoriating criticism. Following Diogenes, Marx's cynicism sought to unveil the worldly *interests* behind philosophical parties. The constant measuring of contingency by essence prompted him to find the relativity in all absolute declarations. Instead of becoming yet another "doctrinaire," Marx mounted a theoretical program based on "a ruthless critique of everything existing."[64] He thereby sought to "help the *dogmatics* to clarify to themselves the meaning of their own positions." The importance of a "ruthless criticism," then, is to cleanse an existing system of its ideological illusions by showing the historically relative "meaning" of positions. So long as critique remains "afraid of its own conclusions," it will remain "infected" by its opposite—by the ideological constraints of the system from which it emerged and which it must, by historical necessity, negate. It was his critical "ruthlessness," in which the principle alone survives, that Marx found a foil to project him beyond Left and Right. But in transforming the "negativity in itself" of dogmatic philosophy into an active "negation," he was also forced to make the final pronunciation of Hegel's "sentence."[65]

The End of the Carnival: Marxist Cynica

The next two years saw Marx building the parameters of his critique and moving further from the coordinates of Hegel. The major works from the 1842–4 period are a critique of Bruno Bauer's political theory and of Hegel's philosophy of right. In these, the turn against the Left Hegelians was transformed into a criticism of Hegel himself. Marx recognized the trace of Epicurus' "abstract-individual self-consciousness" in the abstraction of Hegel. He also began to recognize the urgency of a new, concrete method. During this time, his editorship of the *Rheinische Zeitung* forced Marx for the first time to "take part in discussion on so-called material interests."[66] His engagement with the problem of wood theft in the Rhenish Landtag and the conditions of the Moselle peasantry tested the "ruthlessness" of his approach. His practical engagements made him increasingly impatient with the appetite "to go further" than the facts. In pursuit of a concrete universal, Marx turned to a "positive philosophy" that, methodologically, had more in common with conservative historicist legalists like Friedrich Carl von Savigny and the Hegelian Right than with the theoretics of the Left.[67]

Through the post-dissertation period, the young thinker's main philosophical preoccupation was the relation between the subject and truth as presented by politics and science. This problem was fleshed out first as a criticism of the abstraction of Bauer's liberalism in 1843's *The Jewish Question*. But the decisive movement came in the fragmentary *Critique of Hegel's Philosophy of Right*, which Marx worked on throughout 1843. Under the influence of Ludwig Feuerbach, the eminent leftist critic of religion, Marx turned against Hegel's confusion of the relation between the subject and the world. According to the Marx of the *Critique*'s notebooks, Hegel "makes *subjects* out of *abstract reality, necessity* (or the distinct spheres of substance, *substantiality*; etc.) out of *abstract logical categories*."[68] It isn't too much of a stretch to see Marx's critique of Epicurus moving under this statement. Hegel's self-conscious Spirit is as alienated from reality as the "abstract-individuality" of the Greek. Hegel makes substance the predicate of Spirit, which itself is transformed into a subject. For Marx, this is the wrong way around. In fact, it is "matter," the world of the senses, that primarily constitutes substance. All theoretical abstraction is an alienation from this essence. In a roundabout way, this is perhaps the first statement of Marx's materialism.

The only part of the *Critique* that Marx published was the introduction, which appeared in the *Deutzsche-Franzoische Jahrbücher* in early 1844. In it, he takes materialism beyond the established limits of Left critique. Working with the critical edifice he developed earlier in the notes to the dissertation, he contends that both the "practical" (Right) and "theoretical" (Left) Hegelian parties are ideological outgrowths of a division between the world and philosophy. The attempt by the Right to abolish philosophy fails to realize that "you cannot abolish philosophy without realising it." The Left, on the other hand, fails to recognize that their criticism of the German world relies on a philosophy which "itself belongs to this world."[69] Instead of adopting the "philosophical" or "anti-philosophical" position, one must turn to the practical realization of philosophy. This is only possible by negating all previous philosophy—by abolishing "philosophy as philosophy."[70] Any thought "infected" by the bourgeois, speculative view of the world had to have its "mystifications" revealed. Instead of affirming its theoretical aloofness, Marx sought to "identify" his criticism with "real struggles."[71] Here, philosophy's principle is subordinated to discrete and practical political ends.

This is a distinct movement away from the Epicurean pursuit of ataraxy through theory alone. In the absolute declaration of contingency and the attachment of his philosophy to a practical, nearly prudential, model, however, one can see the glimmer of Epicurus. In the *Critique*, Marx searches for a subject that would achieve universal self-consciousness by fulfilling its own needs. This is a philosophy that searches for a subject whose self-assertion amounts to its own self-negation. For this reason, he develops the theory of a subject with "radical chains," a "class" of people that would overcome the problems of philosophy practically by abolishing the material antagonisms that give rise to abstraction and alienation. In destroying the conditions of their own "universal" sufferings, such a class would seek redress for "wrong in general." The resolution of their demands requires as its foundation the destruction of all classes through the destruction of private property.[72] This class, whose collective search for a kind of ataraxy destroys the foundations of social antagonism, brings the carnival of philosophy to an end. The Epicurean edifice of subjectivism, the humanistic morals of the Left, and the conservative anti-theoretics of the Right are all ushered offstage to the critical laughter of the proletariat.

Conclusion: Universal Chains and Proletarian Genericity

In a neat chiasmus, Marx's reading of Epicurus' reading teaches us something about reading Marx. Understood as the protracted and difficult approach to a "modern point of view," the early works take on significance for Marx's broader career as a revolutionary thinker. In this story, his mobilization of the proletariat in the *Critique* allows him to settle the question of the subject and modernity first opened by the dissertation. In philosophical terms, this resolution is facilitated by the move from "abstract-individual self-consciousness" to "abstract universal self-consciousness." To go from Epicurus' individuated philosophical subject to the universal subject of history transforms *ataraxia* into a revolutionary mechanism.

This, however, is not the whole story. The negation that "abstract universality" performs also urged Marx beyond his youthful Hegelianism. As a solution to the Greek problem of philosophy, the proletariat is not simply a universal class. It is its parodic character as a group whose program fulfills *and* destroys the liberal ideological mystification that allows the proletariat to ironize the foundations of philosophy itself. Their incompatibility with the entire system means that they constitute a point *within* ideology from which its foundations become visible. Generated by the system's own contradictions, they reveal the untruth of its own intellectual apparatus. Marx understood that the theoretical "freedom" of the proletariat meant a *practical* resolution through the destruction of the state and the capitalist system of production. The incompatibility of liberalism with freedom or flourishing makes the entire theoretical-political project of reform legible as an ideological operation of the state itself. The impossibility of self-actualization under capital is the principle that decorates their banners as the proletariat seek ataraxy by the barrel of a gun.

This ironizing of an established reality, the ideological conjuncture of capitalist reproduction, makes the proletariat a *generic* point of thought: a position from which truth is thinkable within a given ideological conjuncture. Generic thought thinks truth as a "hole in knowledge" or a gap in ideology.[73] It looks beyond the regular order that governs politics and language by admitting what these regimes rule as impossible (or "indiscernible"). "The term 'generic,'" in Alain Badiou's definition, "positively designates that what does not allow itself to be discerned is in reality the general truth of a situation, the truth of its being, as considered as the foundation of all knowledge to come."[74] The proletarian view is therefore one that is singularly and scientifically "modern" insofar as its intellectual project is geared to the critique of the interests underlying ideology. It totally relativizes the categories philosophy imagined for itself as absolutes.

Just as Epicurus destroyed the Aristotelian sequence by fulfilling it, Marx simultaneously consummates and annihilates the philosophical question of the subject as it existed through Hegel. The proletarian view overcomes the Epicurean problem of the subjective edifice because the proletariat are yet to be constituted as a subject. They are simply the always-forthcoming answer to the radical theorist's problem of a "universal class." They are what Walter Benjamin recognized in Bertolt Brecht's characters as "virtual revolutionaries."[75] Communist praxis takes the concrete needs of the set of laborers "who live only so long as they find work" and organizes them "*into a class, and consequently into a political party*."[76] This absence of a living subjectivity constitutes their political universality and makes them a possible point of genericity. The generic orientation of thought can be tied to a "definite party position" insofar as the party is completely opposed to the "mediocrity" of the present ideology. The opposition of the immediate interests of the laborers to capitalist production at large makes their position an inherently political one. This means their concrete class-character isn't exhaustive of their political significance. The proletarian subject is not *situated* or spoken-for ahead of time in the figure of the old semiskilled industrial worker. It is a position that can be taken up, a subjectivity that is built in reference to the truths discovered by the critique of ideology. Marx learned from the Left and Right split that subjectivity itself is constituted in advance by ideology.[77] He realized, as he came to see through Hegelianism, that the presence of a subject is nearly fatal for "real and true science." A Marxist science, if it is to go beyond ideology, would have to be turned to precisely what is "unconscious" for the individual historical subject.

Marx declares the contingency of philosophy's categories in a way not entirely unpredictable for a student of Epicurus. By tying theory to its own practical resolution, he stands not only Hegel on his head but the whole of Western thought. He does not, like the Greek ideology, begin with a subject, whose suture is always-already ideological. Instead, the truth as discovered by science must be taken as the point from which a subject is constructed. It is this placement of truth in ontological and temporal priority to the subject that constitutes Marx's advancement on "critique" as such. Though it was not to receive its concretion until the post-1845 works on political economy, it enjoyed its first expressions as early as the dissertation. Marx's self-consciousness as a carrier and a reader of Hegel's philosophy in the iron time allowed him to escape the interpretive crisis of Hegelianism. With his discovery of the proletariat and the development of historical materialism, Marx advanced a nonphilosophical response to the crisis of philosophy.

Notes

1. Marx, "Notebooks on Epicurean Philosophy," in *Marx and Engels Collected Works*, ed. Jack Cohen, Clemens Dutt, and Michael Huds (Laurence and Wishart Electric Book, 2010), 493.
2. Marx, "Notebooks on Epicurean Philosophy," 493.
3. Marx, "Letter from Marx to His Father in Trier," in *The First Writings of Karl Marx*, ed. Paul M. Schafer (New York: IG Publishing, 2006), 80.
4. Althusser, *Lenin and Philosophy*, trans. B. Brewster (New York: Monthly Review Press, 1970), 23.
5. Marx, "Marx on the History of His Opinions" quoted in "Introduction," *The Marx-Engels Reader*, 5; Althusser, *Lenin and Philosophy*, xi.
6. Marx, "Letter to His Father," 73.
7. Marx, "Letter to His Father," 73.
8. Marx, "Letter to His Father," 73.
9. Marx, "Letter to His Father," 73.
10. Marx, "Letter to His Father," 79.
11. Marx, "Letter to His Father," 10.
12. Marx, "The Difference between the Democritean and Epicurean Philosophies of Nature," in *Marx and Engels Collected Works*, 75.
13. Marx, "Philosophies of Nature," 72–3.
14. Marx, "Philosophies of Nature," 30.
15. Marx, "Philosophies of Nature," 84–5.
16. Marx, "To Make the World Philosophical," in *The Marx-Engels Reader*, 11.
17. Marx, "To Make the World Philosophical," 11.
18. Marx, "Philosophies of Nature," 73.
19. Marx, "On the History of His Opinions," 5.
20. Marx, "On the History of His Opinions," 5.
21. The category of the "generic" is drawn from Alain Badiou, *Being and Event*, trans. Oliver Feltham (New York: Bloomsbury, 2013), 69.
22. Marx, "Philosophies of Nature," 29.
23. Marx, "Philosophies of Nature," 30.
24. Marx, "Philosophies of Nature," 30.
25. Marx, "Philosophies of Nature," 36.
26. This conventional view has perservered into the twentieth and twenty-first centuries. For a paradigmatic example, see Felix Cléve's excoriation of Epicurus in *Giants of Pre-Socratic Philosophy* (The Hague: Martinus Nijhoff, 1965), 414.
27. Marx, "To Make the World Philosophical," 10.
28. Mikhail Bakhtin, *The Dialogic Imagination: Four Essays*, trans. Caryl Emerson and Michael Holquist (Austin: University of Texas Press, 1981), 55.
29. Marx, "Philosophies of Nature," 71.

30 Marx, "Philosophies of Nature," 65.
31 To put it shortly, Epicurus raises the value of history above science as a study of the objects of nature. This partly explains his preference for "contingency" over "fate" or "necessity." For Marx, this is a symptom of Epicurus' development of the principle of divinity. "Where the universal and divine begin, the Democritean concept of necessity ceases to differ from chance" ("Philosophies of Nature," 43). Like Hegel, Epicurus elevates what Badiou would call the "singularity" or "ultra-one" of history and the human elaboration of spirit over the "being" of nature.
32 W. J. Oates, ed., *The Stoic and Epicurean Philosophies* (New York: The Modern Library, 1940), 36.
33 Oates, ed. *The Stoic and Epicurean Philosophies*, 36.
34 Oates, ed. *The Stoic and Epicurean Philosophies*, 43.
35 Oates, ed. *The Stoic and Epicurean Philosophies*, 32. This remains the rallying call of contemporary sophism; the "consolations of philosophy" as mediated by Swiss Billionaires and Canadian Tories.
36 Marx, "Philosophies of Nature," 55–6.
37 Marx, "Philosophies of Nature," 55.
38 Marx, "Philosophies of Nature," 73.
39 Marx, "Philosophies of Nature," 34.
40 Marx, "Philosophies of Nature," 73.
41 For a typical criticism of the Epicurean theory on Meteors, see once again Cléve's *Giants of Pre-Socratic Philosophy*, 445–6.
42 Oates, *Stoic and Epicurean Philosophy*, 25.
43 Oates, *Stoic and Epicurean Philosophy*, 27.
44 Marx, "Philosophies of Nature," 71.
45 Marx, "Philosophies of Nature," 65.
46 Marx, "Philosophies of Nature," 71.
47 Marx, "Philosophies of Nature," 72.
48 Marx, "Philosophies of Nature," 72–3.
49 John Stanley, "The Marxism of Marx's Doctoral Dissertation," *Journal of The History of Philosophy* 33.1 (1995): 150.
50 Marx, "Philosophies of Nature," 73.
51 Stanley, "The Marxism of Marx's Doctoral Dissertation," 151.
52 Marx, "Philosophies of Nature," 71.
53 Marx, "Notebooks on Epicurean Philosophy," 491.
54 Marx, "Notebooks on Epicurean Philosophy," 491.
55 Marx, "Notebooks on Epicurean Philosophy," 493.
56 Stanley, "The Marxism of Marx's Doctoral Dissertation," 153.
57 Marx, "Philosophies of Nature," 85.
58 Stanley, "The Marxism of Marx's Doctoral Dissertation," 153–4.
59 Marx, "Philosophies of Nature," 87.
60 Bakhtin, *The Dialogic Imagination*, 55.
61 Stanley, "The Marxism of Marx's Doctoral Dissertation," 153.
62 Althusser, *Lenin and Philosophy*, 109, my italics.
63 Marx, "To Make the World Philosophical," 11.
64 Marx, "For a Ruthless Criticism of Everything Existing," in *The Marx-Engels Reader*, 12–13.
65 Marx, "Notebooks on Epicurean Philosophy," 493.

66 Marx, "On the History of His Ideas," 3.
67 Marx, "On the History of His Ideas," 3. Indeed, the young Marx declared himself against utopian communist ideas germinating in France and began to mount an assault on the groundlessness of his former comrades in Berlin. On this point, Rubin is wrong in claiming that the young Marx was a "Utopian Socialist"; though he certainly had not acceded to "scientific socialism," he was fairly explicit in his criticism of the utopian trend in contemporary thought. See chapter seven of I. I. Rubin, *Essays on Marx's Theory of Value*, trans. M. Samardžija and F. Perlman (Detroit: Black and Red, 1972).
68 Marx, *Early Writings*, trans. Rodney Livingstone and Gregor Benton (London: Penguin, 1975), 72. Italics in original.
69 Marx, *Early Writings*, 58–9.
70 Marx, *Early Writings*, 59.
71 Marx, "For a Ruthless Criticism," 14.
72 Marx, *Early Writings*, 64.
73 Badiou, *Being and Event*, 543.
74 Badiou, *Being and Event*, 345.
75 Walter Benjamin, "Bert Brecht," in *Selected Writings, Vol. 2. Part 1, 1927-1930*, ed. Howard Eiland and Michael W. Jennings (Harvard: Belknap Press, 1999), 369.
76 Marx and Engels, "Manifesto of the Communist Party," 481.
77 Althusser, *Lenin and Philosophy*, 115.

2

Before the *Manifesto*

Märchen and the Impulse to Exorcism

Peter Riley

Specters, exorcism, branding, and a nursery tale: the preamble to the 1848 *Communist Manifesto* immediately conjures up a shadow-world that, according to Marx and Engels, will always haunt bourgeois society. The apparently discrete interests of Pope and Czar, Metternich and Guizot, French radicals and German police spies are united in collective dread of the implied inversion of their own power. "All of the Powers of old Europe have entered into a holy alliance to exorcize this specter."[1] Every affirmation that defines their bourgeois existence; every commodity produced; every factory built; every profit accumulated and protected will summon forth its dialectical antagonist. Now the spectral inversion—communism—has started speaking: collectively, across borders, and in tongues ("to be published in English, French, German, Italian, Flemish, and Danish"). It is "high time," in Samuel Moore's 1888 translation of the original text,

> that Communists should openly, in the face of the whole world, publish their views, their aims, their tendencies, and meet this nursery tale of the Spectre of Communism with a Manifesto of the party itself. [und den Märchen vom Gespenst des Kommunismus ein Manifest der Partei selbst entgegenstellen][2]

At first glance, this reads like Marx and Engels wanting to dispense with nursery tales in order to at last make manifest (the etymological root of "manifesto") the tenets of communism. What is needed now, the passage seems to suggest, is something more concrete: a programmatic clarity to quell the reactionary rumors and abstract generalities. In her 1850 translation of the *Manifesto*, Helen Macfarlane amplified exactly this apparent distinction: the need to dispense with the childish fears that plagued the minds of the powerful. "It is time," we read in her version, "for the Communists to lay before the world an account of their aims and tendencies, and to oppose these silly fables about the bugbear of Communism, by a manifesto of the Communist Party."[3] Ramping up Marx and Engels' satirical tone, Macfarlane draws out an implied image of the Pope and the Czar as little boys terrified in their beds, their bourgeois projections set in opposition to the sober reality of the new political vision.[4] Now is the time to get real, a call that skirts rather closely to the familiar call to temper flights of the revolutionary imagination and reinforce, rather than undermine, the inevitability of a particular historical moment.[5]

Notice, however, that Moore's translation (which was supervised by Engels) softens the sense of any stark contrast between "nursery tales" and "a Manifesto of the party itself." Instead, communists ought to "meet" the nursery tale, rather than necessarily confront, deny, or oppose it. The successive dative and genitive cases ("Märchen vom Gespenst des Kommunismus") make that use of "selbst entgegenstellen" particularly challenging to translate; so much so that it is actually quite tricky to identify what, exactly, is opposing (or standing before) what. In other words, when confronted with the German, Moore decided to opt for a more collaborative and slippery relationship between "Märchen" and "Manifesto"—framing the Manifesto as a Märchen: communism as the raising of a ghost army.

This short chapter draws out some of the implications of this collaboration—this meeting between real and imagined realms—suggesting that Marx and Engel's various "Märchen" should not be treated as cursory or distracting rhetorical flights but as integral and even prior to revolutionary logic. The desire to "exorcize" the Märchen from communism—whether this desire comes from the Right or Left—is as undesirable as it is impossible. Instead of turning away from an apparently imaginary realm of storytelling toward pure political praxis, what the manifesto does so effectively is remind us again and again of the incendiary and world-changing power of fairy tales— and, by extension, the kinds of writing that would eventually be either assimilated or jettisoned by the early twentieth-century conception of the "literary."[6] What follows will attempt to wrestle the *Manifesto*'s Märchen away from the enduring print and pedagogical legacies of Anglo-American modernism and the New Criticism, those movements so at pains to emphasize literature as a qualitatively different substance, worthy of study in its own right.[7] The "literary" quality of the *Manifesto* (as it is so often referred to) is not, this chapter will show, a detachable element-in-itself; it is, rather, a contingent and integrated facet of everything the document attempts to show, inspire, and achieve in the world.

What Marx and Engels apprehend so sharply (and this is what makes the *Manifesto* such an enduring document) is that communism is—from the standpoint of capitalism—a collection of paranoid rumors, half-glimpsed imaginative possibilities, and terrifying ghost stories. It is, ultimately, an inverse projection and a by-product of bourgeois life. Contrary to contemporary political economists and theorists on both the Right and Left (figures such as Adam Smith, Bruno Bauer, or Pierre-Joseph Proudhon), Marx and Engels reject dominant conceptions of the market economy as either benevolent or reformable. As the bourgeois mode of production intensifies, communism's likely contours proliferate in antagonistic and fatal relation to that intensity, in a pattern that will result in violent revolution.

This vision is the culmination of a tendency inbuilt to the work published in the four years preceding the *Manifesto*. Even before meeting Engels, Marx was already rehearsing the structure of this thought in the *Economic and Philosophic Manuscripts of 1844*, in which each affirmation is always accompanied by its agonistic human cost:

"It is true that labor produces for the rich wonderful things—but for the worker it produces privation. It produces palaces—but for the worker, hovels. It produces beauty—but for the worker, deformity."[8] It was, however, only after their initial meeting at the Café de la Régence in Paris in August 1844, and in the run-up to the outbreak of the European revolutions of 1848, when Marx and Engels were forced to move from Paris to Brussels, that they collaborated on the three major works that would outline their materialist conception of history and its world-altering implications. In *The Holy Family* (1845), *The German Ideology* (1845)—to which they appended the "Theses on Feuerbach"—and *The Poverty of Philosophy* (1847), Marx and Engels come into a sense of the implications of their relational and inverted thinking.

In *The German Ideology*, for instance, Marx and Engels put forward the claim that every apparently concrete or discrete idea we can ever have is actually foundationally contingent on a hitherto obscured shadow-world of productive forces:

> We set out from real, active men, and on the basis of their real life-process we demonstrate the development of the ideological reflexes and echoes of this life-process. The phantoms formed in the human brain are also, necessarily, sublimates of their material life-process, which is empirically verifiable and bound to material premises. Morality, religion, metaphysics, all the rest of ideology and their corresponding forms of consciousness, thus no longer retain the semblance of independence. They have no history, no development; but men, developing their material production and their material intercourse, alter, along with this their real existence, their thinking and the products of their thinking.[9]

At such moments, Marx and Engels develop the rhetorical palette that would come to define so much of the later work, and particularly the *Manifesto*. The all-encompassing list of what society takes for truth is no more than a diffusion of "ideological reflexes," "echoes," and "sublimates"—or, more precisely, "phantoms formed in the human brain." In a paragraph such as this, and particularly in that final sentence, our conception of the world shifts from something fixed and inevitable into something malleable and alterable: if men change their behavior, then the ideological reflexes that pass for eternal laws will also change.

The excitements of these ideas and their irresistible force gather pace in the two other significant works of the period. *The Holy Family* takes great delight in experimenting with a new argumentative apparatus, as well as deploying a specifically targeted vocabulary that borrows from the realm of storytelling. The title refers to Bruno Bauer's apparently pious ascription to the Hegelian conception of history and its determining force of Spirit or Geist. Bauer's arguments, particularly those concerning the origins of the French Revolution, are dismissed as tautological, pseudo-spiritual illusions that neglect material realities. "The limitedness of the Mass," we read, "forced 'the Spirit,' 'Criticism,' Herr Bauer, to consider the French Revolution not as the time of the revolutionary endeavors of the French in the 'prosaic sense' but 'only' as the 'symbol and fantastic expression' of the Critical figments of his own brain."[10] Two years later, in 1847, *The Poverty of Philosophy* mounted a critique of Proudhon's reformist economic doctrines and proceeded along similar lines. Marx and Engels repeatedly charged Proudhon with a related proclivity for obscuring the specific relations that generate capital in favor of ethereal argument and speculation. The gothic fairy stories begin to take on a new intensity, even going so far as to compare Proudhon's conception of the driving force of history as a limbless ghost-Prometheus:

> What then, ultimately, is this Prometheus resuscitated by M. Proudhon? It is society, social relations based on class antagonism. These relations are not relations between individual and individual, but between worker and capitalist, between farmer and landlord, etc. Wipe out these relations and you annihilate all society, and your Prometheus is nothing but a ghost without arms or legs; that is, without automatic workshops, without division of labor—in a word, without everything that you gave him to start with in order to make him obtain this surplus labor.[11]

The Communist Manifesto must be read as a culmination and expression of the increasing rhetorical license and flair that Marx and Engels developed in the course of writing these texts. In the months immediately preceding the European revolution of 1848, and at the request of the newly formed Communist League, they set about ratcheting up the ghost stories as an integral feature of their revolutionary logic. Here, and most strikingly of all, are the infamous "sorcerer" and "gravedigger" metaphors:

> Modern bourgeois society with its relations of production, of exchange and of property, a society that has conjured up such gigantic means of production and of exchange, is like the sorcerer, who is no longer able to control the powers of the nether world whom he has called up by his spells.[12]

> The advance of industry, whose involuntary promoter is the bourgeoisie, replaces the isolation of the laborers, due to competition, by their revolutionary combination, due to association. The development of Modern Industry, therefore, cuts from under its feet the very foundation on which the bourgeoisie produces and appropriates products. What the bourgeoisie, therefore, produces, above all, is its own grave-diggers. Its fall and the victory of the proletariat are equally inevitable.[13]

These passages make sure that references to the energies of industry rhetorically produce, or formalize, as gothic Märchen. Marx indulges in these nursery tales because they rehearse the dialectic that organizes his thinking. Communist ideas flourish in relation to the concentration of industry; the more vigorous or successful the industry, the more potently spectral the insurgent imaginary. The bourgeois mode of production places the existing world under such stress that "all fixed, fast-frozen relations" are displaced.[14] Everything on earth becomes subject to capitalism's fundamental law of exchangeability: everything now fights for survival against an inhuman calculus. Capitalist political economy, therefore, produces its own spirit world, upending that which ought to be secure and nurturing (society) with that which is ethereal (the perpetual circulation that defines the market): "society can no longer live under this bourgeoisie, in other words, its existence is no longer compatible with society."[15]

In describing capitalism's sublimating force (solid into air), Marx realizes that it is only, paradoxically, by intensifying the metaphoricity (or, if we must, the "literariness") of his language that he can account for the bourgeoisie's transfiguration of the material world. This will soon become true of one of *Capital*'s (1867) unforgettable and most disturbing ghost stories. "A great deal of capital," we read in that book, "which appears today in the United States without any birth-certificate, was yesterday, in England, the capitalized blood of children."[16] This is a thought Marx would not be able to formulate without the aid of a night-Märchen—a nightmare grounded in a specific material context: the labor of English children, converted into capital, crosses the Atlantic, and circulates within the United States.[17]

Such rhetorical flights do their revolutionary work both externally and internally: externally, in stoking up the indignation (and hopefully organization) of a particular workforce suddenly thrust together on the factory floor. And internally, which is perhaps less frequently noted, in the increasingly paranoid, embattled, and self-defeating mind of the bourgeois subject. The more energetic the capitalist, the more terrifying the specters he summons. "What the bourgeoisie, therefore, produces, above all, is its own grave-diggers": this is a grave being dug by the increasingly united workers of the world, but also by the bourgeois himself, as the various self-summoned nightmares eat away at him. And Marx envisions this defeat as properly humiliating. "No longer able to control the powers of the nether world," the bourgeois will soil the bed in fear of his own night terrors.

A useful companion text to this kind of thinking (and a more obviously literary precursor to the *Manifesto*) is Charles Dickens' *Christmas Carol* (1843). Published five years prior to the *Manifesto*, this story recounts the violent efflux of the spirit world within the consciousness of a capitalist world. A succession of ghosts show the increasingly terrified Scrooge exactly how terrible and misery-inducing his behavior to others has been. A final spirit leads him to a graveyard. The narrator is at pains to emphasize the space as a projection and externalization of Scrooge's own bourgeois practices; an ending of his own making: "It was a worthy place," we are told. "Walled in by houses; overrun by grass and weeds, the growth of vegetation's death, not life; choked up with too much burying; fat with repleted appetite. A worthy place!"[18] The spirit indicates one grave in particular: "Scrooge crept towards it, trembling as he went; and following the finger, read upon the stone of the neglected grave his own name."[19] While this is frightening enough, what really scares Scrooge is the uncertainty of not knowing whether this vision has any bearing on "reality." He pauses:

"Before I draw nearer to that stone to which you point," said Scrooge, "answer me one question. Are these the shadows of the things that Will be, or are they shadows of things that May be, only?"[20]

The spirit refuses to answer. Scrooge promises to change his ways and, at this point in the narrative, Dickens releases the pressure, allowing his protagonist to wake up the following morning filled with the joys of Christmas redemption and charity. He subsequently gives his workforce a pay rise and a bit of holiday. For Dickens, nothing fundamentally changes, whereas Marx and Engels' rewriting of the story stops at the grave: the Scrooges of this world will arrive at their own self-constructed tomb humiliated, terrified, and alone. In answer to the question of whether or not their own particular night-Märchen are real or imagined, they will also receive no answer. Neither will they be given the opportunity to introduce any progressive reforms. Abandoned in a state of vanquished paranoia and self-doubt, they will simply be ended.

So while Marx's night-Märchen delineate the better world to come, they also serve as the canker that eats the capitalist up from within. Bourgeois society is condemned to live with the pressures of being surrounded by an enemy that is at once everywhere and nowhere, inside and outside, rumor and fact, imagined and real. Communism's ghostliness, in other words, is one of its greatest assets, and Marx and Engels take great rhetorical delight in playing on and in that space of suspicion: on stoking and confirming bourgeois anxieties. The second section of the *Manifesto*, "Proletarians and Communists," begins by emphasizing the all-pervasive presence of communism. The opposition between the workforce and the revolutionary movement is a false one. Communism is everywhere: "The Communists do not form a separate party opposed to other working-class parties. They have no interest separate and apart from those of the proletariat as a whole."[21] Having established its all-pervasive presence, Marx and Engels confront a particular rumor (as though, rhetorically, they were about to refute it), only to categorically confirm it. "You reproach us with intending to do away with your property. Precisely so; that is just what we intend."[22] This is, indeed, your worst nightmare, and you ought to be afraid. The section culminates in an articulation of ten general principles—principles that are so audacious in their scope and aims (and so sparse on detail) that they retain the character of Märchen. This is because they are, fundamentally, the night-Märchen of the bourgeoisie, uncontrollable horror stories spewing up out of the darkness and scaring them shitless: "Expropriation of property in land and application of all rents of land to public purposes," "A heavy progressive tax," "abolition of the rights of inheritance," and so on.[23]

At this point, it is worth examining the inevitable gut reaction that would deride such communistic measures as idealistic or vague (two sides of the same reactionary coin)—that such demands are unable to gain political traction because they are too fantastical. This is the kind of response that immediately cedes ground to the anti-revolutionary climate of "realism," the idea that we have to be realistic and compromising in our political demands and temper the fairy tale. Marxist thought has been particularly effective in diagnosing and picking apart the hegemonic force of the "real." Through strategies of repetition and saturation, the status quo reinforces its own objectives by making inequality feel (to use Antonio Gramsci's word) "spontaneous"— commonsensical, "the way it simply is." As Mark Fisher pointed out, capitalism's current neoliberal hegemony thrives on maintaining this state of realism: it is the chief ideological mechanism for ensuring that another, better world remains unimaginable (let alone attainable).[24] More than this, a climate of realism also ensures that capitalists are better shielded from the nightmares that harry and disturb them. This is yet another cue (if any more were needed) to amplify rather than diminish the fairy tales. The more fantastical and monstrous the proliferation, the better. Such imaginings (which are brought into even starker clarity by the squalid realism of the present) constitute the hieroglyphic outline of the world to come, a terrifying or exhilarating (depending on which side you're on) reminder that a different world is possible.

Of course, while the revolutionary fairy tale needs to be implemented materially, its practical application and organization always needs to be carefully separated out from the pervasive call to "get real" or "serious." In the preface to the German edition of 1872, Marx and Engels write that

> the general principles laid down in this Manifesto are, on the whole, as correct today as ever. Here and there some details might be improved. The practical application of the principles will depend, as the Manifesto itself states, everywhere and at all times, on the historical conditions for the time being existing, and, for that reason, no special stress is laid on the revolutionary measures proposed at the end of Section II.[25]

It might seem perverse for the writers of a manifesto to place "no special stress" on the only concrete measures and guidelines contained within the document. Again, such a response is to be in thrall to a realism that would demand policies formalize themselves in the abstract and before particular historical conditions have determined the specific scope and shape of such policies. Marx and Engels know that any attempt to delineate a specific, programmatic account of the future revolution would be to cut ties with history. Thus delimited, the *Manifesto* would consequently become nothing more than an alienated comestible product. At the same time, they realize that they cannot get too embroiled within the contingencies of their present moment. The final section (Section IV) entitled "Positions of the Communists in Relation to the Various Existing Opposition Parties" bears all the hallmarks of a writer (or writers) either up against a deadline (Marx was notoriously bad with deadlines) or ambivalent about addressing any specific political context. It consequently cuts off after a page, impatient with its own stated purpose, and keen to emphasize the broader dialectical pattern: "In short, the Communists everywhere support every revolutionary movement against the existing social and political order of things."[26]

This manifesto can only outline some general possibilities and patterns: even the ten measures that end Section II are as-yet half-glimpsed dialectical shadows, enough to excite and inspire, frighten and panic. Marx and Engels wrestle with the aim of at once needing to maintain contact with specific historical conditions (their entire project depends on a fundamentally dialectical reading of history), but also, paradoxically, wanting to produce a document of lasting significance. Lasting, not in the sense of the "eternal" cultural artifact, but lasting in the sense of being durable enough to speak to multiple contexts both in their present and to come.

Such durability is a characteristic that makes the *Manifesto* vulnerable to the strictly policed borders of academic disciplines and cultural centers, whether that's political economy's attempt to see through and deemphasize Marx's distracting rhetorical or literary sleights of hand, or the publishing industry's repeated framing and ossification of it as part of the cultural sphere (*A World Classic, A Penguin World Classic*). Factor in the pervasive climate of realism (a form of austerity), with its demand that we stop dreaming and "get real," and the *Manifesto* seems to point directly back to its own opening. "All the Powers of old Europe have entered into a holy alliance to exorcise this specter." The powers have altered, but the impulse to exorcize remains—whether that's an urge to extract a pure literariness or abstract revolutionary blueprint or to moderate incendiary demands. As readers of the *Manifesto*, it is incumbent upon those of us interested in making a better world to resist any such impulse toward exorcism. Instead, as subjects who live with the full nightmarish force of bourgeois existence on a daily basis, we ought to sit down to our texts as if before an Ouija board and repossess ourselves with the communistic Märchen that emerge in those crucial years and texts between 1844 and 1848. It is only by nurturing our night-Märchen that we stand any chance of becoming the night-Märchen. Any manifesto that dispenses with its fairy tale—that capitulates to the clarion calls of "compromise," "balance," or "realism"—is a document that can only appease or reinforce the status quo.

In an essay entitled "Opportunism and the Art of the Possible" (1898), Rosa Luxemburg announces a political program in keeping with this law:

> We who oppose the entire present order see things quite differently. In our no, in our intransigent attitude, lies our whole strength. It is this attitude that earns us the fear and respect of the enemy and the trust and support of the people. Precisely because we do not yield one inch from our position, we force the government and the bourgeois parties to concede to us the few immediate successes that can be gained. But if we begin to chase after what is "possible" according to the principles of opportunism, unconcerned with our own principles, and by means of statesmanlike barter, then we will soon find ourselves in the same situation as the hunter who has not only failed to stay the deer but has also lost his gun in the process.[27]

In the current political climate, Luxemburg's views on "intransigence" might be mistaken for a roadmap to political oblivion. If you cannot meet your opponent halfway in compromise, the argument goes, then you inevitably consign yourself to the political margins. But as history lurches toward a new catastrophe—as life on earth as we know it comes to an end—Luxemburg's "no" reminds us of what it sounds like to be a staunch defender and champion of the Märchen that our society is currently so at pains to jettison. Whether we like it or not, anything that falls short of this commitment cannot claim revolutionary credentials; cannot claim to be serious about saving the planet or life thereon. Compromise, opportunism, realism, balance, austerity: reject them all. Each term signals the destruction of our ability to reimagine a future and to terrify our enemies. "Communists should openly," write Marx and Engels, "in the face of the whole world, publish their views, their aims, their tendencies, and meet this nursery tale of the Spectre of Communism with a Manifesto of the party itself."[28] Believe fiercely; encourage our Märchen; be at the ready.

Notes

1. Marx and Engels, "Manifesto of the Communist Party," 473.
2. Marx and Engels, "Manifesto of the Communist Party," 473.
3. Helen Macfarlane's translation was the first in English, and published in the Chartist Newspaper *The Red Republican* in 1850. Long derided as "a somewhat fanciful version," it begins: "A frightful hobgoblin stalks throughout Europe." Marx and Engels, "Manifesto of the German Communist Party," in *The Cambridge Companion to the Communist Manifesto*, eds. Terrell Carver and James Farr, trans. Helen McFarlane (Cambridge: Cambridge University Press, 2015), 270.
4. "Bugbears" in the mid-nineteenth century were not, as they are regarded now, mere annoyances. Rather, they were "an imaginary evil spirit or creature said to devour naughty children; a bogeyman" (*OED*).
5. This sense of the real is also to be distinguished from Georg Lukács' conception of "literary realism," a genre perpetually invested in illuminating the inevitability of epochal supersession through its illumination of historical totality. For an extended treatment of this subject, see Alison Shonkwiler and Leigh Claire La Berge, eds. *Reading Capitalist Realism* (Iowa: University of Iowa Press, 2014).
6. See, for example, Robert Paul Wolff's *Moneybags Must Be So Lucky: On the Literary Structure of Capital* (Boston: University of Massachusetts Press, 1988), 15.
7. In doing this kind of work, I am also rehearsing a Marxian charge against Hegel's hierarchy of art forms and poetry's immateriality in particular. For Hegel, "Poetry is the universal art of the spirit which has become free in itself and which is not tied down for its realization to external sensuous material." See Hegel's *Aesthetics* (Oxford: Clarendon Press, 1998), 89.
8. Marx, "Economic and Philosophic Manuscripts of 1844," in *The Marx-Engels Reader*, 72.
9. Marx and Engels, "The German Ideology," 154.
10. Marx and Engels, "The German Ideology," 161.
11. Marx, *The Poverty of Philosophy: Answer to the Philosophy of Poverty (1847)*. https://www.marxists.org/archive/marx/works/1847/poverty-philosophy/, accessed August 20, 2019.
12. Marx and Engels, "Manifesto of the Communist Party," 478.
13. Marx and Engels, "Manifesto of the Communist Party," 483.
14. Marx and Engels, "Manifesto of the Communist Party," 476.
15. Marx and Engels, "Manifesto of the Communist Party," 483. That great defender of market logic Margaret Thatcher was evidently paraphrasing *The Communist Manifesto* when she famously stated in *Women's Own* magazine (1987) that, under capitalism, "there's no such thing as society."
16. Marx, *Capital*, vol. 1, 920.
17. In saying this, I am extending Keston Sutherland's emphasis on the importance of Marx's idiom. Translations of Marx, Sutherland claims, have tended to try and temper Marx's rhetorical flights, presupposing that they distract from his theoretical diagnosis. But in the use of a word such as "Gallerte" (a substance used to feed the starving industrial poor), Marx attempts to make his readers as uncomfortable as possible; the comparison of the human labor contained within a particular product to a jellied mass of undifferentiated nonhuman tissue is meant to be disturbing and repulsive: a night-Märchen. Keston Sutherland, "Marx in Jargon," *World Picture* 1 (2008): 1–25.

18 Charles Dickens, *A Christmas Carol: And Other Christmas Books* (London: Vintage, 2012), 78.
19 Dickens, *A Christmas Carol*, 78.
20 Dickens, *A Christmas Carol*, 78.
21 Marx and Engels, "Manifesto of the Communist Party," 483.
22 Marx and Engels, "Manifesto of the Communist Party," 486.
23 Marx and Engels, "Manifesto of the Communist Party," 490.
24 See Mark Fisher, *Capitalist Realism: Is There No Alternative* (London: Zero, 2008), 2–4.
25 Marx and Engels, "Manifesto of the Communist Party," 470.
26 Marx and Engels, "Manifesto of the Communist Party," 500.
27 Rosa Luxemburg, "Opportunism and the Art of the Possible" (September 30, 1898), https://www.marxists.org/archive/marx/works/1847/poverty-philosophy/, accessed August 20, 2019.
28 Marx and Engels, "Manifesto of the Communist Party," 473.

3

The Communist Manifesto and the Exhumation of Literature

Alex Niven

The Communist Manifesto of 1848 was written by Karl Marx as a simple statement of aims for the Communist League, in the wake of their Second Congress in London in the last weeks of 1847. On returning to his home in Brussels, Marx wrote quickly and energetically at the start of 1848, polishing and condensing a radically new analysis of bourgeois society, which had been developed partly in collaboration with Friedrich Engels over the previous five years. The end result was a pamphlet of considerable force and originality, which appeared in February just as the so-called Year of Revolution sparked into life with the overthrow of King Louis Philippe in Paris. Written in German and published originally in London, it was soon disseminated in Paris, though its impact was initially felt mainly in Marx's native Germany (and even there its popularity was at first rather limited).

In its style and content, the *Manifesto* is an unremittingly modern document, which demands with passionate intensity that the future be hauled immediately into the present. Proceeding from a famously hyperbolized claim that communism is already striking terror into the hearts of the European great powers, the *Manifesto* offers a précis of the Marxian diagnosis at its point of maturation and breakthrough. A powerful first section, "Bourgeois and Proletarians," sketches a poetic overview of human history, arguing that it amounts to a narrative of nearly ceaseless class struggle. In the second section, "Proletarians and Communists," Marx tentatively outlines communism as a political credo intent on smashing existing property relations, wage labor, the bourgeois family, and nation-states (in a typical aside, he suggests that communism "involves the most radical rupture with traditional ideas").[1] A third section meanders sometimes obscurely over the various sects and subsects of the European left in the 1840s, before a final, short concluding section builds to a stirring finale ("WORKING MEN OF ALL COUNTRIES, UNITE!"[2]) with a series of emphatic bullet points about imminent communist insurgency.

Propelled by a dynamic, idealistic premise—that communists everywhere "support every revolutionary movement against the existing social and political order of things"[3]—the *Manifesto* is plainly one of the foundational modernist texts. Roughly contemporaneous with Baudelaire's first published writings, it initiates a timeline of modern aesthetics that begins with the urbanization and political rupture of the mid-nineteenth century (*modernité*, in the classic definition). But we do not even have to stretch the modernist chronology so far to locate the *Manifesto* in its proper historical period. Perhaps the ultimate slow-burner, like other major philosophical works of the nineteenth century (*The Interpretation of Dreams* [1899], *Thus Spoke Zarathustra* [1883–91]), it was only in the high-modernist moment of critical lore—the febrile years during and after the First World War—that Marx's text began to detonate across the world with truly wide-ranging cultural impact.

More precisely, we might think of the *Manifesto* as a global statement indelibly bound up with 1917, the year of Lenin and the Bolshevik revolution, when this small, well-regarded, radical pamphlet was suddenly transformed into a work of almost literally biblical import. For Leon Trotsky, architect of the Bolshevik breakthrough, the pamphlet was of "greater genius than any other in world literature."[4] Yet it was historically grounded in spite of such claims for transcendence. Indeed, the *Manifesto*'s association in the narrative of its reception with the crossover moment of 1917 puts it in good literary company. This was a watershed year for European modernism, which saw the publication of Ezra Pound's first *Canto*, T. S. Eliot's *Love Song of J. Alfred Prufrock* (in chapbook form), Jean Cocteau's *Parade*, Luigi Pirandello's *Così è (se vi pare)*, and the foundation of Virginia and Leonard Woolf's Hogarth Press. These are—in a significant sense explored throughout this volume—the *Manifesto*'s literary "contemporaries." Beyond questions of simple historical coincidence, the high-modernist period marked the point at which the *Manifesto* finally made good on its opening line ("A specter is haunting Europe—the specter of Communism"[5]) and really did begin to haunt Europe—especially its literary and intellectual culture—in profound and potent ways. European high modernism unfolded consciously alongside the advent of communism, such that we cannot read an exemplary text like W. B. Yeats's "Second Coming" (1919) without being mindful that Yeats' "rough beast [slouching] towards Bethlehem" was, in part, an admission that the new world order would be vitally shaped by Bolshevism and its sacred text.[6]

But it is also true that the *Manifesto*'s modernism was shaped by its revision and reframing of a much deeper and broader intellectual tradition. While it was dedicated to dreaming the new world into being, Marx's communism was also, as Jacques Derrida famously argued, "haunted by what it attempted to foreclose."[7] Written somewhat hurriedly as a parenthesis to Marx's journalism and scholarship, and motivated by an urgent need to condense the whole sweep of human history into a single, lyrical-ethical statement, the *Manifesto* preempted—and in certain concrete ways prepared the way for—the politico-aesthetic revolution of twentieth-century modernism. It did so, as I will suggest in what follows, partly by arguing for the ultimate validity and materiality of the temporal instant, by foregrounding the *moment* itself, a full quarter century before Walter Pater initiated the Aesthetic Movement with a similar gesture in his *Studies in the History of the Renaissance* (1873), wherein the creed of "getting as many pulsations as possible into the given time" was passionately affirmed.[8] But while Pater embraced a very modern kind of atemporality or ephemerality in advocating the pulsating instant, Marx's modernism was subtler, and in the end more prescient, because it arrived at its theory of the transformative moment by reaching back into history as well as forward into a desirable future.

Appraising Marx's peculiar historical sense—his blending of Kant and Hegel, Smith and Ricardo, Rousseau and Proudhon—has long been central to an understanding of his oeuvre, since at least as far back as Lenin's famous assertion that we should look to "classical German philosophy, classical English political economy, and French socialism" for the roots of the Marxist worldview.[9] But when we turn from these sorts of antecedents to Marx's aesthetic inheritance, the picture is much more ambiguous. While Marx's main literary influences are well known, there is less clarity about how these influences were brought to bear in specific ways on his major writings. In what follows, I want to argue that in the case of the short, sharp, poetic shock that is the *Manifesto*, it is Marx's awareness of his literary precedents or hauntings that gives rise to the singularity of this astonishing document.

In seeking to identify the main literary influences on the *Manifesto*, we need not search for obscure, long-forgotten writers and texts. Because Marx was a fairly typical European intellectual of his era, but also because of his profound sympathy for grand narratives and cultural worldhood, the writers he most admired tended to be major world-historical figures. For the purposes of the short overview in this chapter, I will focus on three of the literary figures Marx knew most intimately: Dante, Shakespeare, and Epicurus. By emphasizing its literary backdrop, we gain a strong sense of where the *Manifesto* came from. Even more vitally, we are able to appreciate the manifold complexity of Marx's modernist vision, and how it sublimates a narrative of modernity that long preceded 1848.

Marx and Dante

In the case of the first of these writers, Dante, the influence on the *Manifesto* is palpable in a broad but crucial sense, which can be briefly summarized. We know from Wilhelm Liebknecht's account that Marx knew the *Divine Comedy* inside out, and would regularly recite long sections of it.[10] The prominent Dante quotation at the end of the introduction to *Capital* (1867)—"Segui il tuo corso, e lascia dir le genti" ("Follow your own course, and let people talk")—is perhaps the most famous proof of the centrality of the *Divine Comedy* in Marx's worldview, though this particular phrase is a fairly arbitrary existential motto. A more profound Dantean influence on Marx can be detected in his schematic division of human experience into morally stratified typologies, the basic structural principle of the *Manifesto*. If the *Manifesto* is a lyric work in its minutiae, it uses the scaffolding devices of Dantean epic to bulwark its messianic message at wide range. As William Clare Roberts has recently argued of *Capital*, in terms that might easily be transferred to the *Manifesto*, Marx based his critique of bourgeois society on "a suitably grand literary framework: rewriting Dante's *Inferno* as a descent into the modern 'social Hell' of the capitalist mode of production."[11]

In almost all of its component parts, the *Manifesto* echoes the tripartite structure of the *Divine Comedy* and its central Christian message: that it is only possible to attain spiritual freedom by descending into Hell (*Inferno*), working up through Purgatory (*Purgatorio*), and finally ascending to Heaven (*Paradiso*). Just as the socialist William Morris would later draw on Pre-Raphaelite readings of Dante in positing his "Earthly Paradise," Marx's secularized High Romantic treatments of the *Divine Comedy* to reframe the passage for communist emancipation as a punishing but necessary ascent through historical and contemporary Infernos and Purgatorios up to a utopian world free of nationhood and property. Indeed, we might view the *Manifesto* as the extension of a long-running tradition in European literature, which combined this religious habitus with state-of-the-nation political commentary. Dante and later Milton and Blake proved that they were of a subversive "devil's party" without knowing it, by creating vivid portraits of Hell coupled with rather vague and insipid Paradisos; similarly, one of the striking things about the *Manifesto* is its headlong plunge from the opening line into a gothic world of struggle and nightmare, and the subsequent fact that it never quite manages to rise to a convincingly real evocation of the Earthly Paradise. In this sense, the *Manifesto* resembles a spiritual epic poem treating political themes—and heroically failing to resolve them—far more than a mere political tract.

Given Marx's deeply ingrained knowledge of Dante, it seems implausible that the pattern of the *Divine Comedy* was not somewhere at the root of the suggestion offered in the *Manifesto*: that human history will move inevitably from feudalism through a kind of purgatory (bourgeois society, or at best an imperfect form of socialism) to communism. Again, the literary influence was likely crucial here, and as such it is important to highlight the aesthetic emphasis of Marx's text. The grand narrative sketched in the first two chapters of the *Manifesto* is a highly evocative but somewhat reductive and clearly artificially constructed triptych. Despite a vague, rather anachronistic glance at the "patricians, knights, plebeians and slaves" of ancient Rome in the opening passage, Marx conspicuously neglects to consider the position of human society prior to feudalism in the *Manifesto*, bending many thousands of years of history into an aesthetic schema that seems designed to emulate the movement of upward moral flight that guides the *Divine Comedy*.[12] For all its novel scientific accuracy in diagnosing essential truths about human experience, the *Manifesto* nevertheless relies on fairly traditional epic devices, from its beginning in medias res to its carefully designed progression toward the civic immanence of a communist future.

Marx and Shakespeare

Aside from its reliance on the basic structures of Dantean epic, the main literary mode of the *Manifesto* is undoubtedly Shakespearean. As is fairly well known, Marx's interest in Shakespeare bordered on the obsessive: according to Paul Lafargue, "his whole family had a real cult for the great English dramatist," and Marx himself reputedly read and recited Shakespeare on a daily basis.[13] We can therefore say without hyperbole that the Shakespeare canon—Marx's "Bible" according to his daughter, Eleanor—was a likely background influence on almost every word of the *Manifesto*.[14] At the most elementary level, this means that it is woven from a series of richly poetic phrases, which are lent force and immediacy by a self-consciously "dramatic" mode of address. Derrida drew attention in *Spectres of Marx* (1993) to the parallels between the *Manifesto*'s opening and the first scene of Shakespeare's *Hamlet* (which begins with a mostly wordless visitation by the ghost of Hamlet's father).[15] This is a useful starting point for understanding Marx's indebtedness to a kind of theatrical gothic (precisely the stylistic mode Eliot would later exploit in the high-modernist phantasmagorias of *The Waste Land*). Marx's quotidian intimacy with Shakespeare seems to have surpassed even his obsession with Dante, and it is surely this influence, rather than the more contemporary shadow of Goethean or Heinean romanticism, that lies behind the backdrop of specters, ruins, and gravediggers that dominates the *Manifesto*'s first pages.

More generally, it is the dramatic sweep and knotted lyricism of Shakespeare's history plays that most often haunts Marx's turn of phrase in the *Manifesto*. While the specter motif clearly echoes *Hamlet*'s opening, Marx also derives a maximum effect by imitating a stylistic trick crucial to Shakespeare's best works, whereby a vast historical and moral hinterland is conjured in a powerfully condensed peroration. An obvious example of this is the famous opening of *Richard III*, where the long narrative of the English Wars of the Roses is telescoped in Gloucester's "Now is the winter of our discontent" speech. This, and cognate passages in *Julius Caesar* ("Friends, romans, countrymen"), *Henry V* ("By Jove, I am not covetous for gold"), and perhaps even *Hamlet* again ("Something is rotten in the state of Denmark"), suggests a stylistic basis for the abrupt historicism of Marx's rhetorical statements ("A spectre is haunting Europe," "The history of all hitherto existing society is the history of class struggles," "The proletarians have nothing to lose but their chains"), drawing a line from the archetypes of classical rhetoric at the root of European intellectual culture and education, through Shakespeare to Marx.

Even more important to Marx were the rhythms of debate and disquisition to be found in so-called problem plays like *Timon of Athens, Troilus and Cressida*, and *The Merchant of Venice*. *Timon*, with its commentary on the ill effects of what Marx termed the "visible divinity" of money, and *Merchant of Venice*, with its moneylending antihero Shylock, were canonical texts in Marx's private literary pantheon for obvious reasons. But Marx's gloss on Shakespeare's use of discursive inversion in *Timon* provides a clue to how he channeled Shakespearean skepticism more subtly in the *Manifesto*'s stylistic to-and-fro. Commenting in his manuscripts on *Timon*'s "Gold? Yellow, glittering, precious gold?" monologue, Marx argued that it brings out two properties of money in particular:

1. It is the visible divinity—the transformation of all human and natural properties into their contraries, the universal confounding and distorting of things: impossibilities are soldered together by it.
2. It is the common whore, the common procurer of people and nations.[16]

The Shakespearean high-rhetorical mode is at the forefront of the second point here; but more interesting is the first point, with its emphasis on the "universal confusion and inversion of things" arising out of the capitalist ethic. We are of course familiar with this idea in the context of Marx's theory of dialectical materialism, derived and refined from Hegelian precedent (most fully in the pages of *Capital*). But it is striking that Marx cites Shakespeare as another, more complex and ambiguous influence on his assertion that money transforms "all human and natural qualities into their opposites." While the philosophical basis of Marx's interest in the dialectic came from Hegel, there was also, it seems, a sense in which he derived the stylistic modus operandi of his writing from Shakespeare.

When we turn to the *Manifesto*, we can see the Shakespearean influence manifesting itself as a kind of dialectical style, in which ethical debate is combined with epic historical summary:

> Freeman and slave, patrician and plebeian, lord and serf, guild-master and journeyman, in a word, oppressor and oppressed, stood in constant opposition to one another, carried on an uninterrupted, now hidden, now open fight, a fight that each time ended, either in a revolutionary re-constitution of society at large, or in the common ruin of the contending classes.[17]

In this passage, and throughout the *Manifesto* (especially its dramatic first chapters), there is great synergy between dialectical form and dialectical content. The relentless, deconstructive questioning of Shakespearean drama prefigures Marx's argumentative approach; indeed, Marx's whole philosophical posture mimics a Shakespearean literary texture—a "sickening see-saw rhythm," as L. C. Knights once described *Macbeth*, in a phrase that captures the distinctive storm and stress of the *Manifesto* as well as it does Shakespearian blank verse.[18]

The combination of see-saw philosophy and see-saw style is perhaps best exemplified by the famous monologue on "degree" delivered by Ulysses in Shakespeare's *Troilus and Cressida*, another problem play that seems to have haunted Marx's imagination. Its peroration offers a window into the literary-philosophical feat Marx was attempting in the condensed dramatic epic of the *Manifesto*:

> Take but degree away, untune that string,
> And, hark, what discord follows! each thing meets
> In mere oppugnancy: the bounded waters
> Should lift their bosoms higher than the shores
> And make a sop of all this solid globe:
> Strength should be lord of imbecility,
> And the rude son should strike his father dead:
> Force should be right; or rather, right and wrong,
> Between whose endless jar justice resides,
> Should lose their names, and so should justice too.
> Then every thing includes itself in power,
> Power into will, will into appetite;
> And appetite, an universal wolf,

So doubly seconded with will and power,
Must make perforce an universal prey,
And last eat up himself.[19]

Here we see the lyric immediacy and rhythmic insistence founded in caesura and parallelism, which must have been ringing through Marx's brain from daily readings and recitals of the Shakespearean canon, and which clearly found its way into the struggling, sinewy cadences of the *Manifesto*. But Ulysses' words also suggest a starting point for understanding its singularity, and by implication the entire Marxian worldview. Clearly, Marx did not follow Ulysses and Shakespeare in viewing "degree" or hierarchy as a supreme virtue. But we can go further than this, and say that Marx's intention with the *Manifesto* and his philosophical project in general was to create a kind of inverse or ultimate revision of Shakespearean skepticism, and of its elaborate recoil at a modern epoch in which degree is, apparently, being undermined (for all his occasional utopianism, we are returned time and time again in the Shakespeare canon to this essentially conservative mode). While Shakespeare was content in this passage and elsewhere to play opposites off against one another ("everything includes itself in power, / Power into will, will into appetite"), and derive dramatic effect from the ensuing "oppugnancy," Marx's strategy in the *Manifesto* was to use this literary posture to clear the way for a more substantial endpoint. For Marx, what would be left after the "universal prey" had at last "eat up himself'" was not dramatic sound and fury, but a modern *paradiso*: communism.

Marx the Epicurean

It is highly likely that Marx was delving even further back into Western poetry as he made his grand entrance with the *Manifesto*. As Jonathan Pollock has recently argued, Shakespeare's obsession with the "endless jar" that arises in a world where Divine Providence becomes opaque seems likely to have been gleaned from Lucretius' summary of Epicurean doctrine in *De rerum natura*, which he certainly knew from Montaigne's *Essays* at the least.[20] In responding to Shakespeare's epic dramatization of modern disintegration and struggle in the rallying cry of the *Manifesto*, it is probable that Marx was also harnessing the literary subject he had spent the most time actually studying at close range: that is, Epicurus, the focus of his doctoral thesis.

This literary genealogy suggests the ultimate example of how poetry and philosophy combined to produce the explosive declaration of the *Manifesto*. From Epicurus, Marx appears to have derived the single most important tenet underlying the *Manifesto*'s composition: the sense that amid the rubble of the modern, a new and dynamic combination of parts might emerge to ensure the social liberation of the human individual. Like Shakespeare in prerevolutionary England, Marx could see in the context of 1840s Europe a mise-en-scène of political chaos, collapsing religious and existential wisdoms, and rapid social and technological transformation. Central to this long-running intellectual impulse of disaffection or antagonism with modernity—felt by Marx just as keenly as Shakespeare—was the basic philosophical realization, which they found reflected in Epicurus, that they were inhabiting a European landscape comprised of so many chaotic, warring atoms. If Epicurus had presented the basis of a theory of existence in which nothing could connect with nothing, to paraphrase Eliot's later lament, Marx and Shakespeare proceeded from common intellectual assumptions about the removal of absolute religious certainty, and the corresponding rise of a scientific worldview which would later be characterized by another modernist poet as a desire "to explain the world an atom at a time."[21]

While Shakespeare constructed dramas of skeptical savagery on this atomistic foundation, Marx's contribution to the long humanist conflict with modernity was to use Epicurus as the model for a dynamic, atomistic analysis of social structures, and also as an underlying proof that the clash and fission of these fragments would produce new and better dimensions of experience. In his doctoral dissertation, Marx had argued that Epicurus outlined a theory in which atoms were "opposed to one another as immediate realities."[22] In the *Manifesto*, Marx extends this first principle, sketching a complex web of opposing, interconnected tendencies, from the macro categories of proletariat and bourgeoisie, to the more obscure tangle of contemporary subsects ("petty bourgeois" versus "German" socialism) that was Marx's immediate milieu. This, in a fairly straightforward sense, was what he meant by the radical materialist statement that all human history comprised a struggle between contending classes—a basic reiteration of the atomist premise that the universe is comprised of endlessly colliding and combining particles.

But also key to Marx's reading of Epicurus and its uptake into the *Manifesto* was the yet more radical notion of declination or "swerve"—the idea that atomic parts were not confined to the so-called bonds of fate, nor dissolved into a heady Shakespearean chaos, but rather energized by a generative interplay of compulsion and attraction, which saw them "swerve" out of preexisting categories and fall down into new patterns. For Marx in his doctorate on Epicurus, "the world of appearance can only emerge from the atom which is complete and alienated from its concept"—that is, the declination of atoms from their natural order means that there is now "no obstacle to the thinking subject, no limit, no stumbling-block," leaving the human subject free to perceive anything "which is abstractly possible, which can be conceived."[23] From this radical materialist observation emerges the Promethean basis of Marx's project, underlined by the revolutionary gloss he put on the quotation from Epicurus in the epigraph to his dissertation ("he who affirms of the gods what the multitude believes about them, is truly impious"). This is juxtaposed with Aeschylus' "Better to be the servant of this rock / Than to be faithful boy to Father Zeus," in an obvious presentiment of the *Manifesto*'s final peroration:

> The Communists disdain to conceal their views and aims. They openly declare that their ends can be attained only by the forcible overthrow of all existing social conditions. Let the ruling classes tremble at a Communistic revolution. The proletarians have nothing to lose but their chains. They have a world to win.[24]

And so we arrive finally at something we can confidently term "Marx's modernism." While Shakespeare had, in Trotsky's later formulation, carried "the individual passion ... to such a high degree of tension that it outgrows the individual, becomes super-personal, and is transformed into a fate of a certain kind," Marx's notion of the Epicurean "swerve" suggested a means of going beyond fate and achieving Promethean liberation in the post-religious landscape of the modern (even as Dante provided him with a model of spiritual idealism that could be used to animate the communist hereafter). While Marx's later labors with *Capital* represented one more extensive and intellectually rigorous strand of communist doctrine, the real value of the *Manifesto* lay in its simple instantiation of Epicurean optimism—the sense that a sudden jolt of atoms out of their disposition would result in a shattering of chains, and a historical climacteric in which literally anything was possible.

As mentioned earlier, a similar version of this principle would be articulated in a purely artistic context by the proto-modernist Walter Pater, whose doctrine of the "moment" promised a "quickened, multiplied consciousness" derived from the "poetic passion" of the aesthete (Pater's other great work, *Marius the Epicurean*, made the philosophical source of this literary mode even more explicit).[25] In turn, high-modernist literature more generally—with its *reductio* of writing to the sorts of quasi-scientific metaphors we see in the explosive formulations of Pound and Eliot from the time of the Russian Revolution—would combine a Paterian avowal of the moment with the deeper ethical dimension of Epicurean atomism we see in Marx's writings. While Pound's imagism, Joyce's epiphany, and even Eliot's call for a dynamic poetry in which "feelings are at liberty to enter into new combinations" were all in some sense indebted to the modern world ushered in by Marx in the *Manifesto*, it was the immanent communism of Lenin's revolution that took Marx's intimate knowledge of Dante, Shakespeare, and Epicurus and made of it a truly modern work of art.

Lenin's example reminds us that there are, of course, a number of postscripts to Marx's modernist achievement in the *Manifesto*. As Boris Groys has argued, the Soviet Union and its culture represented one teleology of the sort of literary "foreclosing" Marx was intent on in the *Manifesto*—a collapsing together of the main touchstones of European literature, to create the ultimate, real-world, total work of art.[26] The legacy of that *Gesamtkunstwerk* is, like modernism itself, an ambiguous and contested one. Did the twentieth century's actually existing communism bury "the aesthetic" for good, or did its failure come about because in its historical unfolding—especially during the Stalinist travesty—it was too self-consciously aesthetic? *The Communist Manifesto* will endure as a document that foregrounds this still vital question, and as such will continue to broaden our sense of when modernism began and ended. If it is not quite timeless, its ability to compact literary history into a durable program for human emancipation means that it is, at the very least, an *epic*—and in a way that most other modernist writers could not hope to emulate.

Notes

1. Marx and Engels, "Manifesto of the Communist Party," 489–90.
2. Marx and Engels, "Manifesto of the Communist Party," 500.
3. Marx and Engels, "Manifesto of the Communist Party," 500.
4. Leon Trotsky, quoted in Marx and Engels, *The Communist Manifesto and Its Relevance Today* (Sydney: Resistance, 1998), 19.
5. Marx and Engels, "Manifesto of the Communist Party," 473.
6. W. B. Yeats, *The Poems*, ed. Daniel Albright (London: J. M. Dent, 1994), 253.
7. Derrida, *Specters of Marx*, 47.
8. Walter Pater, *The Renaissance: Studies in Art and Poetry* (Berkeley: University of California Press, 1980), 198.
9. Vladimir Lenin, "The Three Sources and Three Component Parts of Marxism," in *Lenin's Collected Works*, vol. 19 (Moscow: Progress Publishers, 1963), 23.
10. B. Krylov, Preface to *Marx and Engels on Literature and Art* (1976). https://www.marxists.org/archive/marx/works/subject/art/index.htm, accessed August 20, 2019.
11. William Clare Roberts, *Marx's Inferno: The Political Theory of Capital* (Princeton: Princeton University Press, 2018), 1.
12. Marx and Engels, "Manifesto of the Communist Party," 474.
13. Marx and Engels, "Manifesto of the Communist Party," 474.
14. Eleanor Marx-Aveling, "Eleanor Marx on Her Father," in Eugene Kamenka, ed. *The Portable Karl Marx* (New York: Viking, 1983), 50.
15. Derrida, *Specters of Marx*, 4.
16. Marx, "Economic and Philosophic Manuscripts of 1844," 121.
17. Marx and Engels, "Manifesto of the Communist Party," 473.
18. L. C. Knights, *Explorations* (New York: New York University Press, 1947), 23.
19. *Troilus and Cressida*, I.3. 110–25.
20. See Jonathan Pollock, "Of Mites and Motes: Shakespearean Readings of Epicurean Science," in *Spectacular Science, Technology and Superstition in the Age of Shakespeare*, eds. Sophie Chiari and Mickaël Popelard (Edinburgh: Edinburgh University Press, 2017).
21. Basil Bunting, "A Note on *Briggflatts*" (Durham: Basil Bunting Poetry Centre, 1989), no pagination.
22. Marx, "Philosophies of Nature," 49.
23. Marx, "Philosophies of Nature," 44.
24. Marx and Engels, "Manifesto of the Communist Party," 500.
25. Pater, *The Renaissance*, 198.
26. See Boris Groys, *The Total Art of Stalinism: Avant-Garde, Aesthetic Dictatorship, and Beyond*, trans. Charles Rougle (London: Verso, 2011).

4

On France

Revolutions and Communes

Owen Holland

Contrary to popular misconceptions propounded by some of Marx's detractors and vulgarizers, Marx did not arrive at a set of immutable dogmas fixed for all time and in need of retrospective elaboration by a priestly caste of exegetes; on the contrary, he often developed and revised his ideas in response to "the immediate pressure of events."[1] As Étienne Balibar has emphasized, Marx was a conjunctural thinker par excellence. He "wrote in the conjuncture," as Balibar puts it, so much so that the "content of his thought is not separable from his shifts in position," meaning that "one cannot abstractly reconstruct his system."[2] Instead, one has to "retrace his development, with its breaks and bifurcations."[3] Some of these shifts are particularly visible in the series of texts Marx produced in response to the sequence of revolutionary upheavals, and subsequent setbacks and defeats, which took place in nineteenth-century France. From the February revolution and the June Days of 1848 through to the Paris Commune of 1871, Marx acted as a partisan, yet critical, observer of events, seeking to draw conclusions about revolutionary strategy even as he recognized the historical situation as radically in flux. With his eyes turned toward Paris—the city where he had lived in exile between 1843 and 1845, and which Walter Benjamin would describe as "the capital of the nineteenth century"—Marx produced some of his most important political writings in response to the pressure of historical events.[4] Here he grappled with what he had elsewhere referred to as the "bad side" of history.[5] These texts include, most notably, *The Class Struggles in France: 1848 to 1850* (1850), *The Eighteenth Brumaire of Louis Bonaparte* (1852), and *The Civil War in France* (1871), across which he struggled to absorb the impact of contemporary history for his theoretical understanding of the proletariat's world-historical vocation as the sole class capable of leading society toward "the *abolition of class differences in general*, the abolition of all relations of production on which they are based, the abolition of all social relations which correspond to these relations of production, and the revolutionizing of all ideas which stem from these social relations."[6]

There is unfortunately no scope, in this short chapter, to recapitulate or summarize the extensive details of the factional intrigues, spats, opportunist alliances, unprincipled coalitions, and the various wars of position and of maneuvre conducted by the different class fractions of the bourgeoisie—the two monarchist camps (Legitimist and Orléanist), the Bonapartist followers of Napoleon III, the bourgeois republicans, and the democratic socialists and neo-Jacobins of the Montagne—which characterized the politics of the short-lived second French republic (1848–51). Marx's writings on this topic are, in any case, best encountered at firsthand. Comprehending the politics of this period, and Louis Bonaparte's subsequent establishment of the Second Empire, after his coup d'état of December 2, 1851, forms the basis of Marx's extended commentary and analysis in *The Class Struggles in France* and *The Eighteenth Brumaire*. Marx's narration of events is a testament to the panoramic sweep and synthesizing power of his historical imagination. His prose crackles and pulses with bitingly ferocious satire against myriad class enemies, but his writing also lays bare the motivations of the competing actors and bourgeois class fractions with precision and political lucidity. He is particularly incisive, for example, in exposing the stakes of the rivalry between the rival monarchist camps—the Orléanists, who represented the interests of finance capital, and the Legitimists, who represented landed capital, whose competing dynastic claims Marx wittily reveals as a coded expression of their different material and economic interests.[7] Despite their ostensible differences, these two rival factions paradoxically found themselves bound together in the Party of Order, each to "oppose the restorationist and usupatory desires of the other by asserting their joint rule—the *republican form* of bourgeois rule."[8] The "genuine fusion of the Restoration and July monarchies," Marx observed with a fine sense of irony, "was the parliamentary republic, in which the Orléanist and the Legitimist colours were extinguished and the various species of bourgeois disappeared into the bourgeois as such, the bourgeois genus."[9]

Marx's political writings, then, brush against the grain of history, but his reckoning with historical developments did not simply aim at empirical accuracy or the chronicling of events; rather, Marx sought to provide a general orientation with which the revolutionary proletariat could reorganize its forces in response to the experience of political defeat during the June Days of 1848, and then again after the fall of the Commune in May 1871. He deployed a range of rhetorical tactics in this endeavor—making full use of the "weapons of historical research, criticism, satire and wit," as he put it in the 1869 Preface to the *Eighteenth Brumaire*—and he took to task those "so-called *objective* historians" whose "historical construction" of Bonaparte's coup d'état "imperceptibly turns into a historical apology for its hero."[10] Marx, by contrast, wrote history as a partisan of the revolutionary proletariat. His stated aim was to "show how ... the *class struggle* in France created circumstances and conditions which allowed a mediocre and grotesque individual [i.e., Louis Bonaparte in the self-fashioned, unwittingly parodic persona of Napoleon III] to play the hero's role."[11] One might briefly observe, here, both the emphasis Marx places on class struggle as the decisive factor in the movement of history and his recourse to a metaphor drawn from the world of theater, a metaphor he extends throughout the three texts that provide the focus of this chapter. Marx offered concise, and often cutting, thumbnail sketches of the leading personages in the drama of revolution and counterrevolution—from Napoleon III, the "serious clown who no longer sees world history as a comedy but his comedy as world history" to the "monstrous gnome" Adolphe Thiers, whose migrating loyalties saw him don various mantles of Orléanism, Bonapartism, and eventual opposition to the Second Empire, and who was responsible for suppressing the Commune in 1871.[12] But, in Marx's dramatis personae, the proletariat is undoubtedly the key figure, akin to an anonymous, collective protagonist, whose "giant body" bestrides the stage of world history like an animated colossus, playing the leading role in the tragedy of civil war between competing classes.[13]

Marx's extended theatrical metaphor was not incidental. On the contrary, a number of Marx's commentators have paid close attention to his use of metaphor, often noticing the constitutive nature of the relationship between theory and style, and pointing to the way in which "Marx's imagery plays an important role in constructing a political argument."[14] With particular reference to *The Class Struggles in France*, S. S. Prawer has observed that "metaphors from the theatre, from popular entertainments, and from literary parody act as leitmotivs that hold the work together."[15] Toward the beginning of the text, for example, Marx comments that the proclamation of the second republic propelled "all classes of French society . . . into the arena of political power; they were forced to quit the boxes, the pit, the gallery and to act for themselves on the revolutionary stage!"[16] It is almost too obvious to mention that the theater is political, not least because of the way in which the social space of the theater reveals the reality of class division in being partitioned into "the boxes, the pit, the gallery," but Marx here makes the metaphor work in the other direction, suggesting the way in which political action, and particularly revolutionary action, relies upon a performative praxis (or a praxis of performance). Marx uses the theatrical metaphor to formulate an argument about the nature of political agency in a revolutionary situation: all members and layers of society, even those cosseted and ticketed theater-goers who might be more comfortable as passive spectators, are suddenly "forced" into a political arena where choices must be made, and actions taken, even if only to avoid being overtaken by the action of others; but these newly minted actors lack a script, and must therefore extemporize their performance, a process which can often reveal and disclose class interests that might otherwise have been less visible, or harder to detect, in a less volatile historical moment.

The insistence with which Marx returns to this metaphor throughout his political writings on French history is part of the performative work of his own prose, perhaps most famously on display in the opening paragraphs of *The Eighteenth Brumaire* (a passage to which I will return in conclusion), where Marx uses "the categories of literary poetics directly in the construction of his historical argument."[17] Elsewhere, Marx inflects the theatrical metaphor in multiple ways: at one point he likens the replacement of governmental officials to a scene change in a play, where the transformation involves "scenery, costumes, language, actors, supernumeraries, extras, prompters, the position of the parties, the dramatic motifs, the nature of the conflict, the total situation."[18] At another point, the wavering political confidence of sections of the liberal bourgeoisie precipitates a situation in which "the actors cease to take themselves *au sérieux*, and the action totally collapses like a balloon pricked by a needle."[19] If Marx's prose might be thought of as yet another kind of performance, then the reader is cast as a spectator of sorts, but one who is always being invited to take the stage.

Given the central role that Marx accorded to the revolutionary proletariat, he also revised—indeed, he found it necessary to revise—his theoretical positions in response to the lived experience of the proletariat. As a historical materialist, Marx did not formulate his theory in an *a priori* manner, in abstraction from the real struggles and real contradictions he observed around him. Recognizing the juncture of structure and agency, Marx wrote that "[m]en make their own history," as he put it in the opening of *The Eighteenth Brumaire*, "but not of their own free will; not under circumstances they themselves have chosen but under given and inherited conditions with which they are directly confronted."[20] The struggle to *make* history, conceived as a yet-to-be-determined, open field of class confrontation, is also a struggle *against* history, conceived as an ensemble of past events and social relations which confront political agents in the form of "given and inherited conditions"—or the muck of ages, which must be painstakingly scraped off, again and again. Precisely because history does not unfold according to some preordained plan, as Marx clearly intimates here, it can throw up surprises that disturb even the most carefully calibrated theoretical system, therefore necessitating regular revision.

One particularly significant example of such revision concerns Marx's shift in thinking about the bourgeois state in the wake of the Paris Commune, a short-lived workers' insurrection that took place after the Franco-Prussian war, and which disturbed the established order of rival nation-states in proposing a vision of international, working-class solidarity that cut across national boundaries. As Marx wrote in the Preface to the 1872 German edition of *The Communist Manifesto*:

> In view of the practical experience gained, first in the February Revolution [of 1848], and then, still more, in the Paris Commune [of 1871], where the proletariat for the first time held power for two whole months, this programme [i.e., the programme outlined in *The Communist Manifesto*] has in some details become antiquated. One thing especially was proved by the Commune, viz., that "the working class cannot simply lay hold of the ready-made State machinery, and wield it for its own purposes."[1]

Marx here quotes a passage from *The Civil War in France*, his definitive statement on the Commune, drafted at the request of the General Council of the First International, in order to revise an earlier provisional hypothesis about the potential for the proletariat to capture and make use of the bourgeois state to advance progressive policies.[22] Expanding on this revised viewpoint in *The Civil War in France*, Marx comments that "[a]fter every revolution marking a progressive phase in the class struggle, the purely repressive character of the state power stands out in bolder and bolder relief," envisaging history as a process driven by episodes of class struggle, which, depending on their character, can serve to reveal heretofore unrecognized, or under-appreciated, aspects of the state.[23] But such insights are won, Marx knew, at the cost of counterrevolutionary violence and political defeat. If the bourgeois state, as

Marx claims here, is "purely repressive" in character, then the extent to which it can be used as a vehicle for the realization of "progressive" demands begins to appear more doubtful than he had thought to be the case when writing the *Manifesto*—a text written before Marx had witnessed the defeats of 1848 and 1871.

The precise development of Marx's thinking on the state remains an area of considerable controversy within Marxist theory, but it will suffice to note, here, that the Commune precipitated a significant shift in his position. As Vladimir Lenin, one of Marx's foremost interpreters within the revolutionary tradition, aptly commented in *State and Revolution*: "Although the mass revolutionary movement did not achieve its aim, [Marx] regarded [the Commune] as a historic experience of enormous importance, as a certain advance of the world proletarian revolution, as a practical step that was more important than hundreds of programs and arguments."[24] Needless to say, Marx's response to the Commune built upon and developed ideas that he worked through in his earlier writings on preceding periods of revolutionary turmoil in France. In the *Eighteenth Brumaire*, for example, he had suggestively noted that all previous "political upheavals," from the French Revolution to the revolution of 1848, "perfected [the state] machine instead of smashing it," an incipiently anti-statist position that he would develop at much more length in *The Civil War in France*.[25] Indeed, Marx was able to identify what he took to be novel about the Commune—namely, that it was "essentially a working-class government . . . the political form at last discovered under which to work out the economical emancipation of labor"[26]—in part because he could compare it against the historical experience of previous revolutions, drawing upon the insights he had formulated in his earlier texts.

In a remarkable passage in Marx's 1848 article on "The June Revolution," from which he quotes in *The Class Struggles in France*, Marx differentiates between the February revolution and the subsequent rising of the Parisian proletariat during the June Days in terms of the aesthetic categories of the beautiful and the ugly:

> The February revolution was the *beautiful* revolution, the revolution of universal sympathy, because the conflicts which erupted in the revolution against the [Orléanist] monarchy [which had been established in the earlier revolution of 1830] slumbered harmoniously side by side, as yet *undeveloped*, because the social struggle which formed its background had only assumed an airy existence—it existed only as a phrase, only in words. The June revolution is the *ugly* revolution, the repulsive revolution, because realities have taken the place of words, because the republic has uncovered the head of the monster itself by striking aside the protective, concealing crown.[27]

What matters here, for Marx, is the *making visible* of what he takes to be the real nature of the class antagonisms that rive the revolutionary scene. The instability of the coalition between various factions of the liberal bourgeoisie and the proletariat that had seen through the February revolution, toppling the July Monarchy of Louis Philippe and installing a republic in its place, was brutally exposed when the proletariat pushed more radical demands for a social republic during the June Days, only to be met with the full force of bourgeois reaction as their barricades were overrun by the National Guard. The fact that sections of the liberal bourgeoisie chose to support this violent reaction, with varying degrees of reluctance or enthusiasm, in the name of maintaining "order," revealed the limits of their revolutionary rhetoric. Such vacillation on the part of the liberal bourgeoisie also ultimately served to strengthen the Party of Order, paving the way for Bonaparte's coup.

Marx's decision to characterize the "universal sympathy" of the February revolution as "beautiful" is bitingly ironic: he aims to expose the illusion of cross-class unity between the bourgeoisie and the proletariat, which can only have appeared beautiful to those liberals naïve enough to believe in it. By contrast, the June revolution is "ugly" because it punctured those illusions, disclosing the power relations and contradictory class interests that underpinned the February coalition. Marx provides the stark reminder that "[f]raternity lasted only as long as there was a fraternity of interests between bourgeoisie and proletariat."[28] The liberal bourgeoisie would prefer not to confront this "repulsive" state of affairs, but the march of events—and, crucially, the actions of the organized revolutionary proletariat during the June Days—forced the "ugly" truth of class antagonism into the open. Yet even as Marx deploys these aesthetic categories, he implicitly suggests that they are only relevant to those bourgeois actors and observers who would prefer to arrest the course of history in February. Beauty, to recall the cliché, is in the eye of the beholder: the proclamation of the second republic on February 26 would not have appeared particularly beautiful to the Orléanist supporters of Louis Philippe, for example, and Marx himself can hardly have regarded the February revolution as beautiful, given his intention to expose the spuriousness of its alleged universality. In this sense, Marx frames the revolutionary scene in aesthetic terms, but his use of these terms is ironic insofar as it suggests that such an interpretative paradigm is of limited value, and is contingent on the ideological position of the beholder. Indeed, one can almost sense Marx's schadenfreude in imagining the bourgeois recoil from the perceived ugliness of the class struggle. Marx is not so much aestheticizing politics here, as he is revealing the political naivety of those who would attempt to think politics in such terms.

Bearing witness to the historical defeat of the proletariat during the June Days allowed Marx to formulate and sharpen his views. Marx recapitulated the essence of his earlier analysis in *The Civil War in France*, reminding his readers that the "bourgeois republicans, who, in the name of the revolution of February [1848], took the state power, used it for the June massacres, in order to convince the working class that 'social' republic meant the republic ensuring their social subjection."[29] Here, though, Marx's backward glance helps him to establish the novelty of the Commune as "the first revolution in which the working class was openly acknowledged as the only class capable of social initiative, even by the great bulk of the Paris middle class," an analysis he does not figure forth in aesthetic terms.[30] In both cases, his formulations were too late to have any effective capacity to undo the particular circumstances of the defeat, but he sought to enable those who might inhabit a similar conjuncture in the future to prosecute their struggle with a keener awareness of the real nature of the contradictions and antagonisms animating that conjuncture.

Marx was, of course, keenly aware that no conjuncture ever occurs twice, even if certain superficial resemblances might be detectable. His historical writings engage in their own struggle not to be outdone by the ruse of history. The task of reckoning with the actuality of defeat enabled Marx more clearly to delineate the nature, interests, and long-term strategic prospects of the opposing class forces, looking forward to a time when defeat might be transformed into victory. As he put it in the opening paragraphs of *The Class Struggles in France*, "revolutionary progress cleared a path for itself not by its immediate, tragic-comic achievements, but, on the contrary, by creating a powerful and united counter-revolution; only in combat with this opponent did the insurrectionary party mature into a real party of revolution"; he goes on to conclude this introductory section by noting that "[t]o demonstrate this is the task of the following pages."[31] Marx's chief concern, then, in recounting the history of a defeated revolution is to show the ways defeat nevertheless signals a potential realignment and regrouping of the revolutionary forces on a stronger, firmer footing, insofar as the "insurrectionary party" achieves the first goal of any potentially revolutionary force in *recognizing itself as a revolutionary force* as it moves from being a *class-in-itself* to a *class-for-itself*, thus attaining, in the process, a better understanding of the tasks ahead.

After the abdication of Louis Philippe in February 1848, the Paris proletariat agitated for and achieved the proclamation of a republic based on universal suffrage, at a time when sections of the bourgeoisie were willing to settle for some form of compromise in the shape of a differently organized constitutional monarchy. This partial victory led Marx to comment that what the proletariat had "conquered was the ground on which to struggle for its revolutionary emancipation, by no means this emancipation itself."[32] The mere proclamation of the republic secured no concrete material gains for the proletariat, as Marx demonstrates, because the "governmental form of the parliamentary republic" proved to be little more than a means to establish bourgeois dictatorship, as writ large during the massacres of June: "the two great subdivisions of the French bourgeoisie [landed capital and finance capital] could only unite under this form, thus placing on the agenda the rule of their class instead of the regime of a privileged fraction of it."[33] The "parliamentary republic," Marx goes on to observe, "was the only possible form for the rule of the bourgeoisie as a whole."[34]

In the course of his extended engagement with French political history and the socialist ideas that derived from that history—which, according to Lenin, constituted one of the three main sources of Marx's theory, along with classical German philosophy and English political economy—Marx identified the social forces which he deemed capable of revolutionizing bourgeois society, and transforming it into a classless society of freely associated producers.[35] Thus, when Marx identifies the proletariat as the "decisive revolutionary force" in *The Class Struggles in France*, he does so after having borne witness to the containment and ultimate defeat of a particular, historical revolution.[36] Responding to this defeat and imagining how it might have been otherwise, Marx concluded that proletarian hegemony is a necessary but not sufficient condition for successful social revolution. Proletarian hegemony among the revolutionary forces is a necessary condition of social revolution, for Marx, because other potentially revolutionary classes, like the peasantry or the petite bourgeoisie, who might be won to proletarian demands, had proven, in the period following the February revolution of 1848, to be too materially and ideologically vested in the existing economic arrangements to be able to achieve the supersession of the bourgeois status quo in the absence of proletarian leadership. Yet proletarian hegemony is not a sufficient condition for victorious social revolution, however, because the course of any given revolutionary struggle is always contingent upon a set of unforeseen and unforeseeable historical circumstances.

The concept of social revolution—as opposed to a narrow political revolution, whereby one fraction of the dominant class simply replaces another—carried particular significance for Marx, insofar as it envisages the abolition of class society in its entirety. That the French bourgeoisie had manifestly failed to abolish class society during the French Revolution of the late eighteenth century is one of the reasons that Marx regarded the revolution of 1789 as a bourgeois revolution—a term which has elicited much controversy over the years.[37] The concept of social revolution, meanwhile, is, or should be, central to any discussion of aesthetic modernism. As Perry Anderson astutely notes, "the imaginative proximity of social revolution" was an essential coordinate of the "modernist conjuncture," and one which divided most of the early twentieth-century avant-gardes into opposing revolutionary and counterrevolutionary camps—Russian futurism, Berlin Dadaism, and surrealism on the left set against Italian futurism, Vorticism and the "high" modernism of Eliot and Pound on the right.[38] Marx relied upon this concept in the wake of the Paris Commune, which he regarded as the "initiation of the social revolution of the nineteenth century," because, unlike the February revolution of 1848, and the various power struggles that ensured thereafter, Marx saw the Commune as "a revolution not against this or that Legitimate, Constitutional [i.e., Orléanist], Republican or Imperialist [i.e., Bonapartist] form of state power," but as "a revolution against the *state* itself"; the Commune thus figured as "a resumption by the people for the people of its own social life."[39] For Marx, the Commune "was not a revolution to transfer [the state] from one fraction of the ruling classes to the other, but a revolution to break down this horrid machinery of class domination itself," and it was in this respect that the Commune initiated "the social revolution of the nineteenth century."[40] As István Mészáros has commented, the concept of social revolution allowed Marx to formulate "the way of overcoming the problematical relationship between politics and society by consciously superimposing on the political revolution its hidden social dimension."[41] The intense pathos of Marx's political writings on the defeat of the Commune, and the earlier defeat of the proletarian insurrection of June 1848, emerges from the fact that these writings confirm the accuracy of Hegel's dictum that the owl of Minerva only ever flies at dusk.

The act of bearing witness to such defeats cannot undo them, but it can break new interpretative ground in such a way as to provide theoretical and political orientation in the future. Responding to the defeat of the Paris Communards in 1871, Marx wrote:

> The working class did not expect miracles from the Commune. They have no ready-made utopias to introduce *par décret du people*. They know that in order to work out their own emancipation, and along with it that higher form to which

present society is irresistibly tending by its own economical agencies, they will have to pass through long struggles, through a series of historic processes, transforming circumstances and men. They have no ideals to realize, but to set free the elements of the new society with which old collapsing bourgeois society itself is pregnant.[42]

It is worth paying close attention to the turns in this passage's argument, because they neatly illustrate some of the most salient features, and the potential for misunderstanding, of Marx's thinking about revolution and social transformation. One might detect, for example, a strain of determinism in the reference to "economic agencies" that create an apparently irresistible momentum toward a "higher form" of society, intimating a process which seemingly takes place of its own accord, irrespective of human agency or intervention. Yet this reading is undoubtedly complicated by the unambiguous emphasis on proletarian self-emancipation as the crucial element in a "series of historic processes," without which the "higher form" of society will simply be strangled at birth. According to the logic of the metaphor of pregnancy—another of Marx's favorite metaphors—that operates here, the proletariat acts as a kind of midwife to history; it possesses the capability to bring to birth the latent potentiality that exists *within* the present society. This way of conceptualizing social transformation is particularly valuable not least because the *maieutic* approach adopted by Marx avoids both the Scylla of voluntarism and the Charybdis of top-down elitism. The proletariat, according to Marx, does not strive to realize transcendent "ideals" in the form of utopian blueprints or "recipes . . . for the cook-shops of the future," which bear no relation to existing social arrangements, but seeks instead to liberate *existing* society, according to a logic of immanence.[43]

Where, then, might the explicitly Marxian project of social revolution be said to stand today, after the catastrophic failure of numerous twentieth-century versions of self-proclaimed Marxist praxis to live up to the emancipatory promise of Marx's method? Many of the most strident voices of condemnation—anti-communist apostles of bourgeois "freedom," who would seek to consign the entire Marxist tradition to the dustbin of history—have fallen strangely quiet of late, or are at least obliged to hedge their criticism with some sort of gestural acknowledgment toward the deeply precarious position of the present regime of capitalist accumulation. In considering such a vast question, one could do worse than to begin by returning to Marx's memorable and oft-quoted statement from the opening of the *Eighteenth Brumaire*, where he wrote that

> The tradition of the dead generations weighs like a nightmare on the minds of the living. And, just when they appear to be engaged in the revolutionary transformation of themselves and their surroundings, in the creation of something which does not yet exist, precisely in such epochs of revolutionary crisis they timidly conjure up the spirits of the past to help them; they borrow their names, slogans and costumes so as to stage the new world-historical scene in this venerable disguise and borrowed language.[44]

Marx developed this theatrical metaphor to suggest that the leading personages of the 1848 revolution merely parodied the revolutionary traditions of 1789 and 1793–5. Louis

Bonaparte, in assuming the mantle of emperor and styling himself as Napoleon III after the coup of 1851, was repeating, or parodying, Napoleon I's coup d'état of November 9, 1799, in which he overthrew the Directory of the first Republic.[45] In looking back to the French Revolution, regarded by Marx as "the most colossal revolution that history has ever known," the bourgeois protagonists of 1848 simply demonstrated their inability to actualize the progressive potential of the revolution.[46] Instead, they fled from the tasks of the concrete situation, turned against the progressive demands of the proletariat, and "plunged back into an already dead epoch."[47]

However, Marx did not argue that repetition belongs exclusively to the sphere of parody and failure. On the contrary, he noted that the Jacobins themselves looked to the "stern classical traditions of the Roman republic," while "Cromwell and the English people had borrowed for their bourgeois revolution the language, passions and illusions of the Old Testament."[48] In these revolutionary confrontations with feudalism, Marx argued, "the resurrection of the dead served to exalt the new struggles, rather than to parody the old . . . and to recover the spirit of the revolution, rather than to set its ghost walking again," though he added the qualification that the bourgeois recourse to "classical traditions of the Roman Republic" chiefly served to "hide from themselves the limited bourgeois content of their struggles."[49] Donning the heroic mantle of classical republicanism was a form of self-deception (or false consciousness) for the French bourgeoisie insofar as it allowed them to perceive themselves as acting in a revolutionary manner, even as the social and economic content of their activity principally served their own narrow interests. The efficacy of repetition, Marx implies, is itself contingent upon the set of historical conditions in which the protagonists learn their roles, and the nineteenth-century social revolution, Marx argued, "cannot begin its own work until it has sloughed off all its superstitious regard for the past."[50] One might detect a certain superficial resemblance to later modernist assertions of the necessity of rupture, and iconoclastic relinquishments of the past, as in F. T. Marinetti's *Futurist Manifesto* (1909) or Wyndham Lewis' *Blast* (1914), but such aesthetic re-encodings of Marx's elaboration of the tasks facing modern revolution often went together with a corresponding (and frequently reactionary) de-politicization, as Martin Puchner has usefully outlined.[51]

The question facing the present generation, to paraphrase Marx, concerns whether or not the social revolution of the twenty-first century "can only create its poetry from the future, not from the past."[52] If this is true, one might be tempted to agree with Alain Badiou's hypothesis that the historical sequence associated with the terms "Marxism, the workers' movement, mass democracy, Leninism, the proletarian party, the Socialist state—all these remarkable inventions of the twentieth century—are no longer of practical use."[53] On this view, it is necessary to abandon all "superstitious regard" for this past, in order to reinvent communist political praxis in the present.[54] Marx himself, after all, wrote that the protagonists of the nineteenth-century social revolution required no "world-historical reminiscences," and must "let the dead bury their dead"[55]—an allusion, on Marx's part, to Mt. 8:21-22, which rather complicates his assertion of the necessity of an absolute break with the past. But this is surely Marx's point: even when circumstances appear to demand total rupture, patterns of repetition, either conscious or unconscious, remain visible. Even the Commune of 1871, which

Marx celebrated for its novelty, briefly reinstituted the revolutionary calendar of the French Revolution, and took some of its inspiration from the Commune of 1793. According to Walter Benjamin, the Commune even "felt itself to be, in all respects, the heir of 1793."[56] As we look back at the succession of failed twentieth-century revolutions, much as Marx looked back to 1789, 1793–5, 1830, 1848, and 1871, some see only the nightmare of Stalinism, and conclude that Marx should be written off altogether. Others might recall Michael Löwy's cogent warning that "attempts to go beyond Marx frequently end up *falling short* of him."[57] Surveying Marx's engagement with the French Revolution of the late eighteenth century, Löwy also argues that "the legacy of the French Revolution remains, even today, something living, contemporary, and *active*" because it "still has something incomplete about it. It contains a promise not yet fulfilled; it is the beginning of a process that is not yet ended."[58] One might arrive at a similar formula when evaluating the legacy of the twentieth-century communist movement which, in turn, might have a bearing on the way one approaches Marx in the light of this historical dead weight. However one chooses to construe Marx's research project—as critique of bourgeois political economy, as historical materialist analysis of the results of class struggle and prospects for social revolution, or as an unparalleled interpretative framework for reading the runes of modernity—it is hard to dispute that Marxism will remain a *living* tradition, in one shape or another, while the capitalist mode of production lingers on.

Notes

1. Marx, Preface to the Second Edition of "The Eighteenth Brumaire of Louis Bonaparte," in *Surveys from Exile: Political Writings, Volume 2*, ed. David Fernbach (Harmondsworth: Penguin, 1992), 143.
2. Etienne Balibar, *The Philosophy of Marx*, trans. Chris Turner (London: Verso, 2007), 6.
3. Balibar, *The Philosophy of Marx*, 6.
4. See Benjamin, "Paris: Capital of the Nineteenth Century (Exposé of 1939)," in *The Arcades Project*, ed. Rolf Tiedemann, trans. Howard Eiland and Kevin McLaughlin (Cambridge, MA: Harvard University Press, 1999).
5. In analyzing the antagonistic elements at work in feudal production, Marx commented: "It is the bad side which produces the movement which makes history, by providing a struggle." *The Poverty of Philosophy*, ed. C. P. Dutt and V. Chattopadhyaya (London: Martin Lawrence), 103.
6. "The Class Struggles in France" and "The Eighteenth Brumaire" appear in volume two of the Penguin edition of Marx's *Political Writings*. "The Civil War in France" appears in volume three, *The First International and After: Political Writings*, ed. David Fernbach (Harmondsworth: Penguin, 1992). All subsequent references to these editions will appear by volume and page number. Italics in original.
7. Marx, *Political Writings* vol. 2, 138, 173.
8. Marx, *Political Writings* vol. 2, 89.
9. Marx, *Political Writings* vol. 2, 216.
10. Marx, *Political Writings* vol. 2, 144.

11 Marx, *Political Writings* vol. 2, 144.
12 Marx, *Political Writings* vol. 2, 198; Marx, *Political Writings* vol. 3, 191.
13 Marx, *Political Writings* vol. 2, 55. For an extended discussion of the relationship between tragedy and revolution, see Raymond Williams' *Modern Tragedy* (London: Chatto & Windus, 1966). Williams comments that "I see revolution as the inevitable working through of a deep and tragic disorder, to which we can respond in varying ways but which will in any case, in one way or another, work its way through our world, as a consequence of our actions" (75).
14 Terrell Carver, *The Postmodern Marx* (Manchester: Manchester University Press, 1998), 9. For pertinent discussions of Marx's use of metaphor (particularly his vampire metaphor) in *Capital*, see Carver, *The Postmodern Marx*, 14–20; and David McNally, *Monsters of the Market: Zombies, Vampires and Global Capitalism* (Chicago, IL: Haymarket, 2012), 119–20.
15 S. S. Prawer, *Karl Marx and World Literature* (Oxford: Oxford University Press, 1978), 178. For an extended discussion of the literary dimensions of the three texts discussed in this chapter, see Prawer, 178–85 and 352–8.
16 Marx, *Political Writings* vol. 2, 43.
17 Eugene Lunn, *Marxism and Modernism: An Historical Study of Lukács, Brecht, Benjamin and Adorno* (Berkeley: University of California Press, 1982), 19. For further discussion of Marx's literary strategies, see Stanley E. Hyman, *The Tangled Bank: Darwin, Marx, Frazer and Freud as Imaginative Writers* (New York: Atheneum, 1962); and Jeffrey Mehlman, *Revolution and Repetition: Marx/Hugo/Balzac* (Berkeley: University of California Press, 1977).
18 Marx, *Political Writings* vol. 2, 276.
19 Marx, *Political Writings* vol. 3, 179.
20 Marx, *Political Writings* vol. 2, 146.
21 Marx and Engels, "Manifesto of the Communist Party," 470.
22 Marx, *Political Writings* vol. 3, 206. In the *Manifesto*, Marx and Engels outlined a number of measures that a proletarian government might implement in order to "use its political supremacy to wrest, by degrees, all capital from the bourgeoisie, to centralize all instruments of production in the hands of the State . . . and to increase the total productive forces as rapidly as possible." ("Manifesto of the Communist Party," 490). These measures included a heavy progressive income tax, abolition of all right of inheritance, centralization of credit in the hands of the state, free education for children in all public schools, along with various other proposed measures.
23 Marx, *Political Writings* vol. 3, 207.
24 See Lenin, *The State and Revolution* (1917), annotated and introduced by Todd Chretien (Chicago, IL: Haymarket, 2014), 73–4. For some other classic treatments of Marx's writings on the state, see Ralph Miliband, "Marx and the State," *Socialist Register* 2 (1965): 278–96; Hal Draper, "The Death of the State in Marx and Engels," *Socialist Register* 7 (1970): 281–307; and István Mészáros, *Beyond Capital: Toward a Theory of Transition* (London: Merlin Press, 1995), 460–520.
25 Marx, *Political Writings* vol. 2, 238.
26 Marx, *Political Writings* vol. 2, 212.
27 Marx, *Political Writings* vol. 2, 60.
28 Marx, *Political Writings* vol. 2, 60.
29 Marx, *Political Writings* vol. 3, 207.

30 Marx, *Political Writings* vol. 3, 214.
31 Marx, *Political Writings* vol. 2, 35.
32 Marx, *Political Writings* vol. 2, 43.
33 Marx, *Political Writings* vol. 2, 175.
34 Marx, *Political Writings* vol. 2, 210.
35 Lenin, "The Three Sources and Three Component Parts of Marxism" [1913], in *Collected Works* vol. 19 (Moscow: Progress Publishers, 1977), 21-8.
36 Marx, *Political Writings* vol. 2, 121.
37 For recent discussions of this important Marxist concept, see Henry Heller, *The Bourgeois Revolution in France, 1789-1815* (Oxford: Berghahn Books, 2006) and Neil Davidson, *How Revolutionary Were the Bourgeois Revolutions?* (Chicago: Haymarket, 2012).
38 Perry Anderson, *A Zone of Engagement* (London: Verso, 1992), 34.
39 Marx, *Political Writings* vol. 3, 249.
40 Marx, *Political Writings* vol. 3, 249.
41 Mészáros, *Beyond Capital*, 469. See also Max Horkheimer's comment: "Two antagonistic moments, the takeover of state control and the liberation from it, are contained together in the concept of social revolution." Horkheimer, *Walter Benjamin zum Gedächtnis* (1942) quoted in Martin Jay, *Permanent Exiles: Essays on the Intellectual Migration from Germany to America* (New York: Columbia University Press, 1986), 34.
42 Marx, *Political Writings* vol. 3, 213.
43 Marx, "1873 Postface to the Second Edition," in *Capital* vol. 1, 99.
44 Marx, *Political Writings* vol. 2, 146.
45 According to the revolutionary calendar implemented between 1793 and 1805, the date of the coup was 18 Brumaire VIII.
46 Marx and Engels, *The German Ideology, Part One, with Selections from Parts Two and Three*, ed. C. J. Arthur (London: Lawrence & Wishart, 1970), 97. There is no space, here, to broach the question of Marx's various assessments of the French Revolution, but readers are encouraged to consult Michael Löwy's excellent essay on this topic. See Löwy, "'The Poetry of the Past': Marx and the French Revolution," in *On Changing the World: Essays in Political Philosophy, from Karl Marx to Walter Benjamin*, 2nd ed. (Chicago, IL: Haymarket, 2013), 111-26.
47 Marx, *Political Writings* vol. 2, 148.
48 Marx, *Political Writings* vol. 2, 148.
49 Marx, *Political Writings* vol. 2, 148.
50 Marx, *Political Writings* vol. 2, 149.
51 Puchner, *Poetry of the Revolution*, 69-131.
52 Marx, *Political Writings* vol. 2, 149.
53 Badiou, *The Meaning of Sarkozy*, trans. David Fernbach (London: Verso, 2010), 113. He continues: "At the theoretical level, they certainly deserve further study and consideration; but at the level of politics, they have become impracticable" (ibid.).
54 Marx, *Political Writings* vol. 2, 149.
55 Marx, *Political Writings* vol. 2, 149.
56 Benjamin, *Arcades*, 789.
57 Löwy, "The Poetry of the Past," 113.

58 Löwy, "The Poetry of the Past," 123. It is fruitful to compare Jameson's partial endorsement of Jürgen Habermas' "brilliant formula of an incomplete modernity, of 'modernity itself as an unfinished project.'" Habermas' formula, according to Jameson, "remains usefully ambiguous, and allows one to entertain the possibility that modernity is incomplete because it never could be completed by the middle class and its economic system." Jameson, *A Singular Modernity*, 11. For Habermas' argument, see Jürgen Habermas, "Modernity—An Incomplete Project," in Hal Foster, ed. *The Anti-Aesthetic: Essays on Postmodern Culture* (New York: The New Press, 1998), 3–15.

5

Jupiter against the Lightning-Rod

Literary Form in the *Grundrisse*

Dominick Knowles

This chapter is concerned with the literary and aesthetic qualities of the *Grundrisse* (1858) and how its "scientific elaboration of the theoretical foundations of communism" offers not just an analytic framework but a revolutionary method of writing and reading.[1] While Marx has been the subject of numerous recent literary and political-theoretical works, these discussions have tended to focus on either Marx's early writing or his unfinished opus, *Capital* (1867). For instance, S. S. Prawer' *Karl Marx and World Literature* (2011) takes up Marx's preponderant references to Greek, French, and German literatures to develop an aesthetic dimension often ignored by Marxist critics. William Clare Roberts' *Marx's Inferno* (2016) illuminates volume one of *Capital* by envisioning its narrative as an extended Dantean conceit of descent into capitalism's "social hell."[2] Most recently, in his article "Reading Capital, Writing History" and full monograph *Red Modernism* (2017), Mark Steven argues via C. D. Blanton's concept of "epic negation" that dialectical materialism was one of the primary drivers of poetic modernism, in fact comprising its "prehistory."[3] Literature's relationship to the *Grundrisse*, by contrast, has received comparatively little attention since the latter's translation into English in 1973. With the exception of Joshua Clover's work on literature and crisis theory, most scholarship that deals with this relationship appears in the form of either a textual commentary, as in Darko Suvin's "Transubstantiation of Production and Creation: Metamorphic Imagery in the *Grundrisse*" (1982), or a glancing mention, as in Marcello Musto's "History, Production, and Method in the 1857 'Introduction'" (2008).

My aim here is both to re-introduce the *Grundrisse* to literary scholars in the hopes of instigating critical discussion and to re-read it as a formally experimental and speculative work of communist literature. To begin, I'd like to look at two observations by Martin Nicolaus in the introduction to the original English translation: first, that the *Grundrisse* "proclaims its unripeness for print" in its "missing elements of grammar . . . difficult, sometimes awkward, obscure and even altogether inaccurate formulations, endless sentences and paragraphs, irritating digressions and reiterations, etc."[4] For Nicolaus, this unripeness presents a risk that must be heeded by readers: certain ideas developed clearly in *Capital* remain fetal in the *Grundrisse*—among them, Marx's crucial distinction between "labor" and "labor power," as well as the struggle between capital and labor over the working day. The unfinished nature of the manuscript, he avers, can raise "doubts as to what Marx 'really' meant in a given passage. Let the quoter, the exerptor, beware."[5] The second remark from Nicolaus is that Marx's purpose in writing the *Grundrisse* was not just "self-clarification," but "to prepare, to educate the next generation of leaders of the working class in the objective preconditions, possibility and necessity of the historic task." In this way, the *Grundrisse* was not simply a private text; Marx composed it as a guide to the "historic task" of overthrowing capitalism. Nicolaus understands this purpose as occurring *in spite* of the text's roughness: the "deficiencies of form," he writes, "bring with them a powerful compensation."[6] We are compensated for the *Grundrisse*'s irritating formlessness, it seems, by gaining entry to what Roman Rosdolsky calls Marx's "economic laboratory": the author's mind at work, his compositional process that in some ways tells us more about the purposes of communist theory than *Capital* itself.[7]

A crucial feature of *Capital*—its most "scientific" and literary accomplishment—is its polished, crystalline quality, from which the "unripeness" and outright radicalism of earlier drafts have been scrubbed. This is not to make the absurd claim that *Capital* is somehow a reactionary or counterrevolutionary text; as critics such as Keston Sutherland have remarked, *Capital* is brimming with subversive arguments couched in language of political satire. Moreover, its theoretical importance for revolutionaries from Vladimir Lenin to Rosa Luxemburg through James Connolly and Angela Davis surely attests to its use-value in dismantling bourgeois logic. Rather, what I mean to say is that the *Grundrisse*, with its unique structural imperfections, articulates Marx's revolutionary message at the level of literary form. Contra Nicolaus, I argue that Marx's call for the abolition of capitalist social relations bursts through the text of the *Grundrisse* not in spite, but *because*, of its formlessness.

Nicolaus' remarks prompt a reconsideration of the *Grundrisse* in a way consonant of Sutherland's thesis in "Marx in Jargon." Sutherland's essay examines the philological histories behind both the original German and the English translations of *Capital*. Beginning with Marx's anguished review of his own opus' "literary shortcomings," Sutherland argues that *Capital*'s "risks and failures of style are arguments in themselves, irreducible to theoretical propositions."[8] This irreducibility suggests a generative bond between the aesthetic and political valences of Marx's work, in which neither category can collapse neatly into the other. Following Sutherland's line of thought, I want to propose that Marx's messy, digressive sketchbook is not useful just as "pure theory," but must also be regarded as an aesthetic object, a "problem of style."[9] Rather than ignoring or trying to "correct" the work's many digressions, fragments, and redundancies, it might be more productive to understand them as literary-stylistic features that reveal aspects of dialectical thought not present in more polished works like *Capital*, in which the methodological "noise" has been largely silenced. Moreover, I want to channel Steven's intervention by locating the *Grundrisse* in the "prehistory" of modernist poetics. Indeed, reading the *Grundrisse* within and against literary modernism gets us places that other readings—political-economic, theoretical, historical—might not. It lets us reclaim the apparently incidental formal features of

Marx's notebooks as constitutive of his argument; it reframes the *Grundrisse* as a kind of "poem including history," anticipating the works of Ezra Pound and Louis Zukfosky; and, simultaneously, it articulates the composition of the *Grundrisse* as a labor process, a kind of literary praxis toward a communist future. Before making this case, however, it will be necessary to account for the content of the *Grundrisse*, the motivations of its author, and the historical circumstances of its composition.

Prehistory of Modernism's Communism

The *Grundrisse* is the snakeskin left behind by the three volumes of *Capital*. Like a snakeskin, it is a work characterized by fragment and translucence. Never intended for publication, the text comprises a loosely connected series of seven notebooks, drafted from 1857 to 1858. These notebooks roughly correspond to subjects taken up in the unfinished, multivolume project of *Capital*. While the *Grundrisse* is divided into seven notebooks, the two main conceptual divisions are the "Chapter on Money" and the "Chapter on Capital," the latter of which is roughly four times as long as the former. Moreover, outside the notebooks proper, the text is bookended by an introduction and a fragmentary critique of classical economists Claude Frederic Bastiat and Henry Charles Carey. These four sections are in dialogue with one another but do not hang together as a coherent treatise. Yet, as scholars from Antonio Negri to Ellen Meiksins Wood have observed, the *Grundrisse* is not a "rough draft" of Marx's later works—several concepts are mentioned or even developed at length in these notebooks that do not appear anywhere else in Marx's oeuvre. To take the *Grundrisse* as merely preparatory is not only to ignore those qualities unique to it but also to neglect Marx as he thinks through the fundamental arguments that shape his early and mature writings.

For some Marxist scholars, most notably Louis Althusser and Etienne Balibar, Marx's work can be broadly distinguished into two distinct phases. In *For Marx* (1969), Althusser cites the existence of an "epistemological break" that separates the early humanist and the later "scientific" Marx.[10] The first of these categories is represented by the *1844 Manuscripts*, which dealt more prominently with philosophical problems of alienation and humanity's relationship to the natural world. After 1845, Althusser observes, Marx abandons his immature humanism, breaks with Hegel's dialectic, and fully develops his analytic of historical materialism. However, as David McLellan and Antonio Negri have argued in markedly different ways, the *Grundrisse*—which is as much a development of Marx's early philosophical meditations as a critique of political economy—challenged this easy structural distinction. In his introduction to selections from the *Grundrisse* first published in 1971, McLellan derides as "useless" the entire debate over the phases of Marx's development.[11] He argues instead that "Marx's thought is best viewed as a continuing meditation on central themes broached in 1844," which culminates not with *Capital* but the *Grundrisse*, the "completest" of his texts.[12] Negri's *Marx beyond Marx*, a collection of lectures given in 1978 at the École Normale Supérieure, also places the *Grundrisse* at the "dynamic center of Marxian thought"—not for reasons of "completeness" or continuity, but because it is, fundamentally, a "*political* text that conjugates ... revolutionary possibilities ... together with theoretical will."[13] It is this "synthesis" of theory and praxis into a "revolutionary subjectivity" that gives Marx's *Grundrisse* the qualities proper to communist literature.

In essence, the *Grundrisse* is a document responding to a pulverized world economy. Less than a decade after the 1848 revolutions throughout France, Italy, and the Austrian Empire—all of which ended in misery and widespread disillusionment for the working classes—Europe once more found itself embroiled in fiscal crisis. In an article for the *New York Daily Tribune*, for example, Marx blames the "present mania" on the French banking company Credit Mobilier's predatory lending policies, which "universalizes swindling at the same rate that it centralizes it."[14] As havoc spread across Europe and the United States, Marx speculated in his letters to Engels that capitalism's detonating contradictions might undermine industry and finance enough to mobilize the masses. Deportations, police brutality, worker revolts, and assassination attempts punctuated European cities throughout the mid- and late nineteenth century. And while, of course, the revolution never came, this violent social ferment informed Marx's work as he composed the *Grundrisse*, accounting for both its urgency and lack of polish.

If we take seriously Jameson's remark in *A Singular Modernity* (2002) that "fundamental meaning of modernity ... is that of a worldwide capitalism itself," the fact of Marx's writing in the midst of transnational capitalist terror and mass insurrection fixes the *Grundrisse* firmly in the prehistory of modern literature.[15] Modernism, if it means anything at all, is the aesthetic response to these large-scale mutations in the mode of production. More precisely, according to Adorno in "On Lyric Poetry and Society," modernist lyric poetry is "the subjective expression of a social antagonism," in which an apparently private consciousness reveals a "collective undercurrent" of social and political forces.[16] Understood within this dialectic, what Nicolaus described as a series of disjointed notes on economic crisis takes the shape of a poetic attempt to imagine modernity otherwise in the form of a collective subjectivity. The *Grundrisse*, then, is much more than a series of notebooks—it is the imaginative matrix in which modernism's communism begins to emerge.

A Brief Drama of Potential Combatants

At the end of the *Grundrisse*'s 1857 Introduction, Marx stages a battle in which the gods of Greek art struggle against industrial and finance capital:

> Is the view of nature and of social relations on which the Greek imagination ... is based possible with self-acting mule spindles and railways and locomotives and electrical telegraphs? What chance has Vulcan against Roberts & Co., Jupiter against the lightning-rod and Hermes against the Credit Mobilier?[17]

This striking series of images points to one of Marx's central concerns throughout the text, and a foundational tenet of materialism: the dependence of cultural production on the means of economic production. More precisely, it suggests the impossibility of the art and literature from an older mode of production to exist under a more recent one—namely, capitalism. Marx worries, however, that the "difficulty" doesn't lie in the relationship between economic base and politico-cultural superstructure, but in the fact that works of art from an "undeveloped" economy can "still afford us artistic pleasure."[18] The solution he gives—that the "charm of [Greek] art for us . . . is inextricably bound up . . . with the fact that the unripe social conditions under which it rose, and could alone rise, can never return"—feels like wistful nostalgia, substituting "charm" and "pleasure" for the language of struggle.[19] On the other hand, although Marx never returns to this problem in the *Grundrisse*, its strange presence alone should be enough to give pause, as though Marx is waxing less descriptive than speculative, even imaginative: he has given us the brief drama of an obsolete mode of artistic production acting as a potential combatant against capital itself. Even though he implies capital's overwhelming victory, the secondary implication is that it is possible to imagine an art capable of superseding the machinery of capitalism. He notes earlier in the introduction that "the object of art—like every other product—creates a public which is sensitive to art and enjoys beauty," concluding that "production thus not only creates an object for the subject, but also a subject for the object."[20] If we take the violent interaction of art and capital as a subset of class struggle, then the *Grundrisse* seems to suggest a partial reversal of the orthodox Marxist binary in which base determines superstructure. To Marx, artistic production operates in the social arena of the not-quite, its ceaseless drive to conjure a public always caught between dependence and autonomy. The literary problem posed by the *Grundrisse* thus appears as that of producing a subject adequate to the object of revolution, a Hermes who can dismantle the Credit Mobilier.

In fact, Negri's reading in *Marx beyond Marx* detects in the *Grundrisse* a "communist subjectivity" in which "there is no linear continuity, but only a plurality of points of view which are endlessly solicited at each determinant moment of the antagonism" between labor and capital.[21] Such a subjectivity is both internal to the form of the text and external, insofar as it can be seized upon by the masses in moments of crisis. How is this discontinuity expressed internally? First, of course, through the metonymic relation of part to whole, broadly conceived as the chapter divisions and the shorter works that orbit them. Negri describes the structure of the text as a series of "explosive antagonisms" centering around the introduction of two indispensable concepts: the law of surplus value and the theory of exploitation within the reproduction of capital. Taken together, they constitute the "translation of the law of exploitation into the law of crisis and the class struggle for communism."[22] The resulting chain of signifiers contains "a forward movement in the theory" that "permits us to perceive the fundamental moment constituted by the antagonism between the collective worker and the collective capitalist, an antagonism which appears in the form of the crisis." In other words, the text itself takes the "open" form of process, of deliberate generation. *Marx beyond Marx* achieves a singular, if dense, reading of the *Grundrisse*, positing the existence of a revolutionary subjectivity that comes into being in the explicitly political passages, such as the famous "Fragment on Machines," which will occupy the remainder of this argument.

The "Fragment on Machines" is one of the most contested sections of the *Grundrisse*, as well as the most integral: Marx presents the fragment as a series of short, aphoristic arguments about the contradictory role of machinery in the struggle between labor and capital. Unlike conventional tools like a shovel or a drill, which were appropriated by the worker during the process of value-creation, the "automatic system of machinery" "confronts the worker *as capital*."[23] Machines are in this sense the "most complete, most adequate" form of capital because the worker can no longer appropriate it or put it to use as "living labor." In Marx's view, this "metamorphosis" engenders the profoundest rupture between labor and capital:

> The science which compels the inanimate limbs of the machinery, by their construction, to act purposefully, as an automaton, does not exist in the worker's consciousness, but rather acts upon him through the machine as an alien power, as the power of the machine itself. The appropriation of living labor by objectified labor [i.e., the machine itself, the fixed product of previous labor] . . . is posited, in production resting on machinery, as the character of the production process itself, including its material elements and its material motion. . . . Labor appears . . . merely as a conscious organ, scattered among the individual living workers at numerous points of the mechanical system; subsumed under the total process of the machinery itself . . . whose unity exists not in the living workers, but rather in the living (active) machinery, which confronts his individual, insignificant doings as a mighty organism.[24]

What we see here is the complete reversal of Negri's "communist subjectivity": the utter subsumption of labor to capital, the flipping of the terms "living" and "objectified" so that the dead machine resurrects itself as a monstrous "organism" that devours workers' "consciousness" and renders it "insignificant." But notice how the multiple levels of formlessness—the looming colossus of capital, the workers' "scattered" consciousness— reproduce themselves at the microlevel of paragraph, sentence, and clause. The "Fragment on Machines" is riddled with these moments of dialectical parataxis: independent clauses mashed between parentheticals and stacked upon digressive asides comprise its literary structure, as well as structuring the rest of the *Grundrisse*.

Writing of Louis Zukofsky's communist poetics, Ruth Jennison argues that "paratactical strategies permit the emergence of an aesthetic 'unity that knows itself to be inconclusive' and generate precisely the kind of self-knowledge incommensurate with fascist politics."[25] Moreover, she cites Marx's remarks on the "unity of the diverse" in the 1857 Introduction to speculate that Zukofsky's poem might even be in direct dialogue with the *Grundrisse*. Without anachronistically applying "antifascist" politics to Marx himself, we can nevertheless recognize that the literary style of the *Grundrisse* resonates with Jennison's analysis of communist parataxis. The paratactical formlessness and diverse unities here suggest that the apparently total subsumption of labor to capital may in fact drive capital itself toward crisis and dissolution.

Not-labor Time and the Collective Literary Program

This chapter has maintained that, as a document of economic crisis, the *Grundrisse* might fit into the "prehistory" of modernism, prefiguring the actually existing antagonist to capitalism that emerged with the Bolshevik revolution: within the *Grundrisse* there exists a "communist subjectivity" capable of producing an art form to challenge or supersede capital. We can further think through the later sections of the "Fragment on Machines" by invoking Alain Badiou's concept of "subtraction." Badiou writes within and against a Heideggerian philosophical tradition that seeks to reappraise the ontological and epistemological status of the poem; one of the central questions he grapples with involves recovering and elaborating "what remains in spite of the linguistic ruin of almost everything."[26] In *The Age of the Poets*, his 2014 collection of literary criticism, Badiou explains that "subtraction" refers to the compositional process that "assembles the poem with the direct aim of the withdrawal of the object." This process in turn makes the poem into a "negative machine [that] ruins discursivity" while revealing the possibility of a new coherence.[27] Although there are aspects of Badiou's philosophy that can obstruct materialist analysis—among them, his tendency to dehistoricize European and American modernism by referring to "the Poem" as a transhistorical abstraction—the idea of the "negative machine" is a useful method for working through the digressive fragments that span the *Grundrisse*.

In Badiou's formulation, the poem can only exist at the moment "objective reality ... starts to disappear."[28] This act of subtraction recalls Marx's definition of communism in *The German Ideology* (1845): "not a state of affairs which is to be established, an ideal to which reality [will] have to adjust itself ... [but] the real movement which abolishes the present state of things."[29] The process of poetic subtraction parallels the act of abolishing "the present state of things": objective reality has to be withdrawn, as opposed to reformed in the way of the Proudhonian socialists, in order to create the conditions for real communism. Both on the level of form and content, the *Grundrisse* continually dramatizes this subtractive process, repeating, rearranging, negating, and affirming itself in order to, as Nicolaus remarks, prepare us for the "historic task" of revolution. Exploding the logical-mathematical act of "putting arguments in a chain," the communist poem "ruins discursivity" and through this very act of ruination produces its most important and dangerous quality: "a form of thinking without knowledge ... a properly incalculable thought."[30]

Marx alludes to that incalculable thought in the last paragraph of the *Grundrisse* proper, the "Chapter on Capital," which breaks off in the middle of a sentence about the recent rediscovery of "communal property":

> A whole series of economic systems lies in turn between the modern world, where exchange value dominates production to its whole depth and extent, and the social formations whose foundation is already formed by the dissolution of communal property, without[31]

The word "without" hangs anxiously in the blank space of the page as pure negation. It's tempting to read this moment as a kind of enjambment, the end of a "poem including history" in which the formless abyss around the final word abounds with signification and possibility. Earlier, in the "Fragment on Machines," we saw that abyss takes the form of fixed capital's zombie-like re-appropriation of "living labor." The "enjambed" fragment that ends Marx's seventh notebook, however, prompts us to return to the "Fragment" and look for what remains in the ruins of the workers' domination by machines. What we find there is an imaginative leap to a communist future in which the automatic system of machinery, which first dispersed the workers' subjectivity and rendered it useless, becomes the "material conditions to blow this foundation sky-high."[32] This, of course, is a contradiction, and perhaps the highest level of contradiction in all of Marx's work. Because machines usurp labor from the laborer, the production process itself begins to shed its dependence on labor time. Simultaneously, however, capital continues "to use labor time as the measuring rod for the giant social forces" of capitalism.[33] The synthetic collision of these contradictory impulses, Marx argues, is atomic, powerful enough to "blow the foundation" of capital's primary measure of wealth; in its place arises a total subtraction of labor time: "disposable time" or "not-labor."[34]

The general dispersion of "not-labor" time, facilitated by the capitalist mode of production's self-implosion, produces an ontologically new form of subjectivity:

> Free time—which is both idle time and time for higher activity—has naturally transformed its possessor into a different subject, and he then enters into the direct production process as this different subject. This process is then both discipline, as regards the human being in the process of becoming; and, at the same time, practice [*Ausübung*], experimental science, materially creative and objectifying science, as regards the human being who has become, in whose head exists the accumulated knowledge of society.[35]

The idea of a universal not-labor, "a discipline" and a "practice" of becoming human, is the *Grundrisse*'s properly incalculable thought adequate to a collective mode of production. Here, Negri and Badiou collide: the production of disposable time is Marx's imagined process of subtraction, that "affirmative part of negation"[36] that "animates development, crisis, transition, and communism."[37] We also hear echoes of the introduction's "literary problem" in this passage's reference to "experimental" and "materially creative" activity. What kind of literature, which acts of poetry, are adequate to the direct, communal production process? The implication here points us not to individual works, but instead to the "accumulated knowledge of society" or general intellect that articulates the "universal needs which have emerged on the collective but miserable basis of the organization of waged work, but which in a revolutionary way signify the abolition of work, its definitive death."[38] As a "negative machine" in Badiou's sense, the *Grundrisse* then moves dialectically from a total negation or "subtraction" of capital to an affirmation of the subject that surfaces from the text's ruined discursivity.

That subject materializes as a collective literary program, an act of imagination in which individuals exist "in mutual relationships, which they equally reproduce and produce anew."[39] Because not-labor is a "constant process" of "vanishing moments," Marx can only gesture toward the eternally ephemeral character of communist subject-formation.[40] Nevertheless, the *Grundrisse* becomes revolutionary literature through its "materially creative" attempts to imagine this final abolition of wage labor and the incalculable potential of the subject liberated from labor time.

Notes

1. Marx, *Grundrisse: Foundations of the Critique of Political Economy*, trans. Martin Nicolaus (New York: Vintage, 1973), 7.
2. Roberts, *Marx's Inferno*, 1.
3. Mark Steven, "Reading Capital, Writing History: Pound's Marx," *Modernism/Modernity* 24.4 (November 2017): 771–90.
4. Marx, *Grundrisse*, 24.
5. Marx, *Grundrisse*, 25.
6. Marx, *Grundrisse*, 25.
7. Roman Rosdolsky, David Bathrick, and Anson Rabinbach, "Comments on the Method of Marx's Capital and Its Importance for Contemporary Marxist Scholarship," *New German Critique* 3 (1974): 64.
8. Sutherland, "Marx in Jargon," 5.
9. Sutherland, "Marx in Jargon," 3.
10. Althusser, *For Marx*, trans. Ben Brewster (London: Verso, 2006), 192.
11. David McLellan, *Marx's Grundrisse*, 2nd ed. (London: Palgrave, 1980), 12.
12. McLellan, *Marx's Grundrisse*, 15.
13. Antonio Negri, *Marx beyond Marx* (New York: Pluto Press, 1992), 8.
14. Marx, "The Economic Crisis in Europe by Karl Marx 1856" (1856). https://www.marxists.org/archive/marx/works/1856/10/09.htm, accessed August 20, 2019.
15. Jameson, *A Singular Modernity*, 12.
16. Adorno and Paul Kottman, *Notes to Literature*, ed. Rolf Tiedemann, trans. Shierry Weber Nicholson (New York: Columbia University Press, 1991), 45.
17. Marx, *Grundrisse*, 110.
18. Marx, *Grundrisse*, 111.
19. Marx, *Grundrisse*, 111.
20. Marx, *Grundrisse*, 92.
21. Negri, *Marx beyond Marx*, 13.
22. Negri, *Marx beyond Marx*, 4.
23. Marx, *Grundrisse*, 694.
24. Marx, *Grundrisse*, 693.
25. Jennison, *The Zukofsky Era*, 31.
26. Badiou, *The Age of the Poets: And Other Writings on Twentieth-Century Poetry and Prose*, trans. Emily Apter and Bruno Bosteels (London: Verso, 2014), 28.
27. Badiou, *The Age of the Poets*, 29.

28 Badiou, *The Age of the Poets*, 28.
29 Marx and Engels, "The German Ideology," 162.
30 Badiou, *The Age of the Poets*, 33.
31 Marx, *Grundrisse*, 882.
32 Marx, *Grundrisse*, 706.
33 Marx, *Grundrisse*, 708.
34 Marx, *Grundrisse*, 708.
35 Marx, *Grundrisse*, 712.
36 Badiou, *The Age of the Poets*, 84.
37 Negri, *Marx beyond Marx*, 154.
38 Negri, *Marx beyond Marx*, 160.
39 Marx, *Grundrisse*, 712.
40 Marx, *Grundrisse*, 712.

6

The Voices of *Capital*

Poetics of Critique beyond Sentiment and Cynicism

Daniel Hartley

Marx concludes the preface to the first edition of *Capital* (1867) by declaring that "every opinion of his work based on scientific criticism" is welcome, but when it comes to "prejudices of so-called public opinion," his maxim is that of Dante's *Purgatorio*: *Segui il tuo corso, e lascia dir le genti*—"Go on your way, and let the people talk."[1] The line conjures an image of the bold, solitary thinker forging an independent path for science by turning his back on the noisy crowd and the bustle of vulgar opinion. Yet the irony is that the scientific exposition of *Capital* consists precisely in "letting the people talk." *Capital* is, in many ways, nothing but a strategically formed cacophony of voices: from speaking commodities to political economists, exhausted child laborers to heartless manufacturers, from factory reports to Shakespeare and Goethe: *Capital*, as in Mikhail Bakhtin's theory of the novel, is a truly polyphonic work.

The present chapter offers a closer consideration of this multiplicity of voices and suggests certain theoretical and political ramifications of Marx's formal choices. In doing so, it draws on two heterodox ways of reading *Capital*. The first sees it as a discursive intervention in and response to a textually mediated class struggle. This approach was elaborated by Raya Dunayevskaya in *Marxism and Freedom* (1958), and taken up separately by Jacques Rancière, following his break with Louis Althusser, in "Mode d'emploi pour une réédition de *Lire le Capital*" (1973), only to be taken up by Althusser himself in the late 1970s. Where Dunayevskaya stresses those aspects of Marx's *Capital* that were written as a response to increased class militancy in the 1860s, Althusser draws attention to the ways in which the "major" order of exposition of *Capital* is constantly intersected and interrupted by "minor" (dis)orders that have their roots in class struggle (as in the long chapter on the working day or those on primitive accumulation).[2] Rancière, meanwhile, emphasizes the *textual* and *discursive* mediations of such struggles: "reports by police commissioners or public attorneys, inquiries by doctors and economists, sermons, electoral speeches, etc.," as well as "voices in the workshop, rumours in the streets, market-places and labor-exchanges, to the leading ideas of working-class insurrection, by way of the educated forms of working-class literature or the popular forms of street songs."[3] Rancière points to the multiplicity of textual and discursive mediations of class struggle and their effect on Marx's own discourse. In different ways, Dunayevskaya, Althusser, and Rancière each delineate a fourth dimension of Marx's text that is often overlooked: its structural openness to history and its attempt directly to incorporate the voices of contemporary class struggle.

The second heterodox approach centers on what Anna Kornbluh has called the "conceptual agency of literary form," the idea that the form and style in which Marx writes are *constitutive* elements of his theory and cannot simply be set aside as the mere "dress of thought."[4] There is a small but significant tradition of reading *Capital* with an attentiveness to form, from Ludovico Silva's *El Estilo de Marx* (1971) to Robert Paul Wolff's *Moneybags Must Be So Lucky* (1988), by way of S. S. Prawer's monumental *Karl Marx and World Literature* (1976). Most recently, this tradition has been extended by Kornbluh, Fredric Jameson, and Keston Sutherland. Where Jameson reads *Capital* as a series of dialectically unfolding solutions to the problem of representing the unrepresentable (capital), Kornbluh reads it as a Victorian novel that "means what it means not simply through denotative reference, but through the connotative, associative, artful ways the language *works*"—not least through personification and metalepsis.[5] Sutherland, likewise, has argued that *Capital* should not be seen as a work of "pure theory" but rather as a "complicated *satire of social existence under capital* . . . in which risks and failures of style are arguments in themselves, irreducible to theoretical propositions."[6] Taken together, these two approaches alert us to Marx's fundamentally heteroglossic poetics, a mode of presentation in which the systematic unfolding of the logic of capital is always overdetermined by history—a history *charged* by class struggle but suffered, groaned, screamed, and scribed by those unable to escape its nightmare.

Such a perspective has repercussions for how we understand critique. For it may be that *Capital*'s subtitle—"A Critique of Political Economy"—not only signals a post-Kantian *theoretical* interrogation of the historical conditions of possibility of a given discourse but, in Marx's hands, becomes linked to a *poetics*. In other words, the act of critique becomes inextricable from the formal operations in and through which it is elaborated. At the same time, from his early writings onward, Marx consistently connected critique to specific feelings, affects, and dispositions. Having castigated the German social order as a shameful anachronism—"If I negate the situation in Germany in 1843, then according to the French calendar I have barely reached 1789, much less the vital centre of our present age"—Marx proceeds to call for "*a ruthless criticism of all that exists*" [*die rücksichtslose Kritik alles Bestehenden*], one whose "essential pathos" [*wesentliches Pathos*] is "indignation."[7] Yet where the early writings call on critique to induce the very "consistency, acuteness, courage and ruthlessness" that the German bourgeoisie lacks, *Capital* is more concerned with critique's ambiguous relation to the twin affects of sentiment and cynicism, which haunt it from within.[8] Where the former tends toward an immediate humanism that is inadequate to grasping and opposing the mediated totality of capitalism as a system, the latter risks an over-identification with the structural indifference of capital itself. Sentiment was integral to the moral reformism of the Blue Books, while cynicism was the disposition of mature political economy.[9] To avoid both pitfalls, Marx develops a proto-modernist poetics of critique that harnesses the strengths of each position while avoiding their ideological limitations. Ultimately, Marx's critique of political economy is a simultaneously theoretical, formal, and affective operation that is attuned to, and draws its authority from, the voices of contemporary class struggle.

The Commodity Form: Between Sentiment and Cynicism

In the preface to the first edition of *Capital*, Marx makes a concerted effort to distinguish his critique from moralistic recriminations against individual capitalists or landowners, which "make the individual responsible for relations whose creature he remains, however much he may subjectively raise himself above them."[10] Instead, Marx will deal with individuals in *Capital* "only in so far as they are the personifications of economic categories, the bearers [*Träger*] of particular class-relations and interests."[11] In chapter two, he refers to such agents as "the characters who appear on the economic stage [*die Charaktermasken der Personen*]."[12] Capital's impersonal domination thus operates through a system of categorial personifications or "masks" [*Charaktermasken*], which are *indifferent* to the empirical or phenomenological individuality of the agents who "bear" them. Marx then goes on to describe the difference between such personified individuals and the commodities they own: the commodity, he writes, using the figure of prosopopoeia, is a "born leveller and cynic," indifferent to the material specificity of other commodities which merely constitute the form of appearance of its own value. The commodity owner himself, meanwhile, "makes up—with his own five senses—for the commodity's lack of a sense of the concrete body of the other commodity."[13] Commodity owners are thus portrayed as *personifications of economic relations* and *sensual supplements* of a structural lack within the commodity form itself. Capitalism, premised on commodity production, is shown to be *structurally* cynical, yet this cynicism requires constant moral, sentimental, or sensuous supplementation.[14]

This poses severe problems of form and feeling for any project of critique. For the young Marx, as already noted, critique is partly motivated by the "essential pathos" of "indignation"—that is, it is fuelled by specific *feelings*. Yet if the systemic function of "feeling" in general under capital is to supplement a lack in the commodity, then how is it possible for any affect—whether critical or not—ultimately to avoid the status of a reformist moralism, an internalization of capital's fundamental drives, or a momentary lyrical outburst? On the flipside, however, how could critique not be driven by pathos? Indeed, given that labor power is defined as "the aggregate of those mental and physical capabilities existing in the physical form, the *living personality*, of a human being,"[15] the subjective dispositions that make up the "living personality" will clearly be of vital importance to the class struggle. It would seem, then, that what Marx requires will be, first, a way of *formally reproducing* the indifferent impersonality of capital while rejecting its structural cynicism and, second, a way of drawing on the constitutive power of pathos while foregrounding its reformist limitations.

One obvious way he does this is by staging short fictions which directly dramatize the problems of sentiment and cynicism. In chapter seven, for example, he imagines a scenario in which the value of a product is exactly equal to the capital advanced, such that the capitalist has received no surplus value. Switching from expository prose to satirical sketch, Marx stages a meticulously choreographed scene in which the capitalist adopts a range of moral justifications for his claim to surplus value while Marx, in the ironic voice of an interlocutor, proposes a series of moral counterclaims for why the capitalist should be content with his lot. The capitalist proclaims: "Consider my abstinence. I might have squandered the 15 shillings, but instead I consumed it productively and made yarn with it." To which Marx responds: "Very true; and as a reward he is now in possession of good yarn instead of a bad conscience." The capitalist changes tack. Has he not "rendered society an incalculable service by providing [his] instruments of production"? Marx responds: "But has the worker not performed an equal service in return, by changing his cotton and spindle into yarn?" At this point, the capitalist shifts tactics again: he "suddenly takes on the unassuming demeanour of one of his own workers, and exclaims: 'Have I myself not worked? Have I not performed the labor of superintendence . . . does not this labor, too, produce value?'" But then—just as suddenly—"with a hearty laugh, [the capitalist] recovers his composure [*seine alte Physiognomie wieder angenommen*]. The whole litany he has just recited was simply meant to pull the wool over our eyes. He himself does not care twopence for it. . . . He himself is a practical man."[16]

The scene thus stages, in the mode of satire, the subjective effects of the structural cynicism of capital. The capitalist adopts at least three distinct ideological justifications for his right to surplus value: abstinence, service, and the productivity of his own labor. At the same time, Marx ironically mobilizes, in a sort of staged reformism, precisely the same moral discourses to argue *against* the capitalist's right to surplus value. The "pragmatism" to which the capitalist ultimately reverts at the end of the scene—with the "hearty laugh" of the cynic—can then be read as the subjective mediation of the structural "praxis" of capital: namely, the spontaneous ideology generated by the auto-telic activity of capital as "automatic subject."[17] Indeed, the constant changes of the capitalist's physiognomy suggest just how volatile the individual subject position of the capitalist really is; it has to constantly hop and switch between an ideological supplement in which it does not really believe and a pragmatism which it does believe in, but which is, in fact, the subjective mediation of capital's self-valorization. At the same time, the scene exposes the structural inadequacy of moral or sentimental critiques of capital: the "unassuming demeanor" [*anspruchslose Haltung*—literally, the attitude that *makes no claims*] of the worker imitated by the capitalist implies his subjection, one which the worker sublimates by priding himself on the productivity of his own labor (and here one glimpses the structural origin of those spontaneous ideologies which glorify the inherent dignity of labor). There is nonetheless something quite moving about the figure of the "unassuming" worker whom the capitalist grotesquely imitates, a certain fragility that induces a sympathetic identification very much at odds with the otherwise sharp, satirical objectification of the logic of capital in this scene. Marx manages to take the measure of capital's indifference, to foreground the limitations of moral discourse, yet not entirely to surrender the motivating critical power of pathos.

The most significant dramatization, however, comes in the crucial scene at the opening of the chapter on the working day, in which "suddenly, there arises the voice of the worker."[18] The worker's voice, Marx informs us, "had previously been stifled [*verstummen*] in the sound and fury [*Sturm und Drang*] of the production process."[19] The ironic echo here of the German, proto-Romantic literary movement *Sturm und Drang* is unmistakable. Drawing on sentimental and Pietist traditions, Goethe and his peers had fostered a mode of writing that gave voice to a desire for authentic self-realization and engaged in "moral criticism of individuals who hold power."[20] Marx here juxtaposes this idealist proto-Romanticism with its dialectical opposite: the sound and fury of the factory floor. Like a Benjaminian dialectical image, the infernal tempest of the factory is suddenly revealed as the hidden truth of the inadequacy of individual sentiment: the dull throbbing of the machine becomes the hitherto unsounded undertone of the solitary poet's doleful voice. What follows is Marx's extraordinary fictional dramatization of a real historical manifesto written by London building workers who were on strike in 1859. The worker directly addresses the capitalist:

> I therefore demand a working day of normal length, and I demand it without any appeal to your heart, for in money matters sentiment is out of place [*hört die Gemüthlichkeit auf*]. You may be a model citizen, perhaps a member of the R.S.P.C.A., and you may be in the odour of sanctity as well; but the thing you represent when you come face to face with me has no heart in its breast [*schlägt kein Herz in seiner Brust*]. What seems to throb there is my own heartbeat.[21]

The worker has grasped the structural indifference of capital: its intrinsic *heartlessness*. He distinguishes between the capitalist as individual (i.e., as the mediated totality of his unique relation to the state [citizen], civil society [R.S.P.C.A], and the church [sanctity]), and the capitalist as "representative," or personification, of capital. He does not so much reject affairs of the heart as rearticulate them; he identifies a separation effected by capital between sentiment and money, but at the same time recognizes his own imbrication with capital as that which lives, "vampire-like," from his own heartbeat.[22] His demand for a "normal" working day is an attempt to win back at least a portion of his heart from the grip of capital's psychotic love.[23]

This defiant passage sets the tone for a broader consideration of Marx's poetics. For Marx does not, of course, remain within the realm of sympathetic subtleties: one cannot do justice to the style of *Capital* if one fails to register its ferocity. If there are two overriding obsessions in this book, they are the reduction of workers to the status of "slaves" and the terrifying destruction of their bodies. Page after page of *Capital* documents the bodily and existential torture to which the worker is subjected under the despotism of capital. Yet it is important to recall, as Jameson reminds us,[24] that most accounts of such torture—and the moral judgments pronounced upon them—occur in quotations from factory reports. There are vast passages of *Capital* that show Marx to be, not only one of the great writers of the nineteenth century, but also one of the finest *collators*: fifty years before Walter Benjamin would radicalize the practice of citation into a post-Hegelian historiography, Marx developed a citational, "documentary poetics" prefiguring such modernist masterworks as Ezra Pound's *Cantos*, T. S. Eliot's *The Waste Land*, and Louis Zukofsky's *"A."*[25] In this way, Marx prefigured the poetry of the future. As in modernist collage and montage techniques, Marx cuts, arranges, and pastes strategically chosen excerpts from factory reports and works of political economy—an artistically organized polyphony of workers, reformists, and capitalists whose words he arranges into a devastating indictment of capital without ever (or, at least, very rarely) overtly condemning it.[26] Just as the late Althusser in "Marx in his Limits," states that "critique" for the mature Marx can implicitly be understood as the "real criticizing itself," so the very *form* of *Capital* is designed to stage the self-critique of the real through a vast cast of opposing voices.[27] In many cases, the factory reports from which Marx quotes were initially the result of the struggle between the landed aristocracy and the industrial bourgeoisie, the former feigning sympathy for the woes of the factory worker. As Marx writes, "the noisy and passionate dispute between the two factions of the ruling class as to which of them exploited the workers more shamelessly was the midwife of truth on both sides of the question."[28] Marx thus poetically configures the textual traces of this self-critique of the real.

The very system of quotation provides him with a formal solution to the contradiction of cynicism and sentiment: the gap between quoting and quoted instances generates a critical distance that mimetically reproduces capital's apparent indifference to the affairs of the heart. At the same time, however, by including the voices of the workers themselves—albeit in a mediated form—the *Darstellungsweise* [mode of presentation] remains immanent to the pathos fueling critique. Who, for example, would not be moved by the testimony of G. Apsden, a worker in a wallpaper factory who speaks of the suffering of his son in the chapter on the working day.

> That boy of mine . . . when he was 7 years old I used to carry him on my back through the snow, and he used to have 16 hours a day . . . I have often knelt down to feed him as he stood by the machine, for he could not leave it or stop it.[29]

After reading this passage, only the most heartless would disagree that Marx was entirely justified when he wrote that capital spins silk from the blood of children.[30]

On History, the *Darstellungsweise*, and Double-voiced Discourse

This practice of collation is not, however, an aesthetic free-for-all. It is intrinsically limited by the logical "mode of exposition" (*Darstellungsweise*) of *Capital*. Without wishing to enter here into the arcane debates concerning the possible Hegelian provenance of Marx's *Darstellungsweise*,[31] suffice it to say that the *unity* of the order of exposition consists in a conceptual mimesis of the systemic totality of capitalism. Summarizing Gérard Duménil's work on Marx's materialist "thought process," Althusser (in 1978) describes it thus:

> Marx's thought, far from proceeding by the *self-production* of concepts, proceeds rather by *positing* a concept that initiates the exploration (analysis) of the theoretical space opened up and closed off by this positing, after which it posits a new concept, broadening the theoretical field, and so on, until theoretical fields of great structural complexity have been constituted.[32]

It is this process that generates what Althusser refers to as the "major" order of exposition—"from value to capital and capitalist production all the way to the 'concrete' categories of volume 3."[33] Similarly, Jameson has identified "a series of interlinked problems or paradoxes, which, ostensibly solved, give rise to new and unexpected ones, of greater scope":

> The process must then be imagined as a specific proto-narrative form, in which the transformation or recoding of a conceptual dilemma in a new and potentially more manageable way also results in the expansion of the object of study itself: the successive resolutions of the linked riddles or dilemmas lay in place the architecture of a whole construct or system, which is that of capital as such.[34]

Dramatization and collation are thus tendentially subordinated to the rhythm of capital's monstrous self-development; and yet, it is only in and through the textual interpolations—the cacophony of nineteenth-century voices—that this terrifying *Bildung* can unfurl.[35]

At this point, we have to take into account that other great presence in *Capital*: history itself. For it has not gone unnoticed that the logical order of exposition is in fact less unified than at first meets the eye, unfolding like a seeming law of necessity yet constantly intersected and interrupted by different, antagonistic orders of exposition that are irreducible to it:[36] from the momentous class struggle that is narrated in the astonishing long chapter on the working day, to the history of large-scale manufacture, building up finally to the epic panorama of primitive accumulation. How one interprets this overdetermination of the "major" order of exposition by "minor" logics has serious political and theoretical consequences, not least for how we understand critique. The Althusser of *Reading Capital* (1965), for instance, identified the "politicity" of theory (and, by extension, critique) with the "ability to link an ideological result to the contingency of the processes that give rise to it,"[37] and it was this theoretical practice that constituted the precondition of a *political* practice of collective self-extrication from the dominant ideology. In the 1970s, however, Althusser came to locate the preconditions of critique, not in theoretical systematicity itself, but precisely in those "other 'orders of exposition'" that intersect and interrupt the logic of capital portrayed by Marx's *Darstellungsweise*.[38] On this view, class struggle produces realities external to the major order of exposition (namely, the automatic logic of capital), generating "minor" orders that interrupt it. By attuning himself to existing proletarian struggles and the "practical concepts" they produced in the course of their activity, Marx was able to incorporate insights and logics that defied the major order of exposition. Critique is thus conceived by the late Althusser as the theoretical incorporation of thoughts arising from proletarian activity itself—beyond, or against, the purview of the dominant ideology.

Such insights can be usefully reconceived from the perspective of poetics. For just as Althusser's multiple orders of exposition imply an orientation of Marx's discourse to that which lies beyond the logic of capital, what Bakhtin refers to as "double-voiced discourse" denotes "discourse with an orientation toward someone else's discourse."[39] Bakhtin distinguishes between three kinds of double-voiced discourse, all of which are employed in *Capital* to a greater or lesser degree. The first type, which Bakhtin calls "unidirectional," refers to a mode of stylization that works *with* the grain of a style that is being imitated (and which may allow us to reconceive Marx's use of the language of bourgeois political economy as just such an "imitation" that remains only partly internal to that which it imitates), while the second—"vari-directional"—works against it, as in parody. Marx makes constant use of this second kind, especially when ironically deploying the moral discourse of the bourgeoisie to expose its hypocrisy, such as when he writes of the "great compassion" of the manufacturers who generously allow their child employees a good four hours' sleep a night.[40] The third type of double-voiced discourse, however, refers to the influence exerted on a text from another discourse outside it: there is not always a linguistic trace of its presence within the text, but—like a dark sun—its gravitational effects can be felt in every line.

It is perhaps in this (dark) light that we should read the otherwise seemingly outlandish assertion by the late Althusser that Marx himself was not in fact the "author" of *Capital*; the true author, for Althusser, was working-class struggle itself. Marx, he suggests, wrote for, through—and under the insistence of—this "author," according to a model that suggests nothing less than a revolutionary version of the divine muse.[41] Unexpectedly, Dunayevskaya's more historically grounded assertions seem to corroborate Althusser's intuition. In *Marxism and Freedom*, Dunayevskaya makes much of the fact that Marx wrote *Capital* during a period of heightened international militancy, provoked not least by the American Civil War and its effect on the British working class, but also inspired by the Polish insurrection of 1863, which was the initial impetus for the foundation of the First International in 1864. While Dunayevskaya has a tendency to a certain vulgar reductionism—proposing a too immediate connection between popular revolt and theoretical innovation—I find convincing her suggestion that the American Civil War and its international shock-waves had a major effect on the structure of *Capital*, not least in the sudden drafting and inclusion of the chapter on the "Working Day" as late as 1866. As Kevin B. Anderson has written, "In *Capital*, as opposed to the earlier drafts of his critique of political economy, Marx made the voices and the struggles of working people present in a new way."[42] It is as if the "structure of openness" of Marxist critique,[43] its attempt to remain immanent and responsive to the contemporary actuality of working-class struggle, generates an externally oriented attentiveness that is structurally homologous to the double-voiced discourse that

Bakhtin associates—in a very different valence—with such novels as Dostoevsky's *Notes from Underground* (1864). Yet where Bakhtin equates the latter with internal polemic (a constant overdetermination of a given utterance by some inimical voice "outside" the text), Marx attempts to *transcribe* external proletarian vocality so as to undermine the strictly ideological, monologic self-presentation of bourgeois political economy.

What this subterranean current (Dunayevskaya, Althusser, Rancière) of *Capital* reception overlooks, however, is the opposite dialectical pole of proletarian struggle: the constant references to the condition of "slavery" and the destruction of the worker's body. I am referring here less to Marx's historiographic sensitivity to the multiple empirical histories of slavery and their variable imbrications with capitalism,[44] and more to those constant, largely rhetorical references to slavery—either by Marx or those he quotes—that are used as shorthand for the lived experience of the impersonal domination of capital.[45] Unlike the minor orders of exposition, which transpose collective working-class antagonism, these references might be read precisely as a "hidden polemic" (the negative pole of Bakhtin's third type of double-voiced discourse) against the dominant ideology of so-called free labor. That is, they posit an implicit, generic proponent of wage labor as civilized and "free" to which they respond by constantly comparing wage labor to that which it claims to have superseded: slavery and barbarism. This looser, rhetorical use of "slavery," aimed at an external ideological opponent, should alert us to the fact that the line between slavery and free labor is not only historically variable but also the continued object of political dispute.[46]

Yet, even beyond "slavery" in this broader rhetorical sense, there is at work in *Capital* something approaching a metaphysical horror of absolute depersonalization. Where the previous dynamic entailed the transliteration of the voices of workers' struggles into the fabric of critique (as the latter's authorizing ground), its negative antipode incorporates the fractured inoperativity of defeat. Jameson has observed that despite its conceptual centrality in *Capital*, work is—astonishingly—very rarely represented in its positive form at all. *Capital* consists primarily of a narrative that moves from "the impossibility of work at its extremes . . . the body on the brink of exhaustion" in the chapter on the working day, toward the black hole of unemployment.[47] This is what Jameson calls, in his own heightened rhetoric, the "ultimate reality of the unrepresentable, a search which more and more minute moves from statistics and regions to towns, streets, houses, rooms, and finally that last glimpse of the nothingness in the back room, blinding, unbearable, from which we must avert our eyes."[48] He is referring to that long quotation in the chapter on the general law of capital accumulation which describes the desolate condition of unemployed shipbuilders and their families:

> Our next visit was to an iron laborer's wife, whose husband had worked in the yards. We found her ill from want of food, lying on a mattress in her clothes, and just covered with a strip of carpet, for all the bedding had been pawned. Two wretched children were tending her, themselves looking as much in need of nursing as their mother. Nineteen weeks of enforced idleness had brought them to

this pass, and while the mother told the history of that bitter past, she moaned as if all her faith in a future that should atone for it were dead.[49]

This absolute reduction to the present—the dialectical opposite of the "fire of labor" to which Jameson refers as the "supreme present of time"[50]—this total incapacitation of the body, its reduction to "bare life" constitute Marx's vision of absolute social horror. It is under the "insistence" of *this* vision fully as much as the authority of collective struggle that Marx wrote *Capital*.

Conclusion

At this point, however, we seem to have moved beyond the original problem of form and feeling, cynicism and sentiment, from which we set out. The question of the order of exposition as well as the situational logic of double-voiced discourse has expanded the scope of the problem and the horizon of possible solutions. It has recast the relatively static, functionalist relation of supplementarity between cynicism and sentiment as part of a developing response immanent to the rhythms and forces of specific conjunctures. We have seen that Marx's own response in the 1860s entailed a formal experimentation with polyphony enabled partly by the textual traces of the struggle between ruling class fractions and inspired partly by the renewed audibility of workers' voices in the period of the American Civil War. Yet the flipside of this audibility is the relative silence of the suffering, disposable body. It is one of the great theoretical achievements of *Capital* to have demonstrated the structural necessity of unemployment: the dialectical unity of wealth and misery, monstrous productivity, and—at its limit—absolute depersonalization. For in any conjuncture, the path beyond cynicism and sentiment requires the invention of representational and political forms capable of attuning themselves to the voices of emergent revolt and to proactively discovering and representing the emergence of new political subjects, not least those whose social *inclusion* assumes the form of structural *exclusion* (one thinks today, for example, of refugees or the "surplus populations" of the "planet of slums"). Marx may well have invented the modernist poetry of the future, but the future lasts forever: its poetry must be constantly reinvented.

Notes

1   Marx, *Capital* vol. 1, 93. This is a subtle adaptation of Dante's original: "Vien retro a me, e lascia dir le genti"—"Follow me, and let the people talk." The present chapter is a lightly modified version of an article that will appear simultaneously in German translation as "Die Stimmen des *Kapitals*: Poetik der Kritik jenseits von Empfindung und Zynismus," in *Poetik und Ästhetik des* Kapitals. *Marx-Lektüren*, eds. Michael Bies and Elisabetta Mengaldo, trans. Lukas Wolff (Göttingen: Wallstein, forthcoming).

2   See, for example, Althusser, "Preface to *Le concept de loi économique dans 'Le Capital,'* by Geérard Dumeénil," trans. G. M. Goshgarian, *Rethinking Marxism*, 30.1 (2018): 4–24.
3   Jacques Rancière, "How to Use *Lire le Capital*," *Economy and Society* 5.3 (1976): 378.
4   Annah Kornbluh, *Realizing Capital: Financial and Psychic Economies in Victorian Form* (New York: Fordham University Press, 2014), 120.
5   Jameson, *Representing Capital: A Reading of Volume One* (London: Verso, 2011); Kornbluh, *Realizing Capital*, 120.
6   Sutherland, "Marx in Jargon," 1, 5.
7   Marx, *Early Writings*, 245, 207, 246. Italics in original. Translations modified.
8   Marx, *Early Writings*, 254.
9   Marx views the increasing cynicism of political economy as a gradual, historical process: "political economy [became] increasingly *cynical* from Smith through Say to Ricardo, Mill, etc., inasmuch as the consequences of *industry* appeared more developed and more contradictory to the latter." Marx, *Early Writings*, 343.
10 Marx, *Capital* vol. 1, 92.
11 Marx, *Capital* vol. 1, 92.
12 Marx, *Capital* vol. 1, 179.
13 Marx, *Capital* vol. 1, 179—translation modified.
14 Marx thus locates in the commodity form that characteristic combination of cynicism and "strange piety" which Deleuze and Guattari claim constitutes "humanism" as such. Gilles Deleuze and Félix Guattari, *Anti-Oedipus: Capitalism and Schizophrenia*, trans. Robert Hurley, Mark Seem, and Helen R. Lane (London: Penguin, 1977), 225.
15 Marx, *Capital* vol. 1, 270.
16 Marx, *Capital* vol. 1, 298–300.
17 Marx, *Capital* vol. 1, 253.
18 Marx, *Capital* vol. 1, 342.
19 Marx, *Capital* vol. 1, 342.
20 David Hill, "Introduction," in *Literature of the Sturm und Drang*, ed. David Hill (Suffolk: Camden House, 2003), 20.
21 Marx, *Capital* vol. 1, 343.
22 Marx, *Capital* vol. 1, 342.
23 Elsewhere, Marx quotes Goethe's *Faust* when referring to the capitalist valorization process as "an animated monster which begins to 'work,' 'as if its body were by love possessed.'" Marx, *Capital* vol. 1, 302.
24 Jameson, *Representing Capital*, 114.
25 On the notion of "documentary poetics," see Steven, "Reading Capital, Writing History," 771–90.
26 The exceptions are those passages in which Marx succumbs to the very bourgeois moralism he elsewhere castigates, as when he laments the destructive effects of capitalist labor regimes and poor housing on women's morality and the fate of family life. Here, Marx fails to follow his own practice to its ultimate conclusion.
27 Althusser, *Philosophy of the Encounter: Late Writings, 1978-87*, trans. G. M. Goshgarian (London: Verso, 2006), 17.
28 Marx, *Capital* vol. 1, 830–1.
29 Marx, *Capital* vol. 1, 356–7.
30 Marx, *Capital* vol. 1, 406.

31 See *Marx's Capital and Hegel's Logic*, eds. Fred Moseley and Tony Smith (Leiden: Brill, 2014).
32 Althusser, "Preface to *Le concept de loi économique dans 'Le Capital,'*" 14–15.
33 Althusser, "Preface to *Le concept de loi économique dans 'Le Capital,'*" 20.
34 Jameson, *Representing Capital*, 3.
35 On *Capital* as a *Bildungsroman*, see Kornbluh, *Realizing Capital*, 120–9.
36 See, for example, Jason Read, *The Micro-Politics of Capital: Marx and the Prehistory of the Present* (New York: State University of New York Press, 2003); Althusser, "Preface to *Le concept de loi économique dans 'Le Capital,'*"; Fabio Buschi, "Splitting Science: The Althusserian Interpretation of *Capital*'s Multiple Orders of Exposition," *Rethinking Marxism* 30.1 (2018): 25–43.
37 Fabio Bruschi, "Splitting Science: The Althusserian Interpretation of *Capital*'s Multiple Orders of Exposition," *Rethinking Marxism* 30.1 (2018): 32.
38 Althusser, "Preface to *Le concept de loi économique dans 'Le Capital,'*" 20.
39 Bakhtin, *Problems of Dostoevsky's Poetics*, trans. Caryl Emerson (Minneapolis: University of Minnesota Press, 1984), 181–204.
40 Marx, *Capital* vol. 1, 352, n. 22.
41 Althusser, *Philosophy of the Encounter*, 18.
42 Kevin B. Anderson, *Marx at the Margins: On Nationalism, Ethnicity, and Non-Western Societies* (Chicago: University of Chicago Press, 2010), 194.
43 Althusser, *Reading Capital*, 57.
44 From the multiple passages on European colonialism in the chapters on primitive accumulation to the constant references to slavery in the US South. Marx wrote regularly on the American Civil War for the *New York Daily Tribune* and the Viennese newspaper *Die Presse*.
45 These range from the Old Testament-inspired Reverend Montagu Valpy's observation in the *Daily Telegraph* that capitalism is a system "of unmitigated slavery, socially, physically, morally, and spiritually" to the well-known passage in which Marx states that "[t]he overseer's book of penalties replaces the slave-driver's lash"—a forerunner to the more overt reference to wage labor as "veiled slavery" (as opposed to the "unqualified slavery of the New World"). Marx, *Capital* vol. 1, 353, 550, 925.
46 At the time of the American Civil War, this was only too clear.
47 Jameson, *Representing Capital*, 113.
48 Jameson, *Representing Capital*, 126.
49 Marx, *Capital* vol. 1, 825.
50 Marx, *Capital* vol. 1, 289; Jameson, *Representing Capital*, 97.

7

The Dialectics of Utopia

Critique of the Gotha Program

Regenia Gagnier

In May 1875, two German proletarian parties met in Gotha, a small town in Central Germany, to debate strategies about unification in the face of Bismarck's Prussian leadership and crackdown after the Paris Commune. The Eisenach or German Social-Democratic Workers Party led by August Bebel and Wilhelm Liebknecht and the General German Workers Union led by Ferdinand Lassalle drafted a program for a United Workers Party. Marx wrote to the leaders in May what was published by Engels in 1891 as *Critique of the Gotha Program*: a long, ill-tempered letter complaining about the drafters' reification of abstractions and dogmas—rather than, as he wanted, starting from real societies with attention to specific material processes and stages of development; about their absence of attacks on landowners as well as on capitalists; and about their notion of a "free state," which for him reified bourgeois notions of governance. He also criticized "modern mythologies" of rights, "[j]ustice, liberty, equality and fraternity," insisting that revolution had to be won by workers' struggle and economic restructuring.[1] In the midst of his unsparing criticisms and complaints, Marx also expressed one of the few utopian moments in his and Engels' theory and one of the most sublime theories of justice in Western, and probably world, history:

> In a higher phase of communist society, after the enslaving subordination of the individual to the division of labor, and therewith also the antithesis between mental and physical labor, has vanished; after labor has become not only a means of life but life's prime want; after the productive forces have also increased with the all-around development of the individual, and all the springs of co-operative wealth flow more abundantly—only then can the narrow horizon of bourgeois right be crossed in its entirety and society inscribe on its banners: From each according to his ability, to each according to his needs![2]

The salient factors here are the progress in stages from lower to higher forms of communism, when one receives first according to contribution but ultimately according to need; the nature of work in the good society; the requirement of a level of subsistence beyond scarcity (*abundance*); and the abolition of private property (bourgeois *right*). Marx is proposing that in communist society people will contribute according to their individual talents and capacities, that their contribution will be fulfilling in itself as a source of dignity and self-respect, and that everyone's needs within reason will be met. Marx's formulation, "from each according to his ability, to each according to his needs," was not new but familiar within French utopian socialism, as in Etienne-Gabriel Morelly and Louis Blanc. Some trace it back to the biblical New Testament, others to Roman law.

Formally, the *Critique* is Marx and Engels' dialogue with objectionable German party positions, criticizing them in such forms as:

The Lassallean sect's servile belief in the state . . .
It is worthy of Lassalle's imagination that with state loans one can build a new society just as well as a new railway.
Ideological nonsense about right and other trash so common among the democrats and French socialists.
A phrase borrowed from the bourgeois League of Peace and Freedom . . .
Some return to Lassalle's dogma although they must have known that Lassalle *did not know* what wages were . . .[3]

Formally, this chapter will also put Marx and Engels' views in dialogue with other historical and contemporary political-economic positions from the nineteenth through the twenty-first centuries, with particular attention to the kinds of liberalisms and "vulgar socialisms" that Marx opposed in the 1870s. The goal of this chapter will therefore be to emphasize the enduring relevance of Marx's utopianism as a specifically modernizing and potentially modernist project.

Because we are so far today from the vision of "from each according to ability and to each according to need," it is useful to begin with some definitions. Communist society cannot appear while people are alienated from—that is, they do not control—their labor. Labor is sensuous human activity that transforms the world for use. It is our species-being, or what it means to be human. It requires the short working day, so that—in the other utopian moment in Marx and Engels—

no one will have a particular, exclusive sphere of activity, which is forced upon him and from which he cannot escape . . . but each can become accomplished in any branch he wishes, society regulat[ing] the general production and thus mak[ing] it possible for me to do one thing today and another tomorrow, to hunt in the morning, fish in the afternoon, rear cattle in the evening, criticise after dinner, just as I have a mind, without ever becoming hunter, fisherman, herdsman or critic.[4]

In this world, people will not be born into fixed divisions of labor, not even according to gender, but will instead develop according to their individual needs and capacities. They will not become things for others' use (via *objectification* or *reification*) but ends in themselves. Things will not take on magical properties that promise falsely to fulfill our wishes (as in *commodity fetishism*). Rather, nature—the external world, the means of life—will be transformed by human labor and the revolutionizing technologies created by humans (*human history*) will be for the good of all.

Notably, in this vision, private property (bourgeois *right*) is not a relation between a person and a thing, but a relation of power between people. In the studies that became the *Economic and Philosophical Manuscripts* (1844), Marx had noted that money was less a thing than a power or capacity that overturned social relations:

> The extent of the power of money is the extent of my power. Money's properties are my—the possessor's—properties and essential powers. Thus, what I am and am capable of is by no means determined by my individuality. . . I am bad, dishonest, unscrupulous, stupid; but money is honored, and therefore so is its possessor. Money can buy talented people for oneself, and is he who has power over the talented not more talented than the talented? . . . Does not my money, therefore, transform all my incapacities into their contrary?[5]

Like money, capitalism is also a social relation, in which the appropriation of surplus value, or the value appropriated by the capitalist after paying the laborer (*exploitation*), and private ownership of the means of production (rights over machines, land, resources) lead to a class that owns everything and a class that owns nothing except its labor power. Property, commodities, class, and wealth (to which we might add *race* and *gender*) for Marx are not natural *facts* but *social relations*. Soon we shall ask what it says about our contemporary social relations that five men today own as much as half the world.

But let's start with a brief history of Western work. Marx begins the *Critique* with these declarations: "Labor is *not the source* of all wealth. *Nature* is just as much the source of use values (and it is surely of such that material wealth consists!) as labor, which itself is only the manifestation of a force of nature, human labor power."[6] The concept of work has changed over time from biblical toil and trouble to Marx's self-fulfillment and fulfillment of species-being through sensuous human activity, to a commodity bought and sold in competitive labor markets. In the book of Genesis, work is pain contrasted with leisure or pleasure, even for a working deity, God the Craftsman or Clockmaker, and levied on humankind when they fell. "God blessed the seventh day," we read. "Because in it He had rested from all His work" (2:3). "In the sweat of thy face shalt thou eat bread, till thou return to the ground" (3:19). To labor in work was man's punishment and to labor in childbirth was woman's. As Marx and Engels eventually observed, the original division of labor was "in the sexual act," or reproduction.[7]

Under sixteenth-century Protestantism, as has been analyzed since Max Weber's *Protestant Ethic and the Spirit of Capitalism* (1905), effortful labor became a precondition to a good afterlife: workers would be compensated in heaven for their toil and trouble on earth.[8] Nineteenth-century industrialism required disciplined workers and entrepreneurs (capital *undertakers* or investors) and, as political economy developed, workers came to be seen as a factor of production and their labor—their sensuous human activity—came to be seen as a commodity, or something to be bought at a price. What this did to the worker was described by Marx as the alienation or estrangement of work, that sensuous human activity, in the form of wage labor, which was reduced to a mere means to an end, not fulfilling in itself and distinct from our free actions "at home." Marx describes the complete upheaval of alienated labor under the capitalist mode of production:

> First, the fact that labor is external to the worker, i.e., it does not belong to his intrinsic nature; that in his work, therefore, he does not affirm himself but denies himself, does not feel content but unhappy, does not develop freely his physical and mental energy but mortifies his body and ruins his mind. The worker therefore only feels himself outside his work, and in his work feels outside himself. He feels at home when he is not working, and when he is working he does not feel at home. His labor is therefore not voluntary, but coerced; it is forced labor. It is therefore not the satisfaction of a need; it is merely a means to satisfy needs external to it. Its alien character emerges clearly in the fact that as soon as no physical or other compulsion exists, labor is shunned like the plague. External labor, labor in which man alienates himself, is a labor of self-sacrifice, of mortification. Lastly, the external character of labor for the worker appears in the fact that it is not his own, but someone else's, that it does not belong to him, that in it he belongs, not to himself, but to another. . . . As a result, therefore, man (the worker) only feels himself freely active in his animal functions—eating, drinking, procreating, or at most in his dwelling and in dressing-up.[9]

Through the nineteenth and first half of the twentieth centuries, there were many alternative visions of work, if not as immediate self-fulfillment and realization of species-being through creative, unalienated labor then at least through cooperation so that no one had to work ceaselessly all day, alone, in conditions of precarity, or throughout one's entire life, blaming oneself and losing dignity and even identity if unemployed. The Owenite Socialists in England during the 1830s, for example, conceived a program in which the necessary labor of society would be allocated according to age and ability, with children up to eleven years doing less skilled housework; young adults aged twelve to twenty-one years producing the wealth; adults aged twenty-two to twenty-five preserving and distributing goods and services; ages twenty-five to thirty-five supervising, teaching, and forming the character of the rising generation; ages thirty-five to forty-five would shoulder the burdens of governing; and after age forty-five, they would be freed for artistic or intellectual pursuits, tours of other communities and cultures, and so forth. All roles were entirely gender neutral. In this vision, labor was not in one's control, but it was equally socially distributed throughout everyone's early to mid-life, in ways that were variable, shared, and left plenty of time for other pursuits.

Such plans were undermined during the second half of the twentieth century, as the desire for consumption as self-fulfillment ("eating, drinking, procreating [homemaking or 'dwelling'], and dressing-up") replaced that for creative labor and leisure. In the long run, the reduction of labor to a commodity has been in terms of the fulfillment of species-being a disaster. Work is now for most of us a disutility to be traded for an optimal basket of commodities. Assuming—as neoclassical economists typically do—that the satisfaction of every want creates another want or wants, humankind as consumer is known by the insatiability of our desires. Progress in neoliberal consumer society—or societies in which all values, including social welfare, are reduced to market price—means not ethical or political progress but rather inspiring others by envy to desire our desires and imitate our wants, globally.[10]

Turning from the nature of work to the requirement of abundance and abolition of private property, Marx wrote in the *Critique of the Gotha Program* that we must start from real societies and must consider land as well as labor and capital. This is as true today as it was in 1875. In the twenty-first century, the richest 1 percent own 50 percent of world's wealth. Locally, half of England is owned by 1 percent of the population; if the land were distributed evenly across the population, each person would own almost an acre (4,000 square meters).[11] Yet working populations are increasingly migrant, precarious, and forced into continuous reskilling. In neoliberal management speak, we are mobile and flexible. In reality, we are perennially at risk. The family, site of the reproduction of labor power and, at the height of working-class consciousness, haven in a heartless world ("To get the whole world out of bed / And washed, and dressed, and warmed, and fed, / To work, and back to bed again, / Believe me, Saul, costs worlds of pain"[12]), is stretched beyond recognition: parents often work long and incompatible hours and childcare is externalized. While economic independence has no doubt contributed to women's liberation, the increase of wage labor of women and children and the flooding of homes with consumer goods have also increased states' bases for taxation and thus have contributed to capitalist expansion.

In the nineteenth and twentieth centuries, industrial mechanization displaced the peasantry and proletariat. In the twenty-first century, information technology and artificial intelligence displace the working and middle classes: after lorry drivers and delivery vans, programmers, managers, clerks, and administrators too will go. They will be followed by translators and educators, the latter replaced by Google Pixel Buds. As Marx argued, the laborers' final task is to make the machines to replace us.[13] From the standpoint of socialism, however, the idea of being freed from distasteful or boring labor by means of technology was a realizable dream. In Oscar Wilde's "Soul of Man under Socialism" (1891), technology would free up leisure time, letting machines do what humans found uncreative or distasteful. Wilde's comments about industrial machinery resonate today with respect to information technology and tech entrepreneurs:

> Up to the present, man has been, to a certain extent, the slave of machinery, and there is something tragic in the fact that as soon as man had invented a machine to do his work he began to starve. This, however, is, of course, the result of our property system and our system of competition. One man owns a machine which does the work of five hundred men. Five hundred men are, in consequence, thrown out of employment, and having no work to do, become hungry and take to thieving. The one man secures the produce of the machine and keeps it, and

has five hundred times as much as he should have, and probably, which is of much more importance, a great deal more than he really wants. Were that machine the property of all, everyone would benefit by it. It would be an immense advantage to the community.[14]

Under postcapitalist conditions, Wilde writes, "[t]here will be great storages of force for every city, and for every house if required, and this force man will convert into heat, light, or motion, according to his needs."[15] Of course, Wilde writing in the 1890s was less concerned than we are about environmental sustainability or about declining profit as machines come to make the machines, throwing even the human machine-makers out of work.

As early as 1848, John Stuart Mill had felt that production had reached the stage where progressive humankind could turn its attention to distribution: "It is only in the backward countries of the world that increased production is still an important object: in those most advanced, what is needed is a better distribution."[16] In the only passage in Mill that Marx ever praised, the former wrote that it was

> questionable if all the mechanical inventions yet made have lightened the day's toil of any human being. They have enabled a greater population to live the same life of drudgery and imprisonment, and an increased number of manufacturers and others to make fortunes. They have increased the comforts of the middle classes. But they have not yet begun to effect those great changes in human destiny, which it is in their nature and futurity to accomplish.[17]

Mill cited the United States as an example of a society that had failed to progress beyond accumulation, or wealth for wealth's sake, and indeed the amendments to its Constitution had presupposed private property.

Marx, in the *Critique of the Gotha Program*, had little patience with rights per se, and not only with rights to distribution. Just preceding the utopian passage with which we began, he saw them as merely the lower stage of communism that had to evolve within the conditions of capitalism:

> This equal right [to distribution or consumption] is an unequal right for unequal labor. It recognizes no class differences, because everyone is only a worker like everyone else; but it tacitly recognizes unequal individual endowment, and thus productive capacity, as a natural privilege. It is, therefore, a right of inequality, in its content, like every right. Right, by its very nature, can consist only in the application of an equal standard; but unequal individuals (and they would not be different individuals if they were not unequal) are measurable only by an equal standard insofar as they are brought under an equal point of view, are taken from one definite side only—for instance, in the present case, are regarded only as workers and nothing more is seen in them, everything else being ignored. . . . Right can never be higher than the economic structure of society and its cultural development conditioned thereby.[18]

Whether rights are considered as universal aspirations, absolutes, "nonsense on stilts" (Bentham), "politics fossilized into law" (Lord Sumption), or (in Marx's phrase) "never higher than the economic structure of society and its cultural development conditioned thereby," at present, nineteenth-century expectations of labor-saving technology have not materialized. Rather, new technologies still result in increasing the wealth of the wealthy and in unemployment without a safety net, thereby intensifying lack of dignity, homelessness, and a loss of identity for workers. Why is this the case? Or, to ask the more practical question, what prevents the realization of Marx's utopian vision?

Contrary to Mill's, Wilde's, Marx's, and many others' diverse plans for labor-saving technologies to free humankind from drudgery and liberate us into alternative forms of creativity, it is now clear that our new forms of electronic and other technologies under the Great Acceleration of the second half of the twentieth century are ecologically unsustainable. Yet even such an anodyne proposal as Universal Basic Income, which simply allows for workers displaced by machines to be retrained, say, in health or social care, and does nothing to interfere with class hierarchies and capitalist exploitation, has as yet been almost universally rejected by neoliberal governments. Our working and unemployed conditions have given rise to a global crisis in mental health, which is now treated as individual weakness to be cured by big pharmaceutical companies in a chemico-biological depoliticization.

In terms of politics, liberal, informed democracies are challenged by capitalist mass media driven by commodity advertising, career politicians, unlimited campaign donations, and democracy by oligarchy. We have seen the reduction of freedoms to free markets and of choice to consumer choice. In the worst predictions, if we permit the neoliberal agenda to continue in its global path, by 2050 we can expect 50–70 percent unemployment with a tiny robot-owner class immeasurably wealthy. With neoliberalism—having cleared away states, governments, borders, trade unions—we can look forward to de- or under-institutionalized, essentially ungovernable societies of collectively incapacitated individualized individuals making their way under local improvisations.[19] And yet we are told that there is no alternative to capitalism, as if private property, unemployment, and ceaseless, mindless, or useless labor were natural rather than socially constructed relations between people.

Increasing inequality is ignored and even justified by the absolute right to private property, which remains grossly, obscenely concentrated in the hands, now, of mainly technology owners, who appear to believe that this inequality and privatized wealth are natural rather than a peculiar form of social relation. In 1989, Francis Fukuyama argued that "with the triumph of Western economic and political liberalism" we were witnessing the "end of history as such . . . the end point of mankind's evolution and the universalization of Western liberal democracy as the final form of human government." Citing the "spectacular abundance of advanced liberal economies and the infinitely diverse consumer culture made possible by them," he announced that political liberalism would follow economic (neo)liberalism "with seeming inevitability," and that class and race antagonisms were merely "historical legacies of pre-modern conditions" already on the way out.[20] Fukuyama's thesis is now disproven, at least in the short term. Political liberalism—tolerance, respect for diversity, opening up to other cultures, cosmopolitanism—has not followed economic liberalism. Rather, global markets under neoliberal ideology have led to xenophobia and insular nationalisms.

As global trade has caused speedups in developing countries and underemployment and precarity in the global north, right-wing cultures have turned to nationalism and xenophobia, whether in Turkey under Erdogan, Hungary under Orbán, Brazil under Bolsonaro, Israel under Netanyahu, India under Modi, the United States under Trump, or Britain under Brexit. In the *Critique of the Gotha Program*, Marx addressed the relation of national working classes to international trade and empire:

> It is altogether self-evident that, to be able to fight at all, the working class must organize itself at home as a class and that its own country is the immediate arena of its struggle.... But the "framework of the present-day national state," for instance, the German Empire, is itself, in its turn, economically "within the framework" of the world market, politically "within the framework" of the system of states. Every businessman knows that German trade is at the same time foreign trade, and the greatness of Herr Bismarck consists, to be sure, precisely in his pursuing a kind of international policy.[21]

Marx's perception of globalization here was especially prescient. At the time, Central Europe had four massive multiethnic empires: the German, the Austro-Hungarian, the Russian, and the Ottoman. The global industrial crisis called the Great Depression of 1873–96 led to populist discontent as well as to the proletarian party merger that occasioned Marx's letter. It then led world leaders to the so-called Scramble for Africa, as European powers competed for markets, resources, and labor. In 1884, Bismarck would convene the Berlin conference of newly unified European states to distribute Africa between French, British, German, Italian, Portuguese, Belgian, and Spanish interests, forming the new imperialisms that might be resisted by the Communist International.

The other main argument that contributes to the naturalizing of capitalism has always been that humans are naturally selfish. In conditions of genuine scarcity, in which survival is "life's prime want," this may well be true of humans as a species of animal. But once we are above the level of scarcity, "after the productive forces have also increased with the all-around development of the individual, and all the springs of co-operative wealth flow more abundantly," then might we be able to cross "the narrow horizon of bourgeois right," that is, private property, and give up some of our self-interest for the common good? Especially if the collective good meant that the rich would not need to barricade themselves from the increasing numbers of refugees migrating across the globe in search of livable political, economic, and environmental conditions? According to Marx, the productive forces will need to have developed to a point of surplus or abundance before a communist revolution could succeed: communism had to emerge out of capitalism. Yet heretofore most communist or socialist societies have not developed from Marx's or Mill's abundance of productive forces, but rather from agricultural, peasant societies within conditions of absolute scarcity, when life's prime want was survival itself. Without abundance sufficient for everyone to live a life worthy of self-conscious human beings, Marx thought that competing groups would struggle to control the surplus. It is also possible that the rich would never voluntarily give up their privilege. As it happens, both Mill and Mao thought that that would be the case; hence Mill's insistence that only rich and educated societies would be prepared to give up some self-interest for the social good and become communist, and Mao's emphasis on re-education. Marx himself thought that the revolution would develop from the one society he knew—Mill's—that had already reached a stage of abundance. His recipe for revolution was the increasing economic inequality he saw developing under capitalism plus increasing political democracy. We may be getting to this point. On a planetary scale, we may also be getting to the point at which Engels' and Rosa Luxemburg's alternatives of socialism or barbarism might now be socialism or extinction.[22]

Political theorists today are writing about the global political crisis, the failure of representative democracy and political parties as we know them, when people no longer trust traditional liberal or conservative parties to solve the economic, ecological, or social problems confronting them and the future generations. This widespread rejection of electoralism is often seen as a crisis of hegemony, in Antonio Gramsci's sense of a process by which a ruling class makes its domination appear natural by installing its own worldview as social common sense. Nancy Fraser has recently argued, for example, that capitalist hegemonic ("There is no alternative") modes of distribution (financialization, deindustrialization, and corporate globalization) and recognition (either Left multiculturalism or Right ethno-nationalism) have divided the world between Left progressive and Right hyper-reactionary populisms.[23]

What has failed everyone is the neoliberalism not only of Reagan and Thatcher but also, more recently, of Clinton, Blair, Obama, Cameron, and May, which promotes social liberalism within market neoliberalism, or liberalism decoupled from economic redistribution. In other words, capitalism has delivered only liberalism but without redistribution of the means of consumption at least (liberal redistribution) or without redistribution of the ownership of production at best (Marx and Engels' view, socialist revolution). The *Critique* spells out the difference between these processes:

> Any distribution whatever of the means of consumption is only a consequence of the distribution of the conditions of production themselves. The latter distribution, however, is a feature of the mode of production itself. The capitalist mode of production, for example, rests on the fact that the material conditions of production are in the hands of non-workers in the form of property in capital and land, while the masses are only owners of the personal condition of production, of labor power. If the elements of production are so distributed, then the present-day distribution of the means of consumption results automatically. If the material conditions of production are the co-operative property of the workers themselves, then there likewise results a distribution of the means of consumption different from the present one. Vulgar socialism (and from it in turn a section of the democrats) has taken over from the bourgeois economists the consideration and treatment of distribution as independent of the mode of production and hence

the presentation of socialism as turning principally on distribution. After the real relation has long been made clear, why retrogress again?[24]

Marx's view was that workers themselves would seize the moment and expropriate the expropriators. "Between capitalist and communist society," we read, "there lies the period of the revolutionary transformation of the one into the other. Corresponding to this is also a political transition period in which the state can be nothing but *the revolutionary dictatorship of the proletariat.*"[25] Mill, the classic liberal and utilitarian, thought that a liberal education would guide everyone to support the workers, to see that equality with relative abundance would be better for the greatest number than obscene wealth on the part of the few. What would it mean for societies living well above scarcity to give up some self-interest for the common good: to educate children equally, for instance, letting them develop according to their needs and capacities, and then to employ them according to their different abilities? What would it mean for us to shorten the working week, for technology to replace our labor without leaving us bereft of employment and therefore dignity, freeing us to work creatively and enhance our leisure? In the liberal view, in the developed societies Marx envisioned, today we wouldn't even need a revolution. We could begin by paying taxes fairly, without loopholes for the rich. Paying taxes, as Marx says in the *Critique*, would not abolish the class system—"Taxes are the economic basis of the government machinery and of nothing else.... Income tax presupposes various sources of income of the various social classes, and hence capitalist society"[26]—but it would be a step nearer to a welfare state, or the kind of social democracies that preceded the neoliberal take-overs beginning in the 1970s. That tax reform might read as an extreme demand is, perhaps, testament to the accuracy of Marx's diagnosis: to the need for revolution over reform.

Throughout the nineteenth century, *communism* and *socialism* were often used interchangeably, with *communist* in the twentieth century being generally reserved for authoritarian parties, or for absolute, levelling equality versus a democratic "socialist" welfare state, the kind of liberal welfare state that Marx and Engels would have rejected or seen as a lower, transitional form. For Marx and Engels, communism as a social relation entailed the abolition of private ownership of the means of production that required alienated labor, and thus the emergence of creative human nature for all rather than the few. Consumption would follow collective production, not be an end in itself, a separate realm of unequal "tastes" among individuals that bestowed on them commodified identities. Contrary to popular perceptions, Marx and Engels recognized natural inequalities and different capacities among individuals—indeed they recognized individuals even more than do bourgeois liberals with their rights, and they anticipated a stage in the emergence of community through which individuals gain their freedom by taking from each according to their ability, and giving to each according to their needs.

Most functional families live according to this rule: from each according to ability, to each according to need. Whether or not modern complex societies can function with the justice of a family depends on how they are educated, as Mill proposed. Can we be educated to give up some self-interest for the social good? Or, more precisely, can the bourgeoisie who have been born into privilege be educated to abandon some of their feelings of entitlement in order to live in more equal societies? Marx thought not, that the owners of the means of production could not be re-educated because their position was structural and no amount of goodwill, philanthropy, or liberalism would overcome the effects of exploitation. In the *Critique* he explicitly stated that government and religion should have nothing to do with education: all education, both technical and theoretical, should be free for all and provided by the revolutionary party:

> Defining by a general law the expenditures on the elementary schools, the qualifications of the teaching staff, the branches of instruction, etc., and, as is done in the United States, supervising the fulfilment of these legal specifications by state inspectors, is a very different thing from appointing the state as the educator of the people! Government and church should rather be equally excluded from any influence on the school.[27]

Yet without the utopian impulse that Marx expressed, what is the point of education at all? Are we educating children to be docile bodies in the relations of international competition, with ceaseless speedups, precarity, and longer and longer working days as technologies drive us and keep us awake at night? Much of the literature of international modernisms and modernization programs was inspired by precisely the kinds of Marxist humanism captured in the *Critique*: not only the creative modernists associated with various social credit schemes, such as Charlie Chaplin, William Carlos Williams, Ezra Pound, T. S. Eliot, Aldous Huxley, and G. K. Chesterton, but also the modernizing movements such as the Communist Internationals, trade unions, early Zionism, the May Fourth and New Culture movements (China), Meiji Restoration (Japan), the Tanzimat (Turkey), Arab Romanticism, the New Woman, Republican Marxist humanism, Marxist-Leninism of the Sino-Soviet Pact, Chairman Mao's internally focused peasant-centered re-education, Bandung and "Third-World" Internationalisms, Latin American *Modernistas*, the Cuban Revolution, *Zapatistas*, *Sandinistas*, the Black Panthers, the Dalit-bahujans, and so on.

In "The Soul of Man under Socialism," Wilde wrote that any "map of the world that does not include Utopia is not worth even glancing at, for it leaves out the one country at which Humanity is always landing. And when Humanity lands there, it looks out, and seeing a better country, sets sail. Progress is the realisation of utopias."[28] José Martí, founder of the first Cuban Revolutionary party in 1892, called Wilde *El Innovador* or the Innovator. Our future depends less on technological innovation than on keeping such *knowledge* in circulation; that is, the knowledge that there are and have been alternatives to capitalist social relations. Beyond fairer taxation, some so-called new economists are beginning to reconsider a "democratic economy" that puts social needs before economic privilege or "growth," local governments supporting small business before big capitalists, "inclusive ownership" or "market socialism" before such unequal degrees of private property.[29] Yet more revolutionary, and more in line with Marx and Engels' collective redistribution of the means of production, it seems as if some of our more thoughtful millennials, precisely because of their generational losing out in terms of ownership of housing, resources, and the basic means to subsist, "have a far greater instinct for collectivism than any of the postwar generation" and appear to value shared experience over the private accumulation of things.[30] Marx himself died intestate and stateless, privatizing nothing and claimed by no state, except utopia.

Notes

1 See also McLellan, *Karl Marx: His Life and Thought* (New York: Harper and Row, 1973), 430–5.
2 Marx, "Critique of the Gotha Program," in *The Marx-Engels Reader*, 531.
3 Marx, "Critique of the Gotha Program," 525–41.
4 Marx and Engels, "The German Ideology," 160.
5 Marx, "Economic and Philosophical Manuscripts of 1844," 128.
6 Marx, "Critique of the Gotha Program," 525. Italics in original.
7 Engels, *The Origin of the Family, Private Property, and the State* (1884), first articulated in *The German Ideology* (1845). See also Regenia Gagnier and John Dupre, "On Work and Idleness," *Feminist Economics* 1.3 (1995), 96–109; Dupre and Gagnier, "A Brief History of Work," *Journal of Economic Issues* 30.2 (1996), 553–9.
8 Max Weber, *The Protestant Ethic and the Spirit of Capitalism*, trans. Talcott Parsons (Kettering: Angelico Press, 2014).
9 Marx, "Economic and Philosophical Manuscripts of 1844," 66.
10 For the Owenites, see Gagnier, *The Insatiability of Human Wants: Economics and Aesthetics in Market Society* (Chicago: University of Chicago Press, 2000), 76–82.
11 Thirty percent aristocracy and gentry; 18 percent corporations; 17 percent oligarchs/City bankers; 17 percent unaccounted; 8.5 percent public sector; 5 percent homeowners; 2 percent conservation charities; 1.4 percent crown and royal family; 5 percent Church of England. See Guy Shrubsole, *Who Owns England?: How We Lost Our Green and Pleasant Land, and How to Take It Back* (Glasgow: William Collins, 2019).
12 John Masefield, "The Everlasting Mercy" (1911). I first read this poem in Lillian B. Rubin, *Worlds of Pain: Life in the Working-Class Family* (New York: Basic Books, 1976).
13 See Marx, "Chapter Fifteen: Machinery and Large-Scale Industry," in *Capital* vol. 1, 429–643.
14 Oscar Wilde, *The Artist as Critic: Critical Writings of Oscar Wilde* (Chicago: University of Chicago Press, 1968), 268–9.
15 Wilde, *The Artist as Critic*, 269.
16 John Stuart Mill, *The Principles of Political Economy* (London: Routledge, 1848), 496–7.
17 Mill, *The Principles of Political Economy*, 498.
18 Marx, "Critique of the Gotha Program," 530.
19 Wolfgang Streeck, *How Will Capitalism End? Essays on a Failing System* (London: Verso Books, 2016).
20 Francis Fukuyama, "The End of History?" *National Interest* 16 (Summer 1989): 1–18.
21 Marx, "Critique of the Gotha Program," 533.

22 Luxemburg, "The Junius Pamphlet: The Crisis of German Social Democracy" (1915). https://www.marxists.org/archive/luxemburg/1915/junius/index.htm, accessed August 20, 2019.
23 Nancy Fraser, *The Old Is Dying and the New Cannot Be Born: From Progressive Neoliberalism to Trump and Beyond* (London: Verso, 2019).
24 Marx, "Critique of the Gotha Program," 531–2.
25 Marx, "Critique of the Gotha Program," 538.
26 Marx, "Critique of the Gotha Program," 539.
27 Marx, "Critique of the Gotha Program," 539–40.
28 Wilde, *The Artist as Critic*, 269–70.
29 These are all projects under varying degrees of consideration and implementation in the Jeremy Corbyn leadership of Britain's Labor Party. The Labor-run Council of the northern town of Preston under Matthew Brown is often cited as a good example.
30 See Charlotte Church, "Why I Dream of Spending My Twilight Years in a Big House with My Mates," *Guardian G2*, June 24, 2019.

8

Posthumous Publications

Capitalism's Circuits and Reading for Totality

Treasa De Loughry and Miles Link

Approaching volumes two and three of *Capital* in literary terms presents a challenge to cultural critics, not least given the paucity of attention paid to these works. Consider Robert C. Tucker's important *Marx-Engels Reader*, which contains no excerpts from volume two and only two brief extracts from volume three; and, latterly, *The Bloomsbury Companion to Marx* (2019), an anthology that makes no reference to its omission of any chapters on these texts. Much of the problem can be framed in terms of what these volumes supposedly lack: their lack of polish, intertextual richness, and even of a straightforward structure.[1] Ernest Mandel opens his introduction to volume two with quotes from Engels bemoaning the "scientific" and less politically exciting ("agitating") nature of this volume, which, in dry prose, focuses on the market rather than on the factory and concerns itself with the circulation of commodities.[2] "The problem," as David Harvey argues, "is not only one of written style," but also one of structure and argumentation, given Engels' substantial edits and reorganization of Marx's largely unfinished, overlapping, and divergent manuscripts, producing two volumes of arid and frequently repetitious prose.[3]

Yet this view of the latter volumes of *Capital* also contributes to their overshadowing. If we speculate about what is missing from volumes two and three, or what they would have achieved had Marx's ambitions for his works been realized, then we fail to recognize these texts as they are. True, volumes two and three bear the marks of the specific circumstances of their compilation by Engels. But they also extend and deepen Marx's overarching theoretical project: a critique of political economy demanding a rigorous interpretive stance toward what capital appears to be and how it behaves. The latter volumes' departures from the style and presentation of volume one are not accompanied by a departure from this interpretive demand; they raise the stakes from a matter of individual perspective to the workings of social production as a whole.

We can therefore treat volumes two and three as "literary" in that, as they have arrived to us, they are fragmentary, provisional, and resistant to the formation of a coherent whole. We can further describe this literary character as "modernist" in at least two ways: first, in these volumes' demand on the reader to reckon with the "ephemeral, the fugitive, the contingent"[4] elements that Marx's work illuminates, including the various transformations of capital in two, and in the gaps, seams, and artifices that reveal capitalism as anything but "natural" in three. These works can also be regarded as modernist in their emphasis on capitalism as a chronically crisis-ridden, easily disrupted social totality, systemic features that international economic institutions exploited effectively by furthering the consolidation of a global precariat of underemployed reserve laborers.

Volumes two and three are also literary in their emphasis on interpretation, encoding a model of textuality as, first and foremost, a hermeneutics of interpretive activity. For the Marx of volumes two and three, capital is a totality unavailable to any one observer, capitalist or otherwise, and it demands an active mode of analysis. The conditions described by these volumes can be usefully applied to the socioeconomic and ecological phenomena that Marx describes, and in turn to the literary manifestations that emerge from these conditions, as is demonstrated by the close of this chapter in relation to ground rent and oil. However, Engels warns against "look[ing] in Marx for fixed, cut-and-dried definitions that are valid for all time" without examining their "process of historical or logical formation."[5] If, as Franz Mehring asserts, "*Capital* is not a Bible containing final and unalterable truths, but rather an inexhaustible source of stimulation for further study, further scientific investigations and further struggles for truth," then this chapter responds to that critical stimulant by examining how capital activates different modes of interpretation (scientific study, "struggles for truth," and literary interpretation).[6]

Volume Two: The Circuits of Capital and Production of Crisis

Volume two is a studiously dry text and contains few of the rhetorical flourishes that enlivened volume one to a more general audience, with Marx quicker to deploy scientific rather than literary analogies in developing a precise understanding of political economy. Consider, for example, the multiple uses of "latent," an expression borrowed from thermodynamics, as in the description of money hoards as "latent money capital";[7] and, elsewhere, the description of productive capital as existing "in a *latent* state in the production sphere, without functioning in the production process itself, or that it functions in the production process without being involved in the labor process."[8] However, Marx's deployment of this scientific language is a condition, as Stephen Shapiro states, of translation and of "awkward Victorianisms"[9] that can deflect attention away from Marx's meaning, which is that capital metamorphoses or metabolizes through various states or circuits. Thus, these forms of capital are "latent" because their potential as surplus value is a future one, dependent on changes in function from money through productive to commodity capital. For Marx, capital is "in motion"[10] and its function requires an expansive "spiral of growth"[11] as well as the reinvestment or capitalization of surplus value into forms of constant and variable capital. The result is that capital alters function across the three different forms: money, productive, and commodity capital, so that capital exists as "value in motion."

While this is what Marx means by the metaphor of "latency," Harvey aptly describes the three constitutive forms as offering various "patterns of relations"[12] onto the world, differing drastically from the emphasis on class relations and production in volume one. Here "finance and money capitalists" are linked to money capital, "producer capitalists to the functions of production, and merchant (commercial) capitalists to commodity capital."[13] This view of capital and the capitalist classes is more expansive than volume one, both temporally and spatially, as is illustrated by the use of the terms fixed and fluid capital to describe the transformation of the social appearance of commodities throughout capital's various circuits: "An ox, as a draught animal, is fixed capital. If it is eaten, however, it no longer functions either as a means of labor, or as fixed capital."[14] Oxen, when they enter into circulation as a commodity, become fluid or circulating capital. Fixed capital, as in that which is held by machines, largely maintains its constant capital (slowly amortizing over time), in contrast to the value it helps produce. In volume one, Marx uses the terms constant and variable, rather than fixed and fluid, capital. Constant capital refers to the raw materials and machinery that contribute to the production of value, but these materials do not in themselves change in value during production. Variable capital refers to labor power, which produces surplus value. In volume two when Marx focuses on circulations of capital, fixed and fluid become useful terms to describe how a part of the value of a machine circulates in the commodities it helps produce, but a part of the machine's value is always "fixed" in it. "This peculiarity," writes Marx, "is what gives this part of the constant capital the form of *fixed capital*. All other material components of the capital advanced in the production process, on the other hand, form, by contrast to it, circulating or *fluid capital*."[15]

Crucially, for Marx, the appearance taken by the circulation of capital changes depending on one's relation to the system, given that within "a constantly rotating orbit, every point is simultaneously a starting-point and a point of return,"[16] but these circuits or "three different forms of the circulatory process"[17] interlock in a sequential and simultaneous process.[18] They are, in other words, highly interdependent, to such an extent that money hoarding in one circuit will interrupt the others. Capital, then, has *discontinuous* stages or circuits. For capital, circulation and production time are mutually exclusive, with circuits also often separated in space.[19] The marketplace, the farm, the pieceworker, and the industrial factory are in different spaces, just as the nineteenth-century cotton plantation (South Carolina) and the spinning wheel (Lancashire) were physically and geographically separate, but linked by global commodity markets and political solidarity in ways that produce correlative and causative effects: a cotton blockade in one (linked to the production circuit) and starvation in the other (linked to the commodity circuit) led to a flourishing of improvisational and urgent Lancashire "cotton poetry."[20]

For Marx, however, the "rotations" of capital are not available to any one capitalist, and the appearance of capital at any one time is a "merely subjective distinction that exists only for the observer."[21] The reproduction of total social capital is visible only in parts, given the discontinuous nature of capitalist reproduction, its global expansion, and the amnesia through which commodities are presented as stripped of their origins. "Whether the commodities are the product of production based on slavery, the product of peasants (Chinese, Indian ryots), of a community (Dutch East Indies), of state production (such as existed in earlier epochs of Russian history, based on serfdom),"[22] they all enter the "world market"[23] eventually as "world money."[24] Absent from this account, although logically preceding from it, is a cultural analysis of how inflections of class or regional variation impact this relational view on a system that is too differential (temporally and spatially) to be understood by any one person. As Harvey argues, the nature of Marx's "circuits" lends itself to an analysis of the uneven effects of globalization or of how capital's form and mobility advance in varied regions.[25] Critically, a materialist strand of world literature has emerged that responds to this declensionist and totalizing but partial vision of capitalism advanced in volumes two and three. Specifically, this approach is concerned with how the boom-bust dynamic of commodity frontiers in peripheries are starkly visible in the form and content of literary works that consciously and unconsciously register the violent appropriations and privatizations of extraction and accumulation.[26] Such materialist world literary theorists take their cue from world-systems theory and seek to examine how the uneven and combined world-economic system is "discernible in any modern literary work, since the world-system exists unforgoably as the matrix within which all modern literature takes shape and comes into being."[27] To read this way is to advance a comparison based on the recurring features of capitalism's economic long waves or periodicity rather than periodization.

Another major idea in volume two that has informed Marxist cultural critics and writers, including Harvey and Shapiro as well as Michael Heinrich, is that of capitalism as a system prone to crisis. Given the "disequilibrium" between each circuit or stage of capitalism as well as their complex interdependencies, capitalism as a whole is highly susceptible to crises that disrupt, halt, or slow down its reproduction and "turnover" time. Because the consumption of labor or resources is required to produce what the next circuit needs for accumulation and to then complete the turnover of a circuit of capital, material phenomena including strikes, hoarding, scarcity, and overproduction can fatally interrupt the next circuit of capital accumulation and so the system in total. Marx gives the example of slowed transportation "pausing" the realization of the value into profit of the commodities being carried. "If the job is not carried further," writes Marx, "then the means of production and the labor already consumed in its production have been spent to no avail."[28] An interruption of work (by a lack of raw materials) is, however, less systematically harmful than an interruption that intervenes in "an interconnected act of production," because it has a longer term and more varied disruptive effect on the production chain and the creation of value than those interruptions that are "discrete in nature."[29] While capitalists attempt to circumvent critical disruptions by hoarding money, borrowing credit, stockpiling resources, and relying on reserve labor, here we can see that the circuits of capitalism inter-rely on and presuppose the functioning of the other circuits, and together constitute and reproduce capitalism as a process of commodity metamorphoses—or, in short, as social capital in motion.

This emphasis on capitalism's potential crises of reproduction is a complex and less teleological vision that attends to the regressions of capital accumulation or fitful profiteering, and importantly the jarring effects of these disarticulations between each circuit, for ultimately it is the precarious and impoverished worker who suffers. A condition of capital accumulation, both in the past and now, is the creation of a reserve of under-, un-, and mis-employed laborers, as evidenced in the expansive slums of contemporary mega-cities and the constant role of unpaid domestic work in social reproduction.[30] The notion of shock as the withdrawal of reliable work could be married to Benjamin's discussion of the disorienting effects of a rapid, disjunctive modernity;[31] or, contemporaneously, to the state of constant impermanence occasioned by zero-hour contracts;[32] or geopolitically, to recent analyses of "World Bank" and neoliberal world literatures that register the foreshortened horizons, feminization of labor, deskilling of work, and underemployment of the global south produced by Structural Adjustment Programs. Contemporary and, arguably, modernist literature has been preeminently sensitive to these economic short-circuits and their precipitating shocks, as read in Jamaica Kincaid's account of Antiguan precarity and resource scarcity generated by global tourism and free trade agreements in *A Small Place* (1988); Arundhati Roy's searing indictments against the imposition of neoliberal capitalism and mega-dam projects in India's Adivasi regions (2002); or Roberto Bolaño's visceral fictionalization of femicides in Mexico's maquiladora regions in *2666* (2009).[33]

Volume Three: The Unseen, the Natural, and the Necessity of Interpretation

Expanding on the lessons of capitalism as a partially visible and unequal totality in volume two, volume three examines the ways in which the total social capital—the "total mass of surplus-value produced by productive wage-labor"[34]—is redistributed: it seeks "to identify," as Harvey suggests, "the rules of distribution of surplus value as these are achieved through social processes"[35] like the market, and how these rules of distribution come into conflict with the rules governing the production of that very surplus value. The key to this mechanism of redistribution is that capitalists do not directly receive the surplus value extracted from their workers but instead receive a portion of the total social capital that has been valorized (i.e., capital that has realized its value, for example through exchange). Since different economic sectors operate at uneven rates of profit, this means that the total social capital is consequently redistributed unevenly, with more capital going to more profitable sectors. As capitalists within different sectors innovate and expand, or fall behind and dissolve, over time this redistribution reveals a tendency of the average rate of profit to fall, as the organic composition of capital (i.e., its ratio of constant capital to living labor) rises. Marx is notoriously unclear here about whether he is describing the way in which capitalism meets its terminal decline. Nevertheless, it is enough to say that the tendency of the rate of profit to fall is not *the* ultimate crisis but promotes the conditions for such a crisis.

With the mechanism for the redistribution of surplus value thus described, volume three shows how this redistribution is facilitated, manipulated, distorted, and mystified. Marx extends the discussion of the credit system raised in volume two and its role in transferring capital from sectors of declining to increasing rates of profit, and examines how ground rent, though historically necessary for the emergence of the capitalist mode of production, now constitutes a barrier to development, by siphoning off from the total social capital without contributing back to its reproduction. The text concludes with a direct analysis of the "Trinity Formula"[36] (capital—profit, land—rent, labor—wages), in which, for capitalists, landlords, and workers, the source of value takes a magical threefold appearance that nonetheless presents itself as a natural state of affairs. Capital, Marx says, ultimately reveals itself not as a thing but as a social relation.

Grasping that relation at the scale of the total social capital is an exercise in analyzing surface appearances in search of that relation's essential character. Broadly, we can place Marx's work beside the work of Charles Lyell in geology, Charles Darwin in biology, and Sigmund Freud in psychology, or within the larger nineteenth-century realization of the metastatic effects of unseen processes. That is, since the processes involved here do not depend on the direct intervention of a rational actor, they require an interpretive model to become visible at all. In *The German Ideology* (1845), Marx with Engels employs the metaphor of the camera obscura, in which "in all ideology men and their circumstances appear upside-down," just as objects on the retina appear upside-down.[37] In volume three, Marx further draws out this principle of inversion:

> The finished configuration of economic relations, as these are visible on the surface, in their actual existence, and therefore also in the notions with which the bearers and agents of these relations seek to gain an understanding of them, is very different from the configuration of their inner core, which is essential but concealed, and the concept corresponding to it. It is in fact the very reverse and antithesis of this.[38]

For Marx, to remain at the level of capital's appearances inevitably means to accept some mystification, or a partial and self-referential understanding of capital's totality. The concept of commodity fetishism from volume one, in which social relations are reified into objects that appear to determine those relations, is a comparable process at the level of the individual, delivered through the commodities one encounters daily. But just as volume three widens the scope of analysis to the totality of capitalist society, the mystifications identified here similarly work not just on individuals, but on whole classes of actors at various points in capital's transformation. As Heinrich neatly avers, "it is no longer apparent" that the relations of production—capital, land, and labor—"are specific historical relations between people. Rather, these seem to have an objective foundation in the fact that production occurs at all."[39] This occlusion is always a falling-away from the view of the total social capital and how it is distributed; equally, it is only with this totality in mind that we can explain how distribution appears to representatives at various points in the process. Marx is not just revealing what the bourgeois economists have failed to see: he is elucidating the social function of a certain subjective experience.[40]

That such mystifications have a social role to play indicates that we should not equate Marx's "appearances" with simple falsehood. As mentioned, Marx's divisions in volume two of the industrial cycle into cycles according to its various transformations (production, circulation, and money capital) demonstrate that capitalist circuits look different from various angles. Volume three, in turn, demonstrates how these views, however self-serving, assist in capital's valorization and expansion. The assumption that profit arises from buying and selling—the "cheating, cunning, expertise, talent and a thousand and one market conjectures"[41] of the sphere of circulation—obfuscates the true source of value as "congealed labor"[42] but also reduces turnover time and keeps capital in motion. With the development of interest-bearing capital (i.e., money itself as a commodity), the "social relation is consummated in the relationship of a thing, money, to itself";[43] or, as Marx quotes from Goethe's *Faust*: "The money's body is now by love possessed."[44] But even as money in this form has shed "any marks of its origin" and stands free to expand to a limit that "beggars all fantasy,"[45] volume three's analysis of the credit system does not privilege productive or industrial capital over merchant capital and "fictitious" credit, since "wealth exists only as a social process expressed as the entwinement of production and circulation."[46] Credit and banking are not extraneous to the more "genuine" business of production; instead, Marx shows how the reformation of usury, which sapped productive power, into interest-bearing capital, which facilitates turnover and ensures expanded reproduction, was a necessary precondition for the emergence of modern capitalism.

Volume three consistently grounds capital's appearances in historically rooted forms. Marx chides "the off-hand way in which economists always treat distinctions of form"[47] as well as their assumptions in describing the "spontaneous" emergence of money and commodity capital from the production process. Making connections between capital's apparent forms is, by contrast to the positivism of classical economics, a necessarily interpretive act. As Marx famously puts it, "all science would be superfluous if the form of appearance of things directly coincided with their essence."[48] To see the behavior making up the total social capital is to see the process by which what appears as normal and natural is produced in the first place. After all, *Capital* as a multivolume whole continually posits ways in which the capitalist mode of production departs not only from the givenness of the natural world but also from previous schemes of reproduction not predicated on endless expansion: consider, for instance, the disarticulation of circuits enlivened in volume two. Capitalism thus appears in these posthumous volumes as a system dialectically producing runaway transformations, geometric expansions of scale, and critical disruptions of a "natural" order. Such disruptions occur even as, simultaneously, capitalism's purpose is "to maintain the existing capital value and to valorize it to the utmost extent possible,"[49] a goal with which its transformative power frequently comes into conflict. But what natural order is it that is disrupted and transformed here?

Marx throughout volume three outlines the disruptions to what was previously understood as given and natural as capitalism extends its reach. Production itself transforms, growing larger and more voluminous, while economies in production compound themselves (though capital is selective in what it chooses to economize and what it chooses to waste). Living labor is replaced by machinery, and the character of work is mechanized. Relations to nature change with transforming production practices: resources provided by nature free of charge are reinterpreted as the "free natural power of capital."[50] Capital investments develop the productivity of agricultural land—"The earth," we read, "continuously improves, as long as it is treated correctly"[51]—but this improvement comes in unison with a shift from naturally self-limiting economic forms (serfs' payment of rent in labor) to forms with potentially limitless expansive power (money rent and capitalist ground rent).

Marx does not point out these disruptions in order to lament the loss of an organic social and natural stability, however. Instead, all of these disruptive processes expose capitalism as "a historically specific form of the social production process,"[52] thus demanding that capitalism's disruptive power be seized upon and turned toward the potential that lies latent within it: for humans to escape the "realm of necessity" and to realize human freedom. This realm of freedom, says Marx, can only be realized by a society of "associated producers" who will "govern the human metabolism with nature in a rational way."[53] Capitalism's "civilizing aspect"[54] is its power to create the conditions for this realization, a power much greater than that possessed by societies based on slavery and serfdom. And yet, this "tremendous productive power... which is developed within the capitalist mode of production... contradicts the basis on behalf of which this immense productive power operates."[55] Constantly transforming itself, capitalist society cannot, like previous economic forms, "sanctify the existing situation as law and [...] fix the limits given by custom and tradition as legal ones."[56] Ultimately, Marx suggests, the opposite impulse emerges: these disruptions of the "natural" are experienced in terms of alienation and fragmentation. This alienation, carrying us further up the asymptote of expansions of scale, requires that we adopt an interpretive framework to navigate our way across this terrain of enlarging, simultaneous and disarticulated capital circuits. Armed with such a framework and able to observe the distance between the appearance of things and their essence (a situation we experience as alienation), we may apply this interpretive power, in turn, to literary manifestations that emerge from the phenomena Marx describes.

Ground Rent and Reading Resources

While this chapter argues that a return to volumes two and three is important for cultural criticism to refine its accounts of capitalism's "partial" or relational appearance, the critique of resources as rent offers an illustration of how culture registers capitalism as a complex socioeconomic lifeworld. A key condition of historical capitalism is the transformation of social property relations that generates capitalist "laws of motion": "the *imperatives* of competition and profit-maximization, a *compulsion* to reinvest surpluses, and a systematic and relentless *need* to improve labor-productivity and develop the forces of production."[57] Those same "laws of motion" that govern the transitions of the three circuits of capital are critically dependent upon, as Ellen

Meiksins Wood argues via Marx, changes in the "social property relations"[58] of the English countryside, in which estates profited from the surplus of agrarian farmers during the time when subsistence workers became wage laborers. Ground rent arises from this process, and is defined by Marx in relation to farmers who pay landowners "a contractually fixed sum of money (just like the interest fixed for the borrower of money capital), for the permission to employ his capital in this particular field of production."[59] Rent rises because of greater productivity on behalf of the farmer, not strictly because of the addition of extra capital. In the language of Marx's discussion of the Trinity Formula, rent presents land as a "natural" source of income expressed through private property. In the language of commodity fetishism, land becomes, as Bina argues, a "*medium* through which the social relations among people are regularly transformed into *fetishized* relations among things."[60]

Specifically, Marx defines ground rent as surplus value that is "over and above profit"[61] or, more precisely, "over and above a portion of commodity value that itself consists of surplus-value," given the rentier's distance from the processes of labor power and surplus labor, through which agricultural work happens.[62] Algebraically comparable to surplus value, differential rent arises from the gap between rent accrued from the price of capital reliant on a monopolized resource and the capital invested in this production, but it does not rely on any greater efficiencies in production or labor. The surplus value arising from this monopoly is a condition of how the unequal expropriation of resources (Marx gives the example of waterfalls) enables the conditions for surplus value to accrue, or for the landowner "to entice this surplus profit out of the manufacturer's pocket and into his own."[63] In Mandel's words, "more efficient farms and mines enjoy surplus profits which Marx calls differential (land and mining) rent."[64]

Rent is notoriously difficult if not impossible to quantify, given the complexities of informal leasing arrangements. Consider oil and its enforced scarcity through the consolidation of oil production into a few groups, including the Seven Sisters as a corporate monopoly, followed by OPEC as a national and regional entity. Marx's "landed property" here acts as a "barrier to the investment of capital"[65] and high oil prices are achieved due to easily found oil (a potential equivalent is Marx's account of soil fertility and the metabolic rift[66]), and low production costs, thus increasing differential rents.[67] Lower oil yields in the United States, for instance, and the consolidation of oil within global commodity and financial markets from the 1950s onward led to further global conditions of international competition for differential rent.[68] Differential rent thus relies on the monopolization by capital of a natural resource to produce surplus profit, and for Marx "whether a waterfall, a rich mine, fishing grounds or a well-situated building site, the person indicated as the owner of these natural objects . . . seizes this surplus profit from the functioning capital in the form of rent."[69]

This, too, registers for literature. In Abdelrahman Munif's *Cities of Salt* (1987), the arrival of American oil engineers transmutes naphtha from a smoky and unproductive substance to oil as black gold. Previously the inhabitants of Wadi al-Uyoun, a remote desert village in the Arabian Peninsula, viewed water as the scarcest and thus most crucial resource. What changes with the introduction of American oil companies is not merely the technological means of refining oil, the fixed capital involved in energy infrastructure, but also an entire economic and cultural shift in what and how resources are valued: "Gold? How on earth could we find gold unless we toiled to find it and ran all over the place? Oil? The naphtha we find is enough to light these lamps of ours that choke you with fumes before they shed light."[70] The narration occurs at the cusp of a transformation from regional-tribal social formations into the formal and real subsumption of oil, land, and culture within a despotic petro-state linked into global networks of oil extraction. The emergence of a globalized oil marketplace in which sovereign resources are reconfigured by imperial spigots is the contextual framing for this transformation, and illustrates how *Cities of Salt* operates in culturally registering wider global transformations in the monopolization of oil rents.

Recently, energy humanities scholars have sought to theorize oil's invisibility in cultural production, despite its role in geopolitical strife, and as the ur-commodity fueling the rapid and disjunctive kineticism of modernization. If we follow Jason W. Moore in taking capitalism as a lifeworld and ecological regime as well as, but not only, an economic system,[71] then energy's relation with capital exceeds our "economic science of representation."[72] There, oil's "true costs" are "coyly" neologized as the "externalities of its extraction," diminishing both the cost (economic, ecological, social) of oil discovery and its eventual carbon emissions.[73] Put differently, the term "capital fictions" refers to the idea that capitalism reproduces on the basis of fictions taken as fact, "namely," as Karl Polanyi has it, "that we begin to assume that labor, land and nature exist so that they might become commodities."[74] For Marx, owning land (and collecting rent) is as absurd as slavery, and will be seen so from a later historical perspective.[75] Realizing this, through absorbing the critical and interpretive moves of volumes two and three, can offer ways of denaturalizing how capitalism operates as a diegetic and historically contingent system, conditioning the treatment of resources as rent within an extractive ecological regime.

Notes

1 See *The Marx-Engels Reader*; and Jeff Diamanti, Andrew Pendakis and Imre Szeman, eds. *The Bloomsbury Companion to Marx* (London: Bloomsbury Academic, 2019).
2 Engels quoted in Mandel "Introduction," in *Capital* vol. 2, trans. David Fernbach (London: Penguin Books, 1992), 11.
3 David Harvey, *A Companion to Marx's Capital Volume 2* (London: Verso, 2013), 7.
4 Charles Baudelaire, *The Painter of Modern Life and Other Essays*, trans. and ed. Jonathan Mayne (London: Phaidon Press, 1964), 13.
5 Engels, "Preface," in *Capital* vol. 3 (London: Penguin Books, 1991), 103.
6 Franz Mehring, *Karl Marx: The Story of His Life*, trans. Edward Fitzgerald (Covivi: Friede Publishers, 1935). https://www.marxists.org/archive/mehring/1918/marx/ch12.htm#s3, accessed August 20, 2019.
7 Marx, *Capital* vol. 2, 158.
8 Marx, *Capital* vol. 2, 201.
9 Stephen Shapiro, "The Cultural Fix: Social Labor-Power and Capital's Long Spiral," in *Ecologies, Technics, & Civilizations I: Capitalism's Ecologies*, eds. Jason W. Moore

and Diane C. Gildea (Oakland: PM Press, 2020), 12; and see Shapiro's forthcoming monograph *The Cultural Fix: Social Labor-Power and Capital's Long Spiral*.
10 Marx, *Capital* vol. 2, 124.
11 Mandel, "Introduction," in *Capital* vol. 2, 17.
12 Harvey, *Volume 2*, 6.
13 Harvey, *Volume 2*, 50.
14 Marx, *Capital* vol. 2, 239.
15 Marx, *Capital* vol. 2, 238.
16 Marx, *Capital* vol. 2, 180–1.
17 Marx, *Capital* vol. 2, 185.
18 See Shapiro, "The Cultural Fix," 25.
19 Marx, *Capital* vol. 2, 203, 205.
20 See the Cotton Famine project which has uncovered hundreds of previously undiscovered poems written by Lancashire workers suffering the effects of cotton blockades and rising prices during the American Civil War (Simon Rennie, *Poetry of the Lancashire Cotton Famine (1861-5)*, http://cottonfaminepoetry.exeter.ac.uk/). As Marx notes, the American Civil War and its effects on global cotton and jute markets was partly to blame for the 1864 famine in Bengal. Marx, *Capital* vol. 2, 218, n. 7.
21 Marx, *Capital* vol. 2, 181.
22 Marx, *Capital* vol. 2, 189.
23 Marx, *Capital* vol. 2, 190.
24 Thanks to Shapiro for the observation that "World money" is another "Victorianism" that means "foreign exchange" or money that can be converted into multiple currencies.
25 Harvey, *Volume 2*, 73.
26 *World Literature, Neoliberalism, and the Culture of Discontent*, eds. Sharae Deckard and and Shapiro (London: Palgrave Macmillan, 2019); Warwick Research Collective (WReC), *Combined and Uneven Development: Towards a Theory of World-Literature* (Liverpool: Liverpool University Press, 2015).
27 WreC, *Combined*, 20.
28 Marx, *Capital* vol. 2, 308.
29 Marx, *Capital* vol. 2, 308.
30 Mike Davis, *Planet of Slums* (London: Verso, 2006). See also Marx's discussion of labor and surplus populations in volume one of *Capital* and Shapiro's elicitation of a similar point, "The Cultural Fix," 23.
31 See Benjamin, *Illuminations*, trans. Harry Zohn (New York: Schocken Books, 2007), 165–6.
32 See also Shapiro, "The Cultural Fix," 22–3.
33 *World Bank Literature*, ed. Amitava Kumar (Minneapolis: University of Minnesota Press, 2003); *World Literature*; WReC; Roberto Bolaño, *2666*, trans. Natasha Wimmer (London: Picador, 2009); Jamaica Kincaid, *A Small Place* (New York: Farrar, Straus and Giroux, 1988); Arundhati Roy, *The Algebra of Infinite Justice* (London: Penguin Books, 2002).
34 Mandel, "Introduction," in *Capital* vol. 3, 12.
35 Harvey, *Limits to Capital* (Oxford: Basil Blackwell, 1984), 352.
36 Marx, *Capital* vol. 3, 953.
37 Marx and Engels, "The German Ideology," 154.
38 Marx, *Capital* vol. 3, 311.

39 Michael Heinrich, *An Introduction to the Three Volumes of Karl Marx's Capital*, trans. Alexander Locascio (New York: Monthly Review Press, 2012), 184.
40 See Shapiro for his neologism, "relative fixed labor power" as a way of analyzing the composition, stabilization, and reproduction of class subjectivity, in his forthcoming chapter "The Cultural Fix: Capital, Genre, and the Times of American Studies," in *The Fictions of American Capitalism: Working Fictions and the Economic Novel*, eds. Vincent Dussol and Jacques-Henri Coste (New York: Palgrave, 2020), 7.
41 Marx, *Capital* vol. 3, 966.
42 Engels, "Preface," in *Capital* vol. 2, 99.
43 Marx, *Capital* vol. 3, 515.
44 Marx, *Capital* vol. 3, 517.
45 Marx, *Capital* vol. 3, 523.
46 Marx, *Capital* vol. 3, 708.
47 Marx, *Capital* vol. 3, 440–1.
48 Marx, *Capital* vol. 3, 956.
49 Marx, *Capital* vol. 3, 357–8.
50 Marx, *Capital* vol. 3, 879.
51 Marx, *Capital* vol. 3, 916.
52 Marx, *Capital* vol. 3, 957.
53 Marx, *Capital* vol. 3, 959.
54 Marx, *Capital* vol. 3, 958.
55 Marx, *Capital* vol. 3, 375.
56 Marx, *Capital* vol. 3, 929.
57 Ellen Meiksins Wood, *The Origin of Capitalism: A Longer View* (London: Verso, 2017), 36–7. Italics in original.
58 Ibid., 37.
59 Marx, *Capital* vol. 3, 755.
60 Cyrus Bina, "Some Controversies in the Development of Rent Theory: The Nature of Oil Rent," *Capital & Class* 13.3 (1989): 87.
61 Marx, *Capital* vol. 3, 773.
62 As outlined earlier, volume three examines the way in which the total social capital, that is the total surplus value produced by wage labor, is redistributed. Surplus value as used here thus refers to the way in which total social capital is redistributed after capital is valorized through exchange, not its direct extraction by individual capitalists.
63 Marx, *Capital* vol. 3, 786.
64 *Absolute land rent* arises when agricultural labor productivity is low, with surplus value here accruing to landowners and capitalist farmers, without being redistributed.
65 Marx, *Capital* vol. 3, 884.
66 See John Bellamy Foster, *Marx's Ecology Materialism and Nature* (New York: Monthly Review Press, 2000).
67 See Mandel's introduction to volume three, and Raul Delgado Wise, *Oil in the Global Economy: Transformation of the International Oil Industry* (New Delhi: A.P.H. Publishing, 1999), 25. Omitted here is the difference between differential rent I and differential rent II, or the issues of unequal capital investment in differing and unequal lands, and what Cyrus Bina describes as the differing prices resulting from

"the existence of differential productivity and the resultant differential profitability through competition," 93.
68 Bina, "Oil Rent," 106–7.
69 Marx, *Capital* vol. 3, 908.
70 Abdelrahman Munif, *Cities of Salt*, trans. Peter Theroux (New York: Vintage International-Random House, 1987), 95.
71 See Jason W. Moore, *Capitalism in the Web of Life: Ecology and the Accumulation of Capital* (London: Verso, 2015).
72 Jeff Diamanti, "Three Theses on Energy and Capital," *Reviews in Cultural Theory* 6.3 (2016): 15.
73 Vaclav Smil, *Oil* (London: Oneworld Publications, 2017), 2.
74 Ericka Beckman, *Capital Fictions: The Literature of Latin America's Export Age* (Minneapolis: University of Minnesota Press, 2013), x–xi.
75 Marx, *Capital* vol. 3, 911.

Part Two

Marx in Modernism

9

Marx in the Modernist Novel

Julian Murphet

Of all the great intellects of the nineteenth century, was any so well versed in the art of the novel as Karl Marx? Ranging from Cervantes to Walter Scott, Defoe to Dumas, Boccaccio to Balzac, Marx frequently turned to contemporary novelists as his most important peers. He hailed the "present splendid brotherhood of fiction-writers in England, whose graphic and eloquent pages have issued to the world more political and social truths than have been uttered by all the professional politicians, publicists and moralists put together."[1] No writer in any genre was offered as much praise by Marx (or Engels) as Honoré de Balzac, "who is generally remarkable for his profound grasp of reality," and who seemed to both writers to impart more historical knowledge and understanding than "all the professed historians, economists and statisticians of the period together."[2] According to Paul Lafargue, Marx "admired Balzac so much that he wished to write a review of his great work *La Comédie humaine* as soon as he had finished his book on economics"[3]—a study of which we were deprived by the unfinished monument of *Capital* (1867).

That the novel was a form of considerable pedagogic, as well as aesthetic, value was never lost on Marx. The aforementioned formulations clarify the fact that for Marx the specializations and reifications of modernity were pulling apart the fabric of human understanding, a process the novel resisted in its canny interweaving of instruction and eloquence, its mastery of the social field in its living unity. The question for us is what uses it may have been put to in the spread of Marx's own teachings. That *Capital* itself has novelistic qualities cannot be denied; the narrator of this vast textual construction, so lively and distinct a presence (especially when contrasted with the dry-as-dust properties of Smith's or Ricardo's prose), can scarcely refrain from novelistic modes of speech: from the playful prosopopoeia of commodities in Chapter One to the discomfiting allegoresis behind the idea that "the characters who appear on the economic stage are merely personifications of economic relations; it is as the bearers of these economic relations that they come into contact with each other," through comic parodies ("We see then that commodities are in love with money, but that 'the course of true love never did run smooth'"), salient metaphors ("Circulation sweats money from every pore"), and gothic shudders ("Capital is dead labor which, vampire-like, lives only by sucking living labor, and lives the more, the more labor it sucks"), to the grand omniscience of a Balzacian embrace—"Let us therefore, in company with the owner of money and the owner of labor-power, leave this noisy sphere, where everything takes place on the surface and in full view of everyone, and follow them into the hidden abode of production, on whose threshold there hangs the notice 'No admittance except on business'"—*Capital* is enlivened by a prodigious novelistic drive.[4]

That is not to say, however, that the principal lesson of this formidable contribution to knowledge is narrative in essence. Marxism doubtless enjoys certain narratological privileges over other politico-economic theories—as emphatically announced in the *Communist Manifesto* (1848), it delineates a past ("The history of all hitherto existing society is the history of class struggles"[5]), a present ("Society as a whole is more and more splitting into two great hostile camps, two great classes directly facing each other: Bourgeoisie and Proletariat"[6]), and one of two futures, either "the inevitable conquest of political power by the working class"[7] or "the common ruin of the contending classes."[8] Yet it would be obnoxious to contend that this powerful narrative dimension is anything more than a novelistic scaffolding erected around what is the nonnarrative core of Marx's method: the critique of political economy as such. This critique is precisely what distinguishes Marx not only from the economists to whom he applies his method but also from those novelists who, to that point, had been the premier mediators of "political and social truths," and who must now give way to an altogether more powerful mode of analysis. Critique is neither a story nor a terrain of moral indignation (Marx specifically warns against what he calls "an extraordinarily cheap kind of sentimentality"[9]); instead, it represents a total "rupture with every philosophical anthropology or humanism" and stands as "Marx's scientific discovery."[10] It can plausibly be suggested that the narrative moments of *Capital* are theoretically its weakest, and that Marx's method propelled him far from the home ground of that novelistic humanism which had prepared its development.

How, then, will Marx and Marxism enter the novel? We must posit two stages here: first, the tail-end realist phase of naturalism, where the absorptive capacities of the existing form are harnessed to accommodate this new theoretical accomplishment; and second, the modernist phase, during which the world-historical fact of really existing communism fast becomes a dense fold in the social fabric to which the novel must rapidly adapt. Marx is integral to the history of fictional naturalism and intermittently appears as a tutelary figure, as for instance in Zola's *L'Argent* (1891), where he is an acquaintance of the socialist Sigismond, and where a first edition of *Capital* is laid out on a table: "A great work indeed, ten years of the life of my master, Karl Marx, the book on capital that he has been promising us for so long! . . . And now here it is, here is our Bible!"[11] But this is not a Bible in any usual sense; "even when translated it would be properly understood only by a few initiates. It was not a work of propaganda. But what forceful logic, and what a triumphant abundance of proofs."[12] And therein lies the rub: a preponderance of logic over propagandistic force; a proof, not a pamphlet, and with none of a manifesto's catechistic succinctness. It is so much easier to deal with political organization and ideals than with the critique of political economy—as with the International Workingman's Association in London, about which Étienne enthuses in *Germinal* (1885): "Was not that a superb effort, a campaign in which justice would at last triumph? No more frontiers; the workers of the whole world rising and uniting to assure to the laborer the bread that he has earned."[13] Pressed to be more precise, however, matters begin to fray: "He explained it badly . . . in confused phrases which contained a little of all the theories he had successively passed through and abandoned. At the summit Karl Marx's idea remained standing: capital was the result of spoliation, it was the duty and the privilege of labor to reconquer that stolen wealth."[14] Beneath which summit, stolen phrases from Proudhon, Lassalle, and anonymous utopian socialists; nothing is more difficult for the novel to incorporate than the complex logic of historical materialism.

As witness that painfully ironic story of working life in Edwardian Mugsborough in Robert Tressell's *Ragged Trousered Philanthropists* (1914). Housepainter Frank Owen's disappointed efforts to raise the consciousness of his fellow workers, those "philanthropists" who unstintingly give of their very essence to maintain the wealth and privilege of their rulers, run into the usual wall of hostile indifference and wilful deference. In two remarkable chapters, fifteen and twenty-one, pressed by his fellow workers finally to answer the questions that preoccupy them, Owen agrees, and with a hand-drawn charcoal diagram and several chunks of bread begins to explain how money is the true cause of poverty. The demonstration, in which knives represent the means of production, coins represent capital, and bread represents wages, is as good an effort at distilling the labor theory of value and the capital relation as any in the literary tradition; yet the accent on representativity and the classroom ambience of the whole undertaking draw attention to what the episode is not: *novelistic*. "These represent the things which are produced by labor, aided by machinery, from the raw materials. We will suppose that three of these blocks represent—a week's work. We will suppose that a week's work is worth—one pound: and we will suppose that each of these ha'pennies is a sovereign."[15] And so it goes: Owen's laborious instruction requires a suspension of all other narrative business, a swerve to the didactic away from plot, intrigue, and character, and a degree of abstraction that mitigates novelistic concretion. The radioactive core of Marxism is something the novel can only fitfully tolerate, its aesthetically protective Geiger counters squealing warnings the while.

In the United States, naturalism and Marxism found a turbulent series of formal compromises in the works of Frank Norris, Upton Sinclair, and (later) Richard Wright; but the center of aesthetic gravity was shifting thanks to the concerted efforts of vanguard innovators Ezra Pound and Gertrude Stein. It is worth remembering that while Pound was taking English courses at Penn, and Stein was embroiled in her nine-year gestation of *The Making of Americans*, Sinclair was proving remarkably adept at incorporating a Marxist political education into his novels, as in *The Jungle*:

> And so all over the world two classes were forming, with an unbridged chasm between them,—the capitalist class, with its enormous fortunes, and the proletariat, bound into slavery by unseen chains. The latter were a thousand to one in numbers, but they were ignorant and helpless, and they would remain at the mercy of their exploiters until they were organized—until they had become "class-conscious."[16]

Jack London's dystopian *The Iron Heel* would similarly incorporate lengthy tracts of highly concentrated Marxist analysis and exhortation, as in this appeal to some machine-breakers:

> Let us not destroy those wonderful machines that produce efficiently and cheaply. Let us control them. . . . Let us run them for ourselves. Let us oust the present owners of the wonderful machines, and let us own the wonderful machines ourselves. That gentlemen, is socialism, a greater combination than the trusts.[17]

But by this point, one could safely say that such material is generally disposed in the text as so much *content*, ideological as any other, with bearings on the moral growth of a protagonist but with no significant repercussions at the level of *form*. And what Pound and Stein were about to adapt from the domain of painting (and sculpture) into literature was the principle that the real work to be done, in refashioning the arts for the twentieth century, was not in admitting more and more "stuff" within the realist frame, but in shattering the frame itself and rebuilding it from scratch.

In this, they took an unconscious cue from Marx himself, who had written that the "social revolution of the nineteenth century cannot draw its poetry from the past, but only from the future. . . . In order to arrive at its content, the revolution of the nineteenth century must let the dead bury their dead. There the phrase went beyond the content; here the content goes beyond the phrase."[18] The implications of this for our discussion are significant: if the "content" of the innovative literature of the twentieth century is in good part the earthquake set off by the successful Bolshevik revolution under Marx's name in Russia (1917, with its failed precursor in 1905)—including revolutionary sequences in many of the most advanced capitalist nations on earth—then this new content must push serious writing "beyond the phrase" of the settled forms of social narration. The novel, circa 1905, is constrained by various limiting conventions and the humanism encrypted in its DNA—specifically the conventions and ideology of that "splendid brotherhood of fiction-writers" whom Marx had hailed as his closest peers. To break the mould and make room for the "content" of theoretical and historical Marxism, the novel would have to *bury itself* in the sandpit of modernism. What Marx had set in train was nothing less than the conditions of modernism itself. This is the sense in which T. J. Clark intends his aphorism, "there could and can be no modernism without the practical possibility of an end to capitalism existing,"[19] and Perry Anderson's claim that one of the three "coordinates" of "the modernist conjuncture . . . was the imaginative proximity of social revolution."[20]

The problem being, of course, that revolution at the level of form is rarely coincident with socially revolutionary convictions, so that the aesthetic transformations of modernism were frequently undertaken by artists for whom Marxism was political anathema. Marx was thus all-too often reformatted into newly disparaged "content," even in texts that have *gone beyond the phrase*. Knut Hamsun, who (like so many modernists) would later espouse fondness for Hitler, stages a verbal battle between socialism (the character of Hansen) and conservatism (the doctor) in a scene from his proto-modernist novel, *Mysteries* (1892), which at this point morphs into that rather different thing, a "novel of ideas." After a lengthy discussion of Tolstoy, the doctor lets fly against socialist leaders:

> Take any of the socialist leaders! What kind of people are they? Shabby, scrawny types who sit around on wooden stools in their garrets, writing essays on how to improve the world! No one can question their integrity—who can fault Karl Marx on that score? But there he is, this Marx fellow, trying to write poverty out of existence! In theory, that is. Intellectually, he has analyzed every level of poverty, every degree of misery; his brain is full of all the sufferings of mankind. He dips his pen in ink and, full of ardor, writes page after fiery page, covers large sheets with figures, takes from the rich and gives to the poor, redistributes the wealth of the world, revolutionizes world economy, flings millions at the poor, who look up in astonishment. Nothing but science and theory! And then it turns out that in his naïveté he has begun with a false premise—namely, that all men are equal. Bah! What could be a bigger lie![21]

It is not that the text is obliged to identify with this tirade, but that the material settles into a familiar format: the detachable "bit," enjoying no organic consistency with the overarching concerns of the novel, other than as one more bone of ideological contention. But at least, in 1892, the name Marx could still be spoken openly. After 1917 the name itself, blackened by its association with the first successful revolution against the rule of capital, would rapidly fall foul of the censor and be subject to various encryptions and displacements in order to bypass the defenses of a bourgeois reading public.

The most significant exception to this rule is the case of John Dos Passos, of whom a contemporary once remarked that, responding to "Dos Passos' call" in the 1930s, "many of us now returned to reading *Das Kapital* and the brilliant historical analysis of *The Eighteenth Brumaire of Louis Napoleon*."[22] His masterpiece, the central novel of his U.S.A. trilogy, *1919* (1932), includes various references to and riffs upon the thought of Marx himself, nowhere more visibly than in the late narrative section on a young Jewish comrade, "Ben Compton." Here, the text is broken up and signposted by five choice passages, in italics, taken from Marx and Engels' *Communist Manifesto* (1848). Like so many of the narrative portions of *1919*, this one is a potted *Bildungsroman*, detailing the radical education and maturation of a fearless speechmaking communist. "Sunday afternoons he went to the library and read Marx's *Capital*. He joined the Socialist Party and went to lectures at the Rand School whenever he got a chance. He was working to be a wellsharpened instrument."[23] Correlating radical pedagogy and effective militancy, the weakly Compton not only survives a brutal assault on a IWW picnic by an armed mob, but rises to steely distinction in the national anti-capitalist movement. Has any novelist better captured the moment when an individual is gripped and overcome by a truth that is *in him more than him*?

> When his turn came to speak there'd be a moment when all the faces looking up at him would blur into a mass of pink, the hum of the hall would deafen him, he'd

be in a panic for fear he'd forgotten what he wanted to say. Then all at once he'd hear his own voice enunciating clearly and firmly, feel its reverberance along the walls and ceiling, feel ears growing tense, men and women leaning forward in their chairs, see the rown of faces quite clearly, the groups of people who couldn't find seats crowding at the doors. Phrases like *protest, massacron, united working-class of this country and the world, revolution*, would light up the eyes and faces under him like the glare of a bonfire.[24]

Whether or not he is named, however, Marx inevitably suffered indelicate misrepresentations from the virulent anti-communism of many modernists. What is more interesting is that underneath that explicit condemnation, deeper formal and political affinities are discharged and acquitted—affinities that suggest Marx's critical structural place at the very epicenter of the modernist revolt. In the most openly anti-communist effort of that lifelong stalwart of the cause, *The Revenge for Love* (1937), Wyndham Lewis stages a botched seduction-confrontation between bourgeois *salon*-revolutionary "Gillian Communist" and the honest-to-goodness "real thing," the one-legged workingman communist agitator, Percy Hardcaster. For Gillian, communism is above all a matter of the personal, a matter of ethics:

> No thoughts hidden away from you brother-biped but all laid naked to inspection, share and share alike: so that no one could say that anyone was keeping anything away from anyone else, or claiming they had a *self*, as she put it. . . . So nothing must be *kept back* and *locked up*, like a private possession, which is all the self is, she said.[25]

But this crudely bohemian *détournement* of the principles of scientific socialism are a mere preparation for the gloves-off, Strindbergian "battle of the brains" to follow, a misogynist agon all the more satisfying for the naked openness this "mental communism" makes possible.[26] Gillian's parlor "communism" effects significant changes at the level of characterization and dramatization, allowing Lewis to propel "this Communist girl born in the ambassadorial purple" like a bullet at the extreme "misanthropic cynicism" of Hardcatser's militancy, without any of the English civility or restraint that might otherwise drive the political unconscious of the encounter under the surface in a typical English novel.[27] Her mortified vanity, his shame and humiliation, all out fatally in the open—and with it their radical class differences, bringing home the ultimate state of the class struggle to this *salon* farce. Hardcaster's speech to her is one of the most perceptive Marxist analyses of the intrication of the "personal" and the "political" in all fiction:

> For it is *me*, as a member of the working-class [on whose behalf *all* revolution is *supposed* to be set in motion], that *you*, as an enlightened member of the owning-class . . . are *supposed* to be getting so excited about—though, as I am not entirely incapable of putting two and two together, I see quite well that is what you would call *bluff*. Why then—you are about to ask me—do I throw in my lot with proletarian

revolution; or continue in it, once my eyes are opened to the true meaning of all this disturbance—this *class-war* as the greatest middle-class theorist called it? Because, in spite of yourself, you cannot help benefitting us. You are tearing each other to pieces in any case ... if it ever comes to a showdown and if there's a bit of a shoot-up, it will be a matter of complete indifference to me *which* of you—whether you "communist" intellectuals, you fancy salon-revolutionaries, you old-school-tie pinks, or on the other hand your fascist first-cousins—are wiped out.[28]

In spite of himself, Lewis, too, seems unable to "contain" Marxism within the confines of his categorical assault on its principles without giving the devil ("the greatest middle-class theorist") his due. The result is a newly militarized fictional characterology, with all the dramatic personae's darker motivations and antipathies laid bare along the axis of class difference and fruitfully dynamized by the endless friction of that struggle. Humanism has nowhere to hide in the space of this novel, whose modernism is what that absence looks like—a stark, satirical patchwork of brutalities and savage indictments, unleavened by sentiment. A Marxist image of the ruling class.

So, while we may look in vain for overt signs of Marx's legacy in the canonical modernist novels of Woolf, Conrad, Faulkner, and James (who would no more mention Marx than describe a fart), it seems that we have to look for those legacies elsewhere, in the underlying presuppositions of the new approach to form: the decentered character spaces, the wayward or nonexistent plot-lines, the efflorescence of new affective intensities, the inability to close, the sense of a style—none of which has any clear correspondence to the tenets of historical materialism, but all of which are implicated in the thoroughgoing redistribution of aesthetic functions and protocols that Marx made possible in his "poetry of the future." For once the prototypical centrality of the middle-class "self" to fictional procedures is subjected to the topsy-turvy object lesson of *really existing communism*, the novel is unhinged from its presumed documentary function, its humanistic impulse to collate and mediate, and implicated directly in the effort to make a new world out of the ruins of capitalism (which was, and remains, the form's material bedrock).

No novel worked harder at this than James Joyce's *Ulysses* (1922). There is no mistaking the thunderous political climax of the book, at Kiernan's pub, when the towering six-foot ad canvasser, wielding his mighty cigar, serves his choice riposte to the anti-Semitic jeers of the Citizen: "—Mendelssohn was a jew and Karl Marx and Mercadante and Spinoza. And the Saviour was a jew and his father was a jew. Your God."[29] This happy volley of cosmopolitan philosemitism cements Marx in a living tradition of freethinking, dissenting Jewish sages and artists that vouchsafe the vital centrality of Jewish intellectual and spiritual gifts to Western civilization—a tradition in which Bloom openly places himself: "a jew like me."[30] Later on Bloomsday, as the mobile phantasmagoria of Nighttown establishes its Circean provenance, Bloom again finds himself channeling the spirit of the founder of scientific socialism—at least in its more populist accents: "Machines is their cry, their chimera, their panacea. Laborsaving apparatuses, supplanters, bugbears, manufactured monsters for mutual murder, hideous hobgoblins produced by a horde of capitalistic lusts upon our prostituted labor. The poor man starves while they are grassing their royal mountain stags or shooting peasants and phartridges in their purblind pomp of pelf and power"[31] Finally, amid the deep exhaustion of Eumaeus, Bloom quips to Stephen on the occasion of his inebriated charity toward young Corley, "Everyone according to his needs and everyone according to his deeds," which is a free (and clumsy) adaptation of the famous aphorism from Marx's *Critique of the Gotha Program* (1875).[32] Joyce, a socialist, knew very well what he was doing in setting up this recurrent association between the modern hero of his new epic and the author of *Das Kapital*, whose revolutionary prescriptions for a broken bourgeois social order chime well with the all-out war against formal proprieties that *Ulysses* represents.

If Joyce and Dos Passos stand as the Anglophone novelists most open to the "storm blowing from Paradise"[33] that was Marx's poetry of the future, perhaps the greatest upsurge of Marxian-utopian thinking took place in Soviet Russia, in the subgeneric depths of science fiction, where pulp writers like Nikolai F. Fyodorov, Valery Bryusov, and Alexander Bolgdanov blended the materialism of Marx and the engineering genius of Konstantin Tsiolkovsky, to provoke the more mature talents of Andrei Platonov, the Strugatsky Brothers, and Stanislaw Lem into scaling the very heights of speculative fiction. Marx's legacy in the rich tradition of Soviet science fiction is, if not his most enduring fictional imprint, then certainly his most inventive and incandescent, in the one sociopolitical climate on earth that was prepared to endorse and celebrate his immense intellectual achievement. It is a testament to the untapped value of this neglected seam that Roberto Bolaño, in his final work, should devote a memorable section to the provincial Jew, Ansky, who travels to the capital, meets the Bolshevik pulp writer Efraim Ivanov, and enters a creative pact with that spent force, penning a string of timeless masterpieces. It is the fertile admixture of Ivanov's formulaic communist faith and the young man's "peculiar ideas, his Siberian visions, his forays into cursed lands, the plenitude of wild experience,"[34] that push them beyond the formal confines of even continental modernism, to emerge (in the fictionalized words of Maxim Gorky) as "better than Jules Verne. A more . . . mature writer. A writer guided by . . . revolutionary instincts. A . . . great writer. As one could only expect of a . . . Communist."[35] Perhaps the fullest picture of Marx's place in the modern novel lies here, in this speculative image of unwritten sci-fi masterpieces tossed off by bibliophile Jewish Bolsheviks under the red light falling from the proximate star of an achievable, now dormant, future.

Notes

1 Marx and Engels, *On Literature and Art*, 339.
2 Marx and Engels, *On Literature and Art*, 313, 91.
3 Marx and Engels, *On Literature and Art*, 439.
4 Marx, *Capital* vol. 1, 143–4, 176–7, 179, through comic parodies ("We see then that commodities are in love with money, but that 'the course of true love never did run smooth'" 202), salient metaphors ("Circulation sweats money from every

pore" 208), and gothic shudders ("Capital is dead labor which, vampire-like, lives only by sucking living labor, and lives the more, the more labor it sucks," 324), to the grand omniscience of a Balzacian embrace—"Let us therefore, in company with the owner of money and the owner of labor-power, leave this noisy sphere, where everything takes place on the surface and in full view of everyone, and follow them into the hidden abode of production, on whose threshold there hangs the notice 'No admittance except on business'" (279–80)—*Capital* is enlivened by a prodigious novelistic drive.

5   Marx and Engels, "Manifesto of the Communist Party," 473.
6   Marx and Engels, "Manifesto of the Communist Party," 474.
7   Marx, *Capital* vol, 1, 619.
8   Marx and Engels, "Manifesto of the Communist Party," 474.
9   Marx, *Capital* vol 1, 1277.
10 Althusser, *For Marx*, 227.
11 Émile Zola, *Money*, trans. Valerie Minogue (Oxford: Oxford University Press, 2014), 262.
12 Zola, *Money*, 262.
13 Zola, *Germinal*, trans. Larry Duff (London: Wordsworth Classics, 2007), 129.
14 Zola, *Germinal*, 218.
15 Robert Tressell, *The Ragged Trousered Philanthropists*. http://www.gutenberg.org/files/3608/3608-h/3608-h.htm#chap21, accessed August 20, 2019.
16 Upton Sinclair, *The Jungle*, ed. Russ Castronovo (Oxford: Oxford University Press), 262.
17 Jack London, *The Iron Heel* (London: Penguin, 2006), 98.
18 Marx, "The Eighteenth Brumaire of Louis Bonaparte," 597.
19 Clark, *Farewell to an Idea*, 9.
20 Anderson, *A Zone of Engagement*, 34.
21 Knut Hamsun, *Mysteries*, trans. Gerry Bothmer (New York: Farrar, Strauss, Giroux, 2006), 193.
22 Matthew Josephson, *Infidel in the Temple: A Memoir of the Nineteen-Thirties* (New York: Knopf, 1968), 66, 68. "Returned" may be a stretch here.
23 John Dos Passos, *1919* in *U.S.A.* (New York: Library of America, 1996), 725.
24 Dos Passos, *1919*, 732.
25 Wyndham Lewis, *The Revenge for Love*, ed. Reed Way Dasenbrock (Santa Rosa: Black Sparrow Press, 1991), 179.
26 Lewis, *The Revenge for Love*, 179.
27 Lewis, *The Revenge for Love*, 187–9.
28 Lewis, *The Revenge for Love*, 195.
29 James Joyce, *Ulysses* (London: Penguin, 1992), 444–5.
30 Joyce, *Ulysses*, 445.
31 Joyce, *Ulysses*, 602.
32 Joyce, *Ulysses*, 713.
33 Benjamin, "Theses on the Philosophy of History" in *Illuminations*, 257.
34 Bolaño, *2666*, 713.
35 Bolaño, *2666*, 718.

10

Marx and Modernist Poetry

Kristin Grogan

Reading American poetry from the 1930s reminds us that Marxism gave us not lone, singular poems, but an entire culture of verse committed to the project of reimagining the world. This chapter focuses on the Depression-era work of Lorine Niedecker, Langston Hughes, and Muriel Rukeyser, three leftist American poets whose writing was nourished by the productive political-cultural soil of that decade—a decade of class and anti-racist militancy in which poetry enjoyed a rich, perhaps unmatched, cultural relevance.[1] Political journals and mainstream presses alike printed verse, pamphlets were published in large print runs, poems were quoted in strike bulletins and on picket lines and broadcast on the radio. American labor literature thrived, building on the tradition of work songs that had emerged in an earlier period of class militancy—the late nineteenth century—and which in addition to their oral transmission had been popularly distributed in print since the early twentieth century.[2] In the decade following the 1929 crash, certain poets wrote verse that married many of the stylistic innovations of the European and transatlantic avant-gardes—free verse, rhythmic play and metrical innovation, and fragmentation, among others—with homegrown proletarian cultural traditions. In the 1930s and into the 1940s, Lorine Niedecker wrote poetry that draws on both folk and oral culture and modernist concision to critique financialization and the Depression's immiseration of the rural working class. In the same period, Langston Hughes traveled to Russia and China, where he wrote revolutionary verse informed by the Soviet avant-gardes that called forth an international proletarian army. And, in "The Book of the Dead" (1938), Muriel Rukeyser elaborated a documentary poetics that detailed the murderous violence of profit extraction and articulated the responsibilities of Marxist poetic work. All three poets wrote formally responsive verse, engaging with their historical moment alongside their activism by working with and against received poetic forms. To that end, the poets under study here are all interested in forms that are the "common property" of readers and writers: popular forms with histories of collective cultural ownership and/or anonymous authorship, such as Niedecker's nursery rhymes, Hughes' ballads, and Rukeyser's interest in the collective social responsibility of the journalist.[3] The relationship between the individual and the collective, as Raymond Williams reminds us, is a question of literary form, for the "problem of form," he argues, is "a problem of the relations between social (collective) modes and individual projects."⁴ I am interested here in a strain of poetics that is less about the difficulty and obscurity we commonly associate with poetic modernism than in a poetics that sets its sights toward the mass, the popular, and the collective. At the same time, I follow Christopher Nealon's example in *The Matter of Capital* (2011) to steer away from a hard distinction between "form" and "content," and to think instead of capital as not only subject matter but "subject matter given different forms, and expressed as different kinds of content—abridged, abstracted, translated, revised."⁵

This is by no means the whole story of the 1930s, and certainly not of Marxism's imprint on modernist poetry. We only have to turn to Bertolt Brecht or André Breton to see Marxist poetry on the continent or to spend any time with a Mayakovsky lyric to see it within its native revolutionary milieu. As modernist critics have shown, North American poetry beyond the bounds of this chapter was keenly attuned to Marxism. Ruth Jennison argues that Objectivism, spearheaded by Zukofsky and including Niedecker, George Oppen, Charles Reznikoff, and Carl Rakosi, should be treated "as a distinct revolutionary current within modernist poetics, whose practitioners' diverse oppositionalities informed their avant-garde experiments."⁶ Mark Steven argues for the centrality of the modern epic to poetic modernism's engagement with communism, in the poetry of Ezra Pound, William Carlos Williams, and Louis Zukofsky.⁷ In the UK, we feel Marx's imprint on Hugh MacDiarmid and David Gascoyne and, later in the century, in the late modernism of Cambridge School. And this is to say nothing of the Marxist and communist poetry that thrived in Latin America, the Caribbean, or of revolutionary Chinese poetry. Nevertheless, in American poetry from the 1930s we feel the most fully realized imprint of Marxism on Anglo-American poetry, in verse that articulated the impossibility of life in the United States under capitalism and offered us a vision of how it might be lived otherwise.

Niedecker's Depression Lyrics

We begin with a five-line lyric by Lorine Niedecker:

I doubt I'll get silk stockings out
of my asparagus
that grows too fast to stop it
or any pair of Capital's
miracles of profit.⁸

In 1946, Niedecker published *New Goose*, a collection of poems she had written over the previous decade. Some were composed during her period of employment by the New Deal's Works Progress Administration as a researcher and writer for the Federal Writers' Project; she worked on the "American Guide" series, helping to produce *Wisconsin: A Guide to the Badger State* (1941). In *New Goose*, as well as in her unpublished poems from this period, Niedecker shifts away from her early surrealist poems and toward a committed localism. These poems describe farmers, sharecroppers, fishermen, unemployment, and rural poverty, all with a deep investment in the rural economics of Wisconsin and the folk culture of the state's citizens. During this period she was also regularly communicating with Louis Zukofsky, who sent her copies of New Masses and the Daily Worker, and her personal library suggests that around this time she was reading a number of books printed by International Publishers in the 1930s, including Marx and Engels' correspondence (1936), Engels' *Herr Eugen Duhring's Revolution in Science* (1939), Emile Burns' *A Handbook of Marxism* (1935), and Anna Rochester's *Rulers of America* (1936).

Silk stockings, the poem's ostensible subject, were indeed a profit-churning miracle, and the average woman bought ten to fifteen pairs before nylon stockings were introduced to American markets in May 1940.[9] This poem heaps irony on the miraculous. On the face of it, "I doubt I'll get silk stockings" expresses an anxiety about the C–M–C transaction, wherein commodities are exchanged only in order to acquire the money to purchase other commodities. Here the worry is about whether or not enough asparagus of a high enough quality will be grown and sold in order for stockings to be bought. Niedecker reckons with exchange-value and its system of equivalence in the poem's sonic play. In "stockings" we hear "stalks," an echo that sets up the exchange that the speaker will make between the two; we also hear "stocks," which begins the poem's comparison between agricultural life and the stock market. Like the stock market, the asparagus grows too fast. In the Midwest, asparagus is an early season crop which, as Michelle Niemann points out in her reading of the poem, runs the risk of growing to seed if it grows too quickly in warm weather.[10] Asparagus thus becomes a way of thinking about both the unmanageable growth that preceded the stock market crash and the irrationality and waste within market capitalism, in which too much asparagus is grown while immiserated humans are left to starve. The risk and uncertainty, disguised as confidence, of too-rapid growth maps onto the poem's unifying slant rhyme on "stop it" and "profit." The poem's one perfect rhyme, between "doubt" and "out," collapses with the enjambment into the second line and the metrical inelegance of the word "asparagus." Things grow too quickly: asparagus grows too fast, stock markets crash, and we might not find the right word, or the perfect rhyme, to prevent it. By the time the stock market collapsed on October 29, 1929, a decade of rampant speculation and proliferation of investment, trusts, and bank loans had created enormous amounts of fictitious capital. Fictitious capital, Marx explained, is "a title to value"; it is value that takes the form of credit, shares, and speculation; it cannot be converted into commodities, and its catastrophic collapse is inevitable.[11] Equally inevitable following overproduction is unemployment, as capital creates its "reserve army of labor" both to expand industry and to reduce production costs, not least of all as a disciplinary measure utilized both as threat and in real against employed labor. What the poem seems to understand, then, is that unemployment is structural, not aberrant: a constitutive element of capitalist industry.

This poem is short, slight, and self-effacing. With its sing-song rhythm and central rhyme, it draws on the tradition of the nursery rhyme. Niedecker's response to an anxiety about the scale and unknowability of the financial system is an ironic turn to a poetics of smallness and self-erasure. The poem that immediately follows in the collection moves from doubt to deceit:

> To see the man who took care of our stock
> as we slept in the dark, the blackbirds flying
> high as the market out of our pie,
> I travel now at crash of day
> on the el, a low rush of geese over those below,
> to see the man who smiled
> and gave us a first-hand country shake. (103)

At "crash of day," another financial pun, the speaker travels on an elevated railway to see "the man who took care of our stock / as we slept in the dark." In "stock" we hear livestock—perhaps the man was charged with temporary care for a farmer's livestock—as well as suggesting the fictitious capital of the pre-crash stock market. In this case the man is a stockbroker who comes to stand in for the irresponsibility of a class of finance professionals, and even more broadly, for the speculation responsible for the crash. The poem thus moves from individual ethical responsibility to a critique of system forces.

This poem is more obviously a nursery rhyme; it rewrites "Sing a Song of Sixpence" in the language of finance. The undead blackbirds that sing when the pie is opened, despite having been baked—the rhyme's central horror—fly instead of sing, "high as the market of our pie." That nursery rhyme is a fable of ruling class consumption: "wasn't that a tasty dish / to set before a king?" it ends, with some variations swapping out "dainty" for "tasty." In Niedecker's poem, the king becomes a smooth, smiling stockbroker who delivers a "first-hand country shake." "Hand" slips into "shake": perhaps the man's handshake is "first-hand," an example of a genuine, unmediated, and shared country sociality, which sits in opposition to what is second-hand, or sold-off. But I would suggest that the poem's irony settles around that final line and in the disjunction between the speaker who "slept in the dark" and the creepy reassurance of the man's smile and too-sure handshake, an action which suggests the exploitation of sociality. I also hear a suggestion of "shakedown" in that final word. Comparably, Marx's word for the accumulation of fictitious capital was "swindle": writing about the English commercial crash of 1847, he describes how "the entire business community in a country can be caught up in a swindling of this kind."[12] If we read the poem this way—if "country shake" becomes a "country shakedown," a swindle—then the poem articulates, first, the swindling of an entire country and especially its rural poor by the financial class and, second, how rural economies and rural citizens, gathered together under the banner of "the country," were shaken down by metropolitan finance. Niedecker's nursery rhymes give life to the swindle Marx describes.

This, then, is a tale of Depression-era financial deception, and a poetics that attempts to represent the invisible mechanics of capitalism and its inbuilt crises. For Jennison, poetry is a genre that owes its "force" to "the figural and the unseen," and this force makes it "uniquely suited to represent a world financial system that is increasingly conducted in an invisible manner."[13] The nursery rhyme dramatizes the limits of knowledge. Rhymes are made for children, and they work with a child's understanding of the world, which they elaborate into verses that are often uncanny, strange, or surreal, and very often violent. They are also pedagogical, offering moral lessons to children and, often, warnings. Niedecker's nursery rhymes work with this tradition, asking us to sit with the deliberately limited knowledge and obfuscation that was keenly felt at the depths of the Depression. Our next poet, in contrast, works in a countervailing mode, toward a poetics of full disclosure.

Hughes' 'Song of the Revolution'

Where Niedecker focused her poetic gaze on the local and rural, Langston Hughes turned his sights outward, moving from the anti-racist struggles localized in the United States toward global revolution and the struggles of the international proletariat. Hughes' early poetry described the collective life of Harlem, and in his sophomore collection, *Fine Clothes to the Jew* (1927) he turned his attention to labor. His blues poems from the volume describe the lives of busboys, elevator attendants, porters, and other contingent workers. In the early 1930s, his solidarity with labor intensified and his interest in collective life sharpened into a commitment to proletarian internationalism if not yet Marxism proper, which would evolve through the next decade. This sharpening occurred as a result of an eighteen-month period spent in Soviet Russia. Hughes arrived in Moscow in 1932 as part of a group of African Americans hired to make a film about race relations in the South. After the film project was abandoned, Hughes traveled on to China. These experiences form the basis of much of the poetry he wrote in that decade, some of which was collected in his 1938 pamphlet, *A New Song*, printed by the International Workers' Order in a run of 10,000, with an introduction by Mike Gold, editor of *New Masses*. The final poem in *A New Song*, entitled "Union," dramatizes the development of Hughes' poetics from the 1920s to the 1930s and the process of developing a collective consciousness: "Not me alone— / I know now— / But the whole world oppressed / . . . Must put their hands with mine."[14] In those clasping hands, we also see the full scale of Hughes' 1930s internationalism. Not just an interpersonal union, or a named trade union, the union to which the poem's title refers is a global proletariat who will join together and bring about a world revolution.

Many of the poems from this period borrow the visual language and theatrical techniques of the Soviet avant-gardes. Other poems make a move in the opposite direction, toward forms that are familiar, received, and well known. Take, for example, "Song of the Revolution," an uncollected poem from this period:

> Sing me a song of the Revolution
> Marching like fire over the world,
> Weaving from the earth its bright red banner
> For the hands of the masses to unfurl. (232)

So continues the poem's "thunderous shout: / Filled with the strength of youth and laughter." The poem is dominated by gerunds, which describe the action of the personified revolution—its "marching," "weaving," ending," and, in three anaphoric lines, "Breaking the bonds of the darker races / Breaking the chains that have held for years / Breaking the barriers dividing the people." But the poem doesn't break; it generates, and it gathers, in the evenness of its quatrains, its abcb rhyme scheme, and the metrical evenness, dominated by trochaic gerunds. The poem's final stanza describes the "flame of the Revolution" cutting "Fear from the world like a surgeon's knife, / So that the children of all creation / Waken, at last, to the joy of life." Rhyme etches these stanzas into memory and gives them the quality of song. Hughes' calls for global revolution, which he figures repeatedly with the language of destruction, comes in forms that are marked for their stability and evenness. In those final lines, the severity of the "surgeon's knife" is counterbalanced, and perhaps blunted, by the "joy of life" with which it rhymes. That rhyme also reinvests the "knife" with the "joy of life," and so makes an argument for revolution.

These poems are manifestos; as such, they are also invitations. In "Good Morning Revolution," another uncollected poem from this period, Hughes addresses the revolution, personifying it as "the very best friend / I ever had" (224). In his 1930s poetics, Hughes plays with a literal re- or perhaps an over-familiarization, inviting us to greet the revolution as a friend or as kin, to share an intimate space. Yet in changing the category of the revolution from event to person it asks us to conceive of it anew, and the revolution into our lives as vital, organic, and fully embodied. The speaker and the revolution are "buddies," they'll "pal around together from now on," and the poem takes a correspondingly loose style as it invites us to join it in seizing the means of production. "We can take everything," Hughes tells us: "Factories, arsenals, houses, ships, /Railroads, forests, fields, orchards, / Bus lines, telegraphs, radios." "Everything," Hughes repeats, "turn 'em over for the people who work. / Rule and run 'em for us people who work." This call to seize the means of production will be internationally broadcast and cosigned by workers the world over:

Sign it: China
Sign it: Africa
Sign it: Poland
Sign it: Italy
Sign it: America
Sign it with one name: Worker.

Compare Hughes' lines of international revolutionary abundance, registered formally in his lists and his anaphoric lines, to Niedecker's stripped-down descriptions of Midwestern devastation and her poem's refusal to quite make their meanings available to us. Hughes is a maximalist, invested in arguing against artificial scarcity and class-based luxury. In his chants, scripts, and manifestos, he summons an avenging proletarian army who will bring about the abolition of class and inaugurate instead a type of communal luxury. These poems, then, argue for a global revolutionary fight against immiseration, which counters "any notion of the sharing of misery with a distinctly different kind of world: one where everyone, instead, would have his or her share of the best."[15]

Rukeyser's Elegy for Labor

In *The Romance of American Communism* (1978), Vivian Gornick describes the intense emotional lives of the American communists. Gornick writes:

> [The communists] were like everybody else, only more so. What was in them is in all of us, only more so. In them, as in the artist, the proportions of response were writ large. In them, the major spiritual and intellectual currents of their time ran strong instead of weak. . . I think it can safely be said: They feared, hungered, and cared *more*. They were indifferent to nothing, they had opinions on everything, they responded with intensity.[16]

The accusation of feeling in greater quantities and with more intensity is one that is frequently leveled against poets. Our final poet shows how Marxism invests a certain strain of modernist poetry with an intensely felt and collectively held political emotion. Muriel Rukeyser's first collection, *Theory of Flight* (1935), is just such an example. Published when she was twenty-one years old and after she had taken flying lessons, the book's governing metaphor of flight invests it with an ecstatic drive toward freedom: "no more horizons now / no more unvisioned capes, no death; we fly." *Theory of Flight* ends with an orgasmic Joycean command to join in this utopian project: "Say yes, people. / Say yes. YES."[17]

In her second collection, *U.S. 1* (1938), Rukeyser shifts her sights from an ecstatic ode of human potential to an elegy for living labor. The first section of that book, "The Book of the Dead," is a multifarious long poem about the Hawks Nest Tunnel "disaster," an instance of murderous profit extraction. In West Virginia in the early 1930s, a subsidiary of Union Carbide employed workers to dig a tunnel for a hydroelectric project. During the excavation workers found silica, which they were instructed to mine without any protective equipment. Breathing in crystalline silica with no protection meant that hundreds—possibly thousands, the exact number is unknown—of workers died from silicosis, a disease that causes lesions in the lungs. The majority of workers were African Americans from the South. A congressional hearing was held five years after the first silicosis case appeared among the workers. No action was taken against the companies responsible for the deaths.

"The Book of the Dead" has frequently been called a documentary poem; that descriptor underplays just how formally varied the poem is. It encompasses styles from blues songs to lyric addresses, makes uses of testimony from victims and survivors, uses doctors' reports and court transcripts. It draws on Rukeyser's journalistic skill—in 1932 she covered the Scottsboro trial, and in 1930 she would write for the *Daily Worker*, *New Masses*, and other leftist magazines—and on her felicity with metaphor and conceit that she had started to develop in *Theory of Flight*. In "The Book of the Dead" the governing metaphors of glass—which is made from silica—allows Rukeyser to think through problems of transparency and knowledge but also breath, which becomes a figure for a basic access to life. The poem is strikingly similar to chapter ten of *Capital* (1867), "The Working Day," in which Marx's critique moves between excoriation of capital's murderous contempt for human life and elegy for the industrial dead. "Capital asks no questions about the length of life of labor-power," and it obtains its objective of maximizing labor power in a given day "by shortening the life of labor-power."[18] "What experience shows to the capitalist generally," Marx writes, "is a constant excess of population, i.e., an excess in relation to the momentary requirements of surplus-labor-absorbing capital, although this excess is made up of generations of human beings stunted, short-lived, swiftly replacing each other, plucked, so to say, before maturity."[19] He continues:

> And indeed, experience shows to the intelligent observer how rapidly and firmly capitalist production has seized the vital forces of the people at their very roots, although historically speaking it hardly dates from yesterday. Experience shows too how the degeneration of the industrial population is retarded only by the constant absorption of primitive and natural elements from the countryside, and how even the agricultural laborers, in spite of the fresh air and the "principle of natural selection" that works so powerfully amongst them, and permits the survival of only the strongest individuals, are already beginning to die off.[20]

Many of Marx's examples are drawn from glass manufacture and throughout the chapter he pays attention to breath and access to fresh air. He describes London milliners having access to one third of the cubic feet of air they require, not only in their workroom but also their "stifling" bedrooms, such that a doctor would report that the twenty-year-old Mary Anne Walkley died from over work and poor ventilation.[21] "Capital therefore takes no account of the health and the length of life of the worker, unless society forces it to do so," we read. "Its answer to the outcry about the physical and mental degradation, the premature death, the torture of over-work, is this: Should that pain trouble us, since it increases our pleasure (profit)?" "The Book of the Dead" responds to this; its task is to force attention upon the crimes of murderous capital, and like *Capital* it does so through acts of documentary ventriloquism.

I have called "The Book of the Dead" an elegy for labor; it is also an argument about the labor of the poet. A documentary poetics draws attention to the poet's labor—the work of recording speech, of collecting, sorting, and redacting documents, and of spinning verse from this material. This is a poetics that doesn't smooth over its rough edges or close its gaps; instead of participating in the poetic fiction that poems are miraculously smooth, perfect objects, "The Book of the Dead" presents itself as the product of immense labor. At the same time, it also doesn't make a familiar implicit—or explicit—argument for the equivalency of the poet's labor to manual work. Rather, the poem suggests the work that poets can do for labor. A titular poem closes the sequence with a five-page series of tercets, which offers itself up to the murdered workers and makes a declaration for the political work of the poet:

> What two things shall never be seen?
> They : what we did. Enemy : what we mean.

This is a nation's scene and halfway house.
What three things can never be done?
Forget. Keep silent. Stand alone.
The hills of glass, the fatal brilliant plain.[22]

The poem seeks to make visible the "things that shall never be seen." The question that begins the second stanza implies another question: what three things can and must be done? And it offers its own answers. Remember. Speak. Stand together. It elaborates:

Carry abroad the urgent need, the scene,
To photograph and to extend the voice,
to speak this meaning.

Voices speak to us directly. As we move.
As we enrich, growing in larger motion,
This word, this power.[23]

The "Voices" that begin the second stanza suggest both the voice of poetry and the voice of labor. "As we enrich" might be self-reflexive (as we are enriched), or it might follow on to the next line: as we enrich this word. In the latter reading, the poem is asking for an amplification of poetry, to invest it with world-changing power. The end of the poem moves from individual experience and testimony to class solidarity and an intimation of the poet's role. The poet's responsibility is both as participant and mouthpiece. Poetry stands here in service to labor. "The word, this power": the caesura that cuts this line makes a forceful equivalence between its constituent halves. Another Rukeyser poem from the period, "Homage to Literature," describes an intense and uncanny sunset, "the lake of sunset as it runs / boiling," "sea beyond sea after unbearable suns," before telling us that "poems fixed this landscape." Rukeyser's meaning is twofold: poetic description fixes landscape in place, it secures and immortalizes the momentary. At the same time, poems mend, repair, and cure landscape; they have a responsibility toward the things they describe. From Niedecker's attention to financial swindling (in which we hear a call for justice for the rural victims of the Depression) through Hughes' revolutionary internationalism to Rukeyser's galvanizing elegy, these poems are convinced of the revolutionary potential of poetry. Marxist poets sought to invest modernist technique with world-changing power, and set their sights far beyond the poem. Rukeyser makes this point once more in the final line of her poem "Night-Music." That poem described a demonstration and its aftermath, "the few jailed, / the march stampeded, the meeting stopped," and they move to "rooms where horror ends, / strike-songs are sung."[24] After its quatrains, a single line stands alone: "Make music out of night will change the night."[25] The line's effect lies in its verbal strangeness, for what should be an infinite—"to make music out of night"—becomes an imperative instead, as command and consequence are folded into one another. By switching from infinitive to imperative the poem begins with a spondee rather an iamb, bursting from the crisis of its present into the revolutions of the future.

Notes

1 The conditions that created the richness of this period have been well documented—see above all Michael Denning, *The Cultural Front: The Laboring of American Culture in the Twentieth Century* (London: Verso, 2010).
2 See, for example, the first printing of the I.W.W.'s *Little Red Songbook* in 1909. For a collection of labor poetry from the 1930s, see John Marsh, ed. *You Work Tomorrow: An Anthology of American Labor Poetry, 1929-41* (Ann Arbor: The University of Michigan Press, 2010).
3 Williams, *Marxism and Literature* (Oxford: Oxford University Press, 1977), 188.
4 Williams, *Marxism and Literature*, 187.
5 Christopher Nealon, *The Matter of Capital: Poetry and Crisis in the American Century* (Cambridge, MA: Harvard University Press, 2012).
6 Jennison, *The Zukofsky Era*, 5.
7 See Steven, *Red Modernism: American Poetry and the Spirit of Communism* (Baltimore: Johns Hopkins University Press, 2017).
8 Lorine Niedecker, *Collected Works*, ed. Jenny Penberthy (Berkeley: University of California Press, 2002), 103.
9 Lawrence B. Glickman, "'Make Lisle the Style': The Politics of Fashion in the Japanese Silk Boycott, 1937-1940," *Journal of Social History* 38:3 (2005): 579.
10 Michelle Niemann, "Towards an Ecopoetics of Food: Plants, Agricultural Politics, and Colonized Landscapes in Lorine Niedecker's Condensery," *Modernism/Modernity* 25:1 (2018): 143–4.
11 Marx, *Capital* vol. 3, 641.
12 Marx, *Capital* vol. 3, 533.
13 Jennison, "29 | 73 | 08: Poetry, Crisis, and a Hermeneutics of Limits," *Mediations* 28.2 (2015).
14 Langston Hughes, *Collected Works: The Poems 1921-1940*, ed. Arnold Rampersad (Columbia and London: University of Missouri Press), 150.
15 Kristin Ross, *Communal Luxury: The Political Imaginary of the Paris Commune* (London: Verso, 2016), 65.
16 Vivian Gornick, *The Romance of American Communism* (New York: Basic Books, 1977), 22.
17 Muriel Rukeyser, "Theory of Flight," in *The Collected Poems of Muriel Rukeyser* (Pittsburgh: University of Pittsburgh Press, 2005), 47.
18 Marx, *Capital* vol. I, 376.
19 Marx, *Capital* vol. I, 380.
20 Marx, *Capital* vol. I, 380.
21 Marx, *Capital* vol. I, 365.
22 Rukeyser, "The Book of the Dead," in *The Collected Poems*, 107.
23 Rukeyser, "The Book of the Dead," 110.
24 Rukeyser, "The Book of the Dead," 128.
25 Rukeyser, "The Book of the Dead," 128.

11

Marx and Cinema

Angelos Koutsourakis

Classical Marxism embodied a political vision that could complete the unfinished Enlightenment project and overcome the contradictions of modernity, the tensions between town and country, the proliferation of poverty through the accumulation of wealth, and the simultaneous production of development and underdevelopment. Aesthetic modernism reacted against tradition as well as the division of labor between artists and consumers of art that characterized bourgeois society. In prioritizing the labor of style, modernism necessitates the labor of the reader and audience, challenging the neat separations between art and social life putting forward the idea of "art as material intervention."[1] The ultimate dream of modernism is its desire to come to terms with the real by refusing its unreflective reproduction. The emergence of cinema as an art form for the masses reliant on collective labor comes at a pertinent time in history when modernism seeks to reclaim art as part and parcel of social life. No other art form at the time was more suited to accomplish such a project, given that cinema was a new art that did not require literacy skills and could thus easily address a mass audience. As Adolf Behne wrote in 1926: "Film is something essentially new. It is the literature of our times."[2] An art form that becomes synonymous with the new and which can address millions of people irrespective of their educational background would be at the forefront of the Marxist and the modernist projects.

It is not accidental that the first manifestations and theorizations of a radical and revolutionary cinema made use of Marx's dialectical materialism. For the Marxist understanding of the dialectic seeks to show that what appears as unified, concrete, and natural is the product of historically determined social conflicts and the material connections between individuals. The Marxist dialectic is thus antithetical to an abstractly evolutionary understanding of reality, wherein historical development proceeds through conflicting collisions, whose synthesis generates more contradictions. Friedrich Engels argued that the dialectic is the "science of interconnections" that allows us to understand all social conditions as susceptible to change and not as static and universal abstractions.[3] In these terms, dialectical materialism intends to fragment what seems to be unitary and complete, so as to reveal the historical transitoriness of social reality and its potential for radical change. Karl Korsch has described this dynamic, suggesting that for Marx a given socioeconomic status quo assumes the form of "consensus" whose self-evidence is to be attributed to its capacity to conceal the social determinants that have produced it. However, the existing state of affairs faces pressure from new social collisions that lead to further conflicts: "From a harmonious 'consensus' it is at a certain point transformed into a 'dissensus.'"[4]

Indeed, cinema was the quintessential medium that could serve the modernist and Marxist projects of analyzing the given state of affairs so as to envisage an alternative modernity, not least of all because it was a mass medium that refuted the class-laden understanding of art as the expression of cultivated taste. Film and media historians have discussed the culture wars initiated following the emergence of the cinema. Siegfried Zielinski explains that the advent of the new media of storage and transmission in the nineteenth century was received with suspicion.[5] The shift from a literary to a visual mass culture posed threats to Western civilization and culture. Similarly, Sabine Hake explains that cinema posed a threat to bourgeois culture, firstly because it was a collective space where the masses could assemble and encounter themselves, but also because of its reliance on technology that was at the antipodes with the idea of art as individual creativity. We can therefore see how cinema in its early days coincided with the modernist desire to overcome tradition, but also with the Marxist project that aspired to enlighten the masses and do away with the conditions of alienation in modernity. Cinema was seen as a threat because it was an art form made for the masses. The fact that early cinema was an exhibitionist medium that did not rely on the use of verbal language made it more approachable to the urban proletariat. The new art form was therefore synonymous with the establishment of a working-class culture. Noël Burch has famously suggested that the primitive mode of representation (cinema in its early days) can be understood as a narrative and visual form influenced by folk art such as the circus, the cabaret, and vaudeville. Early cinema privileged the autonomy of the shot or tableau rather than narrative coherence and made use of anti-psychological representational tropes. For Burch, the shift to a narrative cinema (the institutional mode of representation) influenced by literary dramaturgy was not the teleological development of an imperfect medium, but an industrial choice that aimed at popularizing the new medium to the bourgeoisie of the time so as to expand its market.[6] Raymond Williams voiced a similar concern arguing that many scholars and students "know surprisingly little about the popular theatre on which, in that phase, it [cinema] drew so heavily. Some people still compare the new medium with such older forms as the bourgeois novel or academic painting, when they ought really to be looking at the direct precedents, with the same urban audiences of melodrama and theatrical spectacle."[7] According to Williams, cinema in its early days was monitored by the state, precisely because of its working-class appeal.

These opening remarks provide a historical hindsight to consider why the key and still influential theorizations of a Marxist cinema did not start from countries in the capitalist West, but in the Soviet Union, whose historical experience of underdevelopment during the Czarist years prevented it from equating art with class-laden cultivated taste. As the 1917 revolution contradicted Marx's prediction that the revolution would start in the industrial West, similarly it was in the same country that the theoretical foundations of a revolutionary modernist cinema would be laid. Sergei Eisenstein and Dziga Vertov are the two central film practitioners who formulated the key theories of political cinema that are still influential in the present. Eisenstein, whose background was in theater, argued for a dramatic revolutionary cinema and his influence is evident on the majority of Marxist-modernist auteurs—including those who opposed the aesthetic of montage—such as Jean-Luc Godard, Alexander Kluge, Straub/Huillet, Miklós Jancsó, Ousmane Sembène, Glauber Rocha, Theo Angelopoulos, and many more. Vertov, on his part, argued for a radical experimental cinema that does away with the theatrical tradition and his influence can be seen in the works of late Godard, Chris Marker, Thomas Heise, Alexander Kluge, and others. Godard, Kluge, Heise, and Harun Farocki have been equally influenced by both traditions.

Eisenstein came from the theater to the cinema and his schooling next to Vsevolod Meyerhold was influential in his formulation of a collective dramaturgy that, not unlike early cinema, relied on the autonomy of the tableau or shot. Meyerhold's aesthetic of biomechanics, his departure from the theater of the individual dramatic hero, and his manipulation of popular art forms such as the circus, commedia dell'arte, and cabaret had a significant impact on Eisenstein's theory and practice. Meyerhold's theater reacted against the dominant naturalist tradition and proposed an episodic aesthetic of attractions that did away with the linear drama, aiming instead to produce meaning out of the power of associations generated by the collision of independent episodes. Commenting on Eisenstein's cinema he explains,

> What prompted Eisenstein to divide his subject-matter into a series of attractions, each with a carefully contrived climax? He developed the technique whilst working at the Proletkult Theatre, but it originated when he was working with me in my theatrical laboratory on the Novinsky Boulevard in Moscow. We were looking for a new type of stage, free from anything which might get in the actor's way. Like myself, Eisenstein needs an arena, a platform, a theatre like Shakespeare's Globe. When interviewers question me about this stage without a stage which I am building, I simply answer that I want an arena in which we can put on everything from variety turns like Uberbrettl to vast spectacles of Shakespearian dimensions like Pushkin's Boris Godunov or Oedipus, the King. It will be possible to alternate these productions with gymnastic displays, ballet and folkdancing, because there will be nothing to separate the spectator from the one thing which matters—the performer himself.[8]

Eisenstein inherited Meyerhold's suspicion of naturalism and formulated a dialectical theory of representation, which aimed at demonstrating the potential for the construction of a counter-reality. Here the influence of Marx and Engels is obvious, given that both argued that social reality might appear as natural and self-evident because it cannot be understood as the unity of positive and negative forces. One recalls the famous segment in *The German Ideology* (1845) where Marx and Engels explain how the reproduction of life has a dual character since it appears as a natural process and as a part of a broader web of social relationships. To study the social quality of life suggests that one can understand its changeability. The crucial step for this is to place one's life within the context of human cooperation and consider how the productive forces affect the lives of the individuals: "Further, that the multitude of productive forces accessible to men determines the nature of society, hence, that the 'history of humanity' must always be studied and treated in relation to the history of industry and exchange."[9] Eisenstein proceeded to achieve this by means of a collective dramaturgy that did away with the dramatic hero and psychological portraiture. In placing the collective as the key protagonist of cinema, he aspired to instill a materialist understanding of history and society to the audience.

In good dialectical fashion, Eisenstein's cinema brings together pathos and reason, so as to show in a Marxist way the connection between intellectual thinking and the practical overthrow of the conditions of alienation. The filmmaker solicits the audience's emotional and rational responses by means of a synecdochic representational style that relies on the collision of episodes rather than on their smooth succession. The fragment is central to Eisenstein's understanding of a dialectical representational approach that seeks to connect the particular with the general. Peter Wollen explains that one of the essays that had a tremendous impact on the Soviet director's thinking was Lenin's "On the Question of Dialectics." One sentence is said to have struck Eisenstein forcefully: "In any proposition we can (and must) disclose as in a 'nucleus' ('cell') the germs of all the elements of dialectics." Eisenstein was able to link this to his concept of the shot as the cell, or later, as his views grew more complex, "the molecule of montage."[10] This is clarified in Eisenstein's seminal essay, "A Dialectic Approach to Film Form," where he distinguishes his own modus operandi from that of other Soviet filmmakers, such as Vsevolod Pudovkin, for whom montage serves mainly as a descriptive principle. Eisenstein instead proposes a constructive understanding of montage produced by the juxtaposition "of independent shots—shots even opposite to one another."[11] It is by means of such a collision that a narrative advances through the conflict of contradictory fragments that operate as clashing theses and antitheses.

One needs to recall here the famous passage from the *Старое и новое* (*The General Line*, 1929), when the farmers test for the first time the cream separator that helps them make butter. The sequence defies verisimilitude by being intentionally prolonged. The camera registers a series of close-ups of the farmers looking at the machine in disbelief. The faces are captured from a variety of angles while visuals of the separator are also interjected. This rapid succession of visuals produces an emotional impact as well as a sense of suspense. Interpolated intertitles ask questions whether this is progress or deception. Eventually the camera cuts to the separator capturing its tubes, followed by low-angle shots of the tubes and a high-angle one of the separator's wheel juxtaposed to the ecstatic faces of Marfa and the Party representative. A series of visuals of the milk exploding in the air like a water fountain—interrupted again by reaction shots of the farmers—succeed one another and the sequence culminates with the intertitles announcing that after this successful demonstration the numbers of the cooperative were increased.

The sequence here operates as the "cum-shot" of socialist cinema since it combines an orgiastic aesthetic of visual excess with a rational conclusion regarding the benefits of collective organization and labor. The sexual connotations of the scene are visibly manifested when the separator starts spilling milk on Marfa's hands and her face followed by visuals of the milk exploding skyward. This, however, should not be confused as pornographic hideousness especially in light of the fact that it is Marfa who has convinced the other farmers to invest in new technologies that can maximize production and render their labor more effective. The sexual connotations of this passage may well be seen as the celebration of a new life as showcased by the culmination of the sequence that privileges the rational conclusion, namely, the success of the cooperative experiment and its endorsement as an index of progress and development against religious prejudice and individualist farming production. This combination of affective engagement and rational deductions is a manifestation of Eisenstein's desire to make the Marxist theory of knowledge palpable and graspable by the masses and not just an abstract theoretical exercise in style that obfuscates the practical effects of the dialectical worldview. What this passage of the film clearly articulates is the shift from a semi-feudalistic mode of agricultural production and labor to a socialist mode of industrial production founded upon the principles of collaboration and collective organization. The dialectic here is in service of demonstrating how cooperative labor is the crucial step for the shift from a semi-feudalistic and patriarchal reality of underdevelopment and prejudice, to a new world of development and socialist rationality.

Unlike his previous classics, *The General Line* includes a key narrative agent, Marfa, who is the one to start the cooperative. Yet, in line with his previous works such as *Стачка* (*Strike*, 1924), *Броненосец «Потёмкин»* (*Battleship Potemkin*, 1925), and *Октябрь (Десять дней, которые потрясли мир)* (*October*, 1928), Eisenstein makes use of typage, a strategy that he also got to learn while working with Meyerhold whose typage aesthetic was influenced by commedia dell'arte. According to Eisenstein, typage is not to be understood solely as the director's approach to the characters, that is, the avoidance of psychological portrayal, and the schematic depiction of them based on their social positions, but "a specific approach to the events embraced by the content of the film."[12] Typage thus extends beyond the depiction of characters to the ways actions are represented as the collision between antithetical social forces and not as isolated conflicts among autonomous individuals whose acts seem to be devoid of social influence, as it was the case with naturalist theater against which Meyerhold reacted. Eisenstein admitted that typage is "rooted in theater," but cinema had the potential to push this further thanks to its technological advancement.[13]

Evident in Eisenstein's representational strategy is an awareness of the Marxist concept of realism summarized in his and Engels' view of the individual as "the ensemble of the social relations" that contradicts the liberal understanding of the individual as a free and autonomous subject who is free to make their choices and achieve their goals irrespective of the social conditions.[14] The radical aspect of Eisenstein's typage and montage aesthetic is precisely this capacity to dramatize social circumstances and conditions, showing clearly the constraints placed upon individuals by repressive regimes, but also the collective's capacity to change these circumstances on the condition that they understand them. The celebrated sequence in *Strike* where the workers' massacre is juxtaposed through parallel editing to the slaughtering of a cow, as well as the renowned "For God and Country" sequence in *October*, and the

Odessa steps passage in *Potemkin* are emblematic in this respect. The first and the third put forward the brutality of the Czarist regime by means of montage effects that combine logos and pathos; the second shows the connection between religion and authoritarian rule by juxtaposing figurines from the Asian, Hindu, and Pacific traditions that culminate in the reconstruction of the statue of the Czar. The collision of thesis and antithesis here reveals how religious and patriotic rhetoric seek to divert the proletarian's attention from the social conditions of their oppression. Consequently, Eisenstein's major intervention was the theorization of a dialectical cinema, which radically challenged the individualistic dramaturgy motivated by the nineteenth-century theatrical traditions; he introduced a dramaturgy that viewed characters as the products of processes taking place on a mass scale, and pointed to their capacity to act collectively to change them. It is fair to suggest that he is the Godfather of Marxist narrative cinema because he managed to dialectize representation by means of an expressive mise-en-scène that enabled the coexistence of entertainment and political critique.

Nevertheless, Eisenstein's background was in theater and his cinema was committed to storytelling. His stories followed the Russian formalist imperative of de-automatizing perception so as to enable the audience in a Shklovskian way not to recognize things but to see them differently and identify the social processes behind the narrated events. This is the reason why it would be interesting to envisage his unrealized film on Marx's *Capital* (1867). The film, which did not materialize, can be imagined as a series of dialectical constellations, where the key protagonists would be neither the proletariat nor its exploiters. He envisaged it as an antiheroic film whose dramatis personae would be the workers' production of surplus value and all the processes that perpetuate the capitalist mode of production. Again, the dialectical method occupies a privileged position in his plan for the film:

> In those "great days" I noted on a scrap of paper that in the new cinema, the established place of eternal themes (academic themes of LOVE AND DUTY, FATHERS AND SONS, TRIUMPH OF VIRTUES, etc.) will be taken by a series of pictures on the subjects of "basic methods." The content of CAPITAL (its aim) is now formulated: to teach the worker to think dialectically. To show the method of dialectics. This would mean (roughly) five nonfigurative chapters. (Or six, seven, etc.) Dialectical analysis of historical events. Dialectics in scientific problems. Dialectics of class struggle (the last chapter). "An analysis of a centimeter of silk stocking." (About the silk stocking as such, Grisha I copied out from somewhere—the silk manufacturers' fight for the short skirt. I added the competitors—the textile masters' for long skirts. Morality. Clergy, etc.) Still very complicated to think "somehow" in "extra-thematic" imagery. But no problem . . . a viendra![15]

Eisenstein repeatedly states that the film should rely on the power of associations and start from the exploration of banal situations to move to more concrete ones, bringing as a model example James Joyce's *Ulysses* (1922). Eisenstein intended to leave behind his theatrical influences without abandoning his commitment to the

Marxist dialectic. "There are," he states in his notes, "endlessly possible themes for filming in CAPITAL ('price,' 'income,' 'rent')—for us, the theme is Marx's method."[16] Far from being outmoded or obsolete, Eisenstein's desire to dramatize Marx's *Capital* is pertinent in the present, at a time in history that finance capitalism obfuscates more and more its own modus operandi, while the shift to an immaterial labor in the capitalist West has obscured the fact that this transition is the product of the West's reliance on material labor outsourced to the global south and industrial semi-peripheries. In these terms, Eisenstein's vision is as relevant today as when it was formulated in the years after 1917.

Unlike Eisenstein's desire to dialectize representation by pushing further experiments initiated in theater, Dziga Vertov epitomizes a filmmaking tradition which aspired to make use of the lessons of the dialectic through a type of cinema that was non-reliant on narrative and theatrical conventions. For Vertov, the collision of independent sequences did not aspire to produce predetermined effects and responses. Although his cinema was very much anchored in the principles of the dialectic, Vertov aimed to do away with cinema's roots in theater and argued for an experimental film style whose dialectical effects would not be foreordained. It is a cinema committed to the Marxist theory of knowledge as manifest through the dialectic but whose ultimate aim is the use of the dialectic as a means of research. It is, as Annette Michelson aptly calls it, a cinema "of epistemological inquiry."[17]

Vertov's work is also committed to a paratactic style, yet the difference is that parataxis becomes anti-narrative and does not serve storytelling. So his modus operandi is grounded in cinema's capacity to capture a material reality, but in a way that discontinuity instead of continuity is foregrounded. For Vertov, this process of recording fragments of reality without describing it is the model for the cinema of the future, a cinema that valorized the superiority of machinic (Kino-eye) over human agency (the human-eye) so as to reveal processes not captured by the human. Consider, for instance, his argument that

> The history of Kino-Eye has been a relentless struggle to modify the course of world cinema, to place in cinema production a new emphasis of the "unplayed" film over the play-film, to substitute the document for mise-en-scene, to break out of the proscenium of the theatre and to enter the arena of life itself.[18]

Literary dramaturgy erects an impediment to radical cinema's desire to identify the connection between visual materials and social phenomena. As he says in an essay written in 1929, "the cinema's chief function is the recording of documents, of facts, the recording of life, the historical processes."[19] The refusal to accommodate preordained narrative effects by means of dramaturgy is linked with his belief that dramaturgy perpetuates the bourgeois understanding of art as individual creativity. Documenting processes without commenting on them invites the audience to discover things and phenomena not visible in everyday life. Vertov's faith is in the power of the camera to engage with material reality and not in the director's individuality and creativity. The abandonment of authorship can liberate the medium from the remnants of the bourgeois aesthetics "the poser-actor, fairy-tale script, those costly toys-sets, and the director high-priest."[20]

Underpinning Vertov's aesthetic is the idea that the camera should not reproduce actions but observe things objectively so as to enable the audience to discover the social processes behind the events. This is the reason why he stressed the role of the cameramen rather than the director. In doing so, he aimed at placing art within the sphere of material production. The cameramen and the filmmaker are to be understood as people who do not create but construct materials from their encounter with the world. This is the reason why he vehemently argued in favor of "filming life unawares" so that the people recorded by the camera would not be aware of its presence and would be captured performing their everyday undertakings unaffectedly.[21] This is certainly the case in Человек с кино-аппаратом (*Man With a Movie Camera*, 1929), where he experimented with the medium to simultaneously produce cinematic and class consciousness through the camera's encounter with the material reality of the new world of the time. Attending to the details of everyday life such as births, marriages, divorces, the working routine, and homelessness, the film is paradigmatic of Vertov's understanding of constructive montage, where the dialectic between observing and recording is not necessarily synthetic. In this film, the audience is not encouraged to reconfirm a preexisting conclusion, but to form their own. As Michelson argues, the film "through the systematic subversion of the certitudes of illusion" proposes an understanding of the filmmaker as an "epistemologist."[22]

Vertov's legacy in experimental political cinema and documentary has been tremendous especially when considering the work of late Godard, Alexander Kluge, Chris Marker, and Thomas Heise. He was a passionate advocate of artistic experimentation against the platitudes of Socialist Realism and a firm believer that one should not flatter but challenge the audience. As he suggested in an article published in 1923,

> One of the chief accusations leveled at us is that we are not intelligible to the masses. Even if one allows that some of our work is difficult to understand, does that mean we should not undertake serious exploratory work at all? If the masses need light propaganda pamphlets, does that mean they don't need the serious articles of Engels, Lenin? . . . The LENIN of Russian cinema may appear in your midst today, but you will not allow him to work because the results of his production will seem new and incomprehensible.[23]

Consistent with the Marxist project of radicalized enlightenment, Vertov's work aspired to elevate the masses and teach them a new method of thinking. At the same time, one needs to acknowledge that with a few exceptions—*Man with a Movie Camera* is an obvious one—many of his films failed to promote the cinematic vision articulated in his manifestos and writings. Films like Шагай, Совет! (*Stride Soviet*, 1926) and Энтузиазм: Симфония Донбасса (*Enthusiasm*, 1930) produced undialectical results that did not comply with the filmmaker's desire to observe reality without describing it. The first, for example, shows through the use of parallel editing the progress of the

Soviet Union following the end of the civil war, so as to affirm the superiority of the present over the past. The dialectic here is devoid of complexity. Equally problematic is the reproduction of the Stalinist mottos of the five-year plan in *Enthusiasm* that deprive the film of any dialectical complexity especially in its depiction of labor at the time. Even key aspects of his aesthetic, such as filming life unawares, are visibly absent since the workers in the film seem to be very conscious of the camera's presence; it is fair to suggest that the filming approach is not one of construction, but of reproduction, possibly a product of the pressures artists faced during the Stalinist years.[24] One also needs to point out how many of his aesthetic approaches can be easily assimilated by the market, especially in the current reality of image saturation. To this, one should add that excessive abstraction can lead to indifference rather than political enlightenment. On these grounds, Viktor Shklovsky was one of the first to call Vertov's project into question:

> Cine-eye and the whole "kinoki" movement do not want to understand the essence of cinema. Their eyes are placed unnaturally far from their brains. They don't understand that cinema is the most abstract of all arts, close in its essence to certain mathematical devices. Cinema needs action and meaningful movement the way literature needs words, the way a painting needs semantic meaning. Without it, the spectator becomes disoriented; his view loses direction. In painting, shadows are a convention, but they can only be replaced by another convention. Cinema needs to accumulate conventions, they'll work the way case endings work in language. The primary material of cinema is not the object, but a particular way of filming it.[25]

Similarly, Eisenstein famously suggested that "I don't believe in kino-eye, I believe in kino-fist" although he later praised Vertov for having invented "musical rhythm in cinema."[26] These criticisms cannot be easily dismissed, especially if the Marxist utopian dream is to use cinema as a public sphere that can change collective perception by means of logical and emotional persuasion. At the same time, Vertov's writings prefigure Godard's argument that artistic and theoretical experimentation can have equal importance as the class struggle itself and Vertov was undoubtedly one of the film practitioners who broke ground in this respect.

It will be worth recalling that modernist art negates the old so as to affirm the singularity of the present and the urgency to place art within the context of material production. This desire to simultaneously negate the old and construct something new links modernism with a manifesto culture initiated by Marx and Engels. Martin Puchner has described the *Communist Manifesto*'s (1848) influence on avant-garde manifestos of the twentieth century. He argues that political modernism and the avant-garde absorb the style and the form of the *Manifesto* and its combination of aphoristic, political, and poetic modes of expression. This is verified not only by the furious reproduction of manifestos on the part of modernism and the avant-garde but also by the eccentric styles of these manifestos and their longing for intervening in what they consider a moment of crisis. As Puchner says, "the avant-garde manifesto is unthinkable without the genre-producing force of Marx and Engels' text, its translations and adaptations. The emergence and breathtaking proliferation of art manifestos rival the proliferation of the Manifesto itself."[27] The polemical force that characterizes modernist literary and artistic manifestos is also evident in the manifestos of politically invested modernist cinema. The influence of the *Manifesto* on these is an area that remains relatively unexplored considering the majority of these texts openly use Marxist terms and rhetoric to envisage the emergence of a new cinema that can shake the cinematic institution and enlighten its audience; the spectators envisaged by these manifestos are like the proletariat of the *Manifesto*: they are a collective subject under construction whose emergence is envisioned as the dialectical other to the emergence of a new cinema.

Eisenstein's 1925 manifesto "The Method of Making Workers' Films" is a good case in point. In it, Eisenstein contends the importance of the cinema of attractions as the route to the making of useful and socially engaged films that can instill class consciousness. This manifesto is significant because it clearly sets forth the need to produce films that employ affective stimulation as a means of producing political enlightenment. It also suggests that political cinema must acknowledge the non-homogeneity of the audience even when it comprises members of the working class, for different types of workers react differently to artistic experiments rendering many of the desired political effects innocuous. One of the examples he brings forward is the famous slaughter sequence in *Strike* that failed to affect peasants for whom animal slaughter is part of their working routine. The modernist desire to encounter the real in its material complexity is aptly articulated in Cesare Zavattini's 1953 manifesto of neorealism, "Some Ideas on the Cinema," which proceeds to differentiate the postwar Italian cinema from Hollywood's illusionism by explaining that whereas the latter turns a blind eye to the complexities of everyday reality, neorealism is concerned with capturing the contradictions of reality as manifested in its raw and unembellished state. Indeed, the characters of neorealism are not the exceptional dramatis personae of commercial cinema but everyday people; this corresponds with Marx and Engels, for whom history is not to be produced by gifted individuals and party leaders, but by the international proletariat.[28] Jean-Luc Godard's 1970 manifesto "What Is to Be Done?" is wholly in keeping with this standpoint. The title is a direct reference to Lenin and the text itself is preoccupied with a desire to explore how making films politically differs from making political films, and yet the text also makes clear that the latter cannot exist without the former. In other words, Godard's manifesto demonstrates how a militant type of cinema counters its bourgeois past, but is at the same time reliant on it in order to overcome it.[29]

An analogous approach can be seen in the manifestos of Third Cinema, a film movement that explicitly sees its cinema as a direct response to conditions of underdevelopment in the global south. Fernando Solanas and Octavio Gettino's 1969 manifesto "Towards a Third Cinema: Notes and Experiences for the Development of a Cinema of Liberation in the Third World" is a good case in point. Reacting against economic, political, and cultural imperialism, the premise of this argument is that the imposition of conditions of dependency in colonized countries produces an image of cultural inferiority. The structures of economic exploitation on the part of the colonizers obfuscate the conditions of economic and political exploitation of the peripheral countries. Paraphrasing Marx and Engel's famous formulation in the *Communist Manifesto* that the bourgeoisie creates an image of the world out of its own image, Solanas and Gettino imply that the colonizers produce a reality structured around their own imperialist historical experience. In effect, the task of the Third Cinema filmmakers is to produce a revolutionary cinema that cannot just deconstruct but also destroy the images that neocolonialism has produced of itself and of the colonized people. It is striking here, the rhetoric of construction through destruction that chimes neatly with the modernist and avant-garde manifestos of the twentieth century, and also with the *Communist Manifesto* to which Solanas and Gettino allude. These parallels have to do with the polemical form of the Third Cinema Manifesto whose ultimate aim is the production of a cinema that radically questions the cinematic institution of the world-system, destroys the cinematic images of colonialism and neocolonialism, and entails a radical critique of the ways capitalism reproduces itself in noncoercive ways through the power of its cinematic institution. It is, therefore, not coincidental that the new cinema proposed is directly linked with the class struggle, anti-colonialism, and dialectical enlightenment as formulated in a direct reference to Marx: "there is no knowledge of a reality as long as that reality is not acted upon, as long as its transformation is not begun on all fronts of struggle."[30]

As these and other manifestos suggest, Marx's influence on filmmakers across the world committed to the modernist project has been indispensable and needs to be rediscovered, rethought, and reexamined. Now that discussions of politics and representation have returned with a vengeance—following scholars' apolitical dalliance with postmodernist clichés and a kind of identity politics that was more an index of neoliberal fragmentation rather than political critique—the relationship between Marx and modernism merits revisiting and can inspire new ways of thinking about cinema and politics. The skeptics could interject that cinema has now lost its cultural force and that modernism has been deradicalized, becoming part of the institution it once criticized. The truth, however, is that audiovisual representation can only become political on the basis that it addresses a collective audience as opposed to isolated individuals binging on films and series alone on their couches, as is encouraged by the current on-demand culture. Similarly, modernist cinema's desire to render reality strange was never more pertinent than in the present, when the plethora of audiovisual objects and choices has not led to the development of audiovisual literacy but its opposite. The study of Marxist-modernist cinema can provoke the types of questions that enable us to reconsider the impermanence and changeability not only of the world in which we live but also of the type of cinema with which we engage.

Notes

1 Terry Eagleton, "Capitalism, Modernism and Post-Modernism," *New Left Review* 152 (1985): 61.

2 Adolf Behne, "The Public's Attitude toward Modern German Literature," in *The Promise of Cinema: German Film Theory, 1907–1933*, eds. Anton Kaes, Nicholas Baer, and Michael Cowan (Berkeley: California University Press, 2016), 393.
3 Engels, *Dialectics of Nature*, trans. Clemens P. Dutt (London: Lawrence and Wishart, 1946), 26.
4 Karl Korsch, *Karl Marx* (Boston, Leiden: Brill, 2016), 135.
5 Siegfried Zielinski, *Audiovisions: Cinema and Television as Entr'actes in History*, trans. Gloria Custance (Amsterdam: Amsterdam University Press, 1999), 16.
6 Noël Burch, "Porter, or Ambivalence," *Screen*, 19.4 (1978): 91–106.
7 Williams, *Politics of Modernism: Against the New Conformists* (London: Verso, 2006), 110.
8 Vsévolod Meyerhold, *Meyerhold on Theatre*, ed. Edward Braun (New York: Bloomsbury, 2016), 327.
9 Marx, "The German Ideology," 157.
10 Peter Wollen, *Readings and Writings: Semiotic Counter Strategies* (London: Verso, 1982), 47.
11 Sergei Eisenstein, *Film Form: Essays in Film Theory*, ed. and trans. Jay Leyda (London and New York: Harvest Book, 1977), 49.
12 Eisenstein, *Film Form*, 8.
13 Eisenstein, *Film Form*, 9.
14 Marx, "Theses on Feuerbach," 145.
15 Eisenstein, "Notes for a Film of 'Capital,'" *October* 2 (1976): 10.
16 Eisenstein, "Notes for a Film of 'Capital,'" 23.
17 Annette Michelson, "From Magician to Epistemologist: Vertov's *The Man with a Movie Camera*," *October* 162 (2017): 123.
18 Jay Leyda, *Kino: A History of the Russian and Soviet Film* (Liverpool, London, Prescott: George Allen and Urwin, 1960), 176.
19 Dziga Vertov, *Kino-Eye: The Writings of Dziga Vertov*, ed. Annette Michelson, trans. Kevin O'Brien (Berkeley: University of California Press, 1984), 101.
20 Vertov, *Kino-Eye*, 71.
21 Vertov, *Kino-Eye*, 71.
22 Michelson, "From Magician to Epistemologist," 132.
23 Vertov, *Kino-Eye*, 37–8.
24 Consider for instance Eisenstein's troubles during Stalinism when he was (undialectically) accused of making films deprived of individual characters by placing too much emphasis on collective actions and processes.
25 Viktor Shklovsky, *Viktor Shklovsky a Reader*, ed. Alexandra Berlina (New York: Bloomsbury, 2017), 361.
26 Wollen, *Readings and Writings*, 41.
27 Puchner, *Poetry of the Future*, 66.
28 Cesare Zavattini, "Some Ideas on the Cinema," in *Film Manifestos and Global Cinema Cultures: A Critical Anthology*, ed. Scott MacKenzie (Berkeley: University of California Press, 2014), 126.
29 Jean-Luc Godard, "What Is to Be Done?" in *Film Manifestos and Global Cinema Cultures: A Critical Anthology*, 169–70.
30 Godard, "What Is to Be Done?" 241.

12

Theatrical Proletarians

Michael Shane Boyle

The line that scholars draw to connect modernism with Marxism often runs through the category of "production." This is especially so when it comes to modernist theater, a field filled with performances of people at work. The modernist theatrical preoccupation with working did not end at the level of representation; it extended as well to the novel methods for producing performance that took their cues from labor process innovations that were then reshaping production in the capitalist and Soviet core.

Consider, for instance, how the rationality and collective synchrony of the assembly line seemed to saturate popular and avant-garde performance alike, from the mass ornaments of the Tiller Girls to the participatory spectacles of Sergei Eisenstein's Soviet pageants or Max Reinhardt's theater of 5,000.[1] Likewise, the influence of factory mechanization on directors and choreographers would seem to suggest that impresarios like Edward Gordon Craig shared with Bauhaus savants László Moholy-Nagy and Oskar Schlemmer the dream of fully automated stages where robots replaced human performers.[2] And then there is the familiar refrain reminding us how Taylorization—itself a choreography for managing worker motions—found theatrical purchase among Soviet artists Vsevolod Meyerhold and Konstantin Stanislavsky.[3] Modernist experimentation, so the grand narrative goes, was a cultural corollary to, if not the actual outgrowth of what Marx called "the revolution in the instruments of labor [that] attains its most highly developed form in the organized system of machinery in the factory."[4] In this story, theatrical production is defined by labor process innovations that, within the world of industry, sought to boost productivity, creativity, and efficiency.

This near-standardized profile of modernist performance calls to mind the "productivist paradigm" that Moishe Postone (among others) argues buttressed both capitalist and Soviet industrialism.[5] The portrait pins to theater a faith in industrialization's potential for developing the productive forces and generating unfettered growth. The promise of what Kathi Weeks calls "the utopia of modernization" found special favor in the Soviet Union, most notably in Lenin's endorsement of "factory discipline" as being essential for the long transition to full communism.[6] It is hard today to not recognize behind such celebrations of worker potential a justification for exploitation and alienation. Modernist performance tends to evince the heroic image of production, one that complements waged labor instead of condemning it. It is obvious why expanding the ranks of those subjected to the wage should appeal to capital, but a similar aspiration also undergirded Soviet ideology. By increasing the population of industrial workers and the unity among them, universal proletarianization was believed to be a strategy for growing workers' power. Instead of abolishing proletarian labor, the dictatorship of the proletariat defended and fostered it.[7] The twin visions of proletarianization that attach to modernist performance—one utopian, the other universalizing—suggest a field of artistic practice that not only failed to imagine a society beyond capital but which also, in an echo of the productivist paradigm, affirmed "central aspects of capitalism itself."[8]

Of course, this is only a partial account of modernism and theater. Alongside avowals of proletarian labor, prominent figures in modernist performance insisted proletarianization be abolished. Here the work of Bertolt Brecht is exemplary. His boldest period of experimentation in the late 1920s and early 1930s is filled with withering accounts that foreground proletarianization as the "precondition" for capitalist accumulation, thus, as something to be scorned and not celebrated.[9] However, the starting point for Brecht's critique was not proletarian labor in general, but the specific proletarianization of theater. His focus on theater may have been tactical, party to an ambivalent desire to not rock the Third Internationalist boat, but it was also practical, reflecting the simple fact of his employment in the theater.

Up until his 1933 exile, Brecht spilled considerable ink trying to explain how the economic reorganization of theater from a place of royal patronage to entrepreneurial and state investment had transformed its social function into that of a business. Theater, Brecht insisted, is not a sphere of artistic activity immune to capital, but a workplace especially suited to capitalist social relations. Just consider, he argued, the ease with which theater had separated its "producers" (an umbrella category for those who make performance, not a specific job) from the means of theatrical production. Theater's inherent infrastructural complexity, not to mention the capital outlays it requires and the range of specialized skills it draws together, makes the theatrical apparatus particularly difficult for producers to directly control, let alone own. As a result, to access the apparatus needed to make theater, producers must be employed by those who own the means of theatrical production. According to Brecht, theater producers exemplify the double freedom that defines proletarianization for Marx. They are *free to* sell their "naked labor power" but also *free from* the means of production. "The migration of the means of production away from the producers," Brecht writes, "signals the proletarianization of the producers."[10]

Himself the recipient of a handsome monthly stipend from his publisher during this period, Brecht did not presume that artists necessarily belonged to a class of proletarian workers: "the proletarianization of an intellectual," observed Walter Benjamin in an essay on Brecht's proletarianized theater, "hardly ever makes a proletarian."[11] Brecht instead argued that manual workers and cultural producers share a structural position within their respective production processes; artists are "virtually proletarianized" due to their separation from the means of production.[12] In disabusing artists of the petit-bourgeois belief that the social relations other workers are subjected to do not apply to them, Brecht explored the opportunities for solidarity that existed between proletarianized artists and the working class.[13] This hardly means that Brecht affirmed theater's proletarianization as historically progressive. Instead he attacks the proletarianized theater for exploiting its producers and alienating them from the products of their labor. Owing no doubt to his own financial security at the time, the latter consequence attracted most of Brecht's attention. He was concerned chiefly with how artists were alienated from and, therefore, lacked control over their work. This is especially consequential for politically inclined artists, since—as Brecht knew from personal experience—an apparatus can easily defang or repurpose even the most radical play.

Brecht's theory of the proletarianized theater is full of historical holes and relies on conceptual leaps that skip over thorny issues related to the "exceptional" character of theatrical commodities.[14] But what matters most for the present chapter is the simple fact of Brecht's hostility toward proletarianization. His theatrical practice, which many claim is synonymous with modernist performance,[15] should remind us today that a Marxist-modernist perspective on proletarian labor need not be affirmative: a Marxist like Brecht could ruthlessly criticize proletarianization without dismissing the necessity for proletarian struggle. This was the central point Brecht learned from reading Marx for the first time in the late 1920s. Likewise this is the lesson he taught in a series of militant and collaborative works completed just before his exile in 1933, from the film *Kuhle Wampe* to the epic plays *Das Mutter* (*The Mother*) and—the focus of the present chapter—*Die Heilige Johanna der Schlachtöfe* (*Saint Joan of the Stockyards*). Brecht's theory was also shaped by his experiences working in Berlin during a time of unprecedented unemployment, when proletarian labor was defined less by being in work than the threat of being excluded from it. But Brecht avoided the trap of conflating the proletariat with the unemployed, refusing to isolate proletarian experience to the sphere of capitalist production. For Brecht, the proletariat was defined by the capacity to struggle *against capital* instead of just the capacity to labor *for it*. As a result, Brecht's work from the period expanded the then-standard portrait of the proletariat to encompass more than the industrial (male) worker, emphasizing as well the proletarian struggles of women, renters, youths, and more. In what follows, I shift attention from Brecht's theory of proletarianized theater to his actual practice, and specifically to a failed attempt to register this expanded view on proletarianization and proletarian struggle theatrically. In what follows, the object of focus is the collaboratively written play, *Saint Joan of the Stockyards*. Finished in late 1931, the play itself was not the failure, but the attempt to have it produced in theater was. In Brecht's lifetime, the play's lessons about proletarian struggle were never staged. Among other things, *Saint Joan* and its historical exclusion from theatrical production remind us why abolishing proletarianized theater is not a political project in itself, but one that requires the abolition and not the avowal of proletarian labor *tout court*.

A Kind of Work-related Accident

Brecht first began reading Marx in 1926 after suffering what he later described as "a kind of work-related accident."[16] The "accident" was not a physical injury sustained working in the theater but a creative block hit while drafting a play about the wheat commodity exchange. Together with his writing partner, Elisabeth Hauptmann, Brecht had extensively researched the stock market for the play, but neither the trade books they read nor the brokers they interviewed "sufficiently" explained its workings.[17] The play that caused Brecht's "accident" is known today as *Fleischhacker*, and was based on Frank Norris' incomplete "Epic of Wheat" trilogy of naturalist novels, *The Octopus* (1901), *The Pit* (1903), and *The Wolf* (which was planned but never completed). Brecht and Hauptmann started the play in 1924, abandoning it in 1929. What Brecht and Hauptmann had set out to do, namely to use the wheat exchange to explain the economy, proved impossible. The underlying logic of capital could not be found in the stock market. "The planned drama was not written," Brecht recalled, "instead I began reading Marx, then and only then did I read Marx."[18] Although the pair did not need Marx to realize their error, Marxism provided guidance on where to look next.

Scholars agree that Brecht's early study of Marx signaled a turning point in his life, but what Marxism turned him into remains up for debate.[19] While some hold Brecht up as the consummate communist artist,[20] others empty his method of its communism thereby rendering "Brechtian" into a timeless "dialectical" system of dramaturgical interpretation.[21] Marxism would mean many things to Brecht over the course of his career; in late Weimar, it provided a perspective from which to examine the period's devastating rise in unemployment.[22] Between the 1929 Wall Street crash and the Nazi takeover in January 1933, the official number of the German unemployed skyrocketed from just below 1.3 million to over 6 million, about one quarter of the working population.[23] During these years, unemployment became a central theme across Brecht's work in film, literature, and theater, from the sobering "death from despair" that opens *Kuhle Wampe*[24] to *Der Brotladen*'s rioting chorus of "Unemployed Persons." A defining moment for both Brecht and the German unemployed came in June 1931, when the Brüning government deepened the social crisis by decimating unemployment benefits in ways that were especially devastating for married women and anyone under the age of twenty-one.[25] Many of those affected responded in kind, taking to the streets in bloody confrontations with cops and fascists throughout the month.

Brecht followed these developments from afar in Le Lavandou, France, while vacationing with several of his closest collaborators, including Hauptmann, Benjamin, Emil Burri, and Carola Neher. Stationed beachside in the Côte d'Azur, the group watched events unfolding back home closely. The uprising had a particular impact on Brecht; as Benjamin would record in his journal, it ended Brecht's belief that "Germany would have to wait years more for a revolutionary situation to arise."[26] The summer of 1931 was a prodigious season for the circle around Brecht, with filming for *Kuhle Wampe* underway and *Das Mutter* being prepped for its winter premiere. But the project that commanded the most attention in Le Lavandou was *Saint Joan*. Brecht and Hauptmann had started it two years earlier, picking up where they had left off with *Fleischhacker*. Burri had since joined on as a co-writer (as did Hermann Borchardt), while others, including Benjamin, contributed notes. The group wrote the eponymous role of Joan for Neher herself.[27]

Saint Joan was an ambitious achievement, recognized today for its Marxist erudition and as Brecht's first full-fledged epic work. But even admirers concede *Saint Joan* is "Brecht's most perplexing play."[28] As Jan Knopf puts it, this "misunderstood masterwork" is simultaneously "obvious" and "chaotic."[29] The *Fabel* (Brecht's preferred term for plot or story) follows Pierpont Mauler, the meat king of Chicago, as he tries to monopolize the city's livestock industry. Standing in his way is Joan Dark, a recent recruit to the Black Straw Hats who spends her time delivering sermons and hot soup to those left unemployed by Mauler's scheming. Mauler desperately seeks Joan's "stamp of approval" to both ease his guilt and burnish his public reputation.[30] After Mauler's ruthless speculating collapses the livestock market, the unemployed organize a general strike. Joan initially joins them before having second thoughts. She worries that a crucial letter the workers ask her to deliver to spread word of the strike will lead to bloodshed. Her nonviolent ethos and petit-bourgeois failure to support the workers allow police to crush the strike and Mauler to restore profitability by slashing the workforce and burning a third of the livestock. As the crisis ebbs and business resumes, Joan dies of pneumonia. In a mordant final scene, Mauler and his fellow factory owners salute Joan's inadvertent support and proclaim her their patron saint.

The play's sundry reception owes in part to how it mixes classical dramatic form with epic dramaturgy. Conversations among the capitalists unfold in verse and rhyme, with a meter that floats from Shakespearean iambic pentameter to Virgil's dactylic hexameter. Entire speeches, and in some cases whole episodes, allude to or even mimic Schiller, Goethe, and Hölderlin.[31] *Saint Joan*'s form is made even more dizzying by its epic structure as a cycle. Inspired by Marx's theory of crisis, economically the play ends where it begins, moving through stages of prosperity, overproduction, stagnation, and crash until—finally—prosperity returns.[32] For many Brecht scholars, like Patty Lee Parmalee, *Saint Joan* is nothing less than a "dramatization of *Capital*."[33] Yet, and perhaps due to the play's formal complexity, the angle from which *Saint Joan* is said to approach capitalism is almost always misunderstood. Theater programs and high theory alike have tended to erroneously describe *Saint Joan* as a stock market play. No less than Theodor Adorno stepped into this interpretive trap, arguing that the play's laudable attempt to capture the abstract "essence of capitalism" is foiled by its focus on market speculation.[34] According to Adorno, *Saint Joan* reduces capital accumulation to a sport-like competition for profit. Ruthless business dealings can make for compelling drama, but they cannot reveal "the inner nature of capitalism." Adorno writes:

> Mere episodes in the sphere of circulation, in which competitors maul each other, are recounted instead of appropriation of surplus-value in the sphere of production compared with which the brawls of cattle dealers over their shares of the booty are epiphenomena incapable of provoking any great crisis.[35]

Adorno's treatment of *Saint Joan* reads like an exemplary genre critique of art that scapegoats financiers. And, while the criticism could be said to suit a film like *The Wolf of Wall Street* (2013), it hardly applies to *Saint Joan*. It is as if Adorno ignored half of the play. To say that *Saint Joan* centers entirely on the actions of capitalists in the "sphere of circulation" requires Adorno to entirely ignore the tens of thousands of proletarians who haunt the play throughout.

Worthless, Superfluous, Even Bothersome

Adorno rightly observes that *Saint Joan* never takes us into the "sphere of production." The closest we get are the factory gates. But this is the play's entire point, not its failing. We never enter the hidden abode because the workers themselves are barred entry. In place of Marx's famous sign, "No admittance except on business," Brecht and company have hung one that simply reads, "Closed for business."[36] Instead of depicting workers exploited for surplus value, *Saint Joan* shows the "precondition" for this exploitation.[37] As Marx writes, the capitalist mode of production compels its subjects to be "free in the double sense," legally free to sell their labor power and free of everything but this labor power.[38] Lacking both "the objects needed for the realization of [their] labor-power" in production and the resources necessary for reproduction, proletarians are left entirely reliant on the market.[39] This is where they sell both their labor power for a wage and, with this wage, purchase the goods needed to live.

When we first meet the workers in *Saint Joan*, they are waiting to get inside Lennox's packing plant, which, unbeknownst to them, Mauler's scheming in the opening scene has forced to close. Frustrated by the wait, the workers, speaking as a chorus, complain among themselves:

> Who do they think we are? Do they expect us
> To stand out here like cattle, ready
> for anything?

After a short spell, ambiguously indicated in the text as "silence," they begin pleading:

> Why don't you open up, you bloodsuckers? Your
> Cattle are here, you butchers, open up! (5)

By comparing themselves to cattle, the workers grimly acknowledge their low status. But in the shift from simile ("like cattle") to metaphor ("your cattle"), they move from identifying as animals to identifying as commodities, even advertising what they have come to sell: their selves. That the workers reify themselves through livestock, the subject commodity of market speculation in the play, calls into question which commodity is essential to the production process. Like much of the play, this scene makes several obvious allusions to *Capital*. For one, when calling the factory owners "bloodsuckers," the workers imply that they themselves are, as Marx puts it, the "living labor" that capital "vampire-like" sucks dry.⁴⁰ The workers, not the livestock, are the lifeblood of capital, supplying the surplus value the system cannot live without. In addition, their professed desire to be treated like cattle calls to mind *Capital*'s "dramatis personae," whose entrance into the sphere of production Marx famously describes in the following way:

> He who was previously the money-owner now strides out in front as a capitalist; the possessor of labor-power follows as his worker. The one smirks self-importantly and is intent on business; the other is timid and holds back, like someone who has brought his own hide to market and now has nothing else to expect but—a tanning.⁴¹

The meat industry as the setting for *Saint Joan* literalizes Marx's comparison of the sphere of production to a slaughterhouse and his gruesome insinuation that those subjugated by capital willingly subject themselves to the butcher. But like *Capital*, *Saint Joan* contends that what appears to be a choice freely made by workers—to sell their labor power—is anything but; given the miserable choices capital puts before them, "tanning" is the least worst option. "Under capitalism," as Michael Denning sums it up with supreme precision, "the only thing worse than being exploited is not being exploited."⁴²

In depicting the workers' failure to "freely'" sell their labor power, *Saint Joan* provides a cruel reminder of capital's second freedom by excluding the workers from the means of production entirely. Upon hearing news of the plant's closure, they wail: "And our tools, a mountain / Of steam hammers and cranes / Locked behind walls!" (11). Proletarianization, *Saint Joan* announces from the start, does not entail a worker's potential to work, but their inevitable exclusion from production. A proletarian, Marx writes, is someone who "produces and valorises 'capital,' and is thrown onto the street as soon as he becomes superfluous to the need for valorisation."⁴³ *Saint Joan* follows Marx's lead by emphasizing that joblessness is a structural fact of capitalism. Demonstrating this was a key aim for Marx in the first volume of *Capital*. He targets classical political economy's premise that joblessness resulted from overpopulation and wilful idleness, themselves supposedly symptoms of the working class' lack of restraint and ambition. The world as imagined by Adam Smith and David Ricardo was one in which demand for labor outstripped supply. If moral failing kept workers from working, then the effects of poverty were the surest means to compel them back to work.⁴⁴

And yet, the process of proletarianization that Marx describes is not just that of unemployment. In other words, and contrary to the recent "scandalous assertion" made by Fredric Jameson, Marx's *Capital* is not "about unemployment."⁴⁵ For one, despite persistent mistranslations, Marx never uses the German equivalent for "unemployment"—*Arbeitslosigkeit*—in *Capital*. In fact, neither the English nor the German term even entered wide usage until the late stages of the Long Depression (1873–96), well after Marx had written the first volume of *Capital* (1867). In English, the term was not even coined until 1887.⁴⁶ The significance of the terminological absence in

Capital is more than etymological. However much we take unemployment for granted today, neither the term nor the condition it describes is natural. Unemployment, as many labor historians insist, had to be "discovered."[47] The concept's historical emergence in the late nineteenth century signaled significant transformations in capitalist society, from the new recognition of joblessness as a social rather than a moral problem to the normalization of waged employment. More specifically, unemployment was a concept perfectly suited for strengthening the social democratic project that strove to measure, insure against, and, more generally, "contain the spectre of wageless life."[48] *Capital*, by contrast, describes a condition broader than that of unemployment, what Marx calls the "multiplication of the proletariat."[49]

Saint Joan, likewise, is not a play about unemployment, as it shows more than a worker failing to find a buyer for their labor power. The play tells how capital, in order to expand, requires the growth of "surplus populations" that are not needed in production, but nonetheless remain necessary to capital. They comprise what Marx calls "the lever of capitalist accumulation," which takes the form of a "disposable industrial reserve army." Capital gains several kinds of leverage by not exploiting "a mass of human material ready for exploitation."[50] In addition to giving firms flexibility to expand or contract production as the market requires, the presence of a reserve army helps capital discipline workers, temper workplace demands, and sow division among the working class as a whole. Expanding the proletariat, which entails growing the absolute number of those "relatively redundant" to production (and likely pauperized as a result), is a sine qua non of capitalism.[51] In arguing that "[a]ccumulation of capital is therefore multiplication of the proletariat," Marx stresses that proletarians are defined not just by a need to work, but, more crucially, by utter reliance on the market for survival.[52] The immiserating contradiction that the absolute number of people who depend on the market increases as the relative number needed for production falls is what Marx describes as the general law of capitalist accumulation.[53]

This "law" provides the solution to the economic crisis in *Saint Joan*. After his speculating causes the price of meat to collapse, Mauler announces to his fellow capitalists that to restore profitability they must destroy a third of the livestock supply and permanently lay off the same percentage of workers. When asked why he does not just give the "worthless" meat to the unemployed who would surely "make good use of it," Mauler smiles:

> you have failed to grasp
> The essence of the problem. All those people
> Standing out there *are customers*
> They may seem worthless, superfluous
> even bothersome, but it cannot
> Escape close scrutiny that *they* are customers
> Though many will not understand, it is
> Essential to lock out a third of all the work force
> For labor too has glutted the market and must be
> Curtailed! (97–8)

Albeit "worthless, superfluous, even bothersome" for the purposes of production, the growing surplus populations in *Saint Joan* are nonetheless indispensable. They supply the lever that keeps workers down, and the demand that keeps the market afloat.

By acknowledging these two functions of the proletariat, *Saint Joan* avoids reifying proletarians as (just) labor power. By extension, the play also refuses to reduce the proletariat to the identity of a worker. In an early bravura scene, we follow Joan on a tour of the stockyards. There we meet unemployed workers with mangled hands and destroyed lungs, as well as an elderly woman who has spent four nights outside Mauler's plant trying to find out what happened to her missing husband. The plant offers her twenty free meals at the company canteen if she ends her enquiries. Mrs. Luckerniddle, who is entirely dependent on her husband's wages, has not eaten for two days. She has no choice but to accept. The scene's climax comes when Mrs. Luckerniddle, while eating her first meal, overhears a worker describe her husband's fate. He fell into a rendering tank and could not be fished out. She grows ill at the thought that she might be eating her husband, but on the way out she informs the server she will return for more.

It is in this way that Mrs. Luckerniddle exemplifies the initial Roman meaning of the proletariat, indicating complete reliance on one's relations. The play implies she is cut off from all possibility of being employed herself, thus, her condition demands we distinguish proletarianization from such categories like employment or unemployment. As Denning argues, "'proletarian' is not a synonym for 'wage labor' but for dispossession, expropriation and radical dependence on the market. You don't need a job to be a proletarian."[54] *Saint Joan* eludes depicting the proletariat as a coherent identity or fixed social category. Like so much of Brecht and Hauptmann's work before their exile, the play went against the grain of the labor movements of its time, which, in affirming the wage earner as the proper political and economic subject, excluded or gravely limited the participation of women, racialized groups, and others who did not conform to the normalized identity of a worker.

There Ought To be More Like Her

Saint Joan respects Marx's expanded understanding of who should be recognized as a proletarian. At the same time, the portrait it paints of the proletariat does risk condemning them to a state of helplessness. The dominant mode *Saint Joan*'s proletariat performs in is that of waiting, be it when the unemployed wait for work or when Mrs. Luckerniddle waits for news of her husband. This approach broke with the template forged by Soviet modernists like Vladimir Mayakovsky or even socialist realists like Leonid Leonov whose depictions of proletarian experience invariably showed the proletariat as movement, either at work or in struggle. But the waiting portrayed in *Saint Joan* parodies another approach to representing proletarian experience found in the two works it explicitly references: George Bernard Shaw's 1905 Salvation Army play, *Major Barbara*, and Upton Sinclair's 1906 muckraking novel about the American meatpacking industry *The Jungle* (which inspired Luckerniddle's death in a rendering tank). Despite their differences, *Major Barbara* and *The Jungle* are committed to displaying proletarian misery for middle-class audiences, the former to elicit pity and the latter to incite moral outrage. *Saint Joan* issues withering critiques of both methods. Consider, for instance, its treatment of Shaw's play, from which Joan and the Black Straw Hats are directly lifted. *Major Barbara* treats its poor as objects of pity unable to help themselves. *Saint Joan* responds to Shaw's endorsement of liberal philanthropy by unmasking the Black Straw Hats as a group hired by the ruling class to persuade the poor to wait for their reward in heaven instead of revolting.

Saint Joan's proletariat are not just waiting. Throughout the second half of the play, they are preparing to strike. When combined with *Saint Joan*'s cyclical structure, however, the fact that the general strike is crushed might seem to condemn the proletariat to a permanent state of waiting. But the play's conclusion is less a solution than a deferral. Fixing the crisis only intensifies the contradiction between capital and the proletariat. In the late 1920s, Brecht himself argued that the "five-act" dramaturgical structure conventionally used to capture the exploits of a bourgeois hero was inappropriate for "today's catastrophes," which, he observed, "do not proceed in a straight line but in cyclical crises."[55] Brecht rarely provided tidy resolution in his plays, opting instead to give lessons needed for the ongoing struggle.

Just as *Saint Joan* implies that the proletarian struggle entails new patterns and rhythms that theater must figure out how to represent dramaturgically, the play also insists that the bourgeoisie and the proletariat require different forms of characterization. This is most evident in the strikingly different formal devices *Saint Joan* uses to depict capitalists like Mauler and proletarians like the unemployed workers. Whereas the latter appear as a chorus, Mauler imitates characters drawn from the pantheon of bourgeois drama. Formally, Mauler mimics the meter and monologues of Hamlet and Faust, but he replaces their heroic content with his own venal machinations. *Saint Joan* shows that the bourgeoisie and the dramatic form suited to them has flipped from revolutionary dynamism into a force of reaction.[56]

The appeal of choral form for representing proletarians is perhaps obvious. A chorus can imply collective endeavor instead of individual venture. It provides an epic collaborative response to the tendency of drama's dialogic form to require collisions and unequal exchanges between isolated characters. Brecht frequently experimented with choral stagings between 1927 and 1933. His own interest owed as well to the popularity of socialist choirs among the working class.[57] Even though *Saint Joan* is eager to find adequate form for the proletariat's revolutionary potential, it takes a cue from Marx's *Eighteenth Brumaire* (1852) to warn against emphasizing form at the expense of communist content—a lesson for both theater and struggle. Choral form appears in many ways in *Saint Joan*, not all of them revolutionary. At the height of the crisis, for instance, the unemployed workers are divided over whether to organize a general strike or to hold out for the plants to reopen. *Saint Joan* represents the impasse by dividing them into competing choruses, both located offstage. There lingers in this technique a remnant of dramatic dialogue, and with it comes the literal division that prevents the proletariat from uniting before it's too late. Furthermore, choral form is not reserved for the proletariat. Other groupings also perform as a chorus, most notably the Black Straw Hats, who enhance their choral form by wearing uniforms, marching in formation, and singing songs that promise to wage war on behalf of the poor. However, their disciplined vanguardism is merely formal, a veneer that disguises a deeply reactionary content: *Saint Joan* unmasks them as being bankrolled by the capitalists and tasked with persuading the workers to pray instead of strike.

Brecht himself is said to have worried that *Saint Joan*'s proletariat lacked the kind of "clear-cut personality" the capitalists and the petit-bourgeoisie had in Mauler and Joan, respectively.[58] While some scholars claim that Brecht was concerned the audience did not have a proletarian to identify with, he also seems to recognize that *Saint Joan*'s proletariat lacks particularity. The pivotal strike scenes include appearances by a pair of union leaders, who are nothing if not brave and selfless until the bitter end. They heroically embody the collective worker, that universal proletarian figure on whose back the utopian future supposedly rests. But they are also faceless. They speak almost entirely in revolutionary clichés. They are all form and no content. Although they lack any distinguishing traits, we can assume they are semiskilled, male industrial workers since, at that time, "the particular identity of the semi-skilled, male industrial worker was seen as having a universal significance."[59] Whether or not Brecht and Hauptmann meant for this particular snapshot of a revolutionary proletarian to be so utterly unsatisfactory is beside the point. No matter the intent, these union leaders prove the complete insufficiency, both then and now, of the belief that the proletariat can be united simply by a universal worker identity.

The play's final revision, completed by Brecht in 1937 ahead of an unrealized production in Copenhagen, gestures toward a possible fix. In hasty additions, Brecht expanded Mrs. Luckerniddle's role to transform her into a key figure in the strike. We learn that following her husband's death, Mrs. Luckerniddle joined the Communist Party, and evidently gained enough authority to be able to vouch for Joan to deliver the strike letter. When Joan betrays the unemployed, Mrs. Luckerniddle valiantly tries to finish Joan's task. But, in the middle of a snowstorm, she is murdered by the military. Her name is forgotten, yet a small group of workers solemnly recalls her heroic act. "There ought to be more like her," they say (102).

The revision has met with lukewarm response, with some dismissing it simply as Brecht's crass attempt to give his partner Helene Weigel a better role to play in the planned Copenhagen production.[60] But the decision that "an old working woman" (102) should personify proletarian struggle is hard to ignore (though there are precedents for this in Brecht and Hauptmann's other plays). In addition to warning against false individualized heroes like Joan, it also adds to the revolutionary proletarian the very kind of particular social experience that was missing. More importantly, the revision expands who the revolutionary proletarian is by looking beyond worker identity. The promotion of Mrs. Luckerniddle nods to the reality of German communist politics in the early 1930s. Women were hit especially hard by unemployment. They suffered the most from Brüning's cuts to benefits and were actively discouraged from searching for work so as to not take jobs from men.[61] Mrs. Luckerniddle's initial role represents this experience, while the revision attests to the profound contributions women made to communist struggle in the Weimar period. As Geoff Eley has chronicled, by the 1930s the "aggressively 'proletarian' identity" of the German Communist Party (KPD) contrasted "starkly with its actual members."⁶² During the KPD's crucial years of growth before 1933, its ranks were increasingly filled by people foregrounding their non-worker identities—women, youths, renters—whose efforts focused on non-workplace issues, from anti-eviction campaigns to agitation for legalizing abortion. Mrs. Luckerniddle might appear "the very opposite of the classically proletarian," but she is the quintessential communist.⁶³

Removed at a Single Blow

For decades *Saint Joan*'s critique of proletarianization and its expanded perspective on proletarian struggle did not have an audience. In a fate poignantly suited to a play so critical of capitalist production, *Saint Joan* was never produced in Brecht's lifetime.⁶⁴ Many factors contributed to the play's non-production, none of them a lack of trying. In November 1931, Brecht submitted the finished stage script to his publisher, and several proposals for production soon emerged. These ranged from a collaboration with Erwin Piscator to a touring production directed by Berthold Viertel that would start in Vienna and end in Berlin. Hitler's seizure of power rendered these and other plans impossible.

The production of *Saint Joan* that came closest to being realized was shut down just two days after the *Machtergreifung*, making it perhaps the first artwork to be banned by the Nazis. On January 25, 1933, the *Darmstädter Tagblatt* reported that efforts were underway to stage *Saint Joan* at a major state-subsidized theater in Hesse, the Landestheaters Darmstadt. Nationalist and fascist pundits around the country, no doubt emboldened by Hitler's appointment as *Kanzler* on January 30, condemned the planned production as "Bolshevik propaganda."⁶⁵ At least one critic targeted *Saint Joan*'s travesty of "Goethe and Hölderlin," presenting the play as proof of a dire internal threat to the German "soul."⁶⁶ On February 2, the matter went to the Hessian state parliament, where liberals and Christian conservatives lined up on the side of the Nazis. Darmstadt's centrist mayor, Rudolf Mueller, spoke out against the production, urging resistance to "political propaganda" that undermined "Germany's public sphere."⁶⁷ Whereas liberals decried the play, Nazis used the occasion to target the Landestheaters Darmstadt itself, issuing calls to cut its subsidy and fire its leadership for, among other things, "jewishing" the theater.⁶⁸ Since the early 1920s, the Landestheaters Darmstadt, led by Gustav Hartung and his dramaturg Kurt Hirschfeld, had been a bastion for modernist experimentation, even premiering multiple plays by Brecht. *Saint Joan* was a golden opportunity for fascists and nationalists to ramp up their war against 'un-German' modernism.⁶⁹

After its boom period in the 1920s, modernist theater in Germany fell on hard times as political and economic fallout from the 1929 crash made it increasingly difficult to mount productions. Attendance plummeted, deficits skyrocketed, and the Far Right mobilized against experimental and leftist performances. A perfect storm of financial woe and right-wing pressure forced the leading light of Berlin modernism, Otto Klemperer's Kroll Opera, to close in 1931.⁷⁰ When the *Saint Joan* script was sent to theaters in November of that year, conditions were hardly auspicious for the kind of large professional production it required. Brecht, Hauptmann, and most of the other contributors to *Saint Joan* fled Germany in early 1933. Speaking on the radio during a trip to Moscow in 1935, Brecht explained what had happened to the play in the following terms: "For an actor, director, or theatre writer to emigrate meant the virtually complete loss of his profession. His means of production were removed at a single blow."[71]

Notes

1. See Kate Elswit, *Watching Weimar Dance* (Oxford: Oxford University Press, 2014), 26–59; Siegfried Kracauer, *The Mass Ornament: Weimar Essays*, trans. Thomas Levine (Cambridge, MA: Harvard University Press, 1995).
2. See Paul Malone, "Cyber-Kleist," in *Mediated Drama, Dramatized Media*, ed. Eckart Voigts-Virchow (Trier: Wissenschafts Verlag Trier, 2000), 57–66.
3. See Jonathan Pitches, *Science and the Stanislavsky Tradition of Acting* (New York: Routledge, 2009), 11–85.
4. Marx, *Capital* vol. 1, 517.
5. Moishe Postone, *Time, Labor, and Social Domination: A Reinterpretation of Marx's Critical Theory* (Cambridge: Cambridge University Press, 1993), 17. For an articulation of this approach applied to modernism writ large, see Owen Hatherly, *Militant Modernism* (London: Zero Books, 2009).
6. Kathi Weeks, *The Problem with Work: Feminism, Marxism, Antiwork Politics, and Postwork Imaginaries* (Durham: Duke University Press, 2011), 83.
7. For an overview of this, see Aaron Benanav and John Clegg, "Crisis and Immiseration," in *The Sage Handbook of Frankfurt School Critical Theory*, eds. Beverly Best et al. (Thousand Oaks, CA: SAGE Inc, 2018), 1629–48.
8. Postone, *Time, Labor, and Social Domination*, 17.
9. Postone, *Time, Labor, and Social Domination*, 270.
10. Bertolt Brecht, "The Threepenny Lawsuit," in *Brecht on Film and Radio*, ed. and trans. Marc Silberman (London: Methuen, 2000), 147–201, 162. Brecht's theory of proletarianized theater is far from systematic, but was developed over several years in scattered publications. For the key texts, see Brecht, "Notes on the opera *Rise and Fall of the City of Mahogany*" and "Notes on *The Threepenny Opera*" both in *Brecht on Theatre*, eds. Marc Silberman, Steve Giles, and Tom Kuhn. (London: Bloomsbury Methuen), 61–70 and 71–80.
11. Benjamin, "Author as Producer," in *The Work of Art in the Age of Its Technological Reproducibility, and Other Writings on Media*, eds. Michael Jennings, Brigid Doherty, and Thomas Levi, trans. E. Jephcott (Cambridge, MA: Harvard University Press, 2008), 79–95; 92.
12. Brecht, "Notes on the Opera *Rise and Fall of the City of Mahogany*," 61.
13. See Benjamin, "Author as Producer."
14. On this, see my essay "Performance and Value: The Work of Theatre in Karl Marx's Critique of Political Economy," *Theatre Survey* 58.1 (2017): 3–23. See also Dave Beech, *Art and Value: Art's Economic Exceptionalism in Classical, Neoclassical and Marxist Economics* (Leiden: Brill, 2015).

15 See Puchner, *Stage Fright: Modernism, Anti-Theatricality, and Drama* (Baltimore: Johns Hopkins University Press, 2011), 139.
16 Brecht, *Große kommentierte Berliner und Frankfurter Ausgabe Vol. 20*, eds. Werner Hecht, et al. (Frankfurt am Main: Suhrkamp, 1988–2000), 138. If not otherwise noted, translations from German are my own.
17 Brecht, *Große kommentierte Berliner und Frankfurter Ausgabe*, 138.
18 Brecht, *Große kommentierte Berliner und Frankfurter Ausgabe*, 139. On the history of *Fleischhacker*, see Patty Lee Parmalee, *Brecht's America* (Columbus: The Ohio State University Press, 1981), 113-33 and Phoebe von Held and Matthias Rothe, "Introduction," in *Brecht and the Writer's Workshop*, eds. Tom Kuhn et al. (London: Bloomsbury Methuen, 2019), 13-23.
19 For a thorough account of Brecht's study of Marx and its significance to his work, see Parmalee, *Brecht's America*, 124-234.
20 See Jameson, *Brecht and Method* (London: Verso, 1998).
21 See David Barnett, "Performing Dialectics in an Age of Uncertainty, Or: Why Post-Brechtian ≠ Postdramatic," in *Postdramatic Theatre and the Political*, eds. Karen Jürs-Munby, Jerome Carroll, and Steve Giles (London: Bloomsbury Methuen, 2013), 47-66.
22 Brecht's particular reading of Marx at this time owed to his first teacher of Marxism, the sociologist Fritz Sternberg. Just before meeting Brecht, Sternberg had published *Imperialism* (1926), which sought to expand Marx's theory of surplus populations. See Fritz Sternberg, *Der Dichter und die Ratio: Erinnerungen an Bertolt Brecht* (Frankfurt am Main: Suhrkamp, 2014).
23 On unemployment in Weimar Germany see: David Abraham, *The Collapse of the Weimar Republic: Political Economy and Crisis*, 2nd ed. (New York: Holmes & Meier, 1986); Richard Evans and Dick Geary, eds., *The German Unemployed: Experiences and Consequences of Mass Unemployment from the Weimar Republic to the Third Reich* (London: Croom Helm, 1987).
24 Chloe Wattington, "Who Owns Tomorrow," in *Commune* 3 (2019). https://communemag.com/who-owns-tomorrow/, accessed August 20, 2019.
25 See Evans, *The German Unemployed*.
26 Benjamin quoted in Erdmut Wizisla, *Walter Benjamin and Bertolt Brecht: The Story of a Friendship*, trans. Christine Shuttleworth (New Haven: Yale University Press, 2009), 37.
27 On the writing of *Saint Joan*, see Gisela Bahr, "Zur Entstehungsgeschichte," in *Die Heilige Johanna Der Schlachthöfe: Bühnenfassung, Fragmente, Varianten*, ed. Gisela Bahr (Frankfurt am Main: Suhrkamp, 1989), 211-16; Burkhardt Lindner, "*Die heilige Johanna der Schlachthöfe*," *Brecht Handbuch*, ed. Jan Knopf (Stuttgart: JB Metzler, 2001), 266-8; Parmalee, *Brecht's America*, 225-64.
28 John Willett and Ralph Manheim, "Introduction," in Bertolt Brecht, *Saint Joan of the Stockyards* (London: Methuen, 1991), vii-xix, xix.
29 Jan Knopf, "Einleitung," in *Brechts "Heilige Johanna Der Schlachthöfe*," ed. Jan Knopf (Frankfurt am Main: Suhrkamp, 1986), 9-18; 9.
30 Brecht, *Saint Joan*, trans. Ralph Mannheim, 62. All quotations from *Saint Joan* are drawn from this translation, which is based on the 1938 Malik Verlag revision. For reasons explained near the end of the essay, I have cross-checked this edition with the 1932 version, which is republished in Bertolt Brecht, *Die Heilige Johanna Der Schlachthöfe: Bühnenfassung, Fragmente, Varianten*, ed. Gisela Bahr (Frankfurt am Main: Suhrkamp, 1989).

31 Much has been written on the play's allusions to classical drama. See, for example, Knopf, "Die literarische Quellen," in *Brechts "Heilige Johanna Der Schlachthöfe,"* 151–65; Roberto Schwartz, "The Relevance of Brecht: High Points and Low," trans. Emiliio Sauri, *Mediations* 23.1 (2007), 27–61.
32 For the best example of this interpretation, see: Käthe Rülicke-Weiler, *Die Dramaturgie Brechts* (West Berlin: Das Europäische Buch, 1976), 138–9.
33 Parmalee, *Brecht's America*, 244.
34 Adorno, "On Commitment," trans. Francis McDonagh, *PAJ* 3.2 (1978): 3–11, 9.
35 Adorno, "On Commitment," 9–10.
36 Marx, *Capital* vol. 1, 280.
37 Postone, *Time, Labor, and Social Domination*, 270.
38 Marx, *Capital* vol. 1, 272.
39 Marx, *Capital* vol. 1, 272–3.
40 Marx, *Capital* vol. 1, 342.
41 Marx, *Capital* vol. 1, 280.
42 Denning, "Wageless Life," *New Left Review* 66 (2010): 79.
43 Marx, *Capital* vol. 1, 764, n. 1.
44 For a review of classical political economy on this topic, see John Garraty, *Unemployment in History* (New York: Harper & Row, 1979), 57–84.
45 Jameson, *Representing Capital*, 2.
46 On the origins of the term, see Alexander Keyssar, *Out of Work: The First Century of Unemployment in Massachusetts* (Cambridge: Cambridge University Press), 1–9.
47 On the "discovery" of unemployment, see Garraty, *Unemployment in History*; William Walters, *Unemployment and Government: Genealogies of the Social* (Cambridge: Cambridge University Press, 2000).
48 Denning, "Wageless Life," 84.
49 Marx, *Capital* vol. 1, 764.
50 Marx, *Capital* vol. 1, 784.
51 Marx, *Capital* vol. 1, 782.
52 Marx, *Capital* vol. 1, 764.
53 This is the title of Chapter 25 of *Capital* vol. 1.
54 Denning, "Wageless Life," 81.
55 Brecht, "On Subject Matter and Form," in *Brecht on Theatre*, 49.
56 For a similar analysis, see Parmalee, *Brecht's America*, 246.
57 Martin Revermann, "Brechtian Chorality," in *Choruses, Ancient and Modern*, eds. Joshua Billings, Felix Budelmann, and Fiona Macintosh (Oxford: Oxford University Press, 2013), 151–69.
58 Quoted in Willett and Mannheim, "Introduction," xviii.
59 Endnotes, "A History of Separation," *Endnotes* 4 (2015). https://endnotes.org.uk/issues/4/en/endnotes-preface, accessed August 20, 2019.
60 Willet and Mannheim, "Svendborg Amendments and Additions," 139–40.
61 Helgard Kramer, "Frankfurt's Working Women," in *The German Unemployed*, 108–41.
62 Geoff Eley, *Forging Democracy* (Oxford: Oxford University Press, 2002), 257.
63 Eley, *Forging Democracy*, 257.
64 The play was finally produced in 1959, directed by Gustav Gründgens in Hamburg. A shortened radio play directed by Burri and starring Neher as Joan was broadcast

on Berlin radio in May 1932. On the troubled production history, see Bahr, "Zur Entstehungsgeschichte," 211–16; Knopf, "Der lange Weg zur Uraufführung," in *Brechts "Heilige Johanna Der Schlachthöfe,"* 217–20.
65 See the news articles from February 1933 collected in Bahr, "Zur politische Debatte," in *Die Heilige Johanna Der Schlachthöfe*, 223–30.
66 Bahr, "Zur politische Debatte," 226.
67 Mueller's speech is republished in Bahr, "Zur politische Debatte," 228.
68 Bahr, "Zur politische Debatte," 230.
69 Hartung and Hirschfeld would go into exile themselves, and while working in Zurich helped to arrange influential productions of Brecht's plays at the Schauspielhaus.
70 For an overview of the decline of modernist theater in Germany, see John Willett, *The New Sobriety: 1917–1933, Art and Politics in the Weimar Period* (London: Thames and Hudson, 1987), 185–210.
71 Brecht, "Draft for a Radio Talk," in *Saint Joan of the Stockyards*, 123.

13

Marx, Music, Modernism

Sarah Collins

It is often observed that Marx never produced a systematic aesthetic theory or philosophy of art, or rather that his direct engagement with questions of aesthetics extended only to a few early commissions to write on the topic, which he either declined or left unfulfilled.[1] A palpable sense of embarrassment seems to attend this observation—how, after all, could a thinker who was so concerned with identifying the forces that structured human consciousness care so little, apparently, about the role of aesthetics? How could a thinker whose work was the catalyst for the development of some of the most powerful and still-pervasive practices in cultural criticism have written so scantily about the implications of artistic expression? Marx did of course write about the artworks he admired, though these reflections show an overwhelming preference for works involving text, either written or spoken, such as literature (particularly the novel), poetry (indeed he tried his own hand at poetry during this early years), and theater (particularly classical Greek tragedy, and Shakespeare), as other chapters in this volume attest. When it came to non-referential or nonimitative arts such as music, however, Marx seemed far more ambivalent.

There are a handful of fleeting references to music in Marx's early poems and letters: in his poem, "Sir (G)luck's Armide," music clinches a comedic moment when the narrator ignores the advances of his female companion during a concert due to his rapture at events on stage ("I sat, lost in the music's spell"); Marx mentions Wagner on several occasions, though only ever refers to his librettos or the cultural impact of Wagner's writings;[2] and there is an oft-quoted anecdote conveyed by Marx's friend Wilhelm Liebknecht (founder of the Social Democratic Party of Germany), about Marx forcefully defending the musical heritage of Germany to a group of inebriated Englishmen during a drinking session in London in the April of 1854[3]—all of which, needless to say, falls far short of evincing a sincere engagement with the art form of music.

Friedrich Engels, on the other hand, had been thoroughly engaged with musical life in Bremen in the late 1830s; had witnessed the hysterical effects of "Lisztomania" when he was stationed in Berlin in the early 1840s; and had even dabbled in composition himself. Yet while, in the preface to a collection of Marx and Engels' jottings on art and literature, the reader is assured that the pair "had an excellent knowledge of world art and truly loved literature, classical music, and painting," the only musical discussion that appears in these writings, in addition to references to Wagner, is to works involving text such as folk and revolutionary song.[4] Likewise, the treatment of these forms is largely concerned with the interpretation of words. Folk song, for Marx and Engels alike, appeared simply as a form of vernacular poetry—a form of expression that embodied the collective imagination and cultural memory of a people. Revolutionary song reflected more specifically the degree to which class consciousness informed previous workers' revolutions. For example, Marx wrote that

> *not one* of the French and English workers' uprisings had such a *theoretical* and *conscious* character as the uprising of the Silesian weavers.
>
> First of all, recall the *song of the weavers*, that bold *call* to struggle, in which there is not even a mention of hearth and home, factory or district, but in which the proletariat at once, in a striking, sharp, unrestrained and powerful manner, proclaims its opposition to the society of private property.[5]

Marx and Engels wrote about Danish songs, German revolutionary song, Cossack song and songs of the Chartists, among others, yet almost exclusively referring only to the lyrical and textual as opposed to sonic or musical elements.

There are important similarities between the way both poetry and music askew the distinction between affective expression and conceptual content, such that an approach to folksong that only considers the words is not as myopic as it first appears. Rather, it points to a particular tension between the temporal arts during this period that had a significant impact on cultural modernism, as we shall explore further. At the very least, Marx's limited engagement with non-referential musical forms in his writing is telling: it is an omission that speaks directly to the uncertain status of aesthetics in his thinking more broadly and one that has several implications for how we understand his modernist afterlives.

Lingering for a moment on Marx's preference for music with text, there is a dearth of political song after Marx that draws explicitly from his ideas and writings, and are directed toward revolutionary purposes.[6] This is a rich tradition that continues to hold vital relevance in ongoing struggles associated with socialist causes globally. Yet Marxist thought after Marx diverged on the question of the role of art in revolutionary struggle, and on the degree to which the political aims of revolutionary art should be made explicit on the surface of the material. On the one hand, art could achieve political results through direct expression—that is, music coupled with words (voice) in a manner accessible to the people (and encouraging collective participation in performance), tonally oriented, and formally generic. This approach was not limited to the popular realm and indeed a number of composers who were otherwise considered aesthetically progressive offered examples of this, such as Hanns Eisler's "Komintern-Lied" (1929–30). On the other hand, however, music's non-referential character seemed to offer the possibility of the ultimate withdrawal from the rationalizing forces of capitalism in the twentieth century; or alternatively, for Marxist modernists like Theodor Adorno, music could (and should) exhibit the underlying conflicts and fractures of contemporary relations. These approaches foregrounded music's so-called autonomy, which was historically associated with purely instrumental music without narrative, programmatic or functional associations, and in its modernist guise favored twelve-tone and serial approaches to composition, such as in select compositions of Arnold Schoenberg and his disciplines, as well as later composers such as Luigi Nono.[7]

It would be a simplification to claim that the idea of direct expression predominated in music composed within the communist bloc, while the focus on music's autonomy predominated among composers with communist sympathies living elsewhere. For a counter-example of the former, we might think of the occluded presence of twelve-tone composition in the Soviet Union,[8] and for a counter-example of the latter we need only look to the political works of the British composer Alan Bush—works that were seen as the unfortunate parts of an otherwise promising avant-garde output.[9] Nevertheless, it is certainly evident that composers with left-wing political sympathies living in Western democracies had a greater latitude to explore more varied forms of political expression in their music.[10] The left-wing avant-garde also pursued what Anne Shreffler calls "hybrid models," examples of which include Kurt Weill's projects in collaboration with Bertolt Brecht, the participant-based composition of Cornelius Cardew and Christian Wolff, the performance art and music of Yoko Ono and Stefan Wolfe's circle, the anarchic tendencies of John Cage and his associates, and we might also include Paul Dessau's blending of Schoenbergian and Brechtian aesthetics.[11]

Much of the historical research in this area has dealt with these kinds of polarized associations—namely the binary of so-called populist and modernist expression, and hybrid combinations thereof, on Shreffler's account—in the music of composers with broadly Marxist sympathies.[12] By contrast, what follows takes its cue from the very ambivalence with which Marx addresses music in his own writings, and from the latency of his aesthetic theory more generally. To wit, rather than asking how Marxist composers envisaged their task and what aesthetic features typify their music, we might instead ask: can Marx's musical afterlives be traced in the physiognomy of musical modernism itself? It is worth surveying two examples of this type of inquiry to forewarn of its varying degrees of persuasiveness.

During the 1970 anniversary celebrations of Beethoven's birth, musicologist Christopher Ballantine reflected upon the rationale for continuing to celebrate the life and music of Beethoven—whom he considered "the first modernist."[13] Ballantine argued that Beethoven's significance lay not so much in the power of his music to conjure the inner essence of the human experience of the infinite, but rather in its sensuous manifestation of Hegel's dialectic (Hegel was born in the same year as Beethoven), an idea that he saw as coextensive with the new sense of historical agency engendered by the French Revolution. The focus of this claim was Beethoven's contribution to the transformation of the sonata principle—a principle of formal musical organization involving the presentation of an exposition, development, and recapitulation, broadly speaking. The sonata principle involves two musical themes bearing particular harmonic relationships being presented sequentially and usually in a contrasting manner. This, according to Ballantine, suggests the conflict between reality and potentiality—a conflict between the themes that spurn a mutual process of development, thereby "dramatiz[ing] the principle whereby something may become something else under the driving force of contradiction."[14]

While this recalls Marx's dialectical materialism, Beethoven's treatment of the sonata principle also bears the imprint of the post-Revolutionary moment, according to Ballantine, and is distinct from the earlier sonata principle deployed by Mozart and Haydn:

> The musical style appropriate to the pre-Revolutionary conception of an unalterable human "nature" was the Bachian principle of extension by varied, motor-like repetition; but the post-Revolutionary view of man as a product [of] his own efforts called for nothing less than the full Beethovenian dialectic, the principle not of extension but of movement, of contradiction rather than repletion, and of thematic transformation rather than variation.[15]

A less generous reading of sonata form might see the process of recapitulation as itself a form of mandated reconciliation or false consensus, overriding the productive contradictions of the initial themes.[16] However, Ballantine insists that Beethoven's recapitulations do not exhibit the subsumption of difference into sameness, but rather that there is something new that arises from the contradiction through development which is not already latent in the initial themes. By Ballantine's account, just as Marx extended Hegel's theoretical speculations into material terms or active practice, Beethoven made sensuous the "spirit" or "speculative thought" that was exhibited by Mozart's idealism, making Beethoven a "materialist" composer. Beethoven offered an "articulation in music of the principle of dialectic in all its rich and splendid logical and affective significance."[17]

While Ballantine discovered Marx's specter in the formal procedures of Beethoven as a logical and historical continuation of the ethos of the French Revolution and Hegel's dialectic, the conservative thinker Jacques Barzun found the imprint of Marx's thought in the structural and melodic innovations of Wagner. In a book that was roundly criticized for its reductive polemics, Barzun drew a broad brush over the intellectual tendencies in science, economics, and art of the late nineteenth century by linking together Marx, Darwin, and Wagner around the year of 1859: the year Marx published his *Contribution to the Critique of Political Economy*, Darwin published *On the Origin of Species*, and Wagner completed *Tristan und Isolde*.[18] Barzun attributed to these three figures the very opposite of the sense of agency and freedom that Ballantine heard in Beethoven's sonata procedures, instead construing them as reducing man to being mechanistic and determined—a view which, according to Barzun, had led directly to twentieth-century totalitarianisms.

For Barzun, Marx's insistence that human consciousness is determined by the relations of production, together with Darwin's evolutionary determinism, could be seen equally in Wagner's technique of the leitmotif. In this reading, the leitmotif, "though it is the germ of a presumably free musical development, is also the sign, in Wagner, of a definite person, idea or object" and is therefore bound inextricably to something beyond its control, governed by the narrative, by dramatic necessities, and by a collective idea that curtails its autonomous nature. The leitmotif seems free but is in fact mechanical and determined and this, combined with Wagner's penchant for themes of redemption through self-destruction and the sensuous wash of his unending melody which deprived the listener of self-awareness, seemed to Barzun as exhibiting the move away from romanticism and vitalism toward ideological realpolitik.[19] Quite apart from the fact that Barzun presents Wagnerian leitmotif as merely an elaborate form of musical "word painting," rather than the interpenetrating technique that it is, it is clear that his real target lay elsewhere. Barzun attributed the troubling central quality of Wagner's music—namely the illusion of freedom at the behest of a hidden source of control—with programme music more generally, hearkening back to the categories of "absolute" and programmatic musical expression that shaped late nineteenth-century debates in music aesthetics. This is what enables him to link concerns about the treatment of music as the mere "handmaiden of poetry" to Darwin and Marx's conflicted relationship with eighteenth-century rationalism.[20]

In focusing on the relationship between music and words, Barzun's attempt to draw Marx (and Darwin) into one of the major debates of late-nineteenth-century music aesthetics echoes the mistaken alignment of Marx with realism historically. In this contrived conflict between words and music, words came to represent all the qualities that modernists (in the now-discredited singular sense) avowedly strove to reject, such as narrative linearity, representation, accessibility, functionality, intelligibility, and instrumentalization. In this context, words were seen by some as degrading impositions upon the otherwise powerfully ineffable quality of musical expression. It is for this reason that even beyond the musical sphere, literary figures strove to emulate in their work the "condition" of music, on Walter Pater's famous maxim, and even later, in the 1920s and 1930s, the modernist literary and musical fields alike can be seen to have been grappling with this challenge of withdrawing the spoken word and music from discursive function. Music and poetry's unavoidably temporal quality meant that this projected distance from discursive association gradually gave way to a predominance of the image as a metonym for the instantaneous and nonlinear, such as in Weill and Brecht's different notions of *Gestus* as much as in Pound and H. D.'s Imagism.

Others sought to evoke the visceral nature of words through musical treatment. In Schoenberg's Foreword to *Pierrot Lunaire* (1912), he wrote that the *Sprechstimme* or speaking voice was to be a type of speech-melody, and that despite the illustrative quality of the music, his instructions were for the singer to respond only to what is found in the music, not in the text. Both Schoenberg and his student Alban Berg indicated particular vocal techniques on their operatic scores that problematized the relationship between sung and spoken text and music.[21] Orientations like these, favoring the dissolution of the distinction between the arts (here the arts of poetry and music), can be arguably seen as an extension upon Wagner's ideas and compositional practice, contrary to a reading that sees this impulse as exhibiting an occluded form of determinism that undermines human freedom. While Barzun's attempt to read Marx's historical materialism into debates about the relationship between music and words was troubling for a range of reasons (related not only to Wagner's leitmotif but also his reduction of Marx's thinking to a specific sense of labor and surplus value), the link may hold other, more promising, interpretive possibilities.

Apart from passing comments in letters and comments about Wagner and folksong, there is one further way in which Marx refers to music in his writings—when music appears elsewhere in Marx's writings it is not generally for its capacity to stir emotions or to reflect or critique prevailing power structures, but rather as a "hard case" in testing certain propositions. The fact that music required concerted labor to compose and perform, and it was clearly part of a system of exchange, yet its product was ungraspable and appealed merely to the senses, was of interest to Marx in his analysis of labor particularly. For example, in Marx's discussion of Adam Smith's distinction between productive labor (namely labor that produces capital) and unproductive labor, and his analysis of the relationship between labor, use-value, and capital more generally, Marx writes that under Smith's definition a piano-maker would be considered productive but not a pianist, yet if the pianist did not exist there would be no need for the piano-maker:

> The piano-maker reproduces *capital*; the pianist only exchanges his labor for revenue. But doesn't the pianist produce music and satisfy our musical ear, does he not even to a certain extent produce the latter? He does indeed: his labor produces something; but that does not make it productive labor in the economic sense; no more than the labor of the madman who produces delusions is productive. Labor becomes productive only by producing its own opposite [namely capital].[22]

Elsewhere, when Marx discusses Smith's conception of labor, musical activity operates as a "hard case" to test the limits of Marx's argument. While Smith views labor as a form of sacrifice or impediment to liberty, Marx argues that this conception is based on a view of labor undertaken under certain conditions only—namely slave labor, bond labor, and wage labor. Marx seeks to move away from a conception of labor as a sacrifice of liberty and happiness toward a view of labor as a primarily creative activity that supports self-realization and is itself an exercise in liberty: an ideal state of labor that "ceases to be human effort as a definite, trained natural force" and is rather purely an expression of the human capacity to shape their natural environment for their survival and pleasure. For Marx this does not mean that labor under these conditions is pure whimsey—and it is here that he points out that "really free labor, the composing of music, for example, is at the same time damned serious and demands the greatest effort"—but rather that it is both social and scientific but also general, not abstracted from other parts of life, and directed toward human fulfillment.[23] This view of labor as a primarily creative task of self-realization is important in order to link Marx's ideas about the alienation of the senses under capitalism to debates about the division of the arts in modernism, and specifically music's relationship with words.

Marx's early writings on the historicity of the senses offer a more nuanced (and more aesthetically oriented) picture of the relationship between determinism and human freedom. In early works such as the *Economic and Philosophic Manuscripts* (1844), Marx historicizes the human senses in a way that has since become influential for accounts of historical techniques of listening[24]—"the *cultivation* of the five senses is the work of all previous history. *Sense* which is a prisoner of crude practical need has only a *restricted* sense."[25] Just as human consciousness is shaped by relations of production, so too are the senses shaped by the same forces of history. Yet, because Marx ascribes a creative aspect to labor, whereby the human becomes the object of their labor and of their sense perceptions, realizing their own contours through each interaction with objects around them. The sensation of seeing, or hearing, establishes the human as an existing object only in relation to other objects. Marx argues that the limitations of an individual's being relate then to the limitations of what they can take in with their senses. For the industrial working classes, however, affirming the human self through the sensuous apprehension of the object is replaced by a sense that an object can only relate to the self in terms of ownership or use (as it is under the conditions of private property).

At this point, human reality comes to be dominated by means rather than ends—"all the physical and intellectual senses have been replaced by the simple estrangement of all these senses—the sense of having."[26] When our relation to things outside of ourselves is purely for want or need, we are unable to sense what is required to create ourselves as human. Here Marx uses music as a passing example:

> only music can awaken the musical sense in man and the most beautiful music has no sense for the unmusical ear, because my object can only be the confirmation of one of my essential powers, i.e., can only be for me in so far as my essential power exists for me as a subjective attribute (this is because the sense of an object for me extends only as far as my sense extends, only has sense for a sense that corresponds to that object). In the same way, and for the same reasons, the senses of social man are different from those of non-social man. Only through the objectively unfolded wealth of human nature can the wealth of subjective human sensitivity—a musical ear, an eye for the beauty of form, in short, senses capable of human gratification—be either cultivated or created.[27]

What is interesting in this essay is the claim that sensing or perceiving objects for their own sake—an aesthetic mindset if there ever was one, clearly evincing the influence of Schiller on the young Marx—is what enables us to recover from our condition of alienation.

From the foregoing we can see that Marx argued that labor is only burdensome when it is a mere means to life rather than a self-creating exercise, and that the senses are only receptive to the extent that they are not instrumentalized. Here we may return to the concern that music's nature is curtailed by the discursive imperative of words, with an awareness that this is only the case when the arts are combined for the purposes of intelligibility, as in the role of text in revolutionary or folk song, or in programmatic attributions to music that predetermine its meaning. Yet the tendencies of the arts to combine in modernism could also serve to dislocate music from discursive function, and indeed allow its sonic logic to dominate and shape its materials in the manner of creative labor. In Igor Stravinsky's opera-cantata *Renard* (1916), for example, the central stage performers—including acrobats and dancers dressed as animals—are themselves largely mute, and the voices that speak for them (two tenors and two basses) stand off to the side and employ nonsensical utterances, all sustained by a hidden pit orchestra. In this way, the different senses engaged in the performance are unaligned: we do not hear what we see and we do not see what we hear. Likewise, while we can follow the narrative of events played out in the work, the disjunctive presentation seems to thwart any sense of narrative. Daniel Albright has likened this form of presentation to instances in the early history of sound film when there were errors in synchronization—a phenomenon that itself evoked otherworldly and dissonant resonances for audiences in the late 1920s and 1930s.[28] This example shows how, while the arts seem to be drawn together during modernism, they are drawn together in ways that eschew a unified reading—that is, in ways that highlight correspondences *and* non-correspondences between sound and sign, between music and text, between word and semantic meaning, such that neither art labors under the character of the other.

There are yet other tendencies within musical modernism that may be seen as undead traces of Marx's ideas (as opposed to Marx*ist* ideas). These include thematizations of alienation and fetishism; works that exhibit on their surface the mode of artistic labor and the means of production that shaped them (Rose reads Marx into this feature of 1920s Constructivist art, though a similar reading might be given to twelve-tone music and other types of pre-compositional device); a conflicted aspiration toward intelligibility tempered by a suspicion of exchange-value (such as in works that enable passive consumption); music that serves the function of critique, unmasking that which seems natural and inevitable (as theorized amply by Adorno); modernist valorization of preindustrial forms of relation (and the music that came with them, such as folk song); and an interest in the relativity of the senses and their capacity to shape action and selves. Marx's ambivalent engagement with questions of aesthetics is usually seen as a logical omission on account of the perceived abstraction of aesthetics from worldly concerns. Yet others have noted that it is the very fact that Marx joins together matters of the practical and everyday with broader structures of consciousness and culture that reflects the way aesthetics underpinned his thinking on economics.[29] The voluminousness of Marxist aesthetic theory—including that generated by musical modernism—is not only in this sense an application of Marx's economic thinking to art but also a testimony to this latent underpinning in his thought itself—his reaching after a state of noninstrumental and therefore unalienated modes of relation to nature, each other, and ourselves—a mode of life that involves a fully embedded (and embodied) form of aesthetic contemplation.

Notes

1 In 1842 Bruno Bauer invited Marx to contribute to a volume that aimed to radically reinterpret Hegel's aesthetics and philosophy of religion in a manner that would cast Hegel as a critic of Christian art and an advocate of Hellenistic art in order to counter the perception that the latter was overly sensuous and immoral (Margaret A. Rose, *Marx's Lost Aesthetic: Karl Marx and the Visual Arts* [Cambridge: Cambridge

University Press, 1984], 58–62). Marx left only fragments of his contribution to this volume, and it was never published in full. His aversion to writing on aesthetics seemed only to increase over time, as in 1857 Marx was invited but refused to write an entry on the topic for the *New American Cyclopaedia*, despite writing other entries for the volume.

2 Engels recalled that in a letter from the spring of 1882, Marx had written in "the strongest possible terms about the utter falsification of primeval times appearing in Wagner's *Nibelung* text," referring to the presentation of incest as immoral without acknowledging the historical relativity of this view. See Marx and Engels, *On Literature and Art*, 217–18. The source of the translations and the editorial work for this collection of Marx and Engels' writings on art and literature is unclear, but the Preface to the collection was written by B. Krylov. Another example appears in a letter that Marx sent to Engels from Karlsbad in August 1876, where Marx commented "everything here is 'the Future' since the rumbling of 'the music of the future' in Bayreuth" (for this and more translated examples see Mark Lindley, "Marx and Engels on Music," *Monthly Review Online*, August 18, 2010).

3 This anecdote was recalled in Wilhelm Liebknecht, *Karl Marx, zum Gedächtniss: Ein Lebensabriss und Erinnerungen* (Nuremberg: Wörlein, 1896), 82–4.

4 Liebknecht, *Karl Marx*, 15.

5 Marx, "Critical Marginal Notes on the Article 'The King of Prussia and Social Reform, By a Prussian,'" in Marx and Engels, *On Literature and Art*, 433. The song was "Das Blutgericht" (The Bloodbath), which was popular during the Silesian textile districts during the 1844 weavers' uprising.

6 To listen to a selective range of Marxist revolutionary song from the early twentieth century, the *Marxists Internet Archive* hosts a list with downloadable mp3s, idiosyncratically categorized into "Soviet Music," "May Day Music," and "Music about Che Guevara" (https://www.marxists.org/subject/art/music/index.htm, accessed August 20, 2019). In the realm of scholarship there has been a recent resurgence of interest in the interaction between music and leftist politics more generally, characterized by a useful expansion in geographical and historical reach (see for example Danijela Š. Beard and Elaine Kelly's special issue of *Twentieth-Century Music* on "Music and Socialism" 16.1 [2019]; and Regula Burckhardt Qureshi, ed. *Music and Marx: Ideas, Practice, Politics* [London and New York: Routledge, 2002]). Other recent contributions to this field include Nicholas Tochka, *Audible States: Socialist Politics and Popular Music in Albania* (New York: Oxford University Press, 2016); Ana Hofman, *Staging Socialist Femininity: Gender Politics and Folklore Performance in Serbia* (Leiden: Brill, 2011); Eric Drott, *Music and the Elusive Revolution: Cultural Politics and Political Culture in France, 1968-1981* (Berkeley: University of California Press, 2011); and Robin D. Moore, *Music and Revolution: Cultural Change in Socialist Cuba* (Berkeley: University of California Press, 2006). Others are discussed further.

7 Schoenberg did partake of direct political expression in works such as his *Ode to Napoleon Buonaparte* (1943), though not generally in support of left-wing causes, and in any case it was specifically *Adorno's* Schoenberg who was seen as exemplary in the sense that is relevant here.

8 See Peter Schmelz, *Such Freedom, If Only Musical: Unofficial Soviet Music During the Thaw* (Oxford and New York: Oxford University Press, 2009).

9 See Joanna Bullivant, *Alan Bush, Modern Music, and the Cold War: The Cultural Left in Britain and the Communist Bloc* (Cambridge: Cambridge University Press, 2017).

10 See Robert Adlington, ed., *Red Strains: Music and Communism outside the Communist Bloc* (Oxford: Oxford University Press, 2013), particularly Anne C. Shreffler's chapter "'Music Left and Right': A Tale of Two Histories of Progressive Music," 67–88.
11 Shreffler, "Music Left and Right," 71 and Martin Brady, "Paul Dessau and the Hard Work of Socialist Music in the German Democratic Republic," *Twentieth-Century Music* 16.1 (2019): 51–66.
12 For a discussion of other Marxist modernist musicians later in the century such as Nikolaus A. Huber and Mathias Spahlinger, among others, see Robert Adlington, "Modernism: The People's Music?" in *The Routledge Research Companion to Modernism in Music*, ed. Björn Heile and Charles Wilson (London and New York: Routledge, 2019), 216–38. Adlington tests Rachel Potter's distinction between the "two genealogies of modernism" against the music and aims of a selection of politically engaged avant-garde composers and performers—figures who variously capitalized on the aesthetics and rhetoric (sometimes more so than the politics) of revolution in the early twentieth century, as well as those who sought to eschew capitalist impulses more generally, such as Bebop musicians in the 1940s and those involved in contemporary free improvisation communities and noise music.
13 Christopher Ballantine, "Beethoven, Hegel and Marx," *The Music Review* 33.1 (1972): 34–46, 45.
14 Ballantine, "Beethoven, Hegel and Marx," 35.
15 Ballantine, "Beethoven, Hegel and Marx," 36.
16 Alternatively, for a feminist reading of the sonata principle see Susan McClary, *Feminine Endings: Music, Gender, and Sexuality* (Minneapolis: University of Minnesota Press, 2002), 68–71.
17 Ballantine, "Beethoven, Hegel and Marx," 34.
18 Jacques Barzun, *Darwin, Marx, Wagner: Critique of a Heritage* (Boston: Little, Brown and Co., 1941).
19 Barzun, *Darwin, Marx, Wagner*, 262 and 145.
20 Barzun, *Darwin, Marx, Wagner*, 281.
21 See Arnold Schoenberg, "Foreword to *Pierrot Lunaire* (1912)," in *Modernism and Music: An Anthology of Sources*, ed. Daniel Albright (Chicago and London: University of Chicago Press, 2004), 38–9. See also Daniel Albright, *Untwisting the Serpent: Modernism in Music, Literature, and Other Arts* (Chicago and London: University of Chicago Press, 2000).
22 Marx, *Grundrisse*, 232.
23 McLellan, *Marx's Grundrisse*, 133.
24 See for example Jonathan Sterne, *The Audible Past: Cultural Origins of Sound Reproduction* (Durham: Duke University Press, 2003).
25 Marx, *Early Writings*, 353.
26 Marx, *Early Writings*, 352.
27 Marx, *Early Writings*, 353.
28 Albright, *Untwisting the Serpent*, 15.
29 See William Adams, "Aesthetics: Liberating the Senses," in *The Cambridge Companion to Marx*, ed. Terrell Carver (Cambridge: Cambridge University Press, 1991), 246–74.

14

Constructing Socialism

Marxism, Modernism, and Architecture

Tyrus Miller

When considering the relationship of Marx, modernism, and architecture, it is worth recalling the strictures that the Marxist architectural historian Manfredo Tafuri set down in the conclusion to his 1973 book, *Architecture and Utopia: Design and Capitalist Development*. "The truth is," for Tafuri, "that just as there cannot exist a class political economy, but only a class criticism of political economy, so too there cannot be founded a class aesthetic, art, or architecture, but only a class criticism of the aesthetic, of art, of architecture, of the city itself."[1] In other words, the Italian historian considered the idea of a "Marxist architecture," or for that matter a "Marxist modernism" or "avant-garde," a contradiction in terms, since Marxism, as he saw it, could only serve to show the limits of art and architecture within modern capitalist society and to debunk the ideologies these disciplines furnish to the ongoing development and rationalization of capitalism.

One logical way of developing this critique was followed by Tafuri and his colleagues, such as the philosopher Massimo Cacciari: pursuing critical history and an autonomous theory of the metropolis in its complex genealogical relationships with capitalist development. Another, followed by radical architectural groups in Italy such as Archizoom and Superstudio, was to design unconsoling estrangements and extreme extrapolations of the capitalist metropolis itself, in order to demystify the capitalist city and suggest possible sites of political struggle for its spaces to be appropriated and used in new ways. This was exemplified, for example, by Archizoom's projection of the supermarket as a paradigm for a large-scale urban design.[2] We may, however, point to more recent critics such as Owen Hatherley who, in *Militant Modernism* and other works, rejects this negative approach to modernist architecture and its socialist aspirations. Hatherley urges us to reconsider, with more redemptive intentions, the intertwinings of modernism and socialist ideals we may rediscover in the twentieth-century landscape of cities, buildings, and architectural ideas.[3] Flawed, partial, now apprehensible mostly in fragments and traces, socialist modernism—as Hatherley generously conceives it—may yet encompass the utopian energies of everything from Wyndham Lewis' vorticist urbanism in *The Caliph's Design* to Georgi Krutikov's proposal for a Soviet flying city to the New Brutalism of 1950s and 1960s British social housing initiatives.

Marx and Engels did not themselves specifically theorize the city as a manifestation of capitalism, much less give detailed consideration to architecture in the capitalist city and its possible socialist transformations.[4] In his 1845 book *The Condition of the Working-Class in England*, Engels devotes a lengthy chapter to the "Great Towns," including London, Dublin, Birmingham, Liverpool, Glasgow, and Manchester, and reports on the dreadful conditions of working-class slum dwellings and the inequalities that have embedded themselves into the spatial structure of cities. In the second volume of *Capital*, in his discussion of rent, Marx notes the massive speculative construction of housing in London, a "revolutionizing" of building spurred by capitalist development.[5] And the mature Engels dedicated a book-length polemic in 1872 to *The Housing Question*. In the course of demolishing the views of Proudhon and others on the problems of housing in the big cities, Engels asserts how problems of housing and living conditions derive from larger structures of capitalist exploitation. As Pier Vittorio Aureli points out, Engels' polemic was taken up again in the 1960s by the Italian activist Claudio Greppi, who in turn exercised considerable influence over the Archizoom architects, to reject social democratic ideas of urban reform.[6] Tafuri's foreclosure of a class-based architecture is, as well, only a sophisticated restatement of Engels' fundamental argument.

In a more generalizing remark, however—which would anticipate Soviet debates around city planning and urbanization or deurbanization—Engels recurs to his early reflections with Marx in *The German Ideology* (1845) on the division of city and countryside, noting that

> The housing question can be solved only when society has been sufficiently transformed for a start to be made towards abolishing the antithesis between town and country, which has been brought to its extreme point by present-day capitalist society. Far from being able to abolish this antithesis, capitalist society on the contrary is compelled to intensify it day by day. On the other hand, already the first modern Utopian socialists, Owen and Fourier, correctly recognized this. In their model structures, the antithesis between town and country no longer exists.... To want to solve the housing question while at the same time desiring to maintain the modern big cities is an absurdity. The modern big cities, however, will be abolished only by the abolition of the capitalist mode of production and when this is once set going there will be quite other issues than supplying each worker with a little house of his own.[7]

While Engels seems to suggest that housing would surely be the least of people's concerns in the midst of a revolutionary transformation of society, the Russian Revolution and subsequent rapid industrialization and collectivization under Stalin posed questions of housing and city development with immediate urgency. As Walter Benjamin, following his two-month visit to the Soviet Union, expounded in a letter to Martin Buber in 1927:

Moscow, as it appears at the present, reveals a full range of possibilities in schematic form: above all, the possibility that the Revolution might fail or succeed. In either case, something unforeseeable will result and the picture will be far different from any programmatic sketch one might draw of the future. The outlines of this are at present brutally and distinctly visible among the people and their environment.[8]

With his fine-tuned sense for reading cities and their spaces "physionomically," Benjamin saw in Moscow a portent of the future, but also a dialectical image of the indetermination of the present, which could descend into ruin or leap into a messianic overcoming of present limits: "In fact, nowhere does Moscow really look like the city it is, rather it more resembles the outskirts of itself. The soggy ground, the wooden booths, the long convoys of raw materials, the cattle being driven to slaughter, the shabby dives can all be found in the most central parts of the town."[9] More directly, in his important intervention into the Soviet planning debate in 1930, *Sotsgorod: The Problem of Building Socialist Cities*, N. A. Miliutin reprised Engels arguments about overcoming the division between city and countryside, but in a way that would be a dialectical reversal of the Moscow-as-village urban landscape that Benjamin observed: "there can be no controversy about urbanization or disurbanization. We will have to settle the problem of the new distribution of humanity after we have eliminated that senseless . . . centralization of industrial production which gives birth to the modern city."[10] In this context, ideas for new city types such as constellations of eccentric and shifting urban nodes and new linear cities that would continuously link chains of existing cities were advanced by Soviet architects, as were new building types like those involving aerial structures such as El Lissitzky's "skyhooks" or Georgi Krutikov's "flying city."[11]

In fact, the visionary writings of the utopian socialists that Engels mentions, especially Fourier with his architectural representation of affective classes and spatialized proportions in his "phalanxes,"[12] might, in light of the early Soviet experience, be seen as a more direct precursor of modernist innovations in architecture than Engels' formally indifferent critique. Tafuri and Francesco Dal Co note—albeit with predictable disapproval—direct reference to Fourier in the idea of the "communal house" in the Soviet discourse of the late 1920s. As they remark about the conceptions of new worker settlements to accommodate accelerated industrialization during the first Five-Year Plans,

> The solutions adopted initially were not too remote from the experimental notions of the avant-garde architects, but very soon the ideas that emerged in the course of the debate over the new socialist way of life lapsed unequivocally into utopianism when confronted with the real conditions of labor in the building industry. On the basis of a contrived return to the ideas of Fourier, pasted together with vague Leninist slogans, L. Sabsovich and Zelenko at the close of the 1920s launched the theory of the communal house; it was to be organized collectively with collective eating and other services, and the individual relations within the family nucleus were to be replaced by socialized ways of life, from which would be forged the New Communist Man.[13]

Sabsovich, taking in a new context Fourier's organization of affective and sexual life in the phalansteries, saw architecture and sexual or family life as essentially inter-translatable elements of the communal home: "When life is organized on a socialist basis each worker may be regarded as a potential 'bachelor' or as a potential 'husband' or 'wife', to the extent that today's bachelor may be tomorrow's husband and today's couple may tomorrow be separated."[14] The architecture of the communal house ensures that postcapitalist family and sexual roles become little more than a matter of opening or closing a door between communicating spaces.

It would of course be an exaggeration to suggest that modernist architecture was universally animated by socialist or utopian ideas, for it is easy to enumerate many influential architects, projects, and theoretical statements for which this is not the case. However, especially in Germany and Central Europe in the 1920s and 1930s, a wide range of architects internalized a broadly socialist ethos and felt it consonant with the new formal and technical languages they were evolving in their projects and buildings. Contributing to this ethos—which could range from an intuitive feeling of solidarity with the popular masses to tangible commitments to programs of socialist and communist politics—were the pervasive atmosphere of revolution and mass politics during these years; the strong association of industry and technology with collectivist social aims; the escalating role of planning in the production sphere, viewed as contrary to capitalist speculation and individualism; increasing engagement with new planning and design tasks such as the construction of standardized workers' housing; and widely shared enthusiasm of intellectuals for the experiment in socialist construction in the Soviet Union.

As iconic a document of modernist architecture as Walter Gropius' 1919 founding "Program of the Staatliche Bauhaus in Weimar" evoked the sentimental humanist socialism shared by other figures in the left-expressionist movement such as Bruno Taut and Adolf Behne in the concluding image of its preamble: "Together let us desire, conceive, and create the new structure of the future, which will embrace architecture and sculpture and painting in one unity and which will one day rise toward heaven from the hands of a million workers like the crystal symbol of a new faith."[15] The program was printed on a four-page leaflet with an expressionist "Cathedral of Socialism" by Lyonel Feininger as its cover image. It is easy to dismiss such abstract and high-flying rhetoric, which would prove short-lived in favor of Gropius' subsequently more sober advocacy of rationalist principles of design and the convergence of art and industry. But if we are justifiably skeptical of the depth of this early evocation of socialism, neither should we see it as a mere momentary enthusiasm or aberration. Gropius had been part of Taut's circle of radical architects sharing utopian plans in their "Crystal Chain" correspondence,[16] and he was also drawn into the political activities of "artist-workers" during the revolutionary events that followed Germany's defeat in the First World War, the *Novembergruppe* (November Group) and the *Arbeitsrat für Kunst* (Work Council for Art). In the early years of the Bauhaus at Weimar, the ex-army officer and rector Gropius also designed a monument—his only work of monumental sculpture—for the victims of a right-wing putsch attempt in 1920, the Kapp Putsch.

In his contribution to the first book publication of the *Arbeitsrat für Kunst, Ja! Stimmen des Arbeitsrates für Kunst in Berlin* (Yes! Voices of the Work Council for Art in Berlin, 1919), Gropius presented the artistic and architectural activity of the present as a transition through the current moment of collapse and chaos toward a new harmonious social order of the "new man":

> Not art nor the work is the most important thing; it is man. Today's artist lives in a creed-less time of dissolution. He stands spiritually alone. The old forms are broken, the petrified world is loosened, the old spirit of humanity has been overthrown, and in the midst of being remolded into a new shape. We waver in space and do not yet recognize the new order. . . . Our work can only consist in preparing the coming unity of a later harmonious time. Perhaps the living artist is called upon much more to live a work of art than to create it, and thus through his new humanity, through his new form of life to construct the spiritual foundation of which the coming art has need. We have urgent need of communion in spirit—for the whole people, but the artist must initiate it.[17]

This was the form of "socialism," an amalgam of expressionist pathos and left-wing utopian communalism, that would dovetail into the founding and early program of the Bauhaus. Through the holistic training of artist-designers in a guild spirit of production, it was to anticipate the coming socialist community of "the whole people." Notably, as the wave of expressionist activism after the First World War ebbed, Gropius' socialist inclinations migrated into concerns about rational, functional design and a closer unity of art and industry, as did those of Adolf Behne, whose book *The Modern Functional Building* (1926) became a touchstone of architectural debates in the 1920s, and of Taut, who in collaboration with Gropius and Martin Wagner designed the six Berlin Modernism Housing Estates including the Hufeisensiedlung, the Uncle Tom's Cabin development, and Berlin Falkenberg.

Even Le Corbusier, whose political inclinations intermittently leaned toward the far right, engaged extensively with the Soviet Union, traveling there in 1928, designing the *Tsentrosoyuz* (Central Union of Consumer Cooperatives) building that was completed in Moscow between 1929 and 1933, submitting plans for the ill-fated Palace of the Soviets in 1931, and forming ideas about new city planning that would inspire his *Ville Radieuse* (Radiant City) concept.[18] What seems to have especially attracted Corbusier about Soviet communism was its concentrated authority to plan, which stood against the anarchy of speculative building and the market forces of capitalism, putatively to realize an intended, socially rational development under the aegis of the proletarian state and party. Indeed, in this light we might see Corbusier's famous formulation "Architecture or Revolution" in his 1927 book *Vers Une Architecture* (Towards an Architecture) as motivated not by anti-socialism as such, but rather by the ideal of a collectivism founded upon strong state authority and rational social planning. At the conclusion of his book, Corbusier evokes a discord between the technological and conceptual means for a rational solution to the problem of human habitation and the "old hostile framework" that confronts today's humanity in the home, city, street, and apartment. By taking up a new architecture, the future "socialist" world, already latent in the new technologies and large-scale urban conglomerations, can be realized, while the violence of a revolution, which Russia was forced to take up in order to arrive at a society of planned development, may yet be foresworn by the West. Corbusier, then, does not so much posit two separate goals for the capitalist West and the communist East, but rather seeks, through modernist architecture and urbanism, the analogous end of a rationally planned ("socialist") society by alternative, nonrevolutionary means.

One of the most important attempts to realize a socialist social and political program in the domain of architecture was the development of "Red Vienna" workers' housing from 1919 until the last-gasp workers' uprising of 1934, which saw armed conflict at the Karl-Marx Hof housing estate and at several other estates in the working-class districts of Ottokring, Meidling, Simmering, and Floridsdorf.[19] In the early 1920s, the municipal Social Democratic administration in Vienna was considered, at least temporarily, friendly to architectural modernists associated especially with the *Siedlung* (settlement) movement and the journal *Der Aufbau (Construction)*. They were on one side of a debate about the appropriate city development form for Red Vienna, advocating for the decentralized and less concentrated horizontal buildings in suburban spaces, and in opposition to the more concentrated, centralized, and vertical housing of the *Gemeindebau* (communal housing).[20] One of the key urban theorists of this tendency, the left-wing Vienna Circle philosopher and social scientist Otto Neurath, had taken part in the so-called gypsy urbanism movement of the immediate postwar years, in which housing and food shortages had led to spontaneous temporary dwellings and gardens popping up on the edges of cities.[21] Though propelled by dire social necessity, such spontaneous urban resettlement put a real face on the utopian fantasies of expressionist visionaries such as Taut, who projected in his eponymous book a "dissolution of the cities" as a way of making the earth a "good place to live."[22] The famous Viennese modernist Adolf Loos headed up the Viennese *Siedlungsamt* (settlement office) from May 1921 to June 1924,[23] before his transplantation to Paris: "in Vienna in particular," Eva Blau writes,

> the *Siedlung* not only had come to be linked with progressive social reform and radical politics but also was seen as one of the key sites of typological and technological innovation in architecture in the 1920s, where new forms of social and spatial organization, new methods of construction and production, and new principles of site planning were being developed.[24]

"[F]or the architects involved in the *Siedlung* movement in Vienna—Adolf Loos, Josef Frank, Margarete Lihotzky, Franz Schuster, and others," Blau concludes, "the *Siedlung* movement was central to the architectural project of cultural modernism in Vienna."[25]

Distinct from the municipal socialist housing projects of Red Vienna were the social housing initiatives of 1920s Germany,[26] with such key figures as architect and city planner Martin Wagner, who oversaw the building of the Berlin modernist housing estates; Ernst May, the major figure behind the "New Frankfurt" movement;

the leftist architect Hannes Meyer, one of the founders of the journal *ABC: Beiträge zu Bauen* (*ABC: Contributions to Building*) with Mart Stam, El Lissitzky, and Hans Schmidt, and director of the Dessau Bauhaus for two years following Walter Gropius' departure in 1928; the ex-expressionist Taut, already discussed earlier; and the outstanding theorist and radical architect Ludwig Hilbersheimer, a former member of the Novembergruppe and the Arbeitsrat für Kunst and a Bauhaus teacher under Hannes Meyer in Dessau and Mies van der Rohe in Berlin, who also contributed regular critical reviews on modern art, cinema, and architecture to the journals *Das Kunstblatt* (*Art Paper*), *G: Material zur elementaren Gestaltung* (*G: Material for Elementary Construction*), and the *Sozialistische Monatshefte* (*Socialist Monthly*). Their planning, building, and theorizing for interwar German social democracy led several of these figures—including May, Taut, and Meyer—to the Soviet Union in the early 1930s.[27] They contributed to the building of new worker cities linked to the rapid development of industry during the first Five-Year Plans (e.g., the famous iron smelting and steel making city of Magnitogorsk, planned by May and his "brigade" of seventeen foreign architects).

In the context of the city planning debates of the late 1920s, Hannes Meyer explicitly proposed a "Marxist architecture" in, for example, his lecture "On Marxist Architecture," probably delivered in the early 1930s at the KOMAKADEMIA (Communist Academy) and his "Theses on Marxist Architecture."[28] Taut even revived his utopian ideas about the "dissolution of cities," originally formulated in an outpouring of expressionist pathos during the German revolutions after the First World War.[29] In his 1930 article in *Sovremennaya Arkhitektura* (*Modern Architecture*), Taut writes:

> To a great degree the joy of the autonomy of thinking about city-building now takes root in the Soviet Union. The disintegration of the city is a clear theory leading to the healing emancipation from the formalist chains of dogmatism, historicism, and eclecticism (whether or not it refers to the old or the new in the West). This disintegration is a consequence of and a parallel to the phenomenon of the liberation of the proletariat from the chains of capitalism.[30]

Soon chastened in their hopes, however, by the conservative outcome of the competition for the Palace of the Soviets in 1932, which had garnered entries from such modernist luminaries as Le Corbusier, Gropius, and Erich Mendelsohn, by the mid-thirties most of the foreign architects had been pushed out, including even Meyer, who had been able to design and build up Birobidzhan, the administrative center of an autonomous Jewish zone in the extreme far east of Russia.[31]

Ludwig Hilbersheimer is of particular interest in this context, because he articulated a direct genealogical relationship between current tasks of modern architecture and urban planning and the modernist revolution in the arts in the first two decades of the twentieth century: "Architecture is the artistic field that can solve the most problems today. This explains the efforts of all modern artistic genres to connect to architecture."[32] Hilbersheimer's guiding conception, most extensively presented in his 1927 treatise *Großstadtarchitectur* (*Metropolis-architecture*), is that of architecture and urban planning as a direct intervention into real social space, with modern art as a study for the intentional design of existence:

> Today it is no longer essential to simply paint paintings, sculpt statues, or create aesthetic arrangements. Rather it is crucial to design reality itself. . . . Because the objective is to order the world and human relationships, to regulate the most important and essential conditions of life.[33]

The goal of design is the total structuring of space, bringing into being an integrated relation between the elemental spatial-architectural unit of the room and the macroscopic social space of the metropolis. "Metropolis-architecture," Hilbersheimer writes,

> is considerably dependent on solving two factors: the individual cell of the room and the collective urban organism. The solution will be determined by the manner in which the room is manifested as an element of buildings linked together in one street block, thus becoming a determining factor of the city structure, which is the actual objective of architecture. Inversely, the constructive design of the urban plan will gain considerable influence on the formation of the room and the building as such.[34]

Modern art, which has increasingly relinquished its reproductive relation to reality, offers the architect and planner crucial insights into how to shape and construct reality using elemental means. Even apparently irrational manifestations of artistic modernism such as Expressionism and Dadaism, Hilberseimer thought, had played a positive role in returning to primitive, elemental realities, free from the accretions of historical culture. Hilberseimer thus saw in Dadaism a liberation from the weight of tradition, "ineffective systems," and the mask of culture.[35]

Even more important, however, had been the work of cubists and especially constructivists in their analytic reduction of their artistic material to the elements of geometry, where they find common ground with architects and urban planners:

> The simple cubic bodies: boxes and spheres, prisms and cylinders, pyramids and cones, purely constructive elements, are the fundamental forms of every architecture. Their corporeal clarity demands clarity of form. Architecture originates from geometry. When geometric entities become proportioned bodies, architecture emerges, revealing diversity within great unity.[36]

The dwelling-cell and the structured metropolis together offer the promise of proportion and shape to urban reality, including the potential for a social democratic planning of society that is, at the same time, Platonic-utopian in its insistence on geometrical, spatial rationality at all scales.

It was, however, in the Soviet Union where the "construction" of socialism and new architectural and urban construction most organically came together as both immediate practical tasks and intensely debated ideological and theoretical issues. As Anatole Kopp notes in his classic study of architecture and urbanism in the early Soviet Union, for architects here "it was clear that 'modern' architecture was the architecture of socialism, and to be an architect, to make architecture, was for them to make their individual contribution to the realization of a policy whose aim was the radical transformation of both society and the way of life that is its expression."[37] Although paralleling in some respects the utopian aspirations of Western European architects to influence human character itself through a new design of buildings and cities, the Soviet architects were deeply marked by the immediate proximity of their practical tasks with the vision of a future socialist world in birth. Architecture was seen as one particularly crucial lever of social transformation. As Kopp notes, the Soviet architects viewed architecture as,

> above all, a tool for "transforming mankind." . . . This new society, this new man, could not develop in the old human dens fashioned in the image of a discredited social order. A special environment and appropriate structures were indispensable. But this environment was not conceived merely as a reflection, or material "translation," of the new society; it had to be created immediately, since only by living in it would man as he was become man as he was to be.[38]

Kopp acknowledges the overestimation by Soviet architects of their role and capacities. Yet he also suggests that it was their passionate focus on designing new spaces as "social condensers" for a new society that spurred their originality of conception.

In conclusion, we may refer to the socialist vision of architecture that El Lissitzky advanced in his book *Russland: Die Rekonstruktion der Architektur in der Sowjetunion* (*Russia: An Architecture for World Revolution*), which appeared in the "Neues Bauen in der Welt" (New Building in the World) book series in 1930, concurrently with books by Richard Neutra on architecture in the United States and by Roger Ginsberger on French modern architecture. In the opening pages, Lissitzky sets out his "basic premises," including the classical Marxist postulate that "[i]t is to this social revolution"—the Russian revolution of 1917—"rather than to the technological revolution, that the basic elements of Russian architecture are tied."[39] This means, however, that "[t]oday, architecture must be judged according to different criteria. The whole field of architecture has become a problem."[40] Soviet architecture, Lissitzky argues, must reconstruct Russia, not just in the sense of restoring the productive capacity lost in the First World War, the revolution, and the civil war that ensued, but also more profoundly by recreating the whole environment of work, everyday life, and culture as expressions of a new social order. "Our new architecture," Lissitzky writes,

> does not just attempt to complete something that has been temporarily interrupted. On the contrary, it is poised on the threshold of the future and committed to more than mere construction. Its task is to comprehend the new conditions of life, so that by the creation of responsive building design it can actively participate in the full realization of the new world.[41]

In this regard, Lissitzky reconceives architecture not simply as an urgent practical task in the construction of socialism, but also, beyond the demands of the day, as a site of enormous future consequence for Marxist theory and practice. For Soviet architecture and the related questions of socialist city planning constitute, in his view, reside at the heart of the matter of Marxist revolutionary change. They promised, Lissitzky believed, an emerging new stage in the human control of the conditions of collective life, and rich nourishment for new capabilities in the epochal struggle for human self-definition and self-overcoming.

Notes

1. Manfredo Tafuri, *Architecture and Utopia: Design and Capitalist Development*, trans. Barbara Luigia La Penta (Cambridge, MA: The MIT Press, 1976), 179.
2. For discussion of Archizoom and Superstudio, see Pier Vittorio Aureli, *The Project of Autonomy: Politics and Architecture within and against Capitalism* (New York: Princeton University Press, 2008), 69–79. See also Andrea Branzi, *No-Stop City: Archizoom Associati* (Orleans: Hyx, 2006); *Superstudio: Opere, 1966-1978*, ed. Gabrielle Mastrigli (Macerata: Quodlibet, 2016); and *Exit Utopia: Architectural Provocations, 1956-1976*, eds. Martin van Schaik and Otaker Máčel (Munich: Prestel, 2005).
3. Hatherley, *Militant Modernism*.
4. For a useful discussion of Marx and Engels' works related to architecture, as well as later Marxist theorists dealing with architecture and metropolitan modernity such as Walter Benjamin, Henri Lefebvre, and Fredric Jameson, see David Cunningham and Jon Goodbun, "Marx, Architecture and Modernity," *The Journal of Architecture* 11.2 (2006): 169–85.
5. Marx, *Capital* vol. 2, 233–4.
6. Aureli, *The Project of Autonomy*, 70.
7. Engels, *The Housing Question* in Marx and Engels, *Collected Works* vol. 23, 1871–74 (London: Lawrence and Wishart, Electric Book, 2010), 347–8.
8. Benjamin, *Moscow Diary*, trans. Richard Sieburth, ed. Gary Smith (Cambridge, MA: Harvard University Press, 1986), 132–3.
9. Benjamin, *Moscow Diary*, 67.
10. N. A. Miliutin, *Sotsgorod: The Problem of Building Socialist Cities*, trans. Arthur Sprague (Cambridge, MA: The MIT Press, 1974), 60.
11. See El Lissitzky, *Russia: An Architecture for World Revolution* [1929], trans. Eric Dluhosch (Cambridge, MA: The MIT Press, 1970), 59–66; and Selim Omarovich Khan-Magomedov, *Georgii Krutikov: The Flying City and Beyond*, trans. Christina Lodder (Barcelona: Tenov Books, 2015).
12. See *Design for Utopia: Selected Writings of Charles Fourier*, trans. Julia Franklin (New York: Schocken Books, 1971) and *Harmonian Man: Selected Writings of Charles Fourier*, trans. Susan Hanson, ed. Mark Poster (Garden City, New York: Anchor Books, 1971).
13. Tafuri and Francesco Dal Co, *Modern Architecture* I, trans. Robert Erich Wolf (Milan: Electa, 1976), 185–6.

14 L. Sabsovich, quoted in Anatole Kopp, *Town and Revolution: Soviet Architecture and City Planning, 1917-1935*, trans. Thomas E. Burton (London: Thames and Hudson, 1970), 171.
15 Walter Gropius, "Program of the Staatliche Bauhaus in Weimar," in *The Bauhaus: Weimar, Dessau, Berlin, Chicago*, ed. Hans M. Wingler (Cambridge, MA: The MIT Press, 1969), 31.
16 For documentation of this circle's activities and correspondence, see *Crystal Chain Letters: Architectural Fantasies by Bruno Taut and His Circle*, ed. and trans. Iain Boyd Whyte (Cambridge, MA: The MIT Press, 1985). For further on Taut and his activist circle, see also Iain Boyd Whyte, *Bruno Taut and the Architecture of Activism* (Cambridge: Cambridge University Press, 1982).
17 Gropius, in *Arbeitsrat für Kunst: Berlin 1918-1921* (Berlin: Akademie der Künste, 1980), 32.
18 For Le Corbusier's Soviet engagements, see Jean-Louis Cohen, *Le Corbusier and the Mystique of the USSR: Theories and Projects for Moscow, 1928-1934* (Princeton, NJ: Princeton University Press, 1992).
19 For historical and critical discussion of Red Vienna politics, architecture, and urbanism, see *Vienna Rossa: La politica residenziale nella Vienna socialista, 1919-1933*, ed. Tafuri (Milan: Electra, 1980); Alfred Georg Frei, *Rotes Wien: Austromarxismus und Arbeiterkultur. Sozialdemokratische Wohnungs-und Kommunalpolitik, 1919-1934* (Berlin: DVK-Verlag, 1984); Helmut Gruber, *Red Vienna: Experiments in Working-Class Culture, 1919-1934* (Oxford: Oxford University Press, 1991); and Eve Blau, *The Architecture of Red Vienna, 1919-1934* (Cambridge, MA: The MIT Press, 1999).
20 See Blau, *The Architecture of Red Vienna*, 98.
21 For Neurath's connection to "gypsy urbanism" and later involvement with Red Vienna urbanism, see Nader Vossoughian, *Otto Neurath: The Language of the Global Polis* (Rotterdam: NAi Publishers, 2008), 16–45. Interestingly, Solita Solano, the partner of Janet Flanner and an associate of Gertrude Stein and Djuna Barnes in the Parisian lesbian modernist circles, reported on the Vienna "settlement" movement in an illustrated article in January 1923 entitled "Vienna: A Capital Without a Nation," *National Geographic* 43.1 (January 1923): 77–102.
22 Bruno Taut, *Die Auflösung der Städte, oder Die Erde eine Gute Wöhnung, oder auch: Der Weg zur Alpinen Architektur* (Hagen: Folkwang Verlag, 1920).
23 Vossoughian, *Otto Neurath*, 17.
24 Blau, *The Architecture of Red Vienna*, 158.
25 Blau, *The Architecture of Red Vienna*, 158.
26 For historical and political context of German left-wing architecture in the 1920s, see Barbara Miller Lane, *Architecture and Politics in Germany, 1918-1945* (Cambridge, MA: Harvard University Press, 1965, 1985).
27 For Taut's activities in the Soviet Union, see Bruno Taut, *Moskauer Briefe, 1932-1933: Schönheit, Sachlichkeit und Sozialismus*, ed. Barbara Kreis (Berlin: Gebr. Mann Verlag, 2006).
28 Hannes Meyer, "Über marxistische Architektur" and "Thesen über marxistische Architektur," in Meyer, *Bauen und Gesellschaft: Schriften, Briefe, Projekte*, ed. Lena Meyer-Bergner (Dresden: VEB Verlag der Kunst, 1980), 92–7 and 97–9.
29 See Taut, "Raspad goroda" ("Auflösung der Städte), *SA: Sovremennaya Arkhitektura* 1–2 (1930): 63–5; and Taut, "Die Auflösung der Städte: Zum Problem der

Zukunftstadt," *Moskauer Rundschau* (March 9, 1930). Note that Taut signals his complete agreement with L. Sabsovich's (Fourierist) conception of housing settlements; see note 14.

30 Taut, "Raspad goroda," English translation from Ross Wolfe's blog post on the Public Philosophy Network site, https://publicphilosophynetwork.ning.com/profiles/blogs/raspad-goroda-bruno-tautthe, accessed August 20, 2019.
31 See Robert Weinberg, *Stalin's Forgotten Zion: Birobidzhan and the Making of a Soviet Jewish Homeland, An Illustrated History, 1928-1996* (Berkeley: University of California Press, 1998). For a fascinating documentary including interviews with some of the original participants in the architect brigades, see Anna Abraham, *Sotsgorod: Cities for Utopia* (New York: Icarus Films, 1999).
32 Ludwig Hilbersheimer, "The Will to Architecture" (1923), in *Metropolisarchitecture and Selected Essays*, trans. and ed. Richard Anderson, with Julie Dawson (New York: GSAPP Books, 2012), 283.
33 Hilbersheimer, "The Will to Architecture," 283.
34 Hilbersheimer, *Metropolisarchitecture and Selected Essays*, 270.
35 Hilbersheimer, "Dadaismus," *Sozialistische Monatshefte*, 26/17 (December 20, 2020): 1120.
36 Hilbersheimer, "The Will to Architecture," 285-6.
37 Anatole Kopp, *Town and Revolution*, 5. See also the critical essays in *Socialismo, città, architettura: URSS, 1917-1937. Il contributo degli architetti europei*, ed. Manfredo Tafuri, 2nd ed. (Rome: Officina, 1972).
38 Kopp, *Town and Revolution*, 12.
39 Lissitzky, *Russia*, 27.
40 Lissitzky, *Russia*, 27.
41 Lissitzky, *Russia*, 27.

15

Marx and Popular Modernism

Esther Leslie

It is typical that historical materialist accounts of the relation between Marx, Marxism, and culture are drawn toward literature and fine arts, as if to consider the popular arts would be a betrayal of the cultural potential of the proletariat, a relinquishing of the demand that they too have access to the cultural forms and spaces that have been denied them. To find Marxist impulses, subversive meanings, and critical values of any sort in comics, cartoons, or throwaway bits of ephemera seems like settling for a place among the trash. Apparently more indicative of the Marxist approach to culture are events and "lines" as voiced at the 1934 Soviet Writers' Congress, which saw Karl Radek promote Realist novels in direct opposition to James Joyce's "cinematographic" approach to everyday life in *Ulysses* (1922). In the 1930s, as Socialist Realism became an officially sanctioned doctrine for art, a form of cultural policing insisted that a particular attitude or line be obvious in the artwork, and also recommended the return to traditional forms of oil painting and novel writing. At the 1934 Congress, the doctrine of Socialist Realism in culture was officially launched and, in a speech titled "James Joyce or Socialist Realism," Radek praised, in contradistinction to Joyce's many genres, many voiced, tangled tale of interiority and public zones, myth and modernity, the Realist novel. For Radek, Joyce lingers in the unappetizing zones of everyday life, rather than aspiring to the grand sweep of "big events," "big people," and "big ideas," which make history in the forceful sense. Radek attacks *Ulysses*, which he describes in these terms: "A heap of dung, crawling with worms, photographed by a cinema apparatus through a microscope—such is Joyce's work."[1]

The notion of writing as "cinematic" is intended to be a great insult. Cinema counteracts literary quality. That a novel must be literary is an unquestionable fact. By extension, painting or sculpture too should follow the codes of a romantically inclined realism, an idealization of what is to be, a proleptic imagination of the liberated future that beckons on the horizon, once the revolution is fully present. Louis Aragon, a surrealist-turned orthodox Marxist, relayed similar sentiments at the Conference for the Defence of Culture in Paris in 1935. He had renamed a leading communist cultural journal *Pour la defense de la culture*. Aragon's essay "Realism, the Order of the Day" (1936) attacked Fernand Léger's use of cinema, radio, montage, and advertising techniques in his art. This was a pushback against the revolutionary aesthetic of certain modernists, closely identified with the Left, who had practiced and theorized against a backdrop of Dada's critical energies and rejection of high culture, and it countermanded surrealism's evaluation of unconscious desires and the significance of the parapraxis, energetic cultural forms forged by new technologies of film and photography, which, in particular, lent themselves to social analysis, and to the critique of culture per se, and as such saw common cause with revolutionaries.

As the insights of Marx are transformed in the writings of those who might be called modernist theorists, especially those who are moved by the establishment of the Soviet Union in 1917 in Marx's name, or those who experience a proximity to the aims of the German revolution of 1919, even in all its failure, a relationship between revolutionary perspectives and visual technologies of reproduction, notably film and photography, is forged. Walter Benjamin's materialist analysis of culture is not an analysis dependent on the vistas opened up by, or reflected blankly in, high literature or fine arts. It sets out from the ways in which humans of the twentieth century have come to be assailed by technology, and in being assailed, are remade as technological subjects with other capacities than they had before, with new types of perceptual experience, new sensibilities, new ways of accessing information or being exposed to cultural material, new collective modes of watching and hearing, and repeating these experiences as they wish. Film, photography, magazines, and cartoons come to meet humans, in new spaces, and they to remake their spaces, because they crack them open through the dynamiting of old-style space and time, broken up by editing and remade in the new auditoria of the cinema space or the room with a gramophone. These new cultural forms, enjoyed by masses, are not simply reflective of the capitalist relations of production that often allow them to come into being. They concentrate something, just as Joyce's dung heap concentrated the contradictory energies of the everyday, its fertility and its decay, its productive capacity and its abhorrent stink.

Benjamin theorized, for example, the ways in which film as a medium mapped out a contradictory space-time. It was a flow that had to be interrupted. Benjamin sought out contradictions in culture, as analogues to contradictions in the social world, or the contradictory tensions of class struggle. Bertolt Brecht's dramatics of Epic Theater demonstrated for him both the valuing of flux and ceaseless change, as well as its contradiction, the breaking-up the flow, interruption, slicing the narrative into scenes and the scenes into *Gestus*, or critical moments, turning points. In one image or in a montage of images appear both the forces of oppression—the flaw of the world— and the possibility of error's supersession—the redemption of reality. In splintering representations by analysis, the possibility arises of worldly reconstitution under new laws, if only temporary ones. Marx and Engels spoke of the revolutionary aspects of bourgeois society in these terms: "All fixed, fast-frozen relations, with their train of ancient and venerable prejudices and opinions, are swept away, all new-formed ones become antiquated before they can ossify."[2] There is now the production of the new, but blindly. There is also the possibility of producing the new, but consciously. Such response to what is, drastically, and the concern to remake it consciously, describes, perhaps, Marxist-infused modernism. The old is negated, polemically and critically. The new is created, as it always is, as old conditions are swept away in the constant revolutionizing of capital, and as the new is created, so is possibility. But the new will always be superseded by the next new thing. Destruction is a hallmark of modernism, as it is of the cycles of life.

The work of the modernist Marxists who engage with an analysis of the structure and feeling of life, everyday life, literary life equally, develops the realm of something called theory. The word "theory" stems from the Greek word *theorein*, which means looking at or things looked at. In other words, the notion of speculation derives from the word for spectator, *theoros*, which is drawn from *thea*, a view and *horao*, to see. Whether a technology-skeptical or a technology-embracing stance, the extension and formulation of Marxist theory, as practiced, for example, by Benjamin and Theodor Adorno, comes as a theory concerned with the mediation of perception. The specific angling of this by Benjamin and Adorno is the addition of the descriptor "critical" to theory, as a circumlocution of Marxism, which also serves to distinguish Adorno's or Benjamin's thinking, from what they and Max Horkheimer deemed "traditional theory." "Critical" is derived from crisis. It is defined as a turning point, an interruption, a change in quality. "Critical theory," in these earlier senses, in relation to seeing or the view and in relation to turning points or interruption, is formalized methodologically in Benjamin's writings in the various notions of "dialectical imagery" or "dialectics at a standstill." Benjamin's concepts propose a method of both describing (seeing) and analyzing (criticizing or interrupting) his objects of analysis. The dialectical aspect relates to movement, history, and the flow of time and change. The other moment, be it image or standstill, arrests what is to be analyzed, taken apart or splintered.

Splinters

Camera lenses, the productions from the regime of profit that is the culture industry, as Adorno calls it, are also not to be trusted. That they might be spaces where the contradictions of capitalism are concentrated in various ways—in terms of actuality and potential, for example, in relation to issues of private ownership and the collectivity of authorship, or formally, as something that is inherently multiple but also limited by commodification—may not be enough to extract these mediators from the snares of capitalist reproduction and ideological enforcement. "The splinter in your eye is the best magnifying glass," notes Adorno in *Minima Moralia* (1951).[3] Adorno distrusts the invented mechanisms of vision, those glassy lenses that intensify, illuminate, and expand vision, providing the image-maker with ever more sophisticated tools for replicating the real in a trajectory that stems from the Enlightenment onward, with its promise of exposure to light as a means to truth. The enlargement achieved by a standard magnifying glass brings back an increased quantity of information. It enlarges details. It makes visible that which has not been seen by the human eye before, or not in that way. It provides a certain knowledge, but it also provides, presumably, if the enigmatic metaphor in Adorno's phrase is unpicked, a knowledge that is no knowledge at all in any meaningful sense. What is seen remains an externality to which the spectator may remain impervious. The splinter in your eye, on the other hand, is a fragment of glass, a broken shard of lens that does not simply look outward into the world, seeing objectively, viewing objectivity, bringing to sight the world through and behind a lens. This splinter of which Adorno speaks does not give a view, as through from a window, onto a stable world out there, transmitting this back into the viewing eye. Rather this splinter conducts between vision, eye, and world—it cuts into the eye that sees. It juts out into the world that is seen. This splintered lens must cause pain, when it cuts into the eyeball, and, as such, in its eliciting of suffering, renders the viewer an involved spectator—or something much more than a spectator—of the scene. The viewer is a casualty of the visioned scene. In fact, the eye with the splinter in it cannot see, in the usual sense. In Adorno's aphorism, the flaw in vision becomes the means to vision. The magnifying glass that cuts into the eye enlarges the error that is the world—an erroneous state that is always present but unseen in usual mechanisms of imagery. Only when directly interpolated—pronged—in the mechanism of vision by the mode of visioning, can we speak of authentic seeing. Sight, then, is insight—turning inward into the self, but it is also insight into the conditions of seeing, into mediation. For Adorno, no sight can be accepted as true if there is no flaw included—a flaw in vision, a flaw in the machine, a flaw in what is seen in a world in which all is flawed.

Adorno's aphorism on the splinter indicated the extent to which the flaw in vision might be truthful in a world that is false. At the dawn of modernism, art circles had been challenged similarly, though more consciously dumbly, by Marcel Duchamp's paradox of art, which hitched blindness to insight. Duchamp was co-editor of a magazine called *The Blind Man*. In the issue of May 1917 he published an anonymous letter—probably written by himself and Beatrice Wood—in support of his much-pilloried readymade *Fountain*, which had originated as a porcelain urinal. The letter was written apparently by a blind reader, who had not been able to see the controversial object, but nonetheless expressed "blind solidarity." The blind apparently "see" the readymade rather than the seeing being blinded by the readymade's refusal to return the spectator's gaze, that is to say, its refusal to provide aesthetic pleasure. *Fountain* does not want to be seen by the seeing, because they see blindly. The blind see differently and in good faith.[4] The failure of vision can be the vision of failure.

Despite their differences, particularly in the matter of the technological mediation of vision, Adorno and Benjamin both present the field of vision as something that evades intention, and yet, in order to make this field meaningful, human, it needs, in some way or another, to be cut into. For Adorno, the cut is, metaphorically, into the eye—disturbing the unmediated activity of seeing, making seeing seen. For Benjamin, the cut is into reality, via technique or technology, in order to not reproduce but produce the image world. The camera's eye falls specifically on excerpted portions of a real, natural world, but it can bring into vision something other than nature's surface, and something other than nature.[5] The image of reality, as specifically represented in film and photography, is an image of the real that has been mediated, subjected to analysis, works with incongruities, destruction, construction, reconstructions. The splintering that, for Adorno, penetrates the eye, for Benjamin is a splintering of the world in film to make an image world:

The cinema then exploded this entire prison-world with the dynamite of its fractions of a second, so that now we can take extended journeys of adventure between their widely scattered ruins.[6]

The world is "laid open," in order to be entered, and viewers come away with an enhanced knowledge of the structure of actuality through exposure to the film's extremely perceptive and analytical eye, as well as the barrage of editing techniques that pick apart the filmic space. Audiences find out secrets contained even in commonplace reality, once it has been splintered into shards, amid which audiences drift and saunter for a while. It should be noted, of course, that film's effect relies upon a flaw in vision: that we do not, at a certain hertz, see the gaps between the still frames, which allows film's snatched moments of time to be restrung through flicker fusion. It is in the most popular forms, in the newest forms, that the world can be known and known as it is, as it has become, and what it might become in the future.

Marxist modernism involves a suspicion of surfaces, the desire to identify what is beneath the surface of what appears, and how this beneath shapes what can and cannot be seen. One statement of this is repeated by Benjamin:

> As Brecht says: "the situation is complicated by the fact that less than ever does the mere reflection of reality reveal anything about reality. A photograph of the Krupp works or A.E.G. tells us next to nothing about these institutions. Actual reality has slipped into the functional. The reification of human relations,—the factory say—means that they are no longer explicit. Something must in fact be built up, something artificial, posed."[7]

Benjamin brings out the question of alienation, here termed "reification," a making thingly. It is this category that enters into the critical inventory of Marxist-modernist theorists as they outline, for the purposes of abolition, the cold world in which they found themselves. It is, of course, not just the modernist Marxists who perceive a widespread alienation of social relations. The perception is made more relevant by being present across other cultural forms, including popular ones, as the theorists themselves observe. Modernist theory of cultural form becomes a theory that can understand popular culture as an expression of discomfort, as well as possibility.

The Infernal Dream of Animation

"The Infernal Dream of Mutt and Jeff," or, alternatively, "When Hell Freezes Over" is a cartoon from 1926. Mutt and Jeff are in beds, parallel to each other. It is freezing. They are freezing. They are poor. Their surroundings are poor. They fight with each other over meagre resources, a tiny threadbare blanket. In this coldness, we might recognize a hint of urban coldness, a suggestion of the kind of urban environment through which a chill wind of alienation and unfriendliness blows. Mutt and Jeff are in Brecht's city, his figurative one as written up in his "Reader for City Dwellers" (1926–7), but also in the actual one, the same place, from a few years before, as represented in his poem "Of Poor B.B." (1921):

> Of those cities will remain what passed through them, the wind!
> The house makes glad the eater: he clears it out.
> We know that we're only tenants, provisional ones
> And after us there will come: nothing worth talking about.[8]

Brecht is not a Marxist, in the sense of having a relationship with the Communist Party, when he writes the poem. His main influence is the Bavarian clown Karl Valentin, who finds bitterly satirical ways of expressing a frustration with the unfairness and brutality of the world, a sensibility that appealed to a young bohemian, such as Brecht. The world is an unfair, brutal, class-ridden place, whether or not its inhabitants are Marxists. In the same year that Brecht wrote his poem, Winsor McCay, in New York, no Marxist either in the card-carrying sense, though certainly a critic of Wall Street capitalism, made two animations based on his comic strip, *Dreams of a Rarebit Fiend*, "The Pet," and "The Flying House." In one, an outsize and insatiable beast masquerades as a domestic pet. In the other, there is a flying sequence where the householders transcend capitalism's emergent hold, with its illusions of rationale and security undermined by the nightmare inculcation into the destabilizing debt-economy. A marauding quadruped trounces New York's newly built skyscrapers and the maverick householders literally fly their house into space to escape their mortgage debt and the suburban grid. They can only be stopped by state military intervention with their new forms of heavy machine artillery, and the dreamers' own salutary return to consciousness. McCay illustrates wish fulfillments, social embarrassment, fear of dying of debt, of the fragile structure of reality collapsing altogether, and of humans going insane. There is a constant awareness of social structure that involves "getting ahead," both as a prevailing cultural imperative and a systematic impossibility. These formations are acted out in the social world and come up against the interpersonal, political, and technological manifestations of the age, including new technologies and the machine violence of the First World War. History enters, loudly, violently. Marxist notions of state violence, alienation, competition, and the reduction of the self pervade the cartoons.

Brecht's poem "Of Poor B.B." projects into a future. It is an apocalyptic one, and it speaks, cynically, of survival of the self:

> In the earthquakes to come, I very much hope
> I shall keep my cigar alight, embittered or no.[9]

The only warmth in Brecht's poem is a tiny point of fire at the end of a cigar. In just such a place, Mutt and Jeff end up: their Hell of 1920s America becomes through a few twists and turns the Hell of the underworld, after they have sought firewood and met the Devil instead. This environment is so cold, even Hell has frozen over. There is one flame left. This flame must be kept alight by the always disobedient, uncouth characters, Mutt and Jeff. What are they keeping alight?—that which should be Hell's dreadful power, but is now a welcome source of energy, a counterforce to the frozen world. This flame is one of the most lively entities within this cartoon of blank surfaces and static backgrounds.

It is animation personified, if Sergei Eisenstein's analysis is followed. Eisenstein seized on the provisional quality of animation, which, for him, protests, in utopian fashion, against the rigidities of the capitalist world. He affirmed animation's ability to range in any direction and embark on any exploit. He saw in its ecstatic, plasmatic nature both the beginnings of time and the ends of things. He associates the protoplasmic forms of primordial matter with the shifting shapes of animation. A plasmatic force deforms all forms through time and stimulates an imagination of the emergence of any and every thing. Fire, observes Eisenstein, "is capable of most fully conveying the dream of a flowing diversity of forms."[10] And so it is the most apt object for animation. The flame produces action, just as it transforms matter. Before our eyes, the impossible can happen—and Hell freezes over. The Devil is spiked. But in the end, we, and they, Mutt and Jeff, are returned to the cold world above, to a dream that is unfulfilled, to a living nightmare, or, alternatively, the counter resets to zero, like the barometer. Hell freezes over, and, at one and the same time, the very precise now of capitalist misfortune brushes up against the ever-longed for Utopia of an untrammeled existence, in which even the Devil might be beaten. Reality bites coldly, and the only warmth is the descendant of that which Marx pinpointed as a miserable agent of disease and punishment, the match that lights a cigarette. In *Capital*, he writes:

> The manufacture of lucifer matches dates from 1833, from the discovery of the method of applying phosphorus to the match itself. Since 1845 this manufacture has rapidly developed in England, and has extended especially amongst the thickly populated parts of London as well as in Manchester, Birmingham, Liverpool, Bristol, Norwich, Newcastle and Glasgow. With it has spread the form of lockjaw, which a Vienna physician in 1845 discovered to be a disease peculiar to lucifer-matchmakers. Half the workers are children under thirteen and young persons under eighteen. The manufacture is on account of its unhealthiness and unpleasantness in such bad odour that only the most miserable part of the laboring class, half-starved widows and so forth, deliver up their children to it, "the ragged, half-starved, untaught children."[11]

Animation is born into industrial capitalism, a punishing, turbulent form of production. It becomes the expression of that form. Punishment and turbulence are its mainstays. Born and grown up alongside the burgeoning forms of industrial capitalism, animation appeared close to machinic life. As much as cartoons presented visions and escapades in the realm of the impossible, they also reflected the rhythms and tensions of the modern world. This is the realist face of cartoons. We see our worlds, in all their brutality and unpredictability, lampooned on the screen, and we are asked to laugh at it. That is some sort of training in what industrial capitalism is about. These streaks of ink, these quickly drawn outlines are our avatars, our selves rendered in even more reduced forms than we might feel ourselves to be. These actors, in their worlds, are little more than marks, points, abridged and, yet, expected to be extremely flexible, and also resilient. A despondent situation, against which the persistent protest of the cartoon is instructive, for it registers that endless, infernal history and it wishes it away, hexes it. It diagnoses and proposes, across an ahistorical history. This is the basis of animation's affinity to subversion, just as it simultaneously represents the most commercialized, commoditized, capitalism-friendly mode of creation. It is nothing but contradictory. And anything that is contradictory has to have some sort of opening onto Marxism. For all the emphasis on animation's quest for liveliness, depth, and development, it remains a movement mobilized by a machine; its vision of the actor in its world is as a mark, a point, a streak, both reduced and extended. And it is in this that animation articulates, in animated overliveliness of everything, or especially of that which is not human, the big secret of commodity-producing society. Things—or commodities—exert more effects on the world than people. The truth of who has agency—who has productive capacity, creativity, and value—is revealed in this mechanism that has been read in relation to Marx's notion of fetishism.

"The Infernal Dream of Mutt and Jeff" renders in black and white for us what makes up the emotional tone and physical insistence of our world, what life is like in the cities of today, what dreams and battles dog contemporary city-dwellers. Animation marks the development of a longer process of management of bodies and beings by industrial capitalism, and its stretches from Etienne-Jules Marey and his proto-machines of motion capture, put to use by the French army, through the rationalizing scientific management systems of the Gilbreths, all entangled with animation and its humorous way of dealing with commodity fetishism, those over-lively objects of our environment, its way, as Walter Benjamin puts it, of demonstrating how "humankind makes preparations to survive civilization," finding modes of survival after human existence in a world, in which "it is not worthwhile to have experiences." All of this, this portrait of alienation, indicates that "the public recognizes its own life" in these minimal strips and they go on recognizing themselves, because fundamentally nothing has changed for a long time. The infernal is the eternal: or what Benjamin terms, in his description of capitalism, eternal recurrence of the ever-same in the guise of the new. Benjamin specified this as the tempo characteristic of industrial capitalist modernity. This is the rhythm of technologically reproduced culture, just as it is that of any commodity: replication that produces heterogeneity. It has its horror-face in the endless production of or conveyor belt commodity production, which in cartooning stamps out again and again the ever-same product with the smallest tweaks as stimulus to sales. It circles and circulates, always on the same spot.

Modernist-Marxist Fairy Tales

Animation is a proposal about the world as it is, horribly, and as it could be. In that respect, animation absorbed the critical and constructive energies of Marxism.

Marxism demands a relationship to history. It is a historical materialism. But animation pushes away any simple sense of the historical. Animation is a dream and a nightmare. Neither of those are historical forms, as such, and yet each has so much of the world translated into it, transformed through it, left legibly but enigmatically there, or traumatically. So too the fairy tale—parallel to the world, but modulated through wish, hope, desire, fears. The genius of Marxist-modernist theory is to understand how the lowly regarded forms of cultural expression, old and new, are registers of social alienation and collective hope. And so Ernst Bloch wrote of the fairy tale that it projects our wishes against a background that has long since disappeared:

> The atavistic and simultaneously feudal-transcendental world from which the fairy tale stems and to which it seems to be tied has most certainly vanished. However, the mirror of the fairy tale has not become opaque, and the manner of wish-fulfilment that peers forth from it is not entirely without a home. It all adds up to this: the fairy tale narrates a wish-fulfilment that is not bound by its own time and the apparel of its contents. In contrast to the legend, which is always tied to a particular locale, the fairy tale remains unbound. Not only does the fairy tale remain as fresh as longing and love, but the demonically evil, which is abundant in the fairy tale, is still seen at work here in the present, and the happiness of "once upon a time," which is even more abundant, still affects our visions of the future.[12]

The freshness remains, exceeds time, communicates across epochs, as across generations and territories. The hero of the fairy tale, perhaps a naïve boy or girl, on a quest for happiness, does not die off. He comes back as Mickey Mouse or, in contemporary idiom, *Frozen*'s Anna. The dreamer persists, and so do the nightmares. Bloch finds the demons of old times returning in the present, his present of writing in 1930, as economic ogres:

> The politics of the leading 200 families is fate. Thus, right in America, a country without feudal or transcendental tradition, Walt Disney's fairy-tale films revive elements of the old fairy tale without making them incomprehensible to the viewers.[13]

Bloch observes how the world of the fairy tale is a world of enlightenment, as much as it is one of magic too, in which Hansel and Gretel, like the modern characters of technological modernity, consider themselves "born free and entitled to be totally happy." They dare to make use of their power of reasoning, and look upon the outcome of things as friendly. He writes that we too must contend with the smoke of witches and the blows of ogres: "The fairy-tale hero is called upon to overcome our miserable situation, regretfully just in mere fairy tales."

Walt Disney cast intense oranges and shining blues out into cinemas, claimed Eisenstein, and these were a promise of something. Disney's output came to represent the epitome of escapism. People went to see the colorful confections in order to escape the greyness of everyday life in the Depression. Along with all the rainbows that arc the screen at the close of films, such as *Father Noah's Ark* (1933) or *Funny Little Bunnies* (1934), the red and orangey yellows of fire and sunsets are, according to Eisenstein, a color explosion to counter "the grey squares of city blocks," "the grey prison cells of city streets," the "grey faces of endless street crowds" outside the cinema in the 1930s. Cinematic culture came to saturate the world. As it develops into a popular commercial form, studio animation becomes increasingly dependent on a high division of labor and an industrialized mode of production—but cartoons are also in the business of manufacturing utopias. Cartoons provide the swelling and shrinking outlines of other places and states of being. Cartoon color brings the film world nearer to the real world of perception, but it also introduces more fantasy, more luminosity. Disney, observes Eisenstein, could command "the magic of all technical means," infiltrating the "most secret strands of human thought, images, ideas, feelings."[14] And he states: "That is why the imagination in them is limitless, for Disney's films are a revolt against partitioning and legislating, against spiritual stagnation and greyness. But the revolt is lyrical. The revolt is a daydream."[15] Eisenstein seized on the provisional quality of animation, which is thrown out, in utopian fashion, against the rigidities of the capitalist world. He affirmed animation's ability to range in any direction and embark on any exploit. He saw in its ecstatic, plasmatic nature, both the beginnings of time and the ends of things. He associates the protoplasmic forms of primordial matter with the shifting shapes of animation. A plasmatic force deforms all forms through time and stimulates an imagination of the emergence of any and every thing. Modernism receives Marxism as the capacity to analyze popular culture as a rendering of the social world in all of its hellish and colorless heartlessness and as a colorful, fiery environment of possibility.

Notes

1. See Jeffrey Segall, "'James Joyce or Socialist Realism?' Marxist Aesthetics and the Problem of *Ulysses*," in *Joyce in America: Cultural Politics and the Trials of Ulysses* (Berkeley: University of California Press, 1993), 12–48.
2. Marx and Engels, "Manifesto of the Communist Party," 476.
3. Adorno, *Minima Moralia: Reflections on a Damaged Life* (London: Verso, 2005), 55.
4. See the discussion of this in John Roberts, *The Intangibilities of Form* (London: Verso, 2007).
5. Benjamin, "Little History of Photography," in *Selected Writings* vol. 2, 510–2.
6. Benjamin, "Response to Oscar A. H. Schmitz," in *Selected Writings* vol. 2, 17.
7. Benjamin, "Little History of Photography," 526.
8. Brecht, "Von armen B.B.," in *Brecht für Unsere Zeit: Ein Lesebuch* (Berlin/Weimar: Aufbau Verlag, 1985), 10.
9. Brecht, "Von armen B.B.," 10.
10. Eisenstein, *Eisenstein on Disney*, ed. Jay Leyda (Kolkata: Seagull, 1986), 24.
11. Marx, *Capital* vol. 1, 356.

12 Ernst Bloch, "The Fairy Tale Moves in Its Own time," in *The Utopian Function of Art and Literature: Selected Essays*, trans. Jack Zipes (Cambridge MA: The MIT Press, 1987), 163.
13 Bloch, "The Fairy Tale Moves in Its Own Time," 163.
14 Eisenstein, *Eisenstein on Disney*, 2.
15 Eisenstein, *Eisenstein on Disney*, 4.

Part Three

Glossary of Key Terms

16

The Commodity

Josh Jewell

For Marx, the commodity is the fundamental building block of capitalist society. Commodities are everywhere, and the story of capitalism is the story of the rapid and exponential increase in their production and circulation. The commodity holds the key to understanding how capitalist society functions, because by thinking about what goes in to making one we begin to see the various strange contradictions of its means of production, and thereby the contradictions of a capitalist society more broadly.

A commodity is anything made by human labor power, that can be both used and exchanged on the market. Marx says, therefore, that a commodity has both use-value and exchange-value. In order to produce something useful, or to produce use-values, a worker needs to use a specific set of skills to make an object of a certain quality such that it will fulfill its desired purpose. For example, a woodworker needs to deploy the skills of sawing, carving, beveling, and joining in order to produce a chair that is stable, the correct height to fit beneath a table, comfortable to sit on, and so forth. But if the same woodworker who made the chair simply keeps it for their own use, the chair is not a commodity. It only becomes a commodity when it is exchanged. Its exchange-value must be realized in the marketplace. But here there is a contradiction. If we realize a commodity's use-value, we cannot exchange it because we are using it. And, if we realize a commodity's exchange-value, we cannot use it because we have exchanged it. We will return to the significance of this contradiction shortly.

How do we determine a commodity's exchange-value? In the marketplace, a chair might be exchanged for four coats or two kilos of iron. Every commodity is exchangeable with every other commodity in some quantity or another. Therefore, Marx reasons that there must be something that all commodities have in common. We have already seen what it is earlier: they all have use-values—and are all the product of a certain quantity of labor time.

So the value of a commodity is determined by the quantity of labor time expended in its production. Does this mean that a worker who produces commodities very slowly makes more valuable commodities? No. Exchange-value is the expression of the average amount of labor time required to produce a commodity under a given set of conditions—the average capability of workers, the sophistication of the machinery, and so forth. But note how, in thinking about exchange, we have moved away from thinking about the quality of individual labor, toward the quantity of many workers' labor—away from what Marx calls concrete labor, toward what he calls abstract labor. A commodity, then, is the physical manifestation of a certain quantity of what Marx defines as "socially necessary labor time."

This definition becomes significant when we remember that use-value and exchange-value, and concrete and abstract labor, are mutually exclusive characteristics of commodities. Exchange-value "does not contain an atom of use-value," as Marx says.[1] In order to make commodities in a capitalist society, then, millions of workers must spend billions of hours of labor producing massive quantities of use-values without any concern for their eventual use. The real outcome of this process is not useful objects, then, but quantities of crystallized human labor time. So while the commodity might appear to be just a physical object that is traded in order to satisfy a particular need, it is in fact a representation of a contradictory social process unique to capitalism. The accumulation of millions of hours of human exertion, pain, and injury takes on what Marx calls a "phantom-like objectivity" in the form of the commodity.[2]

This painful process, however, is largely obscured from view—and increasingly so with time. Whereas at the beginning of the twentieth century a Ford motorcar was fully assembled along a single production line in a factory in Michigan, today an Apple computer or a Nike trainer may be assembled piecemeal in factories across three continents. The result of this international division of labor is that, by the time we buy a commodity at the shops, all traces of the fact that it was produced by human labor have disappeared. So when we look at, for example, a computer on display in a pristine white shop, we are prevented from thinking about the South African miners who extracted the platinum for the circuit boards or the Chinese laborers who assembled the components. Instead, we look at the price tag and think about what the computer is worth in relation to other commodities. Through this process, the social relations we all share with each other as humans become replaced, in our minds, by market relations between commodities. When we have no ability to see that it is human labor power, and not commodities themselves, that produce value: this is what Marx meant when he theorized that we endow commodities with magical properties.

The fact that we think buying an expensive Italian-made item of clothing can turn us into someone more attractive, or professional, or more masculine or feminine, shows that we think of commodities in the same way as medieval people thought about religious relics or "fetishes" that could protect them from evil. Marx called this phenomenon *Warenfetischismus*, or "commodity fetishism." What Marxism enables us to do, then, is turn the capitalist world upside down—to stand it on its head and see that all the power that we give commodities and the market actually derives from our own labors. Once we have demystified the commodity and seen it for what it materially is—a representation of human labor time—the apparently rational and natural system of capitalism begins to seem more and more supernatural and strange. For Marx and Marxists, human society must move beyond the stage where commodity production is its highest purpose.

Notes

1 Marx, *Capital* vol. 1, 127.
2 Marx, *Capital* vol. 1, 128.

17

Labor

Veronica Brownstone

Central to Marx's contribution to economic science was his redefinition of labor as a twofold concept combining both labor and labor power. The move from feudalist to capitalist methods of surplus extraction provoked the analytical need to draw a distinction between these categories, as well as to call attention to an experiential change on the part of the worker, whose labor is now alienated. The category of labor power in particular embodies the change in property relations, for it is only in the face of privatized land that the subject is forced to sell their labor to survive. Surplus product appropriation no longer depends on extra-economic coercion but rather on the employment relation. The significance of labor power is thus born in this shift in the structures of domination.

Labor power denotes the capacity to labor. It exists as "the aggregate of those mental and physical capabilities existing in physical form, the living personality, of a human being," and comes into reality only by being activated through *labor*, which distinguishes itself as the manifest exercise of human productive effort.[1] The categorical emphasis on capacity reminds us that labor power's dependence on the market is historically specific. It is not by natural order that the inborn ability to do good work is commodified and estranged from the possessor and made to be their sole means of subsistence; this scenario occurs exclusively under capitalism, where the ruling class owns the means of production and the laborer has only their labor to sell. Surely enough, the subject has no choice but to sell their labor if they are to access basic human needs like food, housing, clothing, hygiene, fuel, and so forth. The capitalist epoch, Marx writes in a footnote, is characterized by the fact that the worker now sees their capacity to labor as a commodity, as property, and their labor consequently as wage labor.[2]

The wage facilitates labor power's function as capital's ultimate source of value. The reference to power embedded in the term recalls labor power's ontological status as the original and only commodity necessary for the generation of surplus value—and the only material body capable of withholding it. Labor power is the source of surplus value because the price capitalists pay workers will always be smaller than the value that their labor contributes to making the commodity. The value of work is determined by the quantity of labor time necessary to produce both the article and the worker.

While their number and extent will vary depending on historical conditions, these necessary requirements will always include production hours, natural needs (food, housing, etc.), reproductive needs (child rearing, gestation, domestic labor, care work, etc.), and education or training. For the price of labor to equate its value, wages would have to stay above this minimum value of the historically indispensable means of subsistence, otherwise the worker is crippled and the basic maintenance of human life that constitutes the value of labor time is denied.[3] It is nonetheless in the interest of capital to keep wages as close to this minimum as possible; the maximization of profit indeed depends on this process of exploitation.

While the self-conscious resistance of workers in the form of strikes, slowdowns, and collective bargaining, for instance, reflects labor power's permanent ability to negotiate the terms of exploitation, the expanding informalization of global labor under neoliberalism weakens this ability. Labor power's appearance on the market requires a class of "free" laborers: free from slavery and free (i.e., dispossessed) of the means of production. These conditions have historically forced populations to sell their labor through proletarianization. Yet, the growth of a global surplus population, and the dovetailing intensification of informality, migration, and incarceration, suggests that contemporary capital accumulation requires a high degree of wageless, undocumented, and unfree labor. Racialized neoliberal precarity compels a re-examination of how labor and labor power are controlled and structured today. Moving forward, the Marxist critique of political economy must insist on thinking race and class together if it is to account for the experience and politics of work at the threshold of labor markets, stranded in poor urban, exurban, and rural communities as well as in prisons and detention centers.

Notes

1 Marx, *Capital* vol. 1, 270.
2 Marx, *Capital* vol. 1, 274.
3 Marx, *Capital* vol. 1, 277.

18

Value

Rory Dufficy

Marx's concept of value and its status as either an unnecessary metaphysical hangover or an intellectual skeleton key unlocking the mysteries of every aspect of society have meant that accounts of this feature of Marx's work often bewilder in their complexity or, alternatively, their peremptory dismissal. And yet, the difficulties and longueurs associated with this term are, among other things, indicative of our distance from classical political economy, and of the intellectual developments of Marxism through its trajectory in and out of the academy. Any account of value must begin by placing it within the broader conceptual architecture of Marx's mature theory.

Like most aspects of this theory, it emerges directly out of an engagement with classical political economy. As with the foundational metaphysical question "why is there something rather than nothing?" so the foundational question of the great figures of British political economy might be said to be "why are there more things, rather than the same amount?" Thinkers like Adam Smith and David Ricardo recognized that capitalism's potential for exponential growth needed to be explained, and that the current theories of value, such as mercantilism and agriculture-centric approaches (most prominently associated with the physiocrats), were insufficient. Instead, they argued that what truly generated value—more things, in total, rather than merely the redistribution of existing product—was human labor. "Labor," concluded Smith, "is the real measure of the exchangeable value of all commodities." It was this line of enquiry, as Marx saw, that was foundational to their theoretical superiority over the subsequent "vulgar" political economy, which contented itself with examining merely the epiphenomena of capitalism. In Marx's words,

> political economy has indeed analysed value and its magnitude, however, incompletely, and has uncovered the content concealed within these forms. But it has never once asked the question why this content has assumed that particular form, that is to say, why labor is expressed in value, and why the measurement of labor by its duration is expressed in the magnitude of the value of the product.[1]

Where classical political economy had a labor theory of value, Marx developed, as Diane Elison would put it, a value theory of labor.

Marx broadly accepts the labor theory of value, but modifies it in important ways. The most detailed engagement with the relationship between labor and value occurs in the opening three chapters of *Capital*. From the beginning, however, Marx argues that rather than attempt to isolate what it is about labor that creates value, we must instead start with how that wealth "appears" to us in the "capitalist mode of production"—as an accumulation of commodities.

For Marx, every commodity has both use- and exchange-value. A commodity must have a use-value, the "material content of wealth, whatever its social form may be," insofar as it must be of some utility for someone. More importantly, though, "[i]n the form of society to be considered here they are also the material bearers [Träger] of... exchange-value."[2] This latter aspect of value will be crucial for Marx. Exchange-value is the "worth" of a particular commodity in relation to any other commodity it might be exchanged with (this—as Marx will show—logically presupposes money as the representation of this exchange-value). It necessarily denotes something common to all commodities: that they are products of human labor. In this, Marx concurred with classical political economy. For Engels, as for many since, it was the subsequent step Marx took that distinguished his theory. Marx notes that labor has the unique property of adding (exchange) value to a commodity and yet its exchange-value is determined by the cost of reproducing that labor. The difference between the value transferred to the new commodity and the costs of a worker's wage constitutes the surplus value a capitalist will later realize through exchange as profit.

The qualifications Marx introduces of temporality and appearance are crucial to his account of value. Both point to the fact that, for Marx, value is not just something that inheres in a commodity as a kind of transhistorical embodiment of human labor; instead and crucially, commodities' "objective character as values is... purely social."[3] It is this notion of value as a "real abstraction," produced by the social exchange of commodities, that means commodities, as Marx comments sarcastically, "abound in metaphysical subtleties and theological niceties."[4] The purpose of this description is twofold. First, it is intended to scandalize: how is it that the banal detritus of everyday life can shimmer in the empyrean light of ratiocination? Second, and relatedly, Marx is positing the centrality of value-form to the very (mis)apprehension of society. Changing the metaphor, Marx comments: "By equating their different products to each other in exchange as values, they equate their different kinds of labor as human labor. They do this without being aware of it. Value, therefore, does not have its description branded on its forehead; it rather transforms every product of labor into a social hieroglyphic."[5] Here, Marx turns to the language of representation. Value is finally the way in which labor appears under capitalism, and precisely because this is so, it is what distinguishes the capitalist mode of production from those that went before and which might come after. Under capitalism, for the first time in history, the form of the commodity serves to determine and regulate all social life, and it does so under the sign of value.

Notes

1 Marx, *Capital* vol. 1, 174.
2 Marx, *Capital* vol. 1, 126.
3 Marx, *Capital* vol. 1, 139.
4 Marx, *Capital* vol. 1, 163.
5 Marx, *Capital* vol. 1, 166.

19

Money

Marina Vishmidt

The dominance of money is what distinguishes a capitalist society from others. Money is an "all-sided mediation," guaranteeing the universality of alienated social relations through the formal means of general equivalence (the erstwhile "invisible hand" of the market, now perhaps the "invisible algorithm").[1] The cash nexus registers the dependencies of a type of social life founded on the axiom of equivalence—that is, organized *objectively* through the capitalist mode of production and *subjectively* through the fiction of liberal personhood.

Labor time takes the form of money. It is objectified in and mediated by money in order to circulate and accumulate. The mediation of exchange by money is the "asocial sociality" that makes all forms of labor comparable insofar as they can be exchanged for a wage. The exchange of labor for a money wage has a prior condition, namely, the investment of money by a capitalist in an enterprise that only surplus labor can make profitable. The exchange of money for commodities has existed in many different forms of society in time and space. What, therefore, distinguishes a capitalist society is that this exchange is part of an overall dynamic of production and reproduction that pivots on private property, investment, and the expanded cycle of production, circulation, and consumption (M–C–M', wherein money is exchanged for commodities only in order to acquire more money). However, money is always a *vanishing* mediator, disappearing and naturalizing itself in commodity circulation. Until we come to the axiom of financialization, M–M', in which money would beget more money without detouring via the commodity for Marx money is a universal mediation in capitalist social life that is both always present and never there: "money appears only fleetingly, or, its substance consists only in this constant appearance as disappearance, as this vehicle of mediation."[2]

Marx's emphasis on money as a universal mediation, the "concrete universal" of social relations fetishized through the commodity and abstract labor, came to influence modernist aesthetics in a number of ways. Money was the "real abstraction" of the form of value that organized life in capitalist society, but modernist art bore a specifically mediated—ideologically and economically—relation to it. In the era of "high modernism," and even more so now, as asset class art may briefly store capital in the upper echelons of value circulation. Yet, art is not capital or value here, only the form of appearance of capital before it moves back into cycles of investment. Art generally circulates via nonprofit institutions and contexts, and where it interacts with profit-making institutions (dealers, auction-houses, collectors) these are rigorously defined by their separation from a wider capitalist marketplace.

Modernist art, with its challenges to vision and sense, came to illustrate the corrosive effect of capitalist quantification and labor discipline on the old verities of human perception and the lifeworld that sustained them, as Walter Benjamin famously chronicled. It evoked the "solidity" melting into air, the social impact of money on "fast-fixed" traditional relations Marx and Engels identified in 1848, in the space of cultural production. At the same time, modernism seemed to point to a numinous "beyond" the money and commodity form, or indeed any human social forms, as modernist mystics such as Wassily Kandinsky, Piet Mondriaan, and Kazimir Malevich attested. The social ontology of money and art have often been discussed in similar terms by critical theorists who based their materialist aesthetic theory on the shared propensity of art and money to conceal and disavow the social relations of capitalist life, principally labor. Theodor Adorno even called art the "absolute commodity," drawing on this social semblance to make a point about how the lack of use-value brings modernist artworks closer to the ur-form of the capitalist commodity as arbitrary: purely social, purely exchange. We see then that the structural analogy between art and money is that each represents an instance of self-valorizing value, insofar as both are social mediations which are anchored in a self-referential or reflexive circuit of valorization—critical value in art is generated from transactions within its semantic domain, much as in speculative finance (or "fictitious capital," in Marx's phrase) money generates more money through transactions internal to financial markets.

We can thus see how both social and artistic abstraction was highlighted in modernist political aesthetics as a pivot toward the "real" determined by capitalist social forms such as money. Such abstraction was later to be taken up in critical practices in theater, literature, and the visual arts, as a bugbear of bourgeois aesthetics to be eliminated through strategic exposure, as in Brecht's "estrangement effect," or to be swept aside in the appeal to (orchestrated) direct experience, as in participatory theatrical and art practices from the 1950s onward. Such "problematizations" evoked Marx's project in the critique of political economy, to disclose the specifically mediated nature of that which seems to have been always there (money, the commodity, abstract social labor). At the same time, it also became increasingly clear that the parallel between art and money was structural as much as ideological, embedded at the level of its institutions and markets, with art functioning in at least two of the modes commanded by money—as a commodity and as an asset class, or store of value. Ideologically, however, whether or not art thematically concerns itself with economic matters, its distance from the utilitarian and the material is ensured by its exceptional status as a good and as a form of labor. This is the ground that sustains the myth of art's autonomy from the principles and methods of market rationality that makes it such an effective legitimation mechanism for accumulation.

It is here that numerous contemporary political conflicts around the sources of funding and the composition of boards at art institutions have emerged, which look to art both for its critical capacities and its significance for "money laundering" in every sense.

Notes

1 Marx, *Grundrisse*, 156.
2 Marx, *Grundrisse*, 209.

20

The General Formula of Capital

Adam David Morton

Who are the dramatis personae of capital? After exploring the fetishism of the commodity and its secret in *Capital* (1867), Marx turns his attention to the presuppositions from which capital may arise. These presuppositions commence with the metamorphosis of the world of commodities (C) into money (M) that begins to define the dramatis personae of the general formula, marked by the buyer and the seller. However, at this stage we are still in the realm of commodities in the sphere of simple circulation, based on use-values and the satisfaction of human needs; we are, in this formula, treading the path from commodity, to money, to commodity (C–M–C). The pupation of commodities into exchange-value creates the possibility for a continuous movement of commodities as capital—of the perpetuum mobile of capital. Here the obvious and trivial "thing" of a fetishized commodity becomes defined by its social relations and the mass of socially necessary labor time needed to produce it, which is then exchanged through the universal equivalent of money.

A "reflux" occurs here so that the process is inverted from C–M–C, with money now the driving and motivating force of commodity production, into M–C–M. There is a deadly leap—or salto mortale—in the commodity's form in this process, where value presents itself as the surplus value, or the original sum advanced plus an increment, and is converted into the general formula of capital: M–C–M'. For the transformation of money into capital, then, there has to be annexed surplus value, the valorization of value. Thus, for the larval form of the money-owner (M) to become the butterfly of the capitalist extracting surplus value (M'), labor power becomes the pivotal commodity (C). Value, after all, is a congealed quantity of abstract labor and its crystallization into surplus value, which is soaked in the exploitation of labor time. The general formula of capital as M–C–M' is thus the purchase (M) of the commodity of labor power (C) and its metamorphosis into surplus value (M') based on the exploitation of labor time as surplus labor.

Value thus undergoes a "metempsychosis" or transmigration that deserts the consumed body of the laborer to occupy the newly created one of capital in the form of surplus value. It is a transmigration between bodies that involves the materialization of blood into capital, the vampire-like sucking of living labor by capital. Meanwhile, other monsters of the market are left to engage in the horrors of exploitation. Marx considered such acts—from pulmonary disease induced by scrofula in the pottery industry of Stoke-on-Trent to the terrors of the trade in human slaves in the Americas—as tending to surpass the worst excesses of Dante's Inferno. The crucible of this set of social relations is not the surface appearances of the buyer and the seller, owner of money and bearer of labor power, within the sphere of circulation. A change has taken place in the dramatis personae. We have, in apprehending the general formula of capital, moved to the hidden abode of production within which the secret of profit-making is laid bare. It is a world where the money-owner now strides out as the capitalist and the possessor of labor power is the active agent of the worker. The sycophant of capital is "vulgar" political economy and the defense of private property the first negation of common interests. The struggle-driven process for the re-establishment of property on the basis of cooperation and the possession of land in common is the negation of that negation. It is a process still in motion, an alternative perpetuum mobile of class struggle.

21

Class

Elinor Taylor

Even the most casual reader of the *Communist Manifesto* (1848) will be struck by Marx and Engels' declaration that "[t]he history of all hitherto existing society is the history of class struggles"[1] and by the grand dramatic imagery of an imminent, cataclysmic confrontation between two classes, the bourgeoisie and the proletariat. But what is class, and why is it so fundamental to Marxist thought in all its areas of research?

To outline the Marxist conception of class, we must first refer to the most basic concepts in Marx's critique of political economy, those of the *productive forces* and the social *relations of production*. The former refers to everything that is required for the production and reproduction of life in a given society, such as raw materials, labor, and technologies of production. The latter refers to the social organization of those forces for the purposes of production in that society: who owns the raw materials and technologies, who works at what tasks, and whether and how profits are extracted. Classes are one aspect of these relations, and when thinking about class it is vital to emphasize that classes are constituted by their role in the dynamic processes of production and reproduction, rather than by some particular objective attribute (such as level of income) or by any individual's subjective identification, or lack thereof, with a particular class position. Class relations in all but the most primitive societies are relations of property ownership; under capitalism, Marx argues, the fundamental class division is between wage laborers who own only their ability to work (the commodity labor power), and capitalists, who own the means of production, the system through which labor power is purchased in order to extract surplus value, which is then transformed into monetary profit.

Between the productive forces and the relations of production is an antagonism that for Marx is the engine of historical change. As he argued in the 1859 Preface to *A Critique of Political Economy*, once the productive forces reach a certain point of development (the point at which communism becomes possible, for instance), the existing class relations will become intolerable and "then begins an epoch of social revolution," transforming the relations of production in their entirety.[2] For Marx, relations of production are always political since they are always relations of "sovereignty and dependence," but the degree to which a class is conscious of itself *as a class* varies in particular circumstances.[3] Raymond Williams noted the two senses of "class" as category (wage laborers) and social formation (working class) in *Keywords* (1983); both senses are integral to the phenomenon of class as Marx understood it.

Writing in *The Poverty of Philosophy* (1847) about the struggles of the English working class in the 1830s and 1840s, Marx describes how "[t]his mass is . . . already a class as against capital, but not yet for itself";[4] in the division of its interests from those of capital, the class is formed as a class, but it only forms *itself* as a class when its consciousness coheres in a certain way via a recognition that its shared interests are opposed to those of another class. This consciousness develops through the political contestation of class struggle.

At the level of the individual subject, matters are necessarily complex. Marx indicated this in *The German Ideology* (1845) with his discussion of the formation of the French bourgeoisie, arguing that while the bourgeoisie forms itself as a class in the way described above, "the class in its turn achieves an independent existence over against the individuals, so that the latter find their conditions of existence predestined, and hence have their position in life and their personal development assigned to them by their class, become subsumed under it."[5] Here, the bourgeoisie forms itself as a class, but in so doing it also constitutes itself as an alien power over which individuals of that class feel they have no control; this is because its class interests are in the maintenance of the division of labor from which issues a contradiction between the interests of the particular individual and the interest of the community. This contradiction manifests itself in the alien existence of class as an apparently independent phenomenon. Proletarian class consciousness, by contrast, in recognizing that it has no class interest except the abolition of class, private property, and the division of labor, is the necessary condition for an end to the subjugation of diminished individuals to implacable social forms: "The reality, which communism is creating, is precisely the true basis for rendering it impossible that anything should exist independently of individuals."[6]

Notes

1 Marx and Engels, "Manifesto of the Communist Party," 473.
2 Marx, *Preface to A* "Contribution to the Critique of Political Economy," in *The Marx-Engels Reader*, 4–5.
3 Marx, *Capital* vol. 3, 927.
4 Marx, "The Coming Upheaval," in *The Marx-Engels Reader*, 218.
5 Marx, "The German Ideology," 143.
6 Marx, "The German Ideology," 157.

22

Technology

Trevor Strunk

Marx's work on technology can be effectively distilled from three sources: the first section of *Capital*'s fifteenth chapter, "Machinery and Large-Scale Industry"; the fragment on machines from the *Grundrisse* (1858); and the rumored notebooks on technology. As much as a Marxist understanding of technology would be improved with access to those latter, ephemeral texts, they seem to have been lost to time outside few citations and a brief mention by Marx in a January 1863 letter to Engels, in which he says he has "re-read all my note-books (excerpts) on technology."[1] Thus, we are left with the evocative snippets in *Capital* (1867) and the *Grundrisse*, which boil down to Marx's conclusion that "the co-operative character of the labor process is . . . a technical necessity dictated by the very nature of the instrument of labor."[2] In other words, for Marx, there is potential for labor-in-common immanent to technology, but he can only responsibly—and dialectically—understand technology as a process. In a pointedly schematic moment in the *Grundrisse*, Marx defines technology in terms of a kind of fixed capital that confronts the laborer with its strangeness, arguing that the "general aspect" of machinery and technology represents itself only "in so far as the means of labor, as a physical thing, loses its direct form, becomes fixed capital, and confronts the worker physically as capital. In machinery, knowledge appears as alien, external to him; and living labor is subsumed under self-activating objectified labor."[3] Importantly, the worker may appear "superfluous" in this, but only due to their relationship to profit. The machine—what Marx calls the automaton in the *Grundrisse*—does not confront the worker as friend or enemy, but rather as part of an alienated means of production.

The implied potential of technology as owned and operated by labor, not capital, has led many thinkers—most recently but not limited to Aaron Bastani—to a sort of messianic faith in technology's liberatory potential. From this perspective, the movement toward full automation promises a kind of labor-free plenitude, with the means of production not only removed from capitalist control but in fact also removed from the realm of the human entirely; technology, recall, encourages cooperation, and "superfluous labor" is only a concern to the capitalist who demands evermore efficient sources of profit. The laborer and the machine could, in theory, live in perfect harmony. But this hope elides Marx's view of industry, which itself is meant to produce surplus value by way of both living labor—namely, workers—and "dead" labor—namely, the machines the workers themselves have created. When industry reaches a scale such that automation, even at fairly primitive levels, of the machine system presents "an entirely objective organization of production, which confronts the worker as a preexisting material condition of production."[4] The worker, in other words, is never simply granted access to the machine-as-machine, but instead is given the form of appearance of the machine as "more efficient labor," as competition. Thus, the laborer must adapt to the material reality of the machine, whereas previously the machines had to be fitted to the specialized workers who represented the increasingly thinly sliced division of labor. Marx in the *Grundrisse* tells us that the subservience or obsolescence of labor in the face of machinery "holds only in so far as [machinery] is cast into the role of fixed capital, and this it is only because the worker relates to it as wage-worker, and the active individual generally, as mere worker."[5] We can unpack this by saying Marx has given us good news and bad news: the good news is that the relationship of labor to technology is a relationship built not on material absolutes but rather on social relationships; the bad news is that all of labor relations are built, rather sturdily, on these same relationships.

Perhaps it is no surprise that, in *Capital*, Marx begins the analysis of relative surplus-value—the analysis that credits time dilation as the reason for increased productivity within a standardized working day—at the end of his investigation of machinery and large-scale industry. As he notes, capitalist production "develops the techniques and the degree of combination of the social process of production by simultaneously undermining the original sources of all wealth—the soil and the worker."[6] This degree of complexity that Marx first sees in his exploration of technology is undercut when he states the simple end of industry, namely to further alienate workers from their labor and further depress the "productive" value of labor power. Value, here, is relative of course; the worker's material value, realized in wages, may be cut by their employer, but ultimately the money earned is less important for the capitalist than the circulating value—M–M'—that determines profit. Therefore, the transfer of value from machine to worker—value "becoming transferred from the worker to capital in the form of the machine, and his own labor capacity devalued thereby"[7]—is the form of appearance of what Marx calls bourgeois social production.

Machines, used collectively, could create free time, a demystifying commodity that Marx calls "both idle time and time for higher activity," but in their current use by the capitalist class, machines condition the laborer to view all time as labor time and all mechanisms as alienated tools of production.[8] "Labor time," Marx explains, "as the measure of value posits wealth itself as founded on poverty, and disposable time as existing in and because of the antithesis to surplus labor time; or, the positing of an individual's entire time as labor time, and his degradation therefore to mere worker, subsumption under labor."[9] But one gets the feeling toward the end of the fragment on machines that Marx is not entirely sure of his ability to predict the totality of "bourgeois society in the long view and as a whole," and this doubt stems from an inability to see the telos of machinery and technology in the labor process.[10] In his letter to Engels about the notebooks, Marx reiterates this doubt, observing that "mechanics presents much the same problem as languages. I understand the mathematical laws, but the simplest technical reality that calls for ocular knowledge is more difficult for me than the most complicated combinations."[11] If we understand the mathematical laws and imbricated social processes of labor and capital as the subject of Marx's dialectical focus and polemic, then we might understand the sections on industry in *Capital* as insights into the form of appearance of technology, a kind of veneer of "productivity" that obscures the simple tenet at the core of autonomous production under capitalism: labor power must be further devalued to ensure faster and more efficient circulation.

It may seem disappointing that Marx does not have a compelling answer to the question of what is to be done about automation and its heightening of the contradictions in variable surplus value and the circulation of value, but perhaps Marx was wise to be circumspect in his thinking here. The calls for "fully automated luxury communism" in our current moment seem like lovely temptations, but they forget a core lesson from the *Grundrisse*: "As the system of bourgeois economy has developed for us only by degrees, so too its negation, which is its ultimate result."[12] Marx is not indecisive on technology, nor is he bold to the point of being outdated; instead, Marx treats technology as he does all aspects of bourgeois social production: dialectically, with the negation in mind as closely as the positing. Marx could not see the ultimate result of the dialectic of technology and laborer, but he could draft the basic processes of interaction, with hope that this analysis would help us resolve machinery into the cooperative, communal tools needed for a society that cares for the individual worker beyond the contingencies of social production.

Notes

1. Marx to Engels, January 28, 1863. https://marxists.catbull.com/archive/marx/works/1863/letters/63_01_28.htm, accessed August 20, 2019.
2. Marx, "Contribution to the Critique of Political Economy," 62.
3. Marx, *Grundrisse*, 702.
4. Marx, *Grundrisse*, 702.
5. Marx, *Grundrisse*, 702.
6. Marx, *Capital* vol. 1, 637.
7. Marx, *Grundrisse*, 704.
8. Marx, *Grundrisse*, 712.
9. Marx, *Grundrisse*, 708.
10. Marx, *Grundrisse*, 712.
11. Marx to Engels, January 28, 1863.
12. Marx, *Grundrisse*, 712.

23

Family

Kate Montague

The family, as a particular and even "primitive" site of social reproduction, forms an absent center within the work of Marx and Engels. It remains, as many critics have noted, an oblique, underdeveloped, and unevenly treated concept or category in their collected works, but one that is also central to the reproduction of capitalism through accumulation—not just in the biological creation of workers and consumers, or the way in which the family reinforces a gendered division of labor, or the many informal ways that "domestic" labor maintains wage labor, but also in the way the family itself has been subsumed and made productive within the capitalist mode of production. "Marx," writes Shulamith Firestone, "was on to something more profound than he knew when he observed that the family contained within itself in embryo all the antagonisms that later develop on a wide scale within the society and the state."[1] In other words, Marx sensed but did not fully develop a critique of the relationship between the familial reproduction of living labor power and the reproduction of capitalism as a whole, and the way in which the family might engender its own destruction. Drawing these lines together, we can combine what Marx and Engels write about the family (and its relation to the mode and means of production) with more recent feminist critiques of the family.

In *Origins of the Family, Private Property, and the State* (1884), Engels draws on "an old unpublished manuscript written by Marx and myself in 1846," wherein they write: "The first division of labor is that of man and wife in breeding children." Engels then elaborates, "today I may add: The first class antagonism appearing in history coincides with the development of the antagonism of man and wife in monogamy, and the first class oppression with that of the female by the male sex." Here Engels emphasizes the contradiction as one of familial bond. "Monogamy was a great historical progress," he suggests:

> But by the side of slavery and private property it marks at the same time that epoch which, reaching down to our days, takes with all progress also a step backwards, relatively speaking, and develops the welfare and advancement of one by woe and submission of the other. It is the cellular form of civilized society which enables us to study the nature of its now fully developed contrasts and contradictions.[2]

In *Capital* (1867), Marx accounts for social reproduction as a precondition to labor before relegating it away from production and into the hidden abode of domestic life. "Labor power exists only as a capacity of the living individual. Its production consequently presupposes his existence. Given the existence of the individual, the production of labor power consist in his reproduction of himself or his maintenance."[3] Neither "reproduction" nor "maintenance" are given much more exegesis than this, except insofar as reproduction becomes a social zone separate from the sphere of production—a place in which "animal" nature might run free. For Marx, then, the worker under capitalism "no longer feels himself to be freely active in any but his animal functions—eating, drinking, procreating, to at most in his dwelling and in dressing-up, etc.; and in his human functions he no longer feels himself to be anything but an animal." Many Marxist-feminists (from Simone de Beauvoir through Silvia Federici, to Sophie Lewis and Amy De'Ath) have critiqued the contradiction inherent within this figuration of the domestic abode and the family as a site of freedom, arguing that the labor that goes into furnishing these activities, the "eating, drinking, procreating," is precisely a space of unfreedom.

Where Marx thinks more carefully about the division of labor and the gendered dynamic of capitalist reproduction is in the function of the family as it becomes integrated into the formal economy. In the chapter on industry, Marx writes that the labor of women and children was "the first result of the capitalist application of machinery." This is because, "as machinery dispenses with muscular power, it becomes a means for employing workers of slight muscular strength, or whose bodily development is incomplete, but whose limbs are all the more supple." Crucially, machinery "that mighty substitute for labor and for workers" presented to capital "a means for increasing the number of wage-laborers by enrolling, under the direct sway of capital, every member of the worker's family, without distinction of age or sex."[4] This meant the capitalist could purchase the labor power of the entire family at a cheaper rate than the "head of the family," because "four days' labor takes the play of one day's, and the price falls in proportion to the excess of the surplus labor of four over the surplus labor of one."[5] Children and women therefore represent a realm of surplus labor able to be aggressively exploited and, in this way, capital subsumes the older feudal structure of the family as yet another site from which to accumulate. And yet, because women were now undertaking wage labor, the traditional form of the family is gradually eroded, precisely because there is less time for all those "caring" activities. To shift this into a more contemporary setting, the outsourcing of "caring" activities once relegated to the hidden sphere of the family (cooking, cleaning, childcare, and gestation) marks the division between the "market-mediated" and "indirectly market-mediated" spheres of reproductive labor, as the *Endnotes* collective accurately demarcate the division of productive and reproductive work.[6]

That Marx sees this subsumption of the family within the formal economy as a potential site of freedom, this time one of equality between the sexes, renders explicitly the contradiction posed by the family within his writing: "large-scale industry, by assigning an important part in socially organized processes of production, outside the sphere of the domestic economy, to women, young persons, and children of both sexes, does nevertheless create a new economic foundation for a higher form of the family and of relations between the sexes."[7] Freedom can, of course, only be figured as freedom from compulsion, from exploitation, from subsistence within the capitalist sphere of production. And yet, we can also compare the family precisely to "modern industry" insofar as it contains the means of its own destruction. In other words, if modern industry reveals this contradiction via the logic of combination, then we might say that the family preconceives its own destruction via precisely the same means that exploit it as surplus labor: technology. This is an argument Sophie Lewis has developed in her thinking through the outsourcing or marketization of gestation, suggesting that a solution to the exploitation of gendered labor under capitalism is to be found in collectively "seizing the means of reproduction," in order to undo the system of exploitation into which they have been recruited so that "where pregnancy is concerned, let every pregnancy be for everyone. Let us overthrow, in short, the 'family.'"[8]

Notes

1 Shulamith Firestone, *The Dialectic of Sex: The Case for Feminist Revolution* (New York: William Morrow and Company, 1971), 11–12.
2 Engels, *The Origin of the Family: Private Property and the State*, trans. Ernest Untermann (North Charleston: Pantianos Classics, 1891), 47.
3 Marx, *Capital* vol. 1, 274.
4 Marx, *Capital* vol. 1, 517.
5 Marx, *Capital* vol. 1, 518.
6 "The Logic of Gender: On the Separation of Spheres and the Process of Abjection," *Endnotes* 3 https://endnotes.org.uk/issues/3/en/endnotes-the-logic-of-gender, accessed August 20, 2019.
7 Marx, *Capital* vol. 1, 620–1.
8 Sophie Lewis, *Full Surrogacy Now: Feminism against Family* (London: Verso, 2019), 29, 26.

24

Ideology

Harry Warwick

The dilemma that famously confronts students of Marx's theory of economic crises—namely, that his reflections on the subject are disparate and unsystematic—also faces those interested in his theory of ideology, for whom no definitive statement on the nature, operations, and function of ideology exists in Marx's corpus. The most rudimentary Marxist definition of ideology as "false consciousness," a misrecognition of what is truly in one's interest, has little to do with Marx's uses of the term, and derives instead from a letter penned by Engels after Marx's death.[1] Marx thus left the formulation of a theory of ideology to his followers, and yet even here, in the two dominant efforts at such theorizations, one finds contrary points of departure. The first approach, associated with the humanist Marxism of Georg Lukács and, later, Fredric Jameson, begins with fidelity to Marx's analysis of commodity fetishism. The second, associated with Louis Althusser's anti-humanist Marxism, reflects the latter's rejection of that analysis.[2]

For Lukács, the processes of abstraction and objectification that Marx identifies in his critique of fetishism are properties not merely of the capitalist production process, but of capitalist society in toto, which unfolds according to its own internal laws, independent of human activity. The consequence is a state of affairs where form prevails over content, quantities over qualities, objects over subjects—in short, where capital sucks the productive and creative power out of humans and turns it to its own purposes, primarily that of self-valorization.[3] Such a society might properly be considered "false," inverted, and alienated. Terry Eagleton thus describes the Lukácsian notion of ideology as "true thought in a false situation."[4] As much is also implicit in Jameson's definition of ideology (not the only one in his oeuvre) as "the form taken by alienation in the realm of consciousness or thought."[5] On this view, ideology is the cognition of de-subjectivized subjects—of subjects whose agency, will, and creativity have been subordinated to capital.

Louis Althusser's 1970 essay "Ideology and Ideological State Apparatuses" laid the foundations of the second dominant approach.[6] Ideology is an essential object of study for Marxists, Althusser suggests, because it guarantees the reproduction of the relations of production. It ensures proletarians rise every morning equipped with the right attitude for work, that they shuffle into their workplace with minimal fuss, with no need for direct repression. Ideology makes people "work by themselves" through "interpellation": an enigmatic process akin to "hailing" whereby the human organism becomes part of the social order—a subject endowed with a history, personality, identity, and social role. These interpellations are the effect of material social practices, perpetuated by institutions (the church, the education system, the media, etc.), which then function as "Ideological State Apparatuses." Unlike the humanists, for whom ideology reflects capital's objectification of social relations, Althusser sees ideology as the process of subjectivation par excellence.

Unsurprisingly, when pressed into the analysis of cultural texts, each ideology theory generates a different hermeneutic. For Lukács and his followers, ideology tends to manifest itself in the framing devices, or "strategies of containment," that texts deploy to occlude the totality of capitalist social relations.[7] This is the standard by which Lukács rather unsympathetically distinguishes realism and modernism: the former seeks to depict society in its dynamic richness, he argues, while the latter elides history and temporality, fascinates itself with pure style, and represents a basically static and hopeless state of affairs.[8] As for Althusser, his model of ideology found particular favor in 1970s Anglo-French film theory, which began to conceive of the cinema itself as an ideological apparatus "constructing" its viewer, interpellating them as a subject.[9]

Notes

1 Engels to Franz Mehring, July 14, 1893 https://www.marxists.org/archive/marx/works/1893/letters/93_07_14.htm, accessed August 20, 2019.
2 See Marx, *Capital* vol. 1, 163–77. And for a reading of this analysis as an exemplary ideology theory and critique in its own right, see Jan Rehmann, *Theories of Ideology: The Powers of Alienation and Subjection* (Chicago: Haymarket, 2014), 39–40.
3 See especially Lukács' long essay, "Reification and the Consciousness of the Proletariat," in *History and Class Consciousness: Studies in Marxist Dialectics*, trans. Rodney Livingstone (Cambridge, MA: MIT Press, 1971), 83–222.
4 Eagleton, *Ideology: An Introduction*, 2nd ed. (London: Verso, 2007), 104–7.
5 Jameson, *Valences of the Dialectic* (London: Verso, 2009), 321.
6 Althusser's essay is in fact a montage of extracts from a longer manuscript, published in English as *On the Reproduction of Capitalism: Ideology and Ideological State Apparatuses*, trans. G. M. Goshgarian (London: Verso, 2014), and carrying that essay as an appendix.
7 On "strategies of containment," see Jameson, *The Political Unconscious: Narrative as a Socially Symbolic Act* (Abingdon: Routledge, 2002), 37–9.
8 See Lukács, "The Ideology of Modernism," in *Realism in Our Time: Literature and the Class Struggle*, trans. John Mander and Necke Mander (New York: Harper & Row, 1971), 17–46. Nuancing Lukács' analysis, Jameson notes the utopian vocation of modernist abstraction in *The Political Unconscious*, 225–6.
9 See, for instance, Jean-Louis Baudry, "Ideological Effects of the Basic Cinematographic Apparatus," trans. Alan Williams, *Film Quarterly* 28.2 (1974–5): 39–47.

25

Alienation

Ana Tomcic

Alienation (or "estrangement") is the omnipresent psychological consequence of capitalist relations of production as well as a crucial tool of their maintenance and reproduction. In order to understand Marx's conception of alienation, it is first necessary to outline his views on what defines humanity. According to Marx, humans realize their self-worth through work, but work is defined as both a *free* and *creative* activity. Through this type of activity, each individual "duplicates himself" not only intellectually—in their consciousness and imagination—but also actively, by leaving their trace on the external world. When people work in this manner, the world becomes a mirror of their inner needs and desires, both emotional and physical. For Marx, this kind of work constitutes the species essence (*Gattungswesen*) of humankind and is what differentiates the human from the rest of the animal kingdom. While animals produce only when coerced by physical necessity, "man truly produces only when he is free from physical need."[1] Thus, for Marx, freedom to engage in self-directed, creative labor constitutes the basic condition of individual and collective well-being.

Within capitalism, however, labor is reduced to a means of ensuring workers' physical subsistence. Rather than being directly useful to the worker, the product is appropriated from them and sold as a commodity. As compensation for the time spent at work, the worker is given wages (always reduced to the minimum in order to extract maximum surplus value), which are needed to secure shelter and food. Simply put, the worker works to live and the product they produce has no other meaning in the context of their life or the lives of their immediate community. Not only is the product decoupled from their individual wants and wishes, but it was also never meant to belong to them in the first place. Oftentimes, workers cannot even afford the product they helped to produce. This constitutes the first aspect of the worker's alienated existence within the capitalist economy: alienation from the product.

This facet of alienation is inextricably linked to alienation from work as an activity. Since the object of their work is always prescribed, workers cannot decide what they produce or the conditions of production. Even in what are traditionally considered more creative or independent types of work, the workers' freedom is restricted by the demands of the market. These demands, in turn, are substantially streamlined by the owners of the means of production—in our contemporary context, owners of multinational companies who decide which types of projects will get funding. Since labor is not voluntary, but forced, it can no longer function as an extension of the worker's individuality. In Marx's words, the "worker's own physical and mental energy—his personal life" becomes "an activity which is turned against him, independent of him and not belonging to him."[2] The more the workers produce, the less power and independence they have, since their work only serves to increase the profits and, consequently, the property and social status of the capitalist. In capitalist societies, work and its products face the worker as an external force that is, at the same time, alien and hostile. The worker "only feels himself outside of his work."[3]

Since the value of the workers' labor is reduced to time (i.e., working hours), the price of which is set through relations of exchange in the market, the workers themselves become commodities. Indeed, the workers are, according to Marx, "the most wretched of commodities," whose bodies and minds are treated as replaceable objects.[4] Just as commodities are pitted against each other in order to be bought and consumed, or discarded, workers are forced into competition for jobs and wages. If the workers' lack of agency in relation to their work and the product alienates them from their own individuality and their humanity (species essence), competition alienates human from human. Not only are the two classes—the owners of the means of production (the bourgeoisie) and those who sell their work (the proletariat)—estranged from each other through domination and exploitation, the workers are also themselves enticed into a relationship of mutual hostility in order to survive. This is the final aspect of alienation in Marx's social analysis.

How then is alienation to be combated? The answer to this question is suggested in Marx's definition of what work should be like if it is to reflect the worker's individuality. In brief, society would have to be restructured in a way that offers individuals the opportunity to develop their needs and wishes through their work as well as the opportunity to enjoy the fruits of their labor. This can only be attained by giving workers the maximum amount of freedom, both in the choice of their work and in the determination of their working conditions. Evidently, such a situation is unattainable under capitalism, but only becomes possible where workers and community members can collectively voice their needs and reach decisions on how they are best to be addressed. Workers should see their desires and efforts reflected in the life of the community, which would enable them to form meaningful connections to other community members. Instead of a large number of people producing for the benefit of a privileged few, Marx envisions an ideal society in which individuals would produce according to their ability (and desire) and each benefit according to their need.

Notes

1 Marx, "The Economic and Philosophical Manuscripts of 1844," 78.
2 Marx, "The Economic and Philosophical Manuscripts of 1844," 74–5.
3 Marx, "The Economic and Philosophical Manuscripts of 1844," 74.
4 Marx, "The Economic and Philosophical Manuscripts of 1844," 70.

Materialism

Fiona Allen

In its broadest sense, materialism refers to a series of theoretical approaches that assert the primacy of material reality over thought. As a result, it can be distinguished from idealist systems, which seek to prioritize spirituality, consciousness, and the idea. In *Ludwig Feuerbach and the End of Classical German Philosophy* (1886), Engels characterized the history of Western philosophy as a perpetual struggle between these two "great camps," proclaiming his and Marx's allegiance to the materialist cause. Yet rather than presenting his materialism as an extension of this position, Marx viewed it as a partial rupture with the past. "The chief defect of all hitherto existing materialism," Marx argued, "is that the thing, reality, sensuousness, is conceived only in the form of the *object* or of *contemplation*, but not as *sensuous human activity, practice*, not subjectively."[1] Instead of framing human beings as contemplative receptacles of their surroundings, Marx believed that they transform these conditions as well as their consciousness through practical interaction. This emphasis on sensuous praxis (i.e., the reciprocal interaction between practice and consciousness) allowed Marx to adopt a more subtle understanding of human agency—one that avoids the twin pitfalls of voluntarism and determinism. It also led to a socio-historical image of reality that assigned as much weight to human structures, actions, and relations as it did to the natural or physical world. This is the approach that came to be known as historical materialism.

Historical materialism received its first coherent articulation in *The German Ideology*. Broadly speaking, this volume is a polemic against the Young Hegelians—leftist followers of Hegel who retained elements of the philosopher's idealist system in their work. To ground their critique, Marx and Engels begin by establishing the criteria for a materialist approach to history. The first premise is that humans cannot make history without first creating their means of sustenance. Consequently, the questions of how, what, and under which conditions humans *produce* should always take priority. Consciousness, Marx and Engels argue, is secondary to these concerns, making its first appearance as history in language, which emerges from the need to cooperate in production and only acquires a semblance of autonomy through improved productivity and the division between intellectual and manual labor. When understood in these terms, the so-called free intellect appears as the product of a series of class and property relations "in which enjoyment and labor, production and consumption—devolve on different individuals."[2] To view philosophical abstractions or other prevailing ideas as either eternal or foundational is not only to lapse into a series of falsehoods but also to naturalize a worldview that arises from the lived experience of the ruling class, a phenomenon Marx termed "ideology."

Even before writing *The German Ideology* (1845), Marx had declared his allegiance to social revolution and a communist future. However, the conception of history put forward here set these commitments on a new path. Communism, he argued, was neither an ethical ideal nor the product of utopian blueprint: assumptions held by figures such as Robert Owen and Henri Saint-Simon. Rather, its origins lie in the material conditions and contradictions of society. Marx's mature account of the capitalist economy, as outlined in *Capital*, differs from other political-economic doctrines due to its attempt to discover paths to communism in the tensions of the present—an approach that sought to emphasize the antagonisms between labor and capital. Though Marx made only a few tentative comments on how communism might emerge from aspects of current society, for the most part, he assumed that it could only be created by those whose practical conditions gave them an interest in building and fighting for it. Consequently, this responsibility falls largely to the working class.

An earlier attempt to summarize Marx's materialism can be found in the preface to *A Contribution to the Critique of Political Economy* (1859). In one of the more famous passages in the Marxian corpus, this text offers a global account of society comprised of two parts: base and superstructure. Whereas the former includes the forces and relations of production, the latter consists of legal, ideological, and political institutions. For Marx, this superstructure rests on the "real foundation" of the base, the composition and movements of which condition its nature. "The mode of production of material life," we read there, "conditions the social, political and intellectual life process in general."[3] Although this account offers a useful summary of Marx's key ideas, its brevity has produced a number of unfortunate consequences. By emphasizing the physical means and techniques of production, it appears to commit Marx to the technological determinism that he consistently denied. In the hands of orthodox dialectical materialists, it also risks being transformed into a type of economism or a doctrine of universal laws. Nevertheless, the need to challenge these assumptions has served as a major source of creativity for Marxist theory. Different understandings of the relationship between base and superstructure, their relative autonomy and internal composition, have been advanced by thinkers from Raymond Williams to Louis Althusser. Indeed, Marx's decision not to write a dedicated volume on his materialism, but rather outline it in a series of statements, has played a formative role in the development of a Marxist thought.

Notes

1 Marx, "Theses on Feuerbach," 143.
2 Marx, "The German Ideology," 159.
3 Marx, "Preface to A Contribution to the Critique of Political Economy," 5.

27

Colonization

Paul Young

Colonization and primitive accumulation are both central to the way Marx understood the world-historical development of capitalist modernity. Primitive accumulation is the process by which he explained the shift from feudalism to capitalism, whereby class distinctions are drawn between labor power and economic ownership of the means of production. In *Capital* (1867), Marx highlights the Enclosure Movement in Britain as a paradigmatic example of this transformative process. Enclosure dispossessed land from a feudal peasantry, who were thereby forcibly "freed" up for wage labor exploitation by those agricultural and industrial capitalists who came to monopolize the means of production. Where classical economists such as Adam Smith suggested hard work and abstinence led naturally and peacefully to the original accumulation of capital by some individuals and not others, Marx saw socioeconomic reorganization premised upon a violent land grab. This formative moment in the emergence of bourgeois-proletarian relations represented a more general history of expropriation, he noted, that was "written in the annals of mankind in letters of blood and fire."[1]

Marx held that European colonization in Africa, the Americas, and Asia realized primitive accumulation on the global stage. Hence he deployed a similarly brutal, bloody lexicon when he turned his attention to the way industrializing European powers penetrated and profited upon the world beyond Europe. "It compels all nations, on pain of extinction, to adopt the bourgeois mode of production," he and Engels wrote in *The Communist Manifesto* (1848), of the imperial program that used "heavy artillery" to batter down borders and establish market-driven connections everywhere.[2] Here Marx referred to "barbarian and semi-barbarian countries," and elsewhere in his work Marx maintained that "Eastern" societies were lacking the progressive historical energies that distinguished western civilizations. So while Marx was a staunch and vocal critic of colonization and other forms of imperial expansion, he emphasized that such expansion generated the revolutionary momentum required to effect a worldwide socialist destiny. In "The Future Results of British Rule in India" (1853), for example, Britain's dialectically destructive and regenerative impact upon an otherwise "unresisting and unchanging society" was framed as a modernizing "mission." Only once a "great social revolution" had mastered the results of this bourgeois phase of world history, Marx concluded, "will human progress cease to resemble that hideous pagan idol, who would not drink the nectar but from the skulls of the slain."³

Primitive accumulation and colonization are thus for Marx violent processes by which the capitalist mode of production takes hold of the world. Much recent critical interest in their historical significance, however, has been concerned to refute a stadial, Eurocentric account of world-systemic development. Scholars have challenged a diffusionist model of a modern world-system in which Europe is the active source and non-Europe is the passive recipient "of culture, of innovation, of human causality."⁴ Such a challenge occasions work that tracks the "multi-causal, multi-directional, and long-historical processes" that have shaped the economic developments, geopolitical forces, social formations, and cultural forms that characterize globalized modernity and its modernisms.⁵ Other scholars demand that because capitalism "does not smooth away but rather *produces* unevenness, systematically and as a matter of course," we should call into question the idea of primitive accumulation as a foundational but transitory act of appropriative violence, emphasizing instead "the continuous role and predatory practices of 'primitive' or 'original' accumulation within a long historical geography of capital accumulation."⁶ Citing Robin Blackburn's claim that primitive accumulation is "a continuing and relentless process whereby capitalist accumulation battens on pre-capitalist modes of exploitation, greatly extending their scope," Timothy Brennan urges attention be paid to the discursive as well as the material features "of an ongoing colonial system on which capitalism has feasted and continues to feast."⁷ Brennan's concern with the depredation of an ongoing colonial system points toward the enduring operation of racialized regimes of primitive accumulation. But because it also suggests a coercive system oriented toward opening up new areas and opportunities for profit-making, it serves, too, as a reminder that capitalism—and the dispossession, exploitation, and violence that characterizes its power relations—is bound up with the nonhuman world as much as it is the human world. In his analysis of the modern world-system as a world-ecology, Jason W. Moore makes clear that primitive accumulation and colonization must be understood in relation to capitalism's definitive need to produce "Cheap Nature," in ideological as well as material terms: "to make Nature's elements 'cheap' in price; and also *to cheapen*, to degrade or to render inferior in an ethico-political sense, the better to make Nature cheap in price."⁸ To appreciate that the "long historical geography of capital accumulation" has demanded the production of "Cheap Nature"—where Cheap Nature takes the form of people, animals, crops, minerals, soil, and so on—is to recognize that capitalism exerts its pervasive planetary powers in ways that have gone, and continue to go, well beyond the exploitation of wage labor.

Notes

1 Marx, *Capital* vol. 1, 669.
2 Marx and Engels, "Manifesto of the Communist Party," 477.

3 Marx, "The Future Results of British Rule in India," *New York Daily Tribune*, August 8, 1853. https://marxists.catbull.com/archive/marx/works/1853/07/22.htm, accessed August 20, 2019.
4 J. M. Blaut, *The Colonizer's Model of the World: Geographical Diffusionism and Eurocentric History* (New York: The Guilford Press, 1993).
5 Regenia Gagnier, *Literatures of Liberalization: Global Circulation and the Long Nineteenth Century* (Basingstoke: Palgrave, 2018), 7.
6 WReC, *Combined and Uneven Development*, 144.
7 Timothy Brennan, "The Economic Image-Function of the Periphery," in *Postcolonial Studies and Beyond*, eds. Ania Loomba, Suvir Kaul, Matti Bunzil, Antoinette Burton and Jed Esty (London: Duke University Press, 2005), 113.
8 Moore, ed., *Anthropocene or Capitalocene? Nature, History, and the Crisis of Capitalism* (Oakland: PM Press, 2016), 1–13.

28

Nature

Margaret Ronda

Over the past two decades, Marxists have turned increasing attention to the importance of ecological thought in relation to broader theories of political economy, emphasizing Marx's interest in the natural sciences, agricultural and evolutionary theories, as well as his attention to issues of population, deforestation, and colonial land development.[1] Far from disregarding ecological dynamics and natural limits in favor of a progressivist "mastery of nature" ideology, Marx's materialist arguments from the *Grundrisse* (1858) forward are inextricably linked to his materialist conceptions of nature, and his critique of capitalism attends to its ecological as well as economic contradictions.[2] Marx's theories must be understood as socioecological, offering a framework for approaching the relation between capitalism as a world-system and the dynamics of the Earth system. Marx's definition of nature, in turn, is a fundamentally dialectical one, attuned to its material forms, exchanges, and systems as they act upon and are reshaped by human social relations, and to the fundamental alterations that capitalist production creates.

Marx conceives of nature not merely as a passive entity, but as an active and relational force. The key concept employed in his works from the 1850s forward to discuss the fundamental characteristics of nature is *metabolism* (*Stoffwechsel*). Metabolism is a term that emerged in nineteenth-century chemistry and biology to describe the interchanges that regulate the growth and regeneration of individual organisms and broader ecosystems.[3] Nature as a metabolic system is composed of dynamic interdependencies and transfers of energy that facilitate life. Marx argues that humans participate in this "universal metabolism of nature" as biological entities, but are differentiated from other species with regard to the unique capacity to labor. Through the labor process, humans "appropriate" "what exists in nature" to meet their needs, and in this way "mediate, regulate, and control the metabolism" between themselves and nature.[4] At the same time, natural conditions and processes necessarily shape these interactions.

For Marx, both labor and nature are key sources of "material wealth," and their interaction constitutes the grounds of social existence across human civilizations. Yet, as he argues in the *Grundrisse*, this "*unity* of living and active humanity with the natural, inorganic conditions of their metabolic interaction with nature" does not necessitate materialist analysis, but rather the *separation* between these conditions, a "separation which is completely posited only in the relation of wage labor and capital."[5] This historical separation from conditions of production for social need and metabolic stability into conditions governed by the imperative for capital accumulation and value production entails a fundamental transformation in metabolic relations. Capitalist relations not only create the division of labor, divorcing producers from their connection to land and capacities for use-value production, but also generate new methods of extraction, expansion, and scientific and technological development that operate on a scale beyond particular ecological relations or ecosystemic processes, diminishing dependence on these more immediate natural conditions.[6] These modes of alienation combine with new forms of exploitation of both worker and nature, as capitalist production relentlessly pursues surplus value: "Capitalist production, therefore, only develops the techniques and the degree of combination of the social process of production by simultaneously undermining the original sources of all wealth—the soil and the worker."[7]

Marx's analysis of capitalist productive relations attends to the profound effects of this metabolic disturbance on workers as corporeal beings and on natural processes and systems more broadly. Both in his individual writings and his collaborations with Engels, Marx chronicles polluted and deleterious working conditions, various health afflictions and diseases, as well as malnutrition, arguing that capitalist production exhausts the corporeal metabolism of laborers, undermining their capacity to reproduce their conditions of health and vitality. These bodily and environmental health conditions are aligned with the broader transformations to ecological processes and relations that characterize capitalism.

As Marx writes in a discussion of soil exhaustion in *Capital* (1867) volume three, capitalist relations "provoke an irreparable rift in the interdependent process of social metabolism, a metabolism prescribed by the natural laws of life itself."[8] Drawing in particular from the chemist Justus von Liebig's concept of metabolism and his descriptions of the depletion of soil nutrients in capitalist agriculture, Marx argues that the intensification of agricultural production under capitalism "hinders the operation of the eternal natural condition for the lasting fertility of the soil."[9] Marx stresses that industrialized methods of agriculture, which rely on technological innovation in the form of artificial fertilizers, large-scale machinery, and new modes of international trade, will necessarily generate long-term instability and declining productivity. Capitalist production "stands in contradiction" to sustainable agricultural practices that are attuned to natural processes and the longevity of ecosystemic health.[10]

Capitalist production, with its ceaseless revolutionizing of the productive process by way of new methods and markets, approaches the natural world as resources for expropriation. This abstract, profit-oriented vantage instrumentalizes nature's capacities and disregards natural limits or strives to overcome them with new technological innovations and expansion into new terrain.[11] As Marx points out, the contradiction between capitalism's built-in requirements for growth and these natural laws, balances, and limits creates long-term sustainability problems, ecological and economic. This limitless tendency toward expansion and accumulation has allowed capitalism to thrive as a global economic system, while also creating the conditions for crisis at a biospheric level, given the system's structural disregard for ecological concerns. While Marx did not predict the full extent of capitalism's ecological transformations, his writings convey the contradictory, crisis-prone tendencies of capitalist development in a broadly systemic way, discussing ecological matters such as deforestation and famine, the depletion of coal reserves, and the rise of urban waste and pollution across a variety of locales. Nature appears, in these descriptions, as reshaped by and expressive of these alienated and exploitative metabolic interactions, even as its laws and limits present barriers to the accumulation process.

Notes

1. Paul Burkett, *Marx and Nature: A Red and Green Perspective* (London: Haymarket, 2014); John Bellamy Foster, *Marx's Ecology: Materialism and Nature* (Monthly Review Press, 2000); Brett Clark, John Bellamy Foster, and Richard York, *The Ecological Rift: Capitalism's War on the Earth* (Monthly Review Press, 2011); James O'Connor, *Natural Causes* (New York: Guilford Press, 1998): Kohei Saito, *Karl Marx's Ecosocialism: Capital, Nature, and the Unfinished Critique of Political Economy* (Monthly Review Press, 2017); Andreas Malm, *Fossil Capital: The Rise of Steam Power and the Roots of Global Warming* (London: Verso, 2016) and *The Progress of this Storm: Nature and Society in a Warming World* (London: Verso, 2017); Moore, *Capitalism and the Web of Life: Ecology and the Accumulation of Capital* (London: Verso, 2015); and Stefano Longo, Rebecca Clausen, and Brett Clark, *The Tragedy of the Commodity: Oceans, Fisheries, Aquaculture* (New Jersey: Rutgers University Press, 2015) offer influential and innovative considerations of Marx's ecological approaches, extending them to current socioecological conditions.
2. Earlier critical accounts of Marx's conceptions of nature favored such readings of Marx as a progressivist thinker. See Paul Burkett and John Bellamy Foster, *Marx and the Earth: An Anti-Critique* (London: Brill, 2016), for sustained engagement with these first-wave eco-socialist accounts.
3. On the history of metabolism as a concept in nineteenth-century science and natural history as well as in Marx's theories, see Foster, *Marx's Ecology*, 141–77, and Saito, *Karl Marx's Ecosocialism*, 68–97.
4. Marx, *Capital* vol. 3, 949; Marx, *Capital* vol. 1, 283, 290.
5. Marx, *Grundrisse*, 489.
6. For a detailed discussion of these ideas, see Burkett, *Marx and Nature*, 57–68.
7. Marx, *Capital* vol. 1, 637–8.
8. Marx, *Capital*, vol. 3, 949.
9. Marx, *Capital* vol. 1, 637–8.
10. Marx, *Capital*, vol. 3, 754.
11. For more on this subject, see Moore and Raj Patel on Cheap Nature, *The History of the World in Seven Cheap Things* (Berkeley: University of California Press, 2019), 44–63.

29

Revolution

Colleen Lye

Revolution is the qualitative, hard-to-imagine leap from one mode of production to another. And yet the task is not only to describe it but, even more, to help actualize it. It's the ambitious task anyway that Marx set for himself. One factor in his favor was his intuition that capitalism was a mode of production in which the revolution of the future was immanent in the contradictions of the present. Capital's self-valorizing tendency continually depended upon the destruction and transmutation of other lifeworlds, which is why the attainment of a historical view of the transition into capitalism was also key to imagining any transition out of it.

Grasping capital accumulation to have a globalizing logic, Marx attempted to make a study of varieties of capitalist transitions and their modes of combination around the world. He thought that communists needed to support anti-colonial and antislavery causes because proletarian struggle may often first be national in form. Indeed, actual proletarian revolution could not only have its beginnings in one country but a less developed country may also see the prospect of a bourgeois revolution directly passing into a proletarian one. Importantly, though, it could succeed only if it coordinated with proletarian struggles elsewhere, especially in the capitalist core. This is what Marx meant by a "revolution-in-permanence," a phrase which concluded his 1850 address to the Communist League on the necessity of maintaining the autonomy of a proletarian organization.[1] That tactical instruction was counterpart to his view of the combined and uneven nature of global capitalist development, which made it possible for the mid-nineteenth-century German proletariat to take the lead in a bourgeois revolution that might well be more advanced than any that had previously occurred in England and France. And it made it possible to think that the traditional Russian commune in the 1880s might serve as the starting point for communist development in general.

Who comprises the revolutionary proletariat? The revolutionary proletariat is not simply identical with the industrial working class, although the alienation of the wage labor form is certainly exemplary of capital's modern separation of human beings from their capacities. Just as Marx thought that non-European peasants being subsumed into English-led capitalism in the nineteenth century could provide the mass basis for a "proletarian majority," he also thought intellectuals had a role to play in the fomenting of proletarian consciousness. The preservation of a proletarian standpoint even in the midst of an alliance with the enemies of its enemy might well be aided by "a portion of bourgeois ideologists, who have raised themselves to the level of comprehending theoretically the historical movement as a whole."[2] Proletarian revolutions, Marx wrote in the wake of the failed revolutions of 1848, "criticize themselves constantly, interrupt themselves continually in their own course, come back to the apparently accomplished in order to begin it afresh, deride with unmerciful thoroughness the inadequacies, weaknesses and paltriness of their first attempt."[3] A proletarian revolution-in-permanence, involving an objective-class composition that has no template, is thus also a ceaseless revolution, one whose subject is still in the making.

Notes

1 Marx, "Address of the Central Committee to the Communist League," London, March 1850. https://www.marxists.org/archive/marx/works/1847/communist-league/1850-ad1.htm, accessed August 20, 2019.
2 Marx and Engels, "Manifesto of the Communist Party," 481.
3 Marx, "The Eighteenth Brumaire of Louis Napoleon," 597.

30

Communism

Conall Cash

Marx and Engels recognized that, rather than drawing up a program for how society should be run and enforcing its implementation upon the people, communism must be the product of social struggles, constructed by the people who will live within it, and not have it benevolently imposed upon them from without. They thus declare that communism "is for us not a *state of affairs* which is to be established, an *ideal* to which reality [will] have to adjust itself. We call communism the *real* movement which abolishes the present state of things. The conditions of this movement result from the premises now in existence."[1] Engels would later characterize this distinction as a move from "utopian" to "scientific" socialism, since it presents the new society as an end toward which existing society is really developing and which revolutionary theory seeks to express and clarify, rather than an abstract goal that individual political leaders can magically conjure into being. Yet, if it is to be arrived at as the realization of immanent tendencies within capitalist society, rather than as an external break with society as it presently exists, the question of how this new society will be achieved becomes a far more difficult one: for it is not a matter of dreaming up a society and implementing it, but of showing the transition as something that society—or at least a section of it, which is necessarily understood to be becoming a majority—will achieve for itself and by virtue of its self-directed activity. Rather than positing communism as an end to be arrived at through a certain means, in Marx's vision it is the means that construct and cohere the end, an end that could not even be articulated if society were not already in the process of bringing about the means of its achievement.

Because communism is a process rather than a state to be achieved or described in advance, Marx speaks of its immanent development: he wants to outline the stages of a process by which developing social forces are, in pursuit of their own interests and way of life, in the midst of making possible the classless and free society of the future. This conception rests on two crucial suppositions about the nature of social change, which distinguish Marx and Engels' perspective from many other currents in radical thought: first, they determine that social change takes place through political struggle for power by social groups, the most fundamental of which are *classes*; and second, they identify the *state* as the ultimate terrain of this struggle as, in Lenin's words, "an organ for the *oppression* of one class by another."[2] From this, they argue that the initial stage of this transition will involve the proletariat's wresting of state power from the capitalist class and replacing the "dictatorship of the bourgeoisie" with the "dictatorship of the proletariat." Yet while this replacement of the rule of an exploitative minority with the rule of the exploited majority is to be valued in itself, its ultimate significance can only be grasped from the perspective of the stage which exceeds it, which will be full communism. While the first stage will involve the replacement of one form of class rule by another—more democratic—one, the ultimate stage will involve the "withering away" of the state, and the concomitant disappearance of classes themselves and of all means for the oppression of one class by another.[3]

According to this argument, the dictatorship of the proletariat is therefore a historically unprecedented form of class rule, one which will lead to the abolition of class rule as such. While previous class societies relied on a productive class to create social wealth, this class could never unite itself or attain class consciousness except in halting forms. The tremendous development of productive forces within capitalism has made possible the unification of the laboring class in an unprecedented manner: the global proletariat increasingly comes to share a similar condition and shared capacities (given the homogenizing tendency of labor under capitalism), and the development of means of communication and transport render contact among members of this class possible on an unprecedented scale. Thanks to these conditions of its life under capitalism, which it makes use of in the revolutionary struggle itself, the proletariat is able to unite all of its productive capacities in taking state power. In the process, the state that it establishes will not be that of a new minority, but that of the vast majority of people in collective possession of the means of production, involved in democratic decision over what these productive capacities are used for.

For Marx, Engels, and Lenin, this will eventually lead to the "final stage," that of full communism. During the initial period of the dictatorship of the proletariat, the proletariat wields state power *over* those who would seek to return it to its dependent position and reproduce the conditions for capitalism. But ultimately, all of these apparatuses serve the purpose of the functioning of the state. Once there is no structural social division between producers and decision-makers, between manual and intellectual labor, there is no reason to maintain the existence of a state as such, even in democratic form. "The more complete the democracy," argues Lenin, "the nearer the moment when it becomes unnecessary."[4] In knowing ourselves as human in the free, collective creation of the meaning of our lives, we will freely pursue our aims without the need of the institutional forms of state power to mediate our relations to ourselves and each other, as there will no longer be any compulsion toward the development of a force *directing* society other than the internal and collective force of society itself. Marx describes the economic basis of this communist society as the abolition of private property, granting the collective ownership of the means of production to the "associated producers, rationally regulating their interchange with Nature, bringing it under their common control." The "realm of freedom" is thus understood to be the domain of "socialized man," attained through humanity's development in the "realm of necessity" in which humanity reproduces itself and the conditions for its continued life.[5] Communist society, by overthrowing private property and instituting collective ownership and decision-making, makes it possible for a collective humanity to recognize the difference between necessity and freedom, and to work toward the extension of the latter; by contrast, private ownership of the means of production under capitalism requires that producers remain tied to the realm of necessity, producing indefinitely so that the wealth they create can be expropriated by capitalists, without which capitalism could not reproduce itself.

Lenin, during the months prior to the October 1917 revolution, returned to and developed Marx and Engels' theorization of the stages of communism and the withering away of the state in *State and Revolution*. Read in the light of Stalinism, where the transition beyond the state was revoked and the centralized enrichment and power of the Soviet state instead became the ultimate end of economic activity, the tremendous gap separating the revolutionary leader from the subsequent bureaucratic state is abundantly clear. Yet inevitably the question arises as to whether the classical Marxist vision, concretized by Lenin, of the dictatorship of the proletariat enabling the communist withering away of the state, was betrayed by Stalinism, or if it was shown by historical experience to be misguided. Critical analyses from the Left of the Marxist tradition, such as (nonorthodox) Trotskyists and "left communists," have argued that what existed under Stalinism and continues to exist in state socialist countries is a form of "bureaucratic" or "state capitalism," rather than any form of proletarian state; as such, these societies did not "stall" in the first stage of communism, but maintained the basic conditions of capitalism itself, through the entrenched exploitation of proletarian labor for surplus value extraction, now perversely carried out in the name of this same proletariat. The question of whether the dictatorship of the proletariat and the withering away of the state have been disproven by history can thus be said to remain open.

Notes

1 Marx, "The German Ideology," 162.
2 Lenin, *State and Revolution*, 43.
3 The canonical version of this account is in Engels, *Socialism: Utopian and Scientific*, in *The Marx-Engels Reader*, 713. This translation renders "withering away" as the "dying out" of the state, but the former has become the more common expression in English.
4 Lenin, *State and Revolution*, 141.
5 Marx, *Capital* vol. 3, 196–7.

31

Utopia

Cat Moir

Utopia is not originally a modernist idea, but it is a modern one. Though the vision of an ideal society or perfect state of humanity has existed since the earliest times, the genre of utopia, which bridges literature and political theory, came into being in the early modern period with the work of Thomas More (1516). More's *Utopia* was the fictional tale of a European traveler claiming to have visited a near-perfect society located on an exotic island. Despite presenting itself as a real travel report, already with More, utopia became identified with the idea of a society that is possible to imagine, but impossible to realize, an association it has never shaken.

Marx and Engels were suspicious of utopia for this reason, even if their ideas about communism can in some ways be seen as an attempt to realize utopia in practice. In the *Communist Manifesto* (1848), they denounced the attempts of early nineteenth-century utopian socialists Henri Saint-Simon, Étienne Cabet, Charles Fourier, and Robert Owen to establish new societies based on a blueprint. For Marx and Engels, communism was not an "ideal to which reality will have to adjust itself" but the "real movement which abolishes the present state of things."[1] In other words, what they understood by communism would be the result of actual collective social action rather than a model imposed from above. Nevertheless, Marx and Engels' relationship to utopia remains ambiguous. Though Engels explicitly distinguished "scientific" from "utopian" socialism, he still praised the utopian socialists as revolutionaries. Meanwhile, throughout his work Marx adumbrates a vision of communism that many have seen as utopian in the negative sense of unrealizable: a participatory democracy, beyond wages, money, and exploitation, in which human freedom and equality can be fully achieved.

A profound connection between utopia and materialism can be seen in the way the utopian imagination is intimately connected to the historical horizon. In More's era, utopias were spatial fantasies imagined on undiscovered islands, but by the time capitalism had reached every corner of the globe, utopia was beginning to project into the future.[2] The process of modernization—profound sociopolitical change and the advance of science and technology—held out the hope that utopia might become a reality. The impact of fascist and communist attempts to realize political utopias in the twentieth century brought utopia into disrepute. Yet the deep social need to imagine a different world remains.

If utopia was not originally modernist, modernism was perhaps by definition utopian. Expressionists, constructivists, and other modernists saw art as a way to criticize an inadequate status quo and create a better society. Today, speculative fictions in print and on screen continue to thematize social and political questions. Dystopias dominate in a context in which, as Fredric Jameson has noted, it is easier to imagine the end of the world than the end of capitalism.[3] But utopia is far from dead. In the face of twenty-first-century challenges—climate change, social inequality, and injustice—only big ideas will do.

Notes

1 Marx and Engels, "The German Ideology," 162.
2 See Bloch, *The Utopian Function of Art and Literature*, 3, and Reinhart Koselleck, *The Practice of Conceptual History: Timing History, Spacing Concepts*, trans. Todd Samuel Presner (Stanford: Stanford University Press, 2002), 84–99.
3 Jameson, "Future City," *New Left Review* 21 (2003): 76.

Contributors

Fiona Allen is Lecturer in History of Modern and Contemporary Art and Visual Culture at the University of Exeter, UK. Her articles and reviews have been published in a range of journals, including *parallax*, *Art & the Public Sphere*, and the *Oxford Art Journal*.

Giacomo Bianchino is a PhD candidate in Comparative Literature at the City University of New York, USA. He has published on the political economy of free time, the discursive politics of internet spaces, and the literary unity of Kierkegaard's works.

Michael Shane Boyle works in the Department of Drama at Queen Mary University of London, UK. His books include the edited collection *Postdramatic Theatre and Form* (2019) and, forthcoming, *The Arts of Logistics*.

Veronica Brownstone is a PhD candidate in Hispanic Studies at the University of Pennsylvania. Her research examines the intersections of labor and political power in contemporary Central American cultural production.

Conall Cash is a PhD candidate in French at Cornell University, USA. His dissertation is a study of selfhood, reflection, and politics in Merleau-Ponty and literary and cinematic modernism.

Sarah Collins is Associate Professor in Musicology at the University of Western Australia. She is the author of *Lateness and Modernism: Untimely Ideas about Music, Literature and Politics in Interwar Britain* (2019) and editor of *Music and Victorian Liberalism: Composing the Liberal Subject* (2019).

Treasa De Loughry is Lecturer/Assistant Professor in World Literature at University College Dublin, Ireland. She is the author of *The Global Novel and Capitalism in Crisis—Contemporary Literary Narratives* (2020) and various chapters and articles on world literature, waste, food, and revolution.

Rory Dufficy is a researcher and policy adviser at the Australia and New Zealand School of Government. He is currently working on a manuscript entitled *An Epoch of Possibility: The Avant-Garde and the Twentieth Century*. He researches the literatures of political transition, rupture, and stasis.

Regenia Gagnier holds the Established Chair in English Language and Literature at the University of Exeter, UK. Her monographs include *Idylls of the Marketplace* (1986), *Subjectivities: A History of Self-Representation in Britain* (1991), *The Insatiability of Human Wants* (2000), *Individualism, Decadence and Globalization* (2010), and *Literatures of Liberalization* (2018).

Kristin Grogan is Assistant Professor in Poetry and Poetics at Rutgers University, USA. Her essays have appeared in *American Literature* and *Critical Quarterly*. She is completing a book on modernist poetry and labor.

Daniel Hartley is Assistant Professor in World Literatures in English at Durham University, UK. He is the author of *The Politics of Style: Towards a Marxist Poetics* (2017) and has published widely on Marxist theory and contemporary literature.

Owen Holland has taught nineteenth- and twentieth-century literature at Jesus College, Oxford and in the English department at UCL, UK. His first book, *William Morris's Utopianism: Propaganda, Politics and Prefiguration*, was published in 2017, and he has also edited a selection of Morris' political writings. His second book on British responses to the Paris Commune is forthcoming.

Josh Jewell is a PhD student and teaching assistant at the University of Exeter, UK. His research examines the proliferation of informal economies and casualized labor practices in Africa and the Caribbean.

Dominick Knowles is a PhD candidate at Brandeis University, USA, as well as the poetry editor of *Protean* magazine. Their dissertation research explores the relationship between Cold War US poetry and imperialism in Latin America; their essays on literary anti-capitalism have been featured in *Viewpoint* magazine and *Modernism/modernity Print +*.

Angelos Koutsourakis is Associate Professor in Film and Cultural Studies at the Centre for World Cinemas and Digital Cultures, University of Leeds, UK, and an AHRC research leadership fellow. He is the author of *Rethinking Brechtian Film Theory and Cinema* (2018), *Politics as Form in Lars von Trier* (2013) and the co-editor of *Cinema of Crisis: Film and Contemporary Europe* (2020) and *The Cinema of Theo Angelopoulos* (2015).

Esther Leslie is Professor in Political Aesthetics at Birkbeck College, London, UK. Her books include *Liquid Crystals* (2016), *Hollywood Flatlands* (2002), and *Walter Benjamin: Overpowering Conformism* (2000).

Miles Link is a research associate in the School of English at Fudan University in Shanghai, China. He is currently preparing a monograph on disaster and the philosophy of history.

Colleen Lye is Associate Professor of English at UC Berkeley, USA. She is the author of *America's Asia: Racial Form and American Literature, 1893-1945* (2005) and the co-editor of *After Marx* (forthcoming).

Cat Moir is Senior Lecturer in Germanic Studies at the University of Sydney, Australia. Her research specializes in nineteenth- and twentieth-century European thought. She is the author of *Ernst Bloch's Speculative Materialism: Ontology, Epistemology, Politics* (2020).

Kate Montague is Lecturer in 20th and Twenty-first Century Literature at the University of Exeter, UK. Her research is focused on the relationships between literature and labor within the capitalist world-system.

Tyrus Miller is Dean of the School of Humanities and Professor of Art History and English at the University of California, Irvine, USA. His publications include *Late Modernism: Politics, Fiction, and the Arts between the World Wars* (1999), *Singular Examples: Artistic Politics and the Neo-Avant-Garde* (2009), and *Modernism and the Frankfurt School* (2014).

Adam David Morton is Professor of Political Economy at the University of Sydney, Australia. He is the author of *Unravelling Gramsci* (2007), *Revolution and State in Modern Mexico* (2011), and *Global Capitalism, Global War, Global Crisis* with Andreas Bieler (2018).

Julian Murphet is Jury Chair of English Language and Literature at the University of Adelaide, Australia. He is the author of *Multimedia Modernism* (2009), *Faulkner's Media Romance* (2017), and *Todd Solondz* (2019), among other things.

Alex Niven is a writer and editor from Northumberland and currently Lecturer in English at Newcastle University, UK. Formerly he was Assistant Editor at *New Left Review* and his books include *New Model Island* (2019), *Definitely Maybe 33 1/3* (2014), and *Folk Opposition* (2011).

Peter Riley is Associate Professor of Poetry and Poetics at Durham University, UK, and a trade unionist. He is the author of *Against Vocation: Whitman, Melville, Crane, and the Labors of American Poetry* (2019) and *Strandings* (forthcoming).

Margaret Ronda is Associate Professor of English at the University of California-Davis, USA. She is the author of *Remainders: American Poetry at Nature's End* (2018).

Mark Steven is Senior Lecturer in Twentieth- and Twenty-first Century Literature at the University of Exeter, UK. He is the author of *Red Modernism: American Poetry and the Spirit of Communism* (2017) and *Splatter Capital* (2017).

Trevor Strunk is an adjunct professor of English at DeSales University, USA, and an independent videogame critic who podcasts, often, at *No Cartridge Audio*.

Elinor Taylor is Senior Lecturer in Literary and Cultural Studies at the University of Westminster, UK. She is the author of *The Popular Front Novel in Britain* (2017) and a member of the executive committee of the Raymond Williams Society.

Ana Tomcic is currently a tutor and researcher at the University of Exeter, UK. Her research interests include psychoanalysis, modernist literature, women's writing, Marxism, and twentieth-century ideas of progress.

Marina Vishmidt is Lecturer in Culture Industry at Goldsmiths, University of London, UK. She is the author of *Speculation as a Mode of Production: Forms of Value Subjectivity in Art and Capital* (2018) and co-author of *Reproducing Autonomy* (2016).

Harry Warwick is an early career researcher whose interests lie at the intersection of Marxist critical theory, popular culture, and utopian studies. He is currently writing a book on the relationship between the "new enclosures" and Hollywood science-fiction films released between 1973 and 2017. He will begin a Leverhulme Early Career Fellowship, examining post-1960 Anglo-American eco-dystopias, at the University of Warwick, UK, in September 2020.

Paul Young is Associate Professor of Victorian Literature and Culture in the Department of English, University of Exeter, UK. He is author of *Globalization and the Great Exhibition: The Victorian New World Order* (2009) as well as numerous essays and articles on the cultural dimensions of Victorian imperialism.

Index

Adlington, Robert 171 n.12
Adorno, Theodor 6, 9, 67, 150–1, 163, 169, 170 n.7, 186–7, 205
Aeschylus 47
Alighieri, Dante 9, 42–3, 44, 48, 74, 83 n.1, 208
Althusser, Louis 3, 23, 66, 74–5, 79, 80–1, 217–18, 222
Anderson, Kevin B. 81
Anderson, Perry 57, 118
Angelopoulos, Theo 136
Aragon, Louis 184
Aristotle 16, 17
Arrighi, Giovanni 6
Artaud, Antonin 1
Aureli, Pier Vittorio 173

Badiou, Alain 26, 28 n.31, 59, 62 n.53, 70, 71
Bakhtin, Mikhail 19, 23, 74, 81–2
Balibar, Étienne 50
Ballantine, Christopher 164–5
Balzac, Honoré de 9, 115–16
Barnes, Djuna 182 n.21
Barzun, Jacques 165–6
Baudelaire, Charles 40
Bauer, Bruno 23, 24, 31, 32, 169 n.1
Beauvoir, Simone de 215
Beethoven, Ludwig van 164–5
Behne, Adolf 134, 175, 176
Benjamin, Walter 26, 50, 60, 78, 79, 103, 147, 149, 150, 173, 174, 185–6, 187–8, 191, 205
Bentham, Jeremy 92
Berg, Alban 166
Berman, Marshall 1, 7
Blackburn, Robin 224
Blair, Tony 94
Blanc, Louis 87
Blanchot, Maurice 9
Blanton, C. D. 64

Blau, Eva 177
Bloch, Ernst 192
Boccaccio, Giovanni 115
Bolaño, Roberto 103, 122
Bolgdanov, Alexander 122
Bolsonaro, Jair 93
Bonaparte, Louis 51, 55, 58–9
Borchardt, Hermann 150
Brecht, Bertolt 26, 125, 147–58, 164, 166, 185, 188–9, 205
Brennan, Timothy 224
Brown, Matthew 98 n.29
Bryusov, Valery 122
Buber, Martin 173
Buck-Morss, Susan 7
Burch, Noël 153
Burns, Emile 126
Burri, Emil 149–50
Bush, Alan 164

Cabet, Étienne 234
Cacciari, Massimo 172
Cage, John 164
Cameron, David 94
Cardew, Cornelius 164
Cervantes, Miguel de 115
Chaplin, Charlie 96
Chesterton, G. K. 96
Clark, T. J. 6, 7, 10, 118
Clinton, Bill 94
Clover, Joshua 64
Cocteau, Jean 41
Connolly, James 65
Conrad, Joseph 121
Corbyn, Jeremy 98 n.29
Craig, Edward Gordon 146
Cromwell, Oliver 59

Dal Co, Francesco 174
Darwin, Charles 104, 165–6
Daub, Karl 22

Davis, Angela 65
Dean, Jodi 6
De'Ath, Amy 215
Defoe, Daniel 115
Deleuze, Gilles 9
Democritus 19, 20
Denning, Michael 152, 154
Derrida, Jacques 9, 41, 44
Dessau, Paul 164
Dickens, Charles 9, 34–5
Diogenes 23
Disney, Walt 192–3
Dos Passos, John 119, 122
Dostoevsky, Fyodor 82
Du Bois, W. E. B. 2
Duchamp, Marcel 187
Dumas, Alexandre 115
Duménil, Gérard 80
Dunayevskaya, Raya 74–5, 81

Eagleton, Terry 6, 217
Eisenstein, Sergei 135–40, 142, 143, 146, 190, 192–3
Eisler, Hanns 163
Eley, Geoff 156
Eliot, T. S. 1, 41, 44, 47, 48, 57, 69, 79
Engels, Friedrich 3, 4, 5, 9, 13, 30–7, 40, 61 n.22, 67, 86, 87, 88, 94–7, 99, 100, 115, 126, 134, 138, 141–3, 162–3, 170 n.2, 173–4, 203, 205, 211–12, 214, 217, 221, 223, 227, 231–4
Epicurus 9, 17–26, 28 n.31, 42, 46–8
Erdogan, Recep Tayyip 93

Fanon, Frantz 2
Farocki, Harun 136
Faulkner, William 121
Federici, Silvia 2, 215
Feininger, Lyonel 175
Fisher, Mark 35
Flanner, Janet 182 n.21
Foucault, Michel 9
Fourier, Charles 173–5, 234
Frank, Josef 177
Fraser, Nancy 94
Freud, Sigmund 41, 104
Fukuyama, Francis 92
Fyodorov, Nikolai F. 122

Gabler, Johann Philipp 22
Gascoyne, David 125
Gettino, Octavio 143–4
Ginsberger, Roger 180
Godard, Jean-Luc 136, 141–3
Goethe, Johann Wolfgang von 44, 74, 78, 84 n.23, 105, 150, 157
Gold, Mike 128
Gorky, Maxim 122
Gornick, Vivian 130
Gramsci, Antonio 3, 35, 94
Greppi, Claudio 173
Gropius, Walter 175–6, 178
Groys, Boris 7, 48
Gründgens, Gustav 160 n.64
Gustav, Hartung 157

H. D. 166
Habermas, Jürgen 63 n.58
Hake, Sabine 135
Hamsun, Knut 118
Harvey, David 6, 99, 101, 102, 103
Hatherley, Owen 172
Haydn, Joseph 165
Hegel, G. W. F. 15–20, 22–7
Heinrich, Michael 102, 104
Heise, Thomas 136
Hilbersheimer, Ludwig 178–9
Hirschfeld, Kurt 157
Hitler, Adolph 118, 157
Hobsbawm, Eric 2
Hölderlin, Friedrich 150, 157
Horkheimer, Max 62 n.41, 186
Hughes, Langston 124, 128–9, 132
Huxley, Aldous 96

James, Henry 121
Jameson, Fredric 5, 7, 63 n.58, 67, 75, 78, 80, 82, 83, 152, 217, 235
Jancsó, Miklós 136
Jennison, Ruth 8, 69, 125, 127
Joyce, James 48, 121–2, 130, 139, 184–5

Kafka, Franz 1
Kant, Immanuel 42, 75
Kautsky, Karl 3
Kincaid, Jamaica 103
Kluge, Alexander 136, 141
Knopf, Jan 150

Kołakowski, Leszek 1
Kopp, Anatole 180
Kornbluh, Anna 75
Korsch, Karl 134
Krutikov, Georgi 172, 174
Krylov, B. 170 n.2

Lafargue, Paul 43, 115
Lassalle, Ferdinand 86–7, 117
Le Corbusier 176–7, 178
Lem, Stanislaw 122
Lenin, Vladimir 3, 9, 41, 42, 48, 54, 56, 59, 65, 137, 141, 143, 146, 231–3
Lewis, Sophie 215, 216
Lewis, Wyndham 59, 120–1, 172
Liebknecht, Wilhelm 42, 86, 162
Lihotzky, Margarete 177
Lissitzky, El 174, 178, 180–1
London, Jack 118
Loos, Adolf 177
Löwy, Michael 60
Lukács, Georg 38 n.5, 217–18
Luxemburg, Rosa 2, 3, 37, 65, 94
Lyell, Charles 104

McCay, Winsor 189
MacDiarmid, Hugh 125
Macfarlane, Helen 30, 38 n.3
McLellan, David 66
Mandel, Ernest 99, 107
Mao, Douglas 6
Mao, Zedong 9, 94, 96
Marey, Etienne-Jules 191
Marinetti, F. T. 59
Marker, Chris 136, 141
Martí, José 96
Marx, Eleanor 43
May, Ernst 177
May, Theresa 94
Mayakovsky, Vladimir 125
Mehring, Franz 100
Mendelsohn, Rich 178
Merleau-Ponty, Maurice 9
Mészáros, István 57
Meyer, Hannes 178
Meyerhold, Vsevolod 136, 138, 146
Miliutin, N. A. 174
Mill, John Stuart 84 n.9, 91–5
Modi, Narendra 93

Moholy-Nagy, László 146
Montaigne, Michel de 46
Moody, Alys 7
Moore, Jason W. 108, 224
Moore, Samuel 30–1
More, Thomas 234
Morelly, Etienne-Gabriel 87
Mozart, Wolfgang Amadeus 165
Mueller, Rudolf 157
Munif, Abdelrahman 107
Musto, Marcello 64
Nealon, Christopher 125

Negri, Antonio 66, 68, 69, 71
Neher, Carola 149–50
Netanyahu, Benjamin 93
Neurath, Otto 177
Neutra, Richard 89, 180
Nicolaus, Martin 64–5, 67, 70
Niedecker, Lorine 124–8, 129, 132
Niemann, Michelle 126
Nietzsche Friedrich 41
Nono, Luigi 164
Norris, Frank 117, 149

Obama, Barack 94
Ono, Yoko 164
Oppen, George 124
Orbán, Viktor 93
Owen, Robert 89, 117, 173, 222, 234

Parmalee, Patty Lee 150
Pater, Walter 41, 48, 166
Philippe, King Louis 40, 54, 55, 56
Pirandello, Luigi 41
Piscator, Erwin 157
Platonov, Andrei 122
Plekhanov, Georgi 3
Polanyi, Karl 108
Pollock, Jonathan 46
Postone, Moishe 146
Pound, Ezra 41, 48, 57, 66, 79, 96, 117, 118, 125, 166
Prawer, S. S. 52, 64, 75
Proudhon, Pierre-Joseph 31, 32–3, 42, 70, 117, 173
Puchner, Martin 8, 59, 142
Pudovkin, Vsevolod 137

Radek, Karl 184
Rakosi, Carl 125
Rancière, Jacques 9, 74–5, 82
Reinhardt, Max 146
Reznikoff, Charles 125
Ricardo, David 42, 84 n.9, 115, 152, 202
Roberts, William Clare 42, 64
Rocha, Glauber 136
Rochester, Anna 126
Rodney, Walter 2
Rosdolsky, Roman 65
Ross, Stephen J. 7
Rousseau, Jean-Jacques 42
Roy, Arundhati 103
Ruge, Arnold 23
Rukeyser, Muriel 124, 130–2

Saint-Simon, Henri 222, 234
Savigny, Friedrich Carl von 24
Schiller, Friedrich 150, 168
Schlemmer, Oskar 146
Schmidt, Hans 178
Schoenberg, Arnold 1, 164, 166, 170 n.7
Schuster, Franz 177
Scott, Walter 155
Sembène, Ousmane 136
Shakespeare, William 9, 42, 43–6, 47, 48, 74, 136, 150, 162
Shapiro, Stephen 100, 102, 110 n.40
Shaw, George Bernard 154, 155
Shreffler, Anne 164
Silva, Ludovico 75
Sinclair, Upton 117, 154
Smith, Adam 31, 42, 84 n.9, 115, 152, 167, 202, 223
Solanas, Fernando 143–4
Solano, Solita 182 n.21
Stalin, Joseph 3, 9, 48, 60, 142, 145 n.24, 173, 233
Stam, Mart 178
Stanislavsky, Konstantin 146
Stanley, David 21, 23
Stein, Gertrude 1, 117, 118, 182 n.21
Steven, Mark 64–5, 84 n.25, 125
Straub/Huillet 136
Stravinsky, Igor 168
Strugatsky Brothers 122
Sumption, Lord Jonathan 92

Sutherland, Keston 38 n.17, 65, 75
Suvin, Darko 64

Tafuri, Manfredo 172–4
Taut, Bruno 175–6, 178
Thiers, Adolphe 52
Tolstoy, Leo 119
Tressell, Robert 117
Trotsky, Leon 3, 9, 41, 48, 233
Trump, Donald J. 93
Tucker, Robert C. 11 n.11, 99

Varoufakis, Yanis 5
Verne, Jules 122
Vertov, Dziga 135–6, 140–2
Viertel, Berthold 157
Virgil 150

Wagner, Martin 176, 177
Wagner, Richard 162–3, 165–7, 170 n2
Walkowitz, Rebecca 6
Weber, Max 88
Weeks, Kathi 146
Weigel, Helene 156
Weill, Kurt 164, 166
Wilde, Oscar 90–2, 96
Williams, Raymond 61 n.13, 135, 209, 222
Williams, William Carlos 96, 124, 125
Wolfe, Stefan 164
Wolff, Christian 164
Wolff, Robert Paul 75
Wollen, Peter 137
Wood, Beatrice 187
Wood, Ellen Meiksins 66, 106–7
Woolf, Leonard 41
Woolf, Virginia 41, 122
Wright, Richard 117

Xi, Jinping 4

Yeats, W. B. 41

Zavattini, Cesare 143
Zielinski, Siegfried 135
Žižek, Slavoj 8–9
Zola, Émile 116
Zukofsky, Louis 69, 79, 125–6

www.ingramcontent.com/pod-product-compliance
Lightning Source LLC
Chambersburg PA
CBHW072141290426
44111CB00012B/1943